Anthropology

Anthropology

A Continental Perspective

CHRISTOPH WULF

TRANSLATED BY DEIRDRE WINTER,

ELIZABETH HAMILTON,

MARGITTA AND RICHARD J. ROUSE

The University of Chicago Press   Chicago and London

CHRISTOPH WULF is professor of anthropology and philosophy of education and director and cofounder of the Interdisciplinary Center for Historical Anthropology at the Free University of Berlin. He is the author, coauthor, or editor of over one hundred books and has been translated extensively in numerous languages.

The University of Chicago Press, Chicago 60637
The University of Chicago Press, Ltd., London
© 2013 by Christoph Wulf
All rights reserved. Published 2013.
Printed in the United States of America

Originally published as *Anthropologie: Geschichte Kultur Philosophie.*
© Rowohlt, 2004

22 21 20 19 18 17 16 15 14 13   1 2 3 4 5

ISBN-13: 978-0-226-92506-6 (cloth)
ISBN-13: 978-0-226-92507-3 (paper)
ISBN-13: 978-0-226-92508-0 (e-book)

Library of Congress Cataloging-in-Publication Data

Wulf, Christoph, 1944–
   [Anthropologie. English]
   Anthropology: a continental perspective / Christoph Wulf;
translated by Deirdre Winter, Elizabeth Hamilton, Margitta and
Richard J. Rouse.
      pages cm.
   Includes bibliographical references and index.
   ISBN 978-0-226-92506-6 (cloth)
   ISBN 978-0-226-92507-3 (pbk.)
   ISBN 978-0-226-92508-0 (e-book)
   1. Anthropology—Philosophy. 2. Anthropology—History.   I. Title.
   GN33.W8513 2013
   301.01—dc23   2012023057

♾ This paper meets the requirements of ANSI/NISO Z39.48-1992
(Permanence of Paper).

For Rosemarie, Katharina, and Alexander

Contents

Preface

This book is intended as a contribution to the heated discussion on the self-definition of anthropology that has been ongoing in the United States in recent years. To this end, I shall develop the broad outlines of a concept of a historical and cultural anthropology that does not, by definition, distinguish between societies and cultures of varying degrees of development. Today it no longer seems meaningful to limit anthropology or ethnology to the study of so-called primitive peoples, preindustrial and pre-state societies, tribal societies, simple societies, underdeveloped, primitive, scriptless, or non-European-American societies. I proceed from the assumption that all human societies and cultures have equal status. However, there are and must be different areas of specialization within anthropology. The American four-field approach,[1] for example, focuses on four different areas whose coherence and current commensurateness have now once more become the subject of lively debate.

The frame of reference of my investigation is the development of anthropological thought in Europe and particularly in Germany over the last century. This is where I have carried out the historical, ethnographic, and philosophical studies that have contributed to this book. In this work I have been inspired by the epistemological traditions of several disciplines, most importantly history, ethnology, and philosophy, but also sociology, psychology, and literary studies. My aim in this book is to develop a few of the *principles and perspectives of anthropology*, comparing and contrasting them with those that emerge from research on evolution, philosophical anthropology in Germany, historical anthropology in France, and cultural anthropology in the United States and Europe, while also drawing on my own research.[2]

As the influence of normative anthropologies has waned, anthropological research has begun to pay more attention to the body with its natality and mortality,[3] which is both the product and the agent of its own socialization and enculturation. The lived human body is the result of multifarious mimetic processes that include not merely imitation, but an active acquisition of cultural knowledge.[4] In these mimetic processes culture is produced, handed down, and transformed. Here the performativity of the body, how it is staged and enacted, plays an important role.[5] Performativity is of particular significance for language processes, cultural performances, and aesthetics.[6] If rituals are perceived and interpreted only as "texts," they lack a dimension that is associated with their material and bodily aspects. This led me to focus on the performative side of ritual acts in a large research project entitled "Berlin Study on Rituals and Gestures," in which I examined these aspects in detail, taking a close look at how rituals and ritualization contribute to the performative formation of communities and how they shape educational processes and promote learning. In these investigations, the material nature and sensory capacities of the body played a major role. The results revealed that human corporeality is shaped by language and imagination, which have been two of the main focuses of my research.[7]

The fragmentation and "deterritorialization" of contemporary anthropology hold considerable potential for the development of new modes of anthropological reflection and research. They also provide an opportunity to free ourselves from outdated traditions of our discipline and to redefine the horizons of anthropology. In this redefinition, the perspectives that are emerging from globalization are becoming increasingly important. Among other things, they have engendered criticism of the neoliberal economic trends that are marginalizing the social market economy and of the associated tendency for many societies to become more and more alike.[8] Today, giving anthropology a global orientation means to open it up for research in all societies and cultures of the world and to address the issue of what will be the most important conditions of human life in the future.

Anthropology is a decentralized, polycentric science in which problems of representation, interpretation, the construction of deconstruction, and thus also methodological diversity are of central importance. Two contradictory developmental trends clash with each other, one of which is oriented toward a "uniformizing" globalization, while the other points toward the limits of this development and stresses the conditions of cultural diversity. This contradiction is reflected in anthropology by the increasing tensions between more universal statements on human beings and statements that emphasize historical and cultural diversity. If we understand anthropology as a *unitas multiplex*—that is, as a science that brings together a multiplicity of individual disciplines—we are aware that the epistemological and paradigmatic differences in the science of the human being cannot be removed but are inherent in it. Anthropological research must therefore proceed from the assumption that its standpoints are relative without dissolving them in arbitrariness and randomness. In my view, the question also arises as to whether and how it is bound by values and its social and ethical responsibility. I see my own research as embedded within the values of human rights, but I would not deny that human rights are also partly time- and culture-bound and therefore also open to discussion.

In view of the fragmentation of the academic disciplines, the task of an anthropology, as I conceptualize it, must be to contribute to understanding between persons and the process of improving understanding between individuals and peoples in the different parts of the world. An anthropology that assumes this task cannot, by definition, develop a systematic approach to the investigation of human societies and cultures—too broad are the variety and diversity of the disciplines and paradigms that have relevance for this research and can and must contribute to an interpretation of humanity. Such a systematic approach would be so abstract that it would be at risk of becoming devoid of all content. I would therefore like to present a contribution to anthropology that takes into account the historical and cultural context (and does not, of course, claim to cover the entire field of possible research).

Although my research is oriented mainly toward continental Europe and Germany in particular, the principles and perspectives of historical cultural anthropology apply as well to other societies and cultures, as evidenced by my research over the last few years. In one of my research projects on the subject of family happiness, three German-Japanese teams examined how families stage and perform Christmas (in Germany) and New Year (in Japan). We identified the historical and cultural conditions for family happiness in both countries and also a number of transcultural elements that families use to express and display feelings of belonging, well-being, and shared happiness.[9] The studies I carried out with Axel Michaels, *Images of the Body in India, Emotions in Rituals and Performances,* and *Exploring the Senses: Emotions, Performativity, and Ritual*, also revealed what Indian and Western cultures have in common and what makes them different in these domains.[10] The results of these studies show that in non-European cultures as well, historicity and culturality are central dimensions of anthropological research. Through focusing on these dimensions, this research is making an important contribution to human beings' understanding of themselves in the twenty-first century.

In what follows I present an outline of selected *aspects of anthropology* that cannot claim to be complete and will require further explanation and specification. Now that the *abstract anthropological norm* that centered mainly on the ideas, images, values, and norms of European-American culture *has ceased to be binding*, anthropology constitutes an attempt to conduct research on human phenomena in the conditions of a globalized world. As a result of this development, anthropological research is no longer fundamentally restricted to *certain defined cultural areas or individual epochs*. The aim of anthropological research is to contribute to a better understanding and better explanations of human phenomena and problems in our globalized world and thus also to a better understanding between people. The lively debates on the historical involvement of sections of anthropology in colonialism and racism, the problem of representation, and the extent to which the other can "speak back" are evidence of efforts to broaden the horizons of anthropology and open it up for new tasks.

There is a *dual historicity and culturality* in anthropology that arises from the historicity and culturality of the different perspectives of anthropological researchers and from the historical and cultural character of the contents and subjects of the research. The historicity and culturality of the anthropologists themselves form the background against which the phenomena and structures that came into being in a different time or culture are perceived and investigated. New research questions and methodologies develop in a reciprocal relationship as researchers reflect upon this dual historicity and culturality. In anthropological research it is important to think of historicity and culturality as belonging together and not, for instance, to play culturality off against historicity. As early as in the work of Franz Boas, who was familiar with the German historical tradition, we can find important ideas pointing in this direction, which have, however, hardly been pursued to date.[11]

The approach to anthropology that I present here employs both *diachronic* and *synchronic methods* to investigate human societies and cultures. In addition to anthropological issues and the hermeneutic and text-critical methods from the historical sciences that are applied dia-chronically, field research with its numerous qualitative and quantita-tive methods still plays an important role as a method of synchronous anthropological research. The interpretative and reflexive methods, in particular, offer the possibility of lending expression to the individual and subjective perspectives.

Many anthropological research projects are *inter-* or *transdisciplinary* and *multi-* or *transcultural*. Because of their transdisciplinary nature, many studies transcend the limits of traditional disciplines and yield new insight by examining new research questions and objects of research, using new procedures and looking at things from new perspectives. The attempt to include multi- or transcultural aspects in anthropological re-search is also leading to the development of new research questions and perspectives that play important roles, particularly within the context of international anthropological research networks.

One new challenge that anthropologists have long failed to address is how to define the *relationship between general insights and specific insights* relating to human beings as individuals and human beings in general. While in archaeology, biological anthropology, and linguistic anthropology it is permissible to make universal statements about hu-man beings and the human race, in historical and cultural anthropologi-cal approaches the emphasis is more on being able to use hermeneutic methods to make complex statements on particular historico-cultural phenomena. These approaches are oriented toward the investigation and assurance of cultural diversity. However, even when we are concerned with cultural diversity, the question still arises as to *what is common to all human beings*. In these times of globalization it is becoming increas-ingly important for anthropology to investigate the relationship between similarities and differences among human beings, cultures, and histori-cal epochs. In this context the question as to the role of comparison in both diachronic and synchronic research in anthropology has taken on a significance that we urgently need to clarify.

In my view, the aim of anthropological research is not to reduce but to *increase* the complexity of our knowledge about human beings. This requires interpretation, reflection, and self-criticism, and an ongoing, philosophically inspired *critique of anthropology* that must include an ex-amination of the fundamental limits of human self-interpretation. In analogy to a definition of God in theology, there is thus talk of the *homo absconditus*. This term expresses the notion that anthropological insights and findings can only grasp the human condition in part, that is, from various different perspectives and thus incompletely. Anthropological research and discovery is location-related and subject to historical and cultural change. Its starting point is a willingness to wonder or marvel that the world is as it is and not otherwise. Marveling (*thaumazein*) is the beginning of fascination with the mystery of the world and curiosity about the possibilities of anthropological knowledge.

Acknowledgments

I would like to express my gratitude to the many colleagues and friends without whose help I would have been unable to develop my concept of a historical and cultural anthropology. A full list of those who have assisted would be impossibly long because there are so many I have worked with over the years who have given me inspiration in my work. I am particularly grateful to my colleagues and friends in the Interdisciplinary Center for Historical Anthropology, in the Collaborative Research Center "Cultures of the Performative," in the Cluster of Excellence "Languages of Emotion," and in three graduate schools, Die Bildung des Körpers, InterArts, and Languages of Emotion, at Freie Universität Berlin. I would also like to express my appreciation to my colleagues on the Educational Anthropology Commission, which was set up as part of the German Society for Educational Research. Three of my colleagues deserve particular mention: Dietmar Kamper, who helped to establish the research projects in historical anthropology in Berlin; Gunter Gebauer, with whom I worked for many years on the historical, cultural, and social bases of mimetic processes; and Jörg Zirfas, who worked with me on the future trends of anthropology and educational anthropology.

I am also grateful to all my colleagues at numerous universities in Germany, Europe, the United States, Latin America, Asia, and Africa with whom I have worked for many years and who have inspired me with a number of important ideas. In particular, I would like to mention Axel Michaels (Heidelberg); Shoko Suzuki (Kyoto); Yasuo Imai (Tokyo); Bingjun Wang, Hongjie Chen, and Zhikun Zhang

(Beijing); Sundar Sarukkai (Manipal); Padma Sarangapani (Mumbai); Susan Visvanathan (New Delhi); Norval Baitello (São Paulo); Fathi Triki (Tunis); Jacques Poulain and Jacky Beillerot (Paris); Alain and Christiane Montandon (Clermont-Ferrand); and Goulnara Khaidarova and Valerij Savchuk (St. Petersburg). All of them helped me to carry out numerous exploratory studies on key anthropological subjects. I am also indebted to the Deutsche Forschungsgemeinschaft and their evaluators, who have continued to support my anthropological research.

I would like to thank the many undergraduate, graduate, doctoral, and postdoctoral students with whom I have worked at Freie Universität Berlin and worldwide who have repeatedly challenged me to reconsider and refine my thoughts and research. Without them and the discussions they provoked, I would not have been able to write this book.

Finally, I would like to thank the translators, Deirdre Winter, Elizabeth Hamilton, and Margitta and Richard J. Rouse, for their commitment; Dr. Michael Sonntag for his very helpful editing of the text and preparation of the index; Melanie Hillerkus for assistance with the editing; David Brent and the reviewers for their very valuable suggestions and comments.

Christoph Wulf
Berlin, Spring 2012

Introduction

Issues of anthropology play an important role in nearly all branches of science, the arts, and the humanities. Currently, scholars in many disciplines of the humanities and social and natural sciences, as well as literature and cultural studies are discussing what is regarded as a key turning point in anthropology. Expectations regarding this new direction differ widely: in some cases scholars are uncovering new problems and new questions, while in others they are applying fragmentary knowledge to larger problems and contexts. Another aim is to find new points of reference—a matter of vital importance in a time of normative uncertainty. Concepts of what constitutes anthropology differ as widely as opinions on how we should understand anthropology. In this book I make some suggestions about how to address these issues.

If we take an etymological approach, we can describe anthropology as the study of a life-form characterized by its upright gait.[1] This concept of anthropology encompasses the universal and the particular aspects of historical and cultural diversity and is closely related to the development of society, science, and philosophy.

Anthropology, as a term used to designate an academic discipline, does not date back to antiquity; it is a neologism that expresses the new interest in humankind itself which arose between the sixteenth and eighteenth centuries. It was first used as a book title by Galeazzo Capella in 1533 for a book divided into three parts: the first part discusses the worthiness and values of men, the second focuses on the charms of the female, and the third deals with the misery of the human condition.[2] The era in which Capella was writing saw a gradual movement away from the theological body of thought toward a focus on the individual. In Montaigne's essays we find the subject becoming the center of anthropological reflection.[3]

In the course of the development of civil society and Enlightenment philosophy, anthropology became the study of human beings. While the aim of education is to promote the development of individuals,[4] anthropology is committed to improving the conditions of human beings as a species.[5] Kant's *Anthropology from a Pragmatic Point of View*, published in 1798, distinguishes between physiological and pragmatic anthropology. Physiological anthropology studies the condition of being human as dictated by nature, whereas pragmatic anthropology is concerned with the civilization and cultivation of human beings. Pragmatic anthropology considers the extent to which humans have both the possibility and the obligation to take their existence and their future into their own hands.[6] This distinction has become highly significant for the development of anthropology because it draws attention to the fact that in order to survive, human beings, unlike animals, are forced to lead their lives in various different historical and cultural environments and to design themselves. However, this distinction, which appears to be so plausible at first sight, is not really accurate, since what Kant referred to as physiological anthropology is not free of historical or cultural influence. It is thus not possible to draw a clear distinction between these two areas, which have been closely interlinked from the start.

Unlike Kant, Johann Gottfried Herder and Wilhelm von Humboldt emphasized the historical and cultural character of anthropology, establishing an approach that has, via Franz Boas's conceptualization of anthropology, had a great influence on the development of anthropology in the US.[7] In Humboldt's view, comparative anthropology should examine the historical and cultural characteristics of different societies. This should include the study of the differences between societies, cultures, and individuals as well as the search for an "ideal of mankind" from among the various disparities and eventualities of the human race. This requires scientific and historical hermeneutical procedures as well as philosophical reasoning and aesthetic judgment. Carrying out research in various eras and cultures creates a body of anthropological knowledge that contributes to an enhanced understanding of social and cultural developments. Humboldt saw the aim of anthropology as more than gaining knowledge for its own sake; he saw it as a way of initiating educational processes with the aim of improving human beings.

Radicalizing Humboldt's thoughts, Nietzsche and Foucault called for an end to the search for a binding, abstract anthropological norm, thereby expanding anthropological issues and points of reference beyond the scope of European culture and history to include an ethnological perspective. Today's anthropology attempts to relate the historicity and culturality of its concepts, viewpoints, and methods to the historicity and culturality of what is under investigation. Anthropology examines the findings of the human sciences and develops a critique of itself based on historical and cultural philosophy, thereby paving the way for the investigation of new questions and issues. At the heart of these efforts lies a restlessness of mind that cannot be stilled. Research in anthropology is not limited to certain cultural contexts or single epochs. Reflections on the integral historicity and culturality of the research enable the discipline to leave behind the Eurocentricity of the human sciences and to focus on the unresolved problems of the present and the future.

This aim implies skepticism toward all-encompassing and universal anthropological interpretations, such as those occasionally found in biological science, for example. Anthropology is not a single discipline. It touches on many different sciences and disciplines, including philosophy. It cannot be regarded as a closed field of research. It is the result of the interplay between different sciences. Depending on the issue to be examined, the range of disciplines involved can be very different. The object and subject of anthropology can encompass the entire field of human culture in different historical areas and cultures. Anthropology presupposes a plurality of cultures and assumes that cultures are not closed systems; rather, they are dynamic, able to permeate each other, and they have an indeterminate future.

Anthropology can be understood as an academic attitude toward examining issues relating to different times and cultures. This is why anthropological research can be found in many different disciplines, such as history, literature, linguistics, sociology, psychology, and the theory of education. However, the research frequently tends to transcend the boundaries of individual disciplines, thereby becoming transdisciplinary. This results in completely new scientific disciplines and issues that require new forms of scientific interaction and cooperation. Many different research methods are used in these processes. Historical-hermeneutical processes of text interpretation, qualitative social research methodologies, and philosophical reasoning are widely used, the latter being an approach that is difficult to categorize in terms of specific methodology. Some research makes use of artistic and literary materials, thereby transcending the traditional boundaries between science, literature, and art.[8] A growing consciousness of the role of cultural traditions in the development of different research areas, subjects, and viewpoints has made the increasing trend toward crossing international cultural boundaries a central issue of anthropological research. In the light of globalization, this transnational approach to anthropology is becoming increasingly important. It provides the framework that nurtures a spirit of inquiry and a commitment to expanding our knowledge, which in turn lead to the development and testing of new research paradigms.

The demise of a binding anthropological norm has made it necessary to take a fresh look at the most important anthropological paradigms and try to locate their common ground as well as their differences. This has also given rise to a need to define the tasks and procedures of anthropology and to illustrate their importance for research in the humanities as well as the social and cultural sciences.

If the subject of anthropology is research on human beings in history, it seems only logical to include human evolution in the scope of the anthropological examination of the "conundrum of humanity." However, human evolution can only be understood if it is viewed as an integral part of the history of life itself. The irreversibility of human evolution and of the history of life is also an aspect of anthropology; today, this process is seen as a consequence of the self-organization of material. In the same way that anthropology highlights the historical character of its research, evolutionary theory emphasizes the radical time-scale of nature and human evolution. Time and history are therefore central dimensions of evolution. Human evolution is a lengthy process of development that starts with early hominids and includes primordial humans and early humans en route to becoming modern human beings. This process is a multidimensional morphogenesis of interdependent ecological, genetic, cerebral, social, and cultural factors.

Integrating the study of evolution into anthropology raises issues concerning the relationships between all living things and beings and the long duration of human evolution. It also involves a quest to discover general laws of evolution. The central focus of philosophical anthropology, on the other hand, is the special character of human beings as derived from a comparison of humans and animals. According to Max Scheler, this character enables humans to be conscious of the objects around them and to have a concept of the world. Helmuth Plessner sees the uniqueness of humans in their ex-centricity. This term refers to our human capacity to step outside our own bodies by using our imagination. This makes it possible for us to see our bodies not only as something we are, but also as something we possess. For example, in terms of the way we feel and perceive our hands, we sense them as belonging to our bodies and also as organs that we can use as we wish. Arnold Gehlen's anthropology also has the special nature of "man" as its centerpiece. Gehlen developed a theory of humans as "deficient beings" (*Mängelwesen*), building on the idea that the constitutive element of human existence is its insufficiency, which had been formulated by Herder one hundred years before. Humans are obliged to use individual and collective actions to overcome their inadequacies and insufficiencies, and this is the origin of culture, language, and institutions.

In the same way that evolutionary theory searches for a general understanding of life and human beings, philosophical anthropology looks to define the special nature of human beings by comparing them to animals. Scholars of philosophical anthropology often overlook the fact that the basis of their thinking is an abstract, generalized concept of the human being that cannot be found in the historical or cultural world, but it implies that humans could exist outside of their historical and cultural specifications. Historical and cultural anthropology oppose this abstract concept by insisting on the necessity of examining human life within its historical and cultural contexts, as it is precisely the different characteristics of these that make us human.

Since the study of anthropology was taken up in the French Annales School and in French research on the history of mentalities, historical writing has taken a new direction. This complements the new issues and the new methodological procedures used in the depiction and analysis of the history of events and the examination of structural and social history. Concentrating on anthropological issues brings into focus both historical structures of social reality and subjective moments of agency in social subjects; this focus is used for research on the basic conditions of human behavior. The studies carried out by Lucien Febvre and Marc Bloch in France are examples of the successful examination of anthropological issues in the field of history, in which historical knowledge arises from the disputed borders between events and narrative, reality and fiction, structural history and narrative historical writings. These works, which have since become classics of their genre, appeared at the same time as the works on philosophical anthropology and also link to the works of historians such as Fernand Braudel, Emmanuel Le Roy Ladurie, Philippe Ariès, Georges Duby, and Jacques LeGoff.

In Germany, anthropological issues are examined in cultural studies, educational studies, women's and gender studies, and in the history of mentality, as well as in everyday history and microhistory. The scope of these studies encompasses case studies of actual life stories, local and regional history, the history of mentality, and historical cultural anthropology. Different mentalities permeate each other, forming new combinations. They devise actions appropriate to specific situations and provide orientation and decision-making aids for social behavior. They are specific to culture, class, and social group. Mentalities evolve in specific social conditions and structure social behavior in social subjects without giving it a determined, fixed form. They allow individuals to be different and to behave differently. They are subject to change and historical development. Understanding their fundamental historical and cultural nature enables us to grasp the universal openness of history.

Additional important anthropological perspectives are provided by the field of cultural anthropology, or ethnology.[9] This discipline does not view human beings as being "behind" (i.e., responsible for) the diversity of their historical and cultural characteristics but studies them within the context of these characteristics. Therefore it is not sufficient to identify *body*, *language*, or *imagination* as universal cultural entities; they must be examined in the context of different cultures. It is this diversity of culture that enables us to draw conclusions about humans. Comparing culturally different forms of expression results in new ideas and calls some areas of accepted thinking into question. Ethnological research into the heterogeneity of cultures yields important results for cultural anthropology. These findings have had a lasting effect on the understanding of what is different in our own cultures. New developments have resulted in an expanded concept of culture in which both the disparities and the shared characteristics of different cultures play an important role. The globalization of politics, economics, and culture is resulting in the overlapping, blending, and assimilation of features that are global, national, regional, and local. This creates a need for new ways of examining different cultures. The issue of understanding the *limits of our comprehension* of different cultures becomes central. The ethnographic methods developed in social and cultural anthropology on the basis of fieldwork and participant observation lead to forms of knowledge other than those gleaned from historical source interpretation and philosophical reasoning. They not only make us aware of what is different in other cultures but also what is different in our own culture. Therefore the application of the anthropological perspective to the cultures of the world broadens and deepens the scope of anthropological research.

In view of this situation in anthropology in Britain, North America, Germany, and France, I suggest that we try to connect lines of thought from these different mainstreams and, where possible, to develop them into an anthropology that adequately accounts for the historicity and culturality of the researchers and their objects of study. Philosophical reflection can then help to render the results of this research fruitful for our understanding and definition of human beings. I have attempted to achieve this in three large, interrelated anthropological research phases, each of which lasted more than ten years.

In the first phase my aim was to do diachronic research on a number of issues subsumed under the heading "Logic and Passion" that are of major importance for the understanding of European culture and difficult to capture within a single discipline.[10] They include such topics as the soul, the sacred, beauty, love, time, and silence. In some of these studies, literary, sociological, and philosophical research played an important role; it was complemented by reflections on the historicity and culturality of anthropological research itself as well as its contribution to a better understanding of contemporary culture.[11] In the second phase I investigated the history and theory of mimesis and the mimetic bases of social and cultural action.[12] My aim was to show that cultural learning is to a great extent mimetic learning. It is not merely a process of imitation, but a creative process of appropriation and development that follows models. In the third phase, I examined the significance of rituals in child-rearing and education, using ethnographic methods. The project focused on four fields of cultural learning: the family, school, peer groups, and the media.[13] The large empirical studies that were carried out in this context made an important contribution to knowledge about the staging and performance of social action and behavior and about the performative creation of communities.[14]

In addition to this I carried out a cross-cultural study on the happiness of families in Japan and Germany. I also conducted three Indian-European studies on the body, the emotions, and the senses, as well as several investigations of the historical and cultural dimensions of human emotions in Germany, Russia, China, Brazil, and the Moslem world. The aim of these studies was to show how helpful the principles and perspectives of historical cultural anthropology are when researching non-European cultures.

In these three phases of research, I translated my concept of anthropology into a concrete form, which combined three different perspectives—the ethnographic, historical and philosophical perspectives—in a single approach. This anthropological research revealed the importance of the human body for our understanding and interpretation of ourselves as human beings, now that anthropology has to a great extent abandoned its normative stance.

Evolutionary research, philosophical anthropology, anthropology in the historical sciences, and cultural anthropology also place equal emphasis on the human body (see chapter 6). However, these paradigms are based on different understandings and concepts of the human body. The first deals with the human body as part of the history of life, the second with its special nature and different characteristics when compared to the bodies of animals. The two paradigms emphasize the characteristics of the body as formed by society, culture, space, and time. Although the basic conditions and needs of the human body remain the same, they are formed differently both historically and culturally. This applies, for example, to gender, relations between generations, nutrition, and clothing. Concepts of the body and the senses are shaped differently in different cultures and historical periods in relation to fellow humans and the environment. Such influences are central to the mimetic learning processes, with which human beings seek to understand their immediate and wider environments, and they also play an important part in the formation of communities through rituals. Investigating the performative arrangement of the body is essential for understanding the performative character of culture. Even language and imagination are performative and cannot be understood without considering their bodily origins. Ultimately, birth, death, and transience are also related to bodily conditions of human life.

The central role of the body in an anthropology that defines itself as historical and cultural is used as an initial point of reference in studying the significance of mimetic processes, in which humans creatively imitate the world around them, recreating it to aid their own understanding and acquiring it as their own in this way. Culture is created, communicated, and changed in mimetic processes (see chapter 7). No individual development is possible without reference to a past development. Mimetic processes occur in our aesthetic and social spheres. Mimetic learning is cultural learning and involves the body, its senses, and imagination.

Following on this analysis, I show how mimetic processes create different "performative cultures," of which three aspects are important (see chapter 8). One involves the different forms of cultural performances of social aspects; the second relates to the performative character of speaking, which stems from the identity of utterances and actions (e.g., saying "I do" in a wedding ceremony); the third refers to the aesthetic, which is closely related to the staging and performance of the body. In contrast to a view of "culture as text," a performative understanding of culture focuses on its character as a performative arrangement. The practical knowledge required for the performativity of actions is acquired in mimetic processes, in which ritual arrangements play an important part. These ideas take on concrete form when we consider the performative character of perception, media, and gender.

As I show in chapter 9, mimetic and performative processes also play an important role in the staging and performance of rituals. Their significance was long overlooked, particularly with regard to aiding in the success of transitions within or between institutions, enforcing order, and channeling potential violence, as well as forming communities. Rituals enable differences to be settled and provide continuity between the past, present, and future. They create communities and social behavior. Metaphorically speaking, they are windows that allow a glimpse into the structures of society and culture.

Language and symbolism play an important role in all of the processes described above. Our ability to speak arises from an innate capacity (see chapter 10) whose biological prerequisites are the language centers in the brain. All humans are born with the ability to form sentences. However, despite this general ability, humans only learn to speak in individual languages that are characterized by their own histories and cultures. The mimetic, ritualistic, and performative aspects of this process are significant. Language is an area where the findings of anthropology intersect and overlap with finite cultural aspects of anthropology. Speaking results from bodily articulation on occasions when it is needed, and the playful use of language develops in the context of historically and culturally diverse ways of life.

Since imagination plays a central role in the advancement of culture and society,[15] I analyze its importance in the evolution of the human being in chapter 11. Imagination creates images that have their basis within the human body. Anybody wishing to understand the body in its historical and cultural forms can discover a great deal about it by examining the collective and individual images of human beings. The images arising from the imagination require a medium if they are to be visible to others. The materialization and execution of the images depends on the nature of the medium used. The role of media in the creation and development of individual images is one of the most important issues in anthropology. Equally important are the manner in which processes of exchange between collective and individual imaginaries are conducted and the way in which cultural change evolves from these processes. The increasing significance of images in the global network of contemporary cultures has further increased the importance of examining the anthropological implications of images.

The first images of humans to be made were death portraits or death

INTRODUCTION

masks, which were created by making an imprint of the face of the deceased. This imprint brings the deceased back as an image in the present. The image renders present what is absent, representing the deceased person in the community of the living. Whereas the body of every human being is transitory, all humans can be retained in the medium of an image. The grave offerings of the Neanderthals show that their imaginary was concerned with the subject of death and also that they believed in life after death. Concepts and rites of death differ according to culture and historical period (see chapter 12). In the European cultural context, Philippe Ariès differentiates between tamed death and the individual's own death, the death of another person and death inverted into its opposite.[16]

Regardless of how one sees these attempts to identify differences in mentality and attitudes toward death, they undoubtedly show that death is one of the most important topics in anthropology. Given the central role of the body in anthropology, questions of birth and death cannot be avoided. They disconcert us and lead to an intensive contemplation of our history and culture. Just as every body is unique due to its biological conditions, and just as its socialization and culturalization will add further to its special nature, all human subjects experience their lives in their own specific ways and therefore also experience death in their own individual ways. While death and dying have long been among the central issues of the humanities and social sciences, procreation and birth, surprisingly, have thus far been accorded scant attention. Hannah Arendt was the first to note this deficit and called for an intensive and critical examination of the phenomenon of birth. Anthropology must conceive of birth and death as the two fundamental conditions of human life, each of which refers to the other. It must investigate how human beings in different cultures and epochs have dealt with birth and death as the enigmatic boundaries of life, and how they continue to do so.

The complexity and puzzling nature of human life is fundamental to anthropology. The more we know about human beings, the more we realize how much we don't. This problem cannot be resolved in our time, culture, and society. This is clearly illustrated by looking back at history and examining other cultures. In anthropology, it is essential to remember that it is only possible to gain an insight into human life and ways of living if we view them as parts of a much greater whole. A critique of anthropology from the inside is therefore indispensable in the attempt to explore the complexity of human history and culture.

10

Paradigms of Anthropology

ONE

Evolution—Hominization—Anthropology

Today, anthropology includes aspects of research on evolution that have contributed to a fundamental change in our understanding of the world. The evolution of life and hominization are only a small part of the development of the universe. There are still many aspects of evolution that we are far from being able to explain. However, this very lack of conclusive answers makes it important to include these issues in our understanding of humanity. Biology, chemistry, and physics have shown that the cosmos as well as the earth and life upon it *are in a constant process of development.* The concept of *irreversibility* has therefore also assumed a special importance in the natural sciences. Ilya Prigogine, who won the Nobel Prize for chemistry in 1977, describes this development "from being to becoming." First, irreversible processes are just as real as reversible processes and do not correspond to any approximations that we would have to impose on the laws that are reversible in time. Second, irreversible processes play a fundamental constructive role in the physical world; they form the basis for important coherent processes that are clearly manifested on a biological level. Third, irreversibility is deeply rooted in dynamics. According to Prigogine, one could say that irreversibility starts where the basic concepts of classical mechanics and quantum mechanics (such as trajectories or wave functions) cease to be observable.[1] This change in perspective led scientists to take into account the temporality and historicity of the processes they describe. This is another reason why today's anthropology needs to take into consideration both historical and cultural dimensions. This perspective must also be applied to research on evolution and hominization.

Evolution

The Evolution of Life

In terms of evolution, hominization was a late development. Evolution includes the origins and development of the universe,[2] the earth, life, and all its diversity. As far as we know to date, life evolved from non-living material. This was dependent on certain preconditions whose basic structures can be experimentally simulated. From a mixture of inorganic compounds such as ammonia, methane, steam, and other gases, it is possible to create organic compounds with the aid of electrical sparks. While this does not create life forms, it does create the first building blocks of life. The probability that these building blocks will evolve to become the extremely complex molecular compounds of a primitive cell or any of its precursors is negligible. Manfred Eigen, who sees evolution as a game with few fixed rules and an open ending,[3] demonstrated in an experiment that in certain circumstances, matter has the tendency to establish self-reproducing systems. When different material structures (molecules) are present, a selection process always takes place, and the linking of such molecular structures fulfills the basic prerequisites for life.[4] According to the current state of knowledge, *life evolves as a result of the self-organization of matter.*[5]

Ultraviolet light breaks down steam into hydrogen, oxygen, and ozone and leads to the production of organic substances such as amino acids, fatty acids, and so forth. This prebiotic evolution results in the creation of carbon, which can form compounds with itself and is therefore necessary for living organisms.[6] Molecular compounds are formed and lead to more complex systems that can already be described as life forms. The two most important chemical building blocks of life are created in this process: *proteins* as cell components,[7] which consist of even smaller parts, the amino acids, and *nucleic acids*, which contain the programs of life and pass down genetic information from generation to generation.[8] The decoding of the genetic code embodied in proteins and nucleic acids is necessary for the development of every single living organism. While the first life-forms on Earth appeared very early, for a long time they remained microorganisms. When they reproduce, microorganisms create copies of themselves; in this process, variants are created that allow natural selection to take effect. The advent of sexual reproduction led to the development of an enormous genetic variation and, with the aid of natural selection, the evolution of more complex forms of life.[9]

The Development of Life

The first life-forms were single cells that are comparable to bacteria and evolved to produce a great variety of species. The transition from single cells to multicellular organisms that can divide their tasks among different cells was a far-reaching change. There is still much to find out about how they develop. It is possible that multicellular organisms develop out of colonies of single cells. The earliest fossilized evidence of diverse multicellular creatures dates back seven hundred million years.

Whereas previously life-forms were only classified as either plants or animals, today life forms are assigned to one of five different categories or *kingdoms*:

- Prokaryotes or Monera (protozoa without a nucleus): blue-green algae, bacteria
- Protists (protozoa with a nucleus): golden algae, Sporozoa, flagellates
- Fungi: genuine slime fungi, Phycomycetes, sac fungi, bracket fungi
- Plantae: red algae, mosses, vascular plants (ferns, flowering plants)
  Animalia: sponges, flatworms, mollusks (cephalopods, mussels, snails), arthropods (millipedes, arachnids, crustaceans, insects), echinoderms, chordates (especially vertebrates).[10]

The life-forms of these five kingdoms nourish themselves in three different ways. Photosynthesis—the process of turning light into chemical energy—with assimilation of carbon dioxide and nutrition by inorganic substances; absorption of dissolved organic nutrients; and active intake of food by incorporation and the internal processing of (mainly) organic food.

The evolution of the vertebrates was a further step in the history of life on Earth. Their development provided a new building plan with many different subsections. Vertebrates are characterized by the arrangement of their bodies in a head, trunk, and tail and their wide distribution in all climatic zones on Earth. Vertebrates were originally aquatic creatures and first appeared around 450 million years ago. Their osseous internal skeletons and mandibular arches developed roughly 400 million years ago, and research has shown that mandibular arches were present in fish around 300 million years ago.

Life has only been present on land for around 400 million years. The first of these life-forms included algae and Psylophyta. Around 350 million years ago the land plants, often more than twenty meters high, formed the carboniferous forests. By this time, insects and arachnids had also evolved. Amphibians also emerged at this time. Reptiles evolved from the amphibians and then later evolved into birds and mammals.[11]

Today there are approximately 1.5 million known species. The actual number is significantly greater than this and is estimated to be ten to fifteen times as many. Even this figure is comparatively low when we compare it with the total number of species that have existed since life appeared on Earth more than three billion years ago, which is estimated to be around one billion.

Of the species known today, 751,000 are insects (roughly half), 281,000 are other animals, 1,000 are viruses, 4,800 are Monera (bacteria and other similar cells), 69,000 are fungi, 26,000 are algae, 248,000 are higher plants, and 30,800 are protozoa.[12] According to the theory of evolution, all of these life forms are *related* to each other by degrees; that is, they have a common *origin*. Human beings comprise but one species within this colossal spectrum of life.[13]

The Process of Evolution

Evolutionary theory gives nature a *temporality* and a *historicization*, with an associated dynamization. Thus, development can no longer be seen as a static scale but as a *phylogenetic tree* with many branches, which helps us to see the *relationships* between species and to see how they *drifted apart*. It is no longer the similarities between living creatures that are decisive, but their common phylogenetic bonds. Of the biological sciences, biology has special significance for the exploration of evolution. It examines the history of evolution and the processes of change in organisms as well as reconstructing their interrelationships and the forces that have brought about evolution and continue to drive it today.

Four assumptions are central to Charles Darwin's evolutionary theory.[14] According to these postulates, the world is never at a complete standstill but is in constant motion. First, the species are in a constant process of change: some become extinct, and new ones evolve. As shown by fossils, these changes occur as living conditions change. Second, evolution is a gradual and continuous process; it is not subject to sudden leaps. Third, Darwin considered it possible to trace back all living creatures to a single common origin. Fourth, Darwin assumed a process of natural selection; that is, as generations follow on from one another, a wide genetic variation develops. Darwin believed that those who survive are those with the most suitable combination of characteristics for coping with their environment.[15]

Evolution takes place in alternating phases of *stagnation* and *accelerated change*. Genetic material remains constant and only changes during reproduction and mutation.[16] That evolution does not follow a principle of linear progress can be seen from the widely differing ages of the plant and animal species alive today: older species coexist alongside younger ones. The horseshoe crab, which is actually more closely allied to scorpions and spiders than it is to true crabs, is an example of a species that was already present 180 million years ago; the ginkgo tree is the only surviving species of a group of plants that was very widespread between 130 and 180 million years ago; the subdivision of mammals into predators, rodents, and primates took place 20 to 30 million years ago. The following table provides a few examples (all of which have been supported by fossilized evidence) of the differing time scales for the development of plants and animals (the figures are given in millions of years):[17]

Mammals	200	Crustaceans	540
Birds	150	Arachnids	420
Reptiles	300	Snails	580
Amphibians	390	Ginkgophyta	200
Cartilaginous and bony fish	410	Conifers	320

The evolutionary process provides examples of both forces of *conservation* and forces of *innovation*. On the one hand, new species appear at varying rates; on the other hand, old structures are retained and, having proved themselves, survive into the future. The recording and transferring of genetic information, the *genetic code*, has proved to be successful and has remained constant for more than three billion years. It gives every species its *genetic identity* and only changes over very long periods of time. Within one species, the genetic information, which is transferred during ontogeny, is basically similar to that of the parents. Anatomical features, physiological characteristics, and behaviors are continuously transferred from one generation to the other. This fixity of the genotypes of species is opposed by the changes that occur between the generations. New combinations of genes occur in the offspring of one generation of parents, and errors may occasionally occur during ontogeny as the genes are copied. This recombination and occasional mutation lead to the genetic diversity that is essential for evolution to succeed. In addition to preservation and innovation, *adaptation* and *specialization* also play an

17

important role in evolution. This is illustrated by the famous finches of the Galapagos Islands. The original species landed on the Galapagos Islands roughly ten million years ago and found an *ecological niche* there. Over the course of time, many different species evolved, which exploited different sources of food. Some finches became insectivores with long, pointed beaks; others ate grains and had short, powerful beaks; still others found their food on the ground and developed a different shape of beak. In the case of the finches, adaptation and specialization enabled the species to survive. In other cases—for example, giant pandas that feed on bamboo shoots, which are low in nutrients—survival is endangered by specialization and its inherent lack of flexibility.

Evolutionary processes are *irreversible*. Once phylogenetic changes have taken place, they cannot be reversed, except for some minor aspects and individual features.[18] An example of the irreversibility of evolution is the horse. Around sixty million years ago, horses had five toes and were the size of a cat. In the course of its orthogenesis, it reached its current size and developed a single-toed foot. However, such a development cannot be judged purely on the basis of the stage of evolution currently reached. We know today that there is no planning for the future in evolution—only decisions based on the current situation. What is currently regarded as having proven itself in terms of survival counts and is repeated. Everything else dies out—that is, extinction is not due to ecological overexploitation alone. Thus, evolutionary trends can only take place in the form of specific development patterns—not as predetermined developments but as phenomena that occur under some environmental conditions to which the life-forms affected are able to react adequately.

Like individuals and societies, species are also mortal. Countless examples show that no species can survive forever. Mass extinctions are known to have occurred several times in the history of our planet. The most famous of these occurrences was the demise of the dinosaurs around 65 million years ago, which was probably caused by the environmental catastrophe resulting from an asteroid crashing into the earth. An even greater catastrophe took place 250 million years ago and led to the extinction of 80 percent of all creatures alive at the time. However, in terms of scope and speed, the current wave of mass extinctions, in which countless species are being destroyed by the human species, is even greater than either of the examples above.

From this we can conclude that *extinction is a necessary by-product of evolution*, and probably there have been *selective extinctions of species that had nothing to do with the ability of organisms to adapt*. This suggests that Darwin's postulation of natural selection must be modified, because it cannot sufficiently explain the diversity of life. According to evolutionary theories like that of *punctuated equilibrium*,[19] gradual development without leaps, as postulated by Darwin, would have had insufficient time to produce the actual diversity of life. In contrast, unforeseeable major catastrophes led to an extinction of species—that was not based on their inability to adapt—which was then followed by an explosive phase of new development, leading to an acceleration of evolution. One such major evolutionary thrust certainly occurred after the devastating catastrophe at the end of the Cretaceous period. "In the opinion of paleontologists, the rapid rise of mammals is among the most dramatic changes of the Cenozoic period, the new era of today's life forms."[20] After the disappearance of the dinosaurs, mammals were initially quite small, but they eventually developed into many larger forms such as primordial horses, bats, whales, apes, and hominids.

Catastrophes thus play a productive role in evolution. This can also be seen in the evolution of hominids. With the emergence of hominids in the course of the differentiation of mammals after the catastrophe at the end of the Cretaceous period, a form of life arises that for the first time not only has catastrophe to thank for its existence, but also has the ability to cause catastrophes. The history of humankind also offers proof that the phrase *"natura non facit saltum,"* which the gradualists following Darwin insisted upon, is not true. The punctuated character of catastrophes again and again brought forth developments of life that could not be sufficiently explained by the gradual theory of evolution of Darwin and his followers. This insight on the part of those who believe in punctuated equilibrium, emphasizing the significance of individual catastrophes, does not mean that Darwin's theory of evolution is false, of course, but it demands that his theory of evolution be modified to include the theory of punctuated equilibrium.

In the nineteenth century, the theory of evolution was closely linked to the idea of natural progress. Evolution was seen as having the aim of achieving *perfection*, and the development of humans from apes to *Homo sapiens* was regarded as evidence of this. Particularly in cultural anthropology and ethnology, this conceptualization resulted in cultures as being evaluated as "better" or "worse"; this view was part of the underlying thinking of colonialism and is completely untenable from a contemporary viewpoint.[21] Although evolutionary biology assumes a consistent general increase in complexity as part of evolution, the theory of a linear progression of development has now been discarded. The idea of steady evolutionary progress ignores the many side branches of every species— the branches that "break off" the evolutionary tree. It is an abstract idea that excludes many of the different twisting paths evolution may take. Evolution does not simply replace the old and "primitive" with "higher" forms of life.

Forces and Mechanisms of Evolution

One of the more important forces of evolution is selection. This generates genetic diversity through new combinations of genes and mutation and gives evolution its respective directions. As most species have male and female forms and produce their offspring by sexual contact, two different sets of genetic information are mixed, and this genetic *recombination* brings about an extraordinary level of genetic diversity. Sexuality has the consequence that in every generation new combinations of genes are tested by the environment. The enormous potential of the genetic recombination that occurs in sexual reproduction can be clearly illustrated by one salient fact: in species that reproduce sexually, no two individual creatures are genetically identical. The rate of mutation, in which spontaneous genetic changes occur, is very low and plays a much smaller part in the evolution of diversity than new combinations of genes. As well as genetic recombination and mutation, *natural selection* also plays a decisive role in evolution. The combinations that are best suited for their respective environmental conditions are selected from a large number of variants. Unlike their predecessors, today's evolutionary biologists assume that there is no fundamental plan of evolution that controls its progress. But where does this process of selection start—at the level of single genes, individual organisms, communities, or the entire species? This issue has been heavily debated, and many books have been written on it. We still have no clear answer today. It is probable that natural selection can start at different levels, and it is also probable that it might have a wide range of different effects. Regardless of where it starts, and however efficient its mechanisms, one thing is clear—it cannot be said to be pursuing a purpose.

As we have seen with the example of the Galapagos finches, the *environment* plays a central role in the process of selection. Climatic factors and the existence of other life-forms are especially important in the process of selection. Due to specialization and adaptation, natural selection reduces the pressure of competition and thereby contributes to the diversity of species. External factors relating to the environment and internal factors concerning the activity of the particular life-form both play a role in the process of selection. The external and internal factors of selection interact closely and in an extremely subtle manner. Whereas the

FIGURE 1.1 *Archaeopteryx lithographica.* The most famous of all *Archaeopteryx* specimens is the Berlin specimen that is one of the best-known fossils in the world. It is approximately 150 million years old. © Museum für Naturkunde in Berlin, Christoph Hellhake.

former relate to selection conditioned by changes in the environment, the latter refer to the adaptation of organisms to a given environment.[22] If this is not successful, the organisms become less viable or even completely unsustainable, and they generally become extinct. While the changes in a feature such as the different beaks of Darwin's finches can easily be traced, evolutionary *blueprints* still pose many difficult questions. It is due to these blueprints, for example, that all birds have had plumages for more than a hundred and fifty million years. Frequently, both the "older" and "newer" features can be seen at the same time. The archaeopteryx is a good example of such a "mosaic evolution"; its body plan combines older reptilian features with innovations regarding the plumage and the skeleton (fig. 1.1). As mutations cannot be regarded as deliberate changes in the development of a new blueprint for birds, it is probable that developmental requirements in the organisms themselves also play a role.

Put simply, there are three different aspects of evolution, and the diversity of life is explained by the interaction between them. First, every change in the evolutionary process consists of a sequence of steps. The first step consists solely of the creation of genetic diversity. This is completely random, which ensures that the material for evolution remains diverse by means of both mutation and genetic recombination. Second, the randomly evolved genetic variants of the life-forms do not simply differ from each other; they differ in regard to their capacity to survive—especially with regard to their capacity to reproduce successfully. Without following a particular plan, selection favors everything that increases the probability of genetic survival. Third, environmental factors and the structural and functional characteristics of the organisms themselves restrict the possibilities of development; the complex interactions between these two influences steer evolution in certain directions.[23]

Hominization

In the previous section we saw how closely the history of humankind is related to the history of life on Earth. The first mammals evolved two hundred million years ago, probably from a group of predatory therapsids ("mammal-like reptiles"). These were relatively small, weighed less than ten kilograms and belonged to the group of animals that escaped the mass extinction at the end of the Cretaceous period.[24] Only after the dinosaurs became extinct in the Pre-Mesozoic period were these mammals able to become more diverse. Today, mammals range from the blue whale, which is thirty meters long and weighs 140 tons, to the Eurasian pygmy shrew, which is just six centimeters long and weighs only six grams. There are more than two thousand extinct species of therapsids that have been preserved in fossils, compared to roughly one thousand surviving species today. *Homo sapiens* is one of approximately two hundred species of primates and has existed for forty thousand years. *Hominization* refers to the manner in which *Homo sapiens* evolved—the process of becoming human. Research into this field includes important contributions from paleontology,[25] paleoecology, and paleoanthropology, as well as research into genetics, the brain, primatology, sociobiology, and cultural anthropology. Hominization research cannot be categorized as part of a single science but is an interdisciplinary task in which different methods and understandings of science have their roles to play.

The primates go back to the Cretaceous era eighty million years ago. The Messel pit near Darmstadt has produced evidence of 49-million-year-old primates. These primates were similar to today's prosimians; they were arboreal, good climbers, and initially very small. Their feet and hands were suited to climbing and gripping. They probably had good eyes and a relatively large brain, and they were omnivorous and fed on insects and fruit (fig. 1.2). Whereas the roots of advanced primates, the anthropoids, go back as far as the end of the Eocene era (58–37 million years ago), fossilized evidence of anthropoid primates, which differed significantly from prosimians, was found in Fayum, near Cairo, and was dated to the Oligocene epoch (37–25 million years ago). In the light of the currently available evidence, which derives mainly from fossils and their dating, our predecessors, immediate ancestors, early humans, *Homo erectus*, and probably also *Homo sapiens* all evolved in Africa.[26]

Hominid Ancestors

In 1992, a large number of skulls, jaw bones, and skeleton fragments were found near Aramis in Ethiopia. They were dated as being 4.4 million years old. In 1994 an almost complete skeleton was found. At first it was assumed that the findings were australopithecines, which were the predecessors of humans. However, differences were soon discovered that were significant enough to convince researchers that this was a new species of hominid, and it was given the name *Ardipithecus ramidus*.[27] *Ardipithecus* had relatively small molars with thin tooth enamel and premolars that were similar to those of the great apes, or anthropoids.[28] They probably lived in an area on the edge of the tropical rain forest, which was also where the evolutionary lines of anthropoids and hominids parted. Their body structure indicates that they were at an initial stage of the development of the bipedal climbing movement of the australopithecines.

The predecessors of human beings, of the genus *Australopithecus*, originated in the Pliocene epoch, more than five million years ago and only ever existed in small numbers.[29] The oldest fossilized remains of

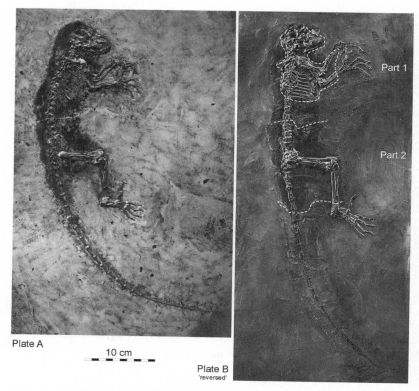

Plate A

10 cm

Plate B
'reversed'

FIGURE 1.2 A 47-million-year-old monkey fossil. "Ida" is the most complete fossil primate ever found. This picture was published by the Public Library of Science. Source: J. L. Franzen, P. D. Gingerich, J. Habersetzer, J. H. Hurum, W. von Koenigswald, and B. H. Smith: "Complete Primate Skeleton from the Middle Eocene of Messel in Germany: Morphology and Paleobiology," *PLoS ONE* 4, no. 5 (2009). This research article was and may still be available on the *PloS ONE* website at http://www.plosone.org/article/info:doi/10.1371/journal.pone.0005723. © Franzen et al. This is an open-access article distributed under the terms of the Creative Commons Attribution License.

australopithecines were found in the Turkana Basin in North Kenya and are more than four million years old. The australopithecines were bipedal and also climbed. Their skulls and brain size were similar to those of anthropoids today. However, it is difficult to distinguish their limbs from those of *Homo sapiens*. As they did not have any tools, they relied on their molars to process their food.

The best-known example of an *Australopithecus*—a 3.6-million-year-old specimen named Lucy (fig. 1.3)—is an example of *Australopithecus afarensis*.[30] Lucy was found in 1974 near Hadar in Ethiopia, and weighed 30–50 kg, was no taller than 1.2 m, and is younger than *Australopithecus*

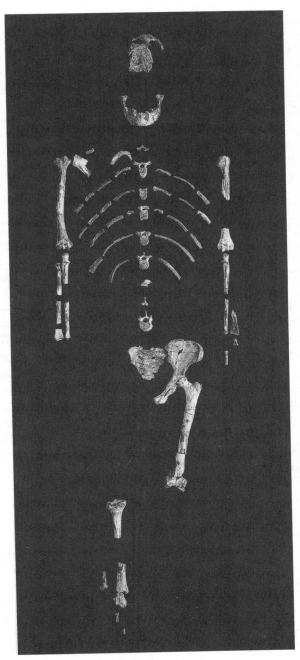

FIGURE 1.3 The fossilized skeleton of Lucy, the *Australopithecus afarensis* specimen that Donald Johanson's team unearthed in 1974 near Hadar, Ethiopia. Lucy lived about 3.18 million years ago and had a skull, knees, and a pelvis more similar to those of humans than to those of apes. © The National Museum of Ethiopia.

anamensis.[31] *Australopithecus afarensis* had already developed an upright gait. Its relative brain size is roughly equal to that of a chimpanzee today. However, its molars are larger and indicate the coarser diet found in the savannahs bordering the rain forest. While its arms were relatively long, its legs were shorter than those of *Homo sapiens*, which indicates that it would have needed considerable energy to move. These australopithecines probably lived in groups in wooded grassland areas in the African reef region three million years ago. According to Friedemann Schrenk, every group member was evidently largely responsible for obtaining its own food, as there is no direct evidence of food-sharing in this time. Finding food should have been a relatively unspecialized process. Fruit, berries, nuts, seeds, shoots, buds, and fungi were all available. Roots and tubers in the ground could be unearthed, and the nutritional value of small reptiles, young birds, eggs, mollusks, insects, and small mammals living in the water and on the ground would not have been ignored.[32] As a result of climate cooling and increasing dryness 2.5 million years ago, their habitats shifted to the banks of rivers and lakes. A selection pressure encouraging the development of hominids with larger molars arose, which may have been so strong that it led to a phylogenetic split of *Australopithecus afarensis* into the robust australopithecines (*Paranthropus*) and the genus *Homo*. According to this hypothesis, there were two different "strategies" for counteracting the worsening climate and the accompanying increase in the intake of harder plant nutrition. In one case we see adaptation to the circumstances of the immediate environment by strengthening of the jaw muscles (in the case of the robust australopithecines), and in the other we see a breaking away from dependence on the immediate environment through the development of tools (in the case of *Homo rudolfensis*).[33]

The Earliest Hominids

Paleoanthropology has still not answered the question of the origins of human beings, and finds are still being made that lead to revisions of previous thinking. However, we can currently assume that *Homo rudolfensis* (2.5–1.8 million years ago) and *Homo habilis* (2.1–1.5 million years ago) were among the earliest species of the genus *Homo*.[34] In both cases we find a mixture of features common to australopithecines and similar to those of humans. *Homo rudolfensis* had a more primitive set of teeth but already had a locomotor anatomy that showed similarities to *Homo sapiens*. *Homo habilis* had a more advanced dental structure with smaller dental roots, but its skeleton was more similar to that of an anthropoid than to that of a human. We still do not have fossilized evidence that would allow us to form clear links between the earlier australopithecines and *Homo erectus*. In contrast to the robust australopithecines, which evolved 2.5 million years ago, *Homo rudolfensis* was more flexible in adapting to its environment. Members of this subspecies also tended toward a more omnivorous diet and showed the beginnings of a tool culture. This enabled them to adapt well to the changes in nutritional circumstances caused by the climate change. They used stones to break up plants and to cut and process the meat of prey. These first forms of cultural specialization, which required only a low physiological specialization, made them increasingly independent of their habitat but increasingly dependent on the stone tools they created. "*Homo rudolfensis* remained native to tropical East Africa partly due to its preference for open habitats in the area of the rain shadow of the Great Rift Valley in Africa and partly perhaps also due to the developing territorial competition with the *Australopithecus (Homo) habilis*. Around 1.8 million years ago, *Homo rudolfensis* evolved to become *Homo ergaster* (working man), the early African variant of *Homo erectus*."[35]

This genus of humans created the first cultural artifacts; stone tools approximately 2.6 million years old have been found in Ethiopia and Tanzania. Their use was accompanied by a refinement in means of communication. Since, according to some researchers, the brain centers that are important for the development of language (the Wernicke and Broca areas) were already present in *Homo habilis* in rudimentary form, the first early forms of language may have developed at this time. The female *Homo habilis*'s readiness to conceive was prolonged until finally a state of continuous readiness to mate arose, which gradually resulted in male group members entering into pair relationships. This led to an intensifying of social relationships, to better rearing conditions for the offspring, and to the first forms of work-sharing, where the males gathered meat and took it to the temporary residence of the group. The first migrations outside of Africa probably took place more than two million years ago.

Early Human Beings (Homo erectus)

Fossils of *Homo erectus* are found in Africa, Asia, and Europe. Its diverse forms encompass early *Homo erectus* (*Homo ergaster*; 2–1.5 million years ago), the late African and Asiatic *Homo erectus* (1.5–0.3 million years ago), and the European *Homo erectus* (*Homo heidelbergensis*; 800,000–400,000 years ago). The predecessor of *Homo erectus* is probably a relatively robust prototype that evolved along with *Homo rudolfensis* in eastern Africa approximately 2.5 million years ago.[36] Compared with *Homo rudolfensis*, *Homo erectus* had physical features that suggest a progressive development toward *Homo sapiens*. This includes especially an increase in the volume of the cranium, alterations in the proportions of the cranium and face, an increase in the cranial base angle, the lower position of the opening of the bottom of the skull (*foramen magnum*), the construction of the jaw joint, and the more rounded dental arch. Where the australopithecines and the early members of the genus *Homo* still have many skeletal characteristics that are very much like those of anthropoids, the anatomy of *Homo erectus* corresponds to that of modern human beings in many specific ways.[37] Hominization is the result of the interaction of a series of factors, in which natural and cultural elements overlap and combine to produce a new level of complexity characteristic of human beings.[38] The contributory factors involved were the brain, the hands, tools, diet, habitat, fire, hunting, language, and culture.

BRAIN   Within about two million years, from early to late *Homo erectus*, the brain underwent considerable development. Whereas the brains of early finds such as the Turkana Boy had a volume of approximately 800–900 cc,[39] roughly one million years ago, brain volume had increased to about 900–1,000 cc; around five hundred thousand years ago, it had reached 1,100–1,200 cc, and today the average is 1,450 cc. If brain size is considered relative to body size, the brains of primates are 1.6–3.1 times larger than those of other mammals. Those of the australopithecines were between 2.4 and 3.2 times larger; those of *Homo erectus* between 4.5 and 5 times larger; and for *Homo sapiens*, the factor is around 7.2.[40] Size is less important for brain performance than the quality of the neuronal network.[41] The neocortex is important for storing and linking information as well as for processing experience. Fossil evidence shows that the neocortex grew considerably during the course of hominization. The cerebellum, which is central to the coordination of motor functions, also expanded considerably during this time, especially in the areas relating to the face and hands.[42] Recent brain research has shown conclusively that the brain undergoes substantial changes after birth under the influence of its (cultural) environment.[43]

HANDS AND TOOL   Upright bipedal gait developed on the borders of the tropical forests as a new strategy for overcoming the spaces between the trees and the earth. This meant that hands were no longer required for locomotion. The interactions between brain growth, the availability of the hands, developments in the anterior portion of the skull, and language led to a new evolutionary complexity that would become characteristic of humans.[44] The new freedom of the hands led to a gradual change in the shape of the hand from the "power grip" of the anthropoids, which were only able to grasp objects between their fingers and thumbs. This became the "grasping hand" and then the "precision grip" of *Homo erectus*, in which the thumb is able to move toward the tips of the other fingers, that is, to take up a position opposite them.[45] This established the anatomical prerequisites for handling smaller objects and more skillful use of tools. However, this transition took a long time to complete. For more than a million years, stone tools were created by chipping off splinters. Many of these simple, scarcely refined tools have been found in the Olduvai valley in Tanzania. The first more refined hand-held axe heads did not appear until about 1.5 million years ago.

DIET AND HABITAT   As diet became increasingly omnivorous, the length of the intestine declined. Carnivores do not need such a long intestine as herbivores. This dietary change meant that energy was freed up for other activities, which benefited the development of the human brain. The meat-rich diet of nursing mothers resulted in better nourished newborns, and their fast-growing brains. The use of stone tools to prepare food relieved teeth of their most demanding tasks and allowed smaller molars. Schrenk notes that the molars of the later *Homo erectus* were very similar to those of the early *Homo sapiens*.[46] This period probably also saw the development of the protruding, cartilaginous nose, hairlessness, and the development of the sweat glands. As *Homo erectus* had developed better methods of gathering and preparing food, which made him increasingly independent of his environment, he was able to migrate from Africa to Asia, America, and Europe.

FIRE AND HUNTING   The first evidence of the use of fire was found in Koobi Fora in East Turkana and is estimated to date from 1.5 million years ago. It is highly likely that early *Homo erectus* was already making use of fire. It would have been used to create warmth, to protect against wild animals, and to prepare meat and preserve it from rotting. Controlling and handling fire required not only technical ability but also social skills for regulating and coordinating its use. The first evidence of the hunting of animals has also been traced to *Homo erectus*. Stone tools and animal bones with traces of cuts have been found together, suggesting that a large number of animals were carved up at collection and distribution points, which could only have been the result of organized hunting. Hunting and the distribution of the spoils require a high degree of dexterity as well as advanced communications and coordination skills. Their significance for the development of the division of labor between men and women and for the formation of human societies can scarcely be overestimated. Serge Moscovici put it in a nutshell when he remarked that it was the hunter who became human and not humans who became hunters.[47]

LANGUAGE AND CULTURE   The growth of the brain and availability of the hands made the first forms of language possible. These were also prerequisites for manufacturing tools. Even if these early humans lacked the ability to create the differentiated sounds that form today's human languages, these early forerunners of language were important for the interaction between physiological and cultural elements in the process of hominization. Parallel to brain growth, methods of tool manufacturing, hunting, and the distribution of meat, a call system developed which made better communication possible. It is not possible to say with any certainty what the possibilities and the limitations of this system were. What is certain, however, is that these forms of linguistic communication played an important role in the development of early forms of culture. This paleoculture was a system that produced a high level of complexity; without it, this complexity would have deteriorated, giving way to a lower level of organization.[48] It consisted of organizational rules, customs, and commandments, the technical knowledge that was required for tool manufacturing, artistic skills, and skills relating to hunting and rearing infants, as well as general knowledge about the environment (e.g. the weather, plants, animals, etc.).[49]

There is widespread agreement that *Homo erectus* originated in Africa, although this is not entirely certain. Tool use, control of fire, hunting techniques, and the associated social skills are important prerequisites for migration to other parts of the world. The late *Homo rudolfensis* or early *Homo erectus* were probably the first to migrate two million years ago. There is also evidence of a concomitant expansion of the food-rich biotopes. The first traces of human life in Java and China go back roughly 1.8 million years. Other migrations took place around 800,000 years ago. Approximately 400,000 years ago *Homo erectus* was widespread in eastern and southern Asia and in central and southern Europe. At some Chinese sites, evidence of early human beings has been found that has been dated as being 280,000 years old. Anatomically, they have an intermediate form between *Homo erectus* and *Homo sapiens* and are therefore classified as "archaic Homo sapiens."[50] They correspond to *Homo heidelbergensis* in Europe, whose anatomical characteristics were a mixture of those of *Homo erectus* and the Neanderthals. In 1997, a new species was found in

Atapuerca in Spain, which was called *Homo antesessor* and is believed to be the common African ancestor of human beings and the Neanderthals.

Homo sapiens (sapiens)

Archaic *Homo sapiens* (*Homo steinheimensis*) evolved in Africa, Asia, and Europe around seven hundred thousand years ago. While its later form, the *Homo steinheimensis*, evolved into the Neanderthal (*Homo sapiens neanderthalensis*) in Europe, at the same time in Africa *Homo sapiens sapiens* was evolving. After Neanderthals and modern human beings first came together in the Middle East around ninety thousand years ago, they existed alongside and together with each other for roughly fifty thousand years, until the Neanderthals disappeared completely around thirty thousand years ago—an event that has given rise to a great deal of speculation.[51] Fossils of early Neanderthals dated to between one hundred and eighty thousand and ninety thousand years ago have been found in Croatia, Italy, and Gibraltar. The remains of classical Neanderthals dated as thirty thousand to sixty thousand years old have been found in Germany in the Neander Valley and in Salzgitter-Lebenstedt. Similar fossils have also been found in Spy in Belgium, at many sites in France, and also in Israel and Kurdistan. At 1,600 cc, the brains of the Neanderthals were larger than those of modern human beings but smaller in terms of overall body weight. At approximately 1.6 m tall and weighing 75 kg, the Neanderthals were somewhat smaller, but they were powerfully built and thus heavier than modern human beings.[52] Their short stature is indicative of a habitat in colder climate zones; if the body surface is reduced in proportion to the body volume, less body heat is lost. This is evident in the present-day inhabitants of Greenland. Since living conditions were harsh during the last ice age, malnutrition was widespread. The climate was six degrees colder than today's climate, which limited the availability of herbivorous food and made meat the most important part of the diet. The Neanderthals had developed tool culture, and they used the tusks of the woolly mammoth to form weapons and tools. As well as axe blades, scrapers, and pointed tools, they also made single-sided knives.

The burial offerings that were placed in the graves of the Neanderthals give us an important insight into their culture. These offerings included paints, equipment, and provisions, indicating that the Neanderthals believed in life after death. The remains of a man, a woman, and three children have been found in Ferrasie in France, the children having been sprinkled with ochre. In the Shanidar cave in Kurdistan, pollen from

roses, carnations, and hyacinths was found on and underneath the skeletons, indicating that the dead were buried on beds of flowers. From these
finds we can conclude that the living took care of the dead and felt that
they belonged to them just as they had done when they were living. They
knew pain and grief and had ideas about human mortality, for which
they sought to compensate by believing in life after death. The Neanderthals not only had distinct ideas about past and future, but also notions
of an imaginary world and the idea that the dead could continue to live
in an afterworld. This already reveals an awareness of death and its significance for human life, which is still today one of the most important
conditions for creating culture and human self-understanding.[53]

Our current levels of knowledge seem to indicate that *Homo sapiens
sapiens* also originated around one hundred and twenty thousand years
ago in Africa and subsequently migrated and settled in the Middle East,
Asia, and Europe. Finds in Border Cave, River Mouth in South Africa,
and in Omo/Kibish in Ethiopia provide evidence of its African origins.
These were preceded by fossils of the early and the late archaic *Homo
sapiens*.[54] This disproved the long-held view that *Homo sapiens sapiens*
evolved in Europe. This view had originated from the discovery in 1868
of five skeletons in the rock shelter, or *abri* of Cro-Magnon in the Dor-
dogne in the south of France. The skeletons differed significantly from
those of the Neanderthals and were anatomically classified as belonging
to modern humans, *Homo sapiens sapiens*. The term *Cro-Magnon man*
was coined as a result of the discovery of these roughly twenty-five-
thousand-year-old fossils, yet some similar fossils found in Borneo and
China are forty thousand years old, and some found in America are
thirty thousand years old. However, it is unlikely that modern human
beings originated in several different regions. Modern humans, who
came to central Europe around forty thousand years ago, did not live in
caves but in tents in the entrance areas of their places of worship, protected against the cold with skins and furs. Modern humans were more
advanced than the Neanderthals in tool technology. Evidence has been
found not only of knives, scrapers, and digging implements made in the
Aurignacian period, 28,000–22,000 years ago, but also of spears, bows,
and arrows dating from the same era. In the Gravettian culture, which
existed 28,000–20,000 years ago, spearheads were attached to wooden
shafts. The Magdalenian era around 18,000–11,500 years ago saw the
production of spear throwers and aesthetically pleasing artwork.[55] The
discovery of metalworking a few thousand years ago brought an end to
2.5 million years of stone tool-making. Compared to the Neanderthals,

modern human beings were, in particular, better at making use of natural resources. Their social organization was more advanced, they developed customs and traditions, their skeletons and musculature consumed less energy, and infant mortality was lower. In general their lives were was less hazardous, they lived longer, and they were more fertile.[56] At this point, the evolution of *Homo sapiens sapiens* becomes the history of humankind.

As a result of the discovery that humans and chimpanzees have 98 percent of their genes in common, interest is currently focused more on the shared characteristics of humans and animals than on their differences.[57] This emphasis is also shared by primatology research,[58] the discoveries in this field over the last few decades having produced a more complex picture of animals. We now see more traces of evolutionary behavior in our actions than before.[59] This change in perceptions of the relationship between humans and animals has resulted from the findings of evolutionary research and also from the basic difficulty of establishing from evidence of fossils and other remains at which stage of development we can start talking about human beings. This is why human beings have birthdays, but not humankind. Human beings did not result from a single act of creation, but came into being through a long process involving the interaction of many factors and culminating in human beings as we know them today. Hominization is a temporal and historical process in which natural and cultural elements are indissolubly and inextricably linked. It is not individual factors but the net result of many very different factors that produced human beings.

Hominization can be understood as a multidimensional morphogenesis arising from the interplay between ecological, genetic, cerebral, social, and cultural factors. Current understanding is that this process necessitated three types of change. The first were *ecological changes* that led to the expansion of the savannah and thus to an "open" biotope. Second, a *genetic change* took place in the highly developed primates, which were already walking upright. Third, there was a *change in social self-reproduction* due to the splitting off of young groups and the use of new territories. The new biotopes led to significant increases in the requirements for dexterity and communication skills for the two-handed, bipedal life-forms, which were already able to use and manufacture simple tools. These hominids, who had become omnivores, had to develop new levels of alertness, watchfulness, and cunning to cope with the demands of hunting. They needed new forms of cooperation and social responsibility to protect themselves against predators, search for food, hunt, share their prey, and rear their young. This led to a further development in cerebral capabilities. It was therefore the new ecosystem—the savannah—that triggered the dialectic between the feet, hands, and brain and became the source of technology and all other human developments.

As these processes unfolded, a paleosociety developed with a culture-based division of work between men and women and the development of hierarchical social relations. Language and culture became gradually more complex. The process of hominization was intensified by a prolonged youth, or neoteny; incomplete development of the brain at birth; and prolonged childhood, with longer affective ties between the generations and associated potential for comprehensive cultural learning. The cerebralization, prolonged youth, and increased social and cultural complexity were mutually dependent. The complexity of the brain requires a corresponding sociocultural complexity. The creative potential of the brain can only be expressed and develop in a sociocultural environment that grows in parallel. This dialectic relationship means that humans have been cultural beings from the very beginning; that is, their "natural" development is cultural. The final stage of this process of hominization is, in fact, also a beginning. The human species, which, for the time being, has reached its completion in *Homo sapiens*, is youthful and child-like; our brilliant brains would be feeble organs without the apparatus of culture, and all our capabilities need to be bottle-fed. Hominization thus was, in a sense, "completed" with the irreversible and fundamental creative incompleteness of human beings. The course not of hominization but of human history clearly illustrates that *Homo sapiens*, from *sapientia*, and *Homo demens*, from *dementia*, are inseparably linked, and the great achievements of humankind have their downside: the horrors and atrocities perpetrated by the human race.

Review and Outlook

As the study of human beings, anthropology covers the evolution of life and the history of the development of the human species (hominization). If it failed to include these aspects, it would omit dimensions of the anthropological body of knowledge that are in fact integral to it. Our understanding of evolution and hominization is determined by the current state of the art, which must take into account the historicity of both the subject matter of the research and the research itself, which are closely interrelated. What is now seen as valid in paleontology and evolutionary research is the cumulative result of knowledge that has evolved in the course of history. It may, however, change again in light of new discoveries and research results and the conclusions drawn from them.

Incorporating the evolutionary perspective into anthropology results in a shared reference point, which is important for how we understand ourselves as human beings. This perspective envisions the creation of human beings not as a single act, but as the result of a natural process of the evolution of life and hominization; thus it involves temporality and historicity.

Whereas evolutionary theory used to be closely associated with the idea of constant progress, today most researchers in this field no longer assume that there is a blueprint inherent in nature that is oriented toward perfection. It is now accepted that genetic recombination, mutation, and natural selection—both internal and external—are the main mechanisms of evolution.

The idea that hominization followed a single principle is now considered outdated. It is currently agreed that evolution involves the interaction of several factors and that social and cultural issues played a decisive role from a very early stage. Biological and cultural mechanisms had synergistic effects, the biological and cultural elements affecting the overall process to differing degrees at different times, depending on the area in question. Today, however, the role played by the cultural elements is increasing. The spectrum of cultural development includes the use of tools, communication, social behavior, cognition, brain structure, anatomy, and locomotion.

With our deliberate interventions, we modern human beings are effecting lasting changes in nature. Our actions are causing the biggest mass extinction that has ever occurred on Earth and are causing climate changes whose destructive effects are becoming increasingly apparent, but there have not yet been any fundamental changes in the behavior of human beings. The nonrenewable resources on Earth, which make human life possible, are being carelessly exhausted. *Sustainable development* is as yet but a catchphrase among groups committed to promoting it.[60] Humans are now in a position to intervene directly in the process of evolution by means of genetic modification, but the undesired side effects of genetic engineering are impossible to estimate.

The complexity of human life has further increased as a result of science and technology and global economics and communications, as well as worldwide political, social, and cultural networks. In the light of this development, the efforts of anthropological research to contribute to interpretations and knowledge about human beings are gaining in importance. If we are successful in bringing together universal and individual perspectives and in rendering visible the complexity of anthropological relationships, this research can make an important contribution to the processes of individual, social, and global self-understanding.

TWO
—

Philosophical Anthropology

Evolutionary research, as we have seen, is a discipline that
originated in the nineteenth century. Initially, it was associated with the established belief in the continuous progress
of historical development while, like all the sciences in this
field, defining itself as an empirically oriented natural science. Hominization was examined in the context of the history of life and the relationship between all living things.
Philosophical anthropology grew up after the First World
War in an era in which human beings had begun to question their belief in general progress and in themselves and
were endeavoring to use biological knowledge and comparisons between humans and animals to establish a basis
for understanding themselves. The centerpieces of philosophical anthropology are the anthropological works of
Max Scheler (1874–1928), Helmuth Plessner (1892–1985),
and Arnold Gehlen (1904–1976).[1] Despite considerable differences between these authors, their works from the first
half of the twentieth century are referred to collectively as
philosophical anthropology. Their common purpose was to
establish how human beings differ from animals, to determine what the specific conditions of being human are, and
to define the human condition. Despite their differences,
all three authors agreed that the central focus of anthropology is the *human body*, which is in itself the starting point
for differentiating between humans and animals. In a time
when humans had come to have grave doubts about themselves and were aware of this, it was hoped that knowledge
gleaned from the natural sciences by focusing on the body
could serve as a starting point for a revalidation of human

nature.[2] This orientation was associated with a rejection of idealism and the philosophy of consciousness and focused heavily on the human body as the starting point for anthropological thinking. Philosophy was no longer interested in reason, but in the creative diversity of life.

In 1927, Max Scheler gave a lecture in Darmstadt entitled "The Human Place in the Cosmos" (*Die Sonderstellung des Menschen*), which was published in 1928 under the title *Die Stellung des Menschen im Kosmos* and is regarded as the beginning of philosophical anthropology.[3] When Scheler died in the same year, he left no concrete preparatory material for the anthropological work he had intended to publish in 1929. The philosopher and biologist Helmuth Plessner also published his main anthropological work, *The Levels of Organic Being and Man* (*Die Stufen des Organischen und der Mensch*), in 1928. Despite large differences in material and argument, Scheler's article and Plessner's book share the assumption that organic life is structured in levels. Arnold Gehlen's work, *Man: His Nature and Place in the World* (*Der Mensch: Seine Natur und seine Stellung in der Welt*), which was revised in 1947 and cleansed of traces of National Socialist thought, took a different approach and focused on humans as acting beings.

The Human Place in the Cosmos

The starting point of Scheler's anthropology was the understanding that the history of human beings had never been as problematic as it was at the time he was writing.[4] This view was the basis for his attempt to determine the special position of human beings within the different levels that form the cosmos—a position that he believed to derive from their metaphysical rootedness. Plants, animals, and human beings are separated from the inorganic world by the urge that manifests itself in the first level of existence—the *urge to live*. This is not centered on a self and is therefore oriented toward the external world, without sensory awareness or consciousness. Scheler believed that every living thing has a soul; in addition to a side that pushes toward the outside world, there is also a side that is turned inward and is inaccessible.

The relationship between humans and animals begins to come into play with *instinct*, the second level of life. In comparison with the behavior of humans, whose instincts are weak, animals' behavior is to a great extent predictable due to the control exerted by their instincts. Animals' innate instincts control the way in which they live and their relationships with their environments. This instinct-driven invariability is largely lacking in humans due to the weakness of their instincts. At the same time, this deficiency is also a strength that permits instinct-free, spontaneous human action. In Scheler's view, which Freud and Gehlen shared, the lack of instinctive control over our drive impulses is the cause of the excess of drive that is characteristic of human beings. In order to behave suitably in social situations and social structures, humans must control their surplus drive energies by repressing and sublimating them.

Human beings also share with animals the third level—the capacity for *associative memory*. This ability is linked to instinctive behavior, drives, and needs, and here conditioned reactions and the reproduction of behavior play an important part. In associative memory we have a capability that is not merely instinct-bound. As a result, human actions are less determined by instinct, as the associative principle permits us to experience things on an individual level and to organize our intentions and actions on the basis of our experiences. This principle also means that individuals are increasingly released from physical limitations.[5]

The fourth level, which is also certainly shared by humans and primates, comprises *practical intelligence* and *choice*. These are the highest forms of biophysical functioning. We need practical intelligence in order to satisfy our human needs by taking the requisite actions. This requires selection processes involving evaluative assessments that we use to direct our actions toward achieving our intentions. If we are to act practically, we need to be able to anticipate objectives that relate to fulfilling our needs. Practical knowledge plays an important role here (see chapter 7).

These four levels of biophysical functioning, which some animals also have, differ from the final level—the mind—to which only humans have access. Unlike animals, which are bound by their drives and environments, humans can reach beyond their natural restrictions, are independent of their environments, and can adapt to the world around them and its changes. *Such a thinking being "has the world,"* that is, it can grapple with, use, and shape the world in accordance with its own intentions. In contrast to animals, which perceive their environments in terms of their drives and instincts, human beings' weak instincts and the hiatus they experience between perceiving and fulfilling a drive enable them to be intelligent, or "mental beings" (*geistige Wesen*). They can thus also grasp the essence of objects, and therefore the world, as opposed to seeing only a specific environment. According to Scheler, the mind or spirit permeates and influences all areas and actions of human life. Although it has the power to shape the areas of life that humans share with animals, it does not have the strength required to do so. Rather, it has to rely on vital energy to exercise its power. The spirit may be able to say no; however, it can only reject wishes and needs with the help of the vital force. Human beings' spirit makes them "ascetics of life." The ultimate goal is the breathing of life into the spirit and the sublimation of life to the spirit.[6]

The pivotal characteristic of human beings' relationship to the world is *openness toward the world*. Whereas animals are only able to perceive their environments as dictated by their instincts, human beings are also capable of perceiving the objects of the world without depending on their drives and instincts. This makes us receptive and open to quite different types of experience that enable us to perceive the world as objects. This is both a potential and a task. It is made possible by shaking off the fetters of the environment and by the existential release from the sphere of the organic. Thus the objects of resistance, which the human organism perceives in the outside world, are transformed into mere objects. Since humans are mental (or intelligible) beings, they are capable of completely understanding the essence of these objects, without any of the limitations that are imposed on the objective world or its actuality by the system of vital drives or the antecedent sensory functions and sensory organs. This is how Scheler characterizes our lack of dependence on our environment, our ability to objectify, and openness toward the world. He does not distinguish between our attitudes toward objects and our attitudes toward the essence of objects. Scheler's characterization of the capacity to experience things as objects, or "objectify" them, as the openness toward the world that sets human beings apart does not suffice to explain some important issues. The ability to objectify arises from historical and cultural attitudes, which are themselves the outcome of a long process of civilization. They enable us to perceive the world in functional terms in our contemporary culture. The ability to see things solely in terms of their functions, to grasp objects in a distanced manner, cannot be seen as the acme of openness toward the world. Because of this openness toward the world, humans are able to recognize the limitations of their distancing objectification and are then able to transcend them, although it was initially this very openness toward the world that was the basis for human beings' capacity for such detached objectivity. Openness toward the world evolved as part of the series of responses that human beings have developed to overcome the challenges of the world, thereby changing their own existence. In Scheler's view, when examined in a formal manner, this issue seems to be a balancing act: sometimes human beings give themselves more weight and are aware of having the power to dominate, and sometimes they recognize the weight of the world by adapting to it. However, in reality the relationship is dialogical.[7]

Scheler's ideas on philosophical anthropology have been criticized for not advancing beyond the views expressed in his previous works. He has also been charged with failing to resolve the dichotomy between body and mind that has been a recurring theme since Plato and Aristotle. Rather, his work has been seen as perpetuating the Cartesian divide between consciousness and the body. Scheler's work has also been criticized for being too heavily anchored in a phenomenological intuition of essences (*Wesensschau*) and eidetic ontology (*Wesensontologie*). Drawing on a traditional view of the person and the world, his writings have been described as being too strongly rooted in the philosophy of the time and not paying sufficient attention to the empirical data provided by the natural and human sciences.[8]

The Levels of Organic Being and Human Beings

Plessner's major work, *The Levels of Organic Being and Man* (*Die Stufen des Organischen und der Mensch*), published in 1928, takes up the idea of levels of organic life and develops it into a multifaceted outline of philosophical anthropology that is not easy to understand and for a long time was not accorded the consideration it deserves. It starts by differentiating between organisms and inanimate objects. Organisms have an insoluble boundary that can be perceived from inside and out. In contrast to inanimate objects, living bodies have a relationship to their boundaries that fulfils a double function: the boundary both closes the organism to the outside world and opens it up to it. The boundary can only be adequately understood if it is viewed from *both* "outside" and "inside." This *dual perspective* also covers the question as to the relationship between the organism and its environment. This boundary links plants, animals, and humans together in the realm of the living, in contrast to inanimate objects. According to Plessner, this boundary constitutes the minimum condition for life. Living things are bodies that have boundaries and are aware of them. In terms of appearance, living organisms differ from inanimate objects in that they can assert themselves in space rather than simply fill it. In the terms of systems theory, the boundary both separates an area from *and* connects it to its external world, and juxtaposes a substantial internal world to its external position, field of action, and environment. Thus it functions both to close off and to open up. It runs through the organism and creates opposing forces within it.[9] Living things are "things that are aware of and create boundaries." As such, they are positioned in time and space. *Positionality* describes the positioning of the living body, its position within time and space, and therefore also its temporal-spatial character. Plessner uses this term to characterize and differentiate living organisms. He thus uses the term *centric positionality* to distinguish animals and human beings from plants.[10]

Plants have no center and are distinguished by their open form. Human beings and animals, on the other hand, are characterized by their closed form—their centrality. Whereas the noncentered, open form of plants, and especially their lack of mobility, are associated with a position within a closed field, the closed, centered form of animals and humans is linked to an open field of movement in which they can position themselves. Plants, which lack the organs needed to create movement, are firmly rooted in their environments in an "unmediated" way. Lifeforms which have a center are only integrated in their environment in a "mediated" fashion. They can move away from it. In this context Plessner uses the term *mediated immediacy*. Centric positionality implies facing head-on, confrontation with an environment structured by objects, and "spontaneity," readiness for action.[11] This centric positionality involves a differentiation between the diverse aspects of the body and its center. The dependence of the body on its center, which arises in this confrontation, makes it possible to experience the body as controllable in terms of a mode of "having a body." Switching between the modes of having a body and being a body is characteristic for life-forms with a closed organizational form. It enables these life-forms to take a detached view of their own bodies. Unlike human beings, animals live within the center of their positionality, out of which they also act, but are not aware of it.

By contrast, human beings live as centers, in an ex-centric mode as selves. They are able to access the center of their positionality. They are ex-centric in that they can take a detached view of themselves. They are then on both the near and far sides of the gap that results from this act of distancing. They are bound within their bodies and their psyches (*Seele*), yet they are also without location, beyond all relation to space and time. Human life cannot transcend its centricity, yet its ex-centricity arises from it. Ex-centricity is an expression of humans' direct confrontation with their environments. As persons, human beings are determined by their bodies, the interiors of their bodies, their psyches, and by their view of the body and psyche from the outside. Plessner also terms the sphere of the psyche the *mind* (*Geist*). Plessner uses the general term *person* (*persona*) for this triad of body, psyche, and mind. The original Latin word *persona* refers to the mask that both conceals and reveals; it is the appropriate manifestation for a substance that is an indeterminate option. The concept of the person is especially suitable for expressing the oscillation between disclosing and hiding. The word person can also be used to refer this ex-centricity of human beings that is revealed in oscillation. The ex-centric position of human beings is associated with an ambiguity that is frequently characterized as being rootless, out of balance, unfathomable, essentially alienated; without location or timeless, placed in a void; seeking a means of expression, being in the ambiguous position of being a thing among things and the absolute center. Yet other ways of putting it are "living a predetermined life" (i.e., being forced to make oneself into something that one already is), "leaving a mark of one's own restlessness and productivity on history," and, finally, "leading an existence that cannot be exhausted by itself" (*Homo absconditus*).[12]

Human beings are therefore characterized by the following features:

- having a body and using it to experience the opposing external world;
- being in the body with a psyche and an inner life;
- being able to perceive the two other modes and the ineluctable interchange between the internal and external from an unreal position outside the body.

This is tantamount to dividing the world into three dimensions: *outside world, inside world,* and *social world* (*Mitwelt*). The outside world is created by the continuum of the objects in space. It cannot be transformed into the environment of animals, just as this environment cannot be turned into the external world of human beings. The reason for this is that as a result of the "dual aspectivity" that arises from human ex-centricity, "inside" and "outside" are perceived simultaneously. Because of this human ability, the inside world parallels the outside world, in a dual aspectivity of psyche and experience. In the inside world there is also a difference between the way objects appear and the way they are experienced by the individual. Here it can also be said that one *is* and one *has* one's experiences. Accordingly, the spectrum ranges from the detached mode of self-reflection to experiences of pain and ecstasy, which lead to a dissolution of the self. Plessner conceives the actual inner world as the state of self-dissolution, from which there is no escape and for which there is no escape.[13] The social world (*Mitwelt*) arises from the eccentric positionality of human beings. It does not surround them like the external world, it does not fill them like the internal world, and it makes it possible for them to be persons. It is the world of social life, without which human beings would not exist. Plessner saw *Mitwelt* as the form of their own position that human beings perceive as the sphere of other people (375). It is the world of mind (*Geist*), and as such it is to be differentiated from the outside and inside worlds, from the psyche, the subject, and consciousness. Human beings have bodies and psyches because they *are* these and *live* them. In contrast, mind is the sphere through which we live as people (377–78).

On the basis of the outline of a theory of the "living" (*das Lebendige*), Plessner developed three anthropological structural formulas on the principles of *natural artificiality, mediated immediacy*, and *utopian location* (383ff.). The principle of *natural artificiality* refers to the fact that culture is constitutive for human beings. They thus have an antinomic task. Because they are forced by their form of existence to live the life that they live, that is, to make themselves what they are (just as they only exist when they act), they need something to complement it that is non-natural or non-intrinsic). Thus they are *artificial* by the very form of their existence. Plessner's position differs significantly from that of Gehlen, who assumes that human beings can use culture to overcome their constitutional weaknesses, thus attributing a complementary function to culture. In Plessner's view, human nature is not deficient, but needs to be complemented by something that cannot be reduced to nature. The relationship between human beings and the world is formed by their discoveries and inventions. Human beings invent nothing that they have not discovered (384). Their inventions come about as part of an exchange with nature; they invent what they have discovered. Animals, on the other hand, can only find and not invent. Human beings are not only driven by an urge to live, but because of their ex-centricity, they can also assume a position in relation to this urge, place demands on themselves, and thus manage their lives. This does not result in a lasting equilibrium, because every certainty attained serves as the starting point for new processes of invention and construction.

Because of their ex-centricity, the relationship between human beings and the world is not direct, but mediated by many processes, resulting in a *mediated immediacy*. The ex-centricity of human beings implies both an involvement with the world and the ability to draw boundaries and distance them. In their relationship with the outside world, humans conduct communications by means of the senses, with the aid of stirrings of the psyche in the internal world, and by relating to other people in the social world. Human beings' expressive actions are communicated by language, images, and gestures. They therefore result from mediated immediacy and can only be understood as a paradox. Plessner sees them as an adequate externalization of inner concerns in the form of a vital impulse that really brings them out *and also* as essentially inadequate and broken as a mode of implementing and giving shape to depths of life that are never themselves revealed (410). Mediated immediacy is also evident in culture and history. The ex-centricity of human beings is the reason for their ambiguous and unfathomable nature.

Unequivocality, security, and certainty mean reduction, a lessening, self-limitation, and lack of productivity. Human beings are thus timeless and placeless beings in time and space and can therefore only have a *"utopian position."* This is linked to the contingency of human experience and actions and the associated openness to the world. This utopian location of humans can be endangered by religion or other attempts to find security where none is to be found. Plessner thus concludes that anyone who wants to go home, back to the homeland, where there is security, must sacrifice himself to his belief. "But he who remains true to the spirit will not go back" (420).

Helmuth Plessner was forced to leave Germany after the National Socialists seized power, and it was a long time before his work received the attention it deserved. Although Plessner's later anthropological writings became very well known shortly after his return from the Netherlands, it is only in the last few years that the situation has changed with regard to his main work. Gradually, detailed critical analyses of this study are appearing, which, while highlighting Plessner's common ground with Scheler's anthropological thinking, also emphasize its independent and original character. Interest in Plessner's work has been steadily growing for some time.[14]

Plessner's thought on eccentric positionality represents an advance on Scheler's less well substantiated positing of the spirit or mind as the defining characteristic of human beings, but a few questions remain unanswered. Plessner's differentiation between "being a body" and "having a body," this "internal position of my self in my body," which results from human beings' ex-centric position, begs the question as to how it can be ascertained whether the body self is identical with the self that has the body. It cannot be shown with any certainty that the two parts of the self form one unified self. There is no inner criterion for the sameness of inner entities. The intrapsychic identifiability of internal events or identities can be claimed but not proven. This had already been pointed out in Wittgenstein's private-language argument.[15]

The Nature of Man and His Place in the World

In contrast to Scheler and Plessner, who situate human beings within the framework of a theory of living creatures and see the spirit or eccentric positionality as the defining feature of human beings, Gehlen regards this attempt to develop a doctrine of levels of living things with the aid of concepts such as psyche and mind as not particularly promising.[16] Instead, he attempts to develop a conceptualization in which human beings can be explained in terms of themselves. Influenced by the American pragmatists of his time, Gehlen centers his theory on the concept of *action*, taking the view that it is action that shapes human beings.

Gehlen sees actions as serving to overcome the deficiency that is fundamental to the nature of human beings. He uses Herder's philosophy to support this thesis.[17] Similar ideas can also be found in the work of Nietzsche, who describes human beings, for example, as the "most botched of all the animals."[18] By comparison with other animals, they are inadequately endowed, and this places them at risk. It is only by taking action that human beings can overcome what must be seen as their constitutional deficiencies in comparison with animals.[19] This enables them to compensate for their morphologically deficient condition and make use of it to reach perfection.[20] In the process of action, human beings express, objectify, and institutionalize themselves. Indirectness, mediatedness (*Vermitteltheit*), and alienation are the inevitable consequences. As beings at risk, humans require cultural and institutional safeguards, self-stabilization, and discipline. With freedom from instinct and excessive impulses and under biological pressure, action is configured in such a way that it becomes increasingly mediated and symbol-laden. Gehlen's view is that drive dynamics are restructured and thus become increasingly indirect, so that human behavior is "relieved" or released in accordance with the principle of *Entlastung*. For instance, small children "must" first touch things and even put them in their mouths in order to experience their materiality. Later a single glance is enough to find out what they are made of, what shape they are and how they disclose themselves. It is no longer necessary to enter into interactions with them. This releases energies that can be used for other actions. These processes, together with the correct functioning of institutions, guarantee security of action.[21] According to Gehlen, the deficient nature of human beings results from their peculiar biological position. The central anthropological concepts of his theory are *neoteny* and the *extrauterine year, reduction of the instincts, excess of impulses, openness to the world, relief,* and the *institution.*

NEOTENY   Referring to the works of Louis Bolk,[22] who compared the morphology of newborn apes and human children and their differing patterns of development in later stages of life and formulated the hypothesis that human morphology is fetalized (i.e., in humans a fetal stage is retained), Gehlen came to the conclusion that human development must be considered to be slowed over the entire life cycle. Gehlen explains this with reference to our exceptionally long childhood, protracted adolescence, and long period of old age. Whereas, according to Haeckel's hypothesis, ontogeny recapitulates phylogeny (i.e., the development of the individual human being recapitulates the entire history of humanity in a condensed form), the hypothesis of *neoteny* draws attention to the fact that the early stages of human development are particularly long. Compared to what happens in other primates, in humans many ontogenetic and phylogenetic developments occur much later or not at all. In this view, what is characteristic of human beings is not the speed but the slowness of their development. Phylogenetically, this even applies to the human organs, which Gehlen sees as retaining developmental features that other primates have left behind long ago. Following Bolk, Gehlen postulates the existence of endocrine disturbances in human beings, which he suggests may be responsible for the differences in their development. This assumption also has the advantage that it does not contradict the evidence that humans and other primates are very similar biochemically.

This theory of neoteny certainly has some explanatory value, but it should not be overestimated. A number of characteristics of human morphology are not subject to slowed development. For example, Gehlen points out that the anatomical proportions of the trunk and extremities in apes are much closer to their fetal condition than they are in humans.[23] The development of the legs, in particular, is accelerated in humans. Similar delays in developmental processes have now also been discovered in other animals and even plants, and thus it is no longer possible to speak of humans as having a special status on account of their slow developmental processes. Neoteny is also not incompatible with the conventional explanations of evolutionary theory, since under certain circumstances it can be a phylogenetic advantage.[24]

THE EXTRAUTERINE YEAR   Gehlen takes a further argument for the special status of human beings from the research of Adolf Portmann, which focuses on pregnancy, birth, and the first year of life of humans and other primates.[25] Portmann differentiates between "nidicolous" (nest-dependent or bound) and "nidifugous" (free-moving) animals and tries to demonstrate that humans have a special position in comparison with these two groups. Insectivores and rodents are examples of nidicolous animals. Their gestation is short, and each birth results in a litter of many young. The young have no hair, and their eyes and ears are closed. They cannot leave their "nests" or feed themselves. They are therefore completely dependent on the help of their parents in every respect. Portmann classifies hoofed animals, whales, and apes as nidifugous (i.e., as leaving the family nest early). Their young complete the nest-dependent stage while still in the womb. Gestation takes longer, and the number of young in each litter is considerably smaller. The newborn young can hear and see, move independently, and interact with the mother almost immediately after birth. For example, foals and young elephants can stand and walk after a very short time.

Humans cannot be classed as either remaining in the "nest" for a long time or as fleeing it at an early age. Although human beings could be classified as nidifugous creatures based on the features named above, in many ways the newborn human resembles the nest-dependent creatures. It is only after one year (the *extrauterine year*) that humans reach the levels of development that the nest-fleeing creatures have already attained at birth. In fact, human pregnancy ought to take considerably longer. For this reason Portmann and Gehlen see human beings as a special case and classify them as "secondarily nidicolous creatures." Gehlen concludes from this that human beings therefore require a high degree of rearing and socialization; that is, they need to have culture imparted to them and are not viable without it. This initial helplessness of humans makes it possible for them to undergo a combination of somatic, psychic, individual, and social development. This is highly significant for the development of small children. Brain research and recent research into the cultural development of human thought have confirmed the importance of this early extrauterine phase of development for ontogenesis.[26] However, there are doubts about Gehlen's use of neoteny to support his thesis of the human being as deficient and to use it to justify the notion of a biologically related special status of human beings.

INSTINCT REDUCTION   In Gehlen's view, the character of humans as "deficient beings" is due not only to neoteny and the extrauterine year, but also to a reduction of instinct and an excess of impulses. This rudimentary instinctual equipment, which is also central to Scheler's and Plessner's work, has numerous consequences. It is evident in the involuntary movements during feeding (sucking, chewing, swallowing), sexuality (intercourse, birth, typical responses to children), and reactions to sudden danger (panic, taking flight, etc.). Otherwise there is no innate connection between a drive and certain objects and movements. Humans do react to certain key stimuli that give them the feeling of needing to do something; however, they are not at the mercy of these feelings and can resist them. Human behavior is characterized by the hiatus between a drive and the corresponding response, which gives humans the option of distancing themselves from these urges and saying no to them. Gehlen interprets this loss of control by the instincts as proof for his theory of the deficient human being and as a precondition for the central significance that learning plays in human life. However, as several recent primate studies have shown, other primates learn much more than Gehlen thought.[27] The differences between groups of apes of the same species that inhabit different biotopes are considerable and can be explained on the basis of their learning processes. In the fall of 1953 a female belonging to a group of macaques in Japan washed a sweet potato in sea water for the first time. This behavior has continued in this group to this day and has been adopted by successive generations, whereas it has still not been seen in another group of macaques living not far away. If, in the history of evolution, open patterns of behavior result in an advantage in terms of development, they frequently replace the closed patterns. Thus the residual instinct present in human beings would appear to be not a deficiency but an advantage in terms of development. To be able to benefit from this advantage and to live accordingly, more complex genetic systems are required than for the closed patterns.[28] Human beings are not deficient in terms of instinct.[29] This suggests that human beings do not have less genetic preprogramming than all other animals, but more. If it were possible to calculate the absolute figures, we would see that humans have more behavioral dispositions in their genetic makeup than animals. Their relative influence on the ensuing actual actions is smaller, however, because the other side—the behavioral components acquired by culture—has become stronger.[30]

EXCESS OF IMPULSES   Gehlen does not assume that humans have several drives but postulates a single, undifferentiated drive. This drive is not subdivided into specific drives relating to different groups of functions, such as reproduction and feeding. Rather, it permeates all areas of human action and emotions such as aggressiveness and efforts to establish power and dominance. Unlike the sex drive of animals, human sexuality is not subject to seasonal cycles. It is permanently present and articulates itself in a constant drive that is accompanied by an insatiable need. Gehlen describes it as an almost inexhaustible, directed energy and considers that "all forms of learned activity have the potential to be invested with impulses."[31] This structure of human inner life results in an excess of impulses (*Triebüberschuss*), and Gehlen refers to Freud and Scheler in an effort to refine his definition. In his view, as "deficient beings," human beings need the excessive impulses, since they require vigorous energy in order to take advantage of the many behavioral options that result from reduced instinct.

The excess of impulses results from neoteny. According to Buytendijk, in human beings the drive energies are present, but because human development is retarded, there is a long delay in the development of children's motor functions and sexuality. During the long phase of child and adolescent development, this excess is also associated with many actions, such as play and exploratory behavior, which do not have a specific aim.

In Gehlen's view, this results in behavior that is biologically paradoxical. He takes the view that the drive potentials released from the excess energy push us beyond our aim of self-preservation. Without this capacity, human beings would never have been able to evolve any further. Human beings are beings at risk, but they also seek risk.[32] This situation gives rise to the need for enforced regimentation and domestication. The hiatus between stimulus and reaction makes it possible and necessary to monitor and control the excess of impulses. The monitoring and controlling is achieved with the aid of culturally created and communicated images, which serve to develop and shape the structure of human needs, so that needs are satisfied by the communication of images. As a result, human behavior becomes less and less direct. In addition to images, language also plays a central role in this process. Impulses are given another form by language. The inside world is structured in terms of language, resulting in a linguistic and grammatical structure of the psyche. It seems necessary that the inner life should become largely expressible in language. According to Gehlen, human beings who are not successful in constantly and actively structuring their needs and building up an architecture of interests that is open to the world fall into self-destructive addictions in the face of the pressing urge of their excess of impulses.[33] As a linguistically structured internal outside world develops in the imaginary, the boundary between the outside and inside world becomes permeable. This results in an enrichment and differentiation of human feelings. In his later works, Gehlen modified his views of the monistic character of human impulses (*Antrieb*).[34]

OPENNESS TO THE WORLD Like Plessner and Scheler, Gehlen starts from the assumption that, due to their residual instinctual structure, human beings are receptive to and open toward the world, unlike animals, which are tied to their proper, that is, species-specific environment. Humans have less specialized sense organs, and they lack hair on most parts of their bodies. This makes them specially sensitive to touch and is a prerequisite for human beings' greater potential for mimicry. According to Gehlen, even the brain is not a special organ, as it could not have developed without a corresponding morphological basis.[35] From an evolutionary viewpoint, upright gait developed at a far earlier stage than the hypertrophic development of the brain, which only began to exceed the size of the brains of other primates to a significant degree half a million years ago. Gehlen sees the brain as a "paradoxical organ" because it has, along with the hands, made the specialization of all other organs superfluous.[36] He therefore agrees with Konrad Lorenz, who spoke of the human being as the specialist in being a nonspecialist.[37] As there is a correspondence between environments and the specialization of organs, the reverse is also true. Since humans do not have a species-specific environment, they do not have any specialized organs.

This view goes back to Uexkuell's insight that animals could not be viewed independently of their environments because they are tied to them by a series of functional cycles.[38] From the point of view of animals, there are only factors that are important for survival. This also applies to the perception and behavior of animals. Uexkuell transfers this thinking to human beings and shows that human beings' perceptions of their environments depend on their particular perspective. The forester sees the woods in a different way from a person going for a walk for pleasure. However, unlike animals, humans can perceive the same environment in many different ways and change their perspective within their current environment. Human beings are not therefore bound by their environments, but open to the world; their lives are not conducted in a closed cycle of function(ality) but in an open cycle of action. Whereas Scheler saw human beings' openness to the world as based in the mind, Gehlen sees it as resulting from a deficient biological constitution. Culture, which humans must create themselves with the aid of language and work, takes the place of an animal's environment. Since human beings are not preprogrammed with regard to how they create cultural figurations, they are open to the world. Constitutional, historical, and cultural conditions limit this openness to the world. However, when human actions lead to the destruction of nature, this openness toward the world is turned on its head.[39]

RELIEF [*ENTLASTUNG*]   Relief of action, or the releasing of energies through the development of behavioral routines, has played an important role in the phylogenetic development of human beings. It helps to coordinate perception and movement. Patterns of behavior develop, and, if they prove satisfactory, they are practiced and automatized and are then available without the need for attention and reflection. During such processes, habits that provide security are developed. Behavioral patterns evolve that make behavior reliable.⁴⁰ Only an everyday life simplified by habits and routines can free human beings to take productive action.⁴¹ If there were no such facilitation or relief, human beings would constantly be preoccupied by their high levels of drive and would thus have only a limited capacity for other actions.

Technology and institutions also aid this relief. Technology takes the place of organs and eases the burden on humans in their daily confrontations with nature. Institutions provide orderly structures and protect people against insecurity. They establish habits, create continuity, and ensure that the community runs smoothly. They protect human beings from being overwhelmed by outside stimuli and provide relief from the demands of their excess of impulses. In addition to technology and institutions, art also contributes to the relief of human beings. Art encourages human beings to develop an aesthetic attitude that is based on a relationship to the world that has been liberated from the demands of excessive impulses. These processes lead to an avoidance of physical effort, create distance, and take place unconsciously. However, if behavior is relieved from the demands of an excess of impulses, there is a danger that it might become rigidified in habits and routines.

THEORY OF INSTITUTIONS   The most controversial part of Gehlen's anthropological work is his theory of institutions. In his view, institutions perpetuate actions that can compensate for human deficiencies. Institutions provide internal and external support that helps human beings to deal with threats from the outside world and, on the other hand, to control the drive-related upsets and insecurities of the inner world. This makes them guarantors of stability and security. According to Gehlen, ever-increasing individuality and subjectivity have caused institutions in the modern world to lose their power to guide and structure. In his view, a culture of subjectivity is inherently impossible to stabilize and doomed to end in massive, ephemeral surplus production.⁴² Institutions stabilize societies by putting their "guiding principles" into practice. This occurs regardless of the intentions of individuals, their rational decisions, and the rule of law. By ensuring the permanence of social structures even outside of democratic control, institutions serve to relieve the burden on society. The institutions, which Gehlen initially called "systems of leadership," are given the task of interpreting the world, shaping actions, and providing security for people. Among these institutions, the state plays a special role in the continuity and social stability of a society. As the importance of the state and other institutions declines, they play a smaller role in the shaping of individuals. Instead, individuals end up wedged between the kind of superstructures that are produced by globalization of corporations and other organizations, neither of which are obliged to adhere to normative guiding principles.

Gehlen fails to include a critical appraisal of the role of historical change in his evaluation of institutions and the prerogative they exercise to subordinate and order individuals. Accordingly, his theory of institutions fails to include any notion of legitimization through democratic processes. Gehlen's nonhistorical belief in a fixed structure and function of institutions fits in with his idea of *post-history* (*post-histoire*). He believed that although there may be quantitative progress in many areas of human life, this does not necessarily lead to actual innovations in culture and society. Rather, a typical cultural crystallization occurs, which has the effect that no genuinely new artistic work can be created. The term *post-history*, which is taken from Kojève's lectures on Hegel, does not refer to the end of time, or humankind, or historical events. It simply means that there will no longer be any real cultural innovations or any new political systems or ideas that an individual could use to influence the superstructures of the present. According to Gehlen, political action is in its truest sense a conservative attempt to convince oneself that one has a chance of controlling a metahuman process that has already exempted itself from this very control.[43]

Review and Outlook

The philosophical anthropology of the first half of the twentieth century lacks a coherent approach. While there are some similarities between Scheler's and Plessner's starting points and also between some of their arguments, Scheler's accusations of plagiarism against Plessner were untenable. The differences between their theories and Gehlen's model are substantial. While Scheler and Plessner sought to determine the position of human beings within an overall theory of living creatures, Gehlen wanted to develop a theory of human beings out of the structural principle of action. The diversity of this field has been broadened by the works of authors such as Michael Landmann,[44] who have made stimulating contributions of their own to philosophical anthropology.

Whereas Scheler and Plessner were influenced by Dilthey's hermeneutics, Husserl's phenomenology and Heidegger's fundamentology,[45] the background to Gehlen's theory of action is mainly American pragmatism. Where Scheler and Plessner used biological research to establish the special status of human beings among living creatures, Gehlen used it to develop his theory of the human being as a "deficient being."

While Scheler's stage model of the cosmos remains rooted in the traditional separation of body and mind, Plessner, in his *Stufen des Organischen*, succeeds in making some progress toward overcoming this dualism by differentiating between open and closed form; centric and ex-centric positionality, with the possibility of distancing oneself from one's self; and a dual relationship to the body (being a body and having a body). No final conclusion has been reached as to the extent of the progress Plessner made in this direction.

Where philosophical anthropology was based on the biological knowledge of the time, it can certainly be said to have advanced the thinking of its time. However, as some of this biological knowledge has since been shown to be incorrect, some of the findings of philosophical anthropology must be modified. This is clear, for example, with regard to Gehlen's overestimation of neoteny and the extrauterine year.

Recent biological research has also called into question Gehlen's plausible thesis that humans are "deficient beings," even though it is only used to explain their dependence on culture and upbringing and to demonstrate that they lead their own lives and therefore have to act. It is more commonly believed today that the factors that led Gehlen to postulate that human beings are deficient creatures have, in fact, been beneficial effects of evolution right from the start. Whether or not one shares Gehlen's emphasis on the importance of culture, of child-rearing and education, and of institutions and structures of order for the creation and preservation of societies that he derives from his theory of human beings' deficiency, some of his insights into the connections between the biological prerequisites of human beings and their actions are still worthy of consideration.

Gehlen's theory of institutions is also open to criticism. While it does include many thought-provoking aspects, its nonhistorical slant and the laying down of a specific character and function of institutions are unacceptable. Moreover, Gehlen's overemphasis on the principle of the relief [*Entlastung*] of life, his undervaluing of individualization and subjectivity, and his provocative theses on modern art and "post-history" invite contradiction and criticism.

Although different in many ways, in their later works both Plessner and Gehlen turned more toward sociology and history and published many fascinating case studies in these areas. However, the resulting expansion of or modifications to their models of anthropology were only partially satisfactory.

In their anthropological work, Scheler, Plessner, and Gehlen reflected little upon the historicity or culturality of their own research. They therefore failed to develop a critical view of anthropological thought. Of the three, only Plessner took this into account to any significant extent. In one of his later works, he developed the concept of the *Homo absconditus*, which contains a critique of anthropology and takes into account the fragmentary and provisional nature of all anthropological knowledge.

Due to its focus on the human being as an individual, philosophical anthropology fails to address the historical and cultural diversity of human beings in the plural. This is the inevitable consequence of the interesting attempt to develop a single coherent concept of "Man," which failed to capture the diversity of human life and could hardly have achieved its ambitious goals. To investigate this is the aim of a branch of historical science that is oriented toward anthropological issues, which was initially developed by the French school of the *Annales* and later continued by the *nouvelle histoire* movement. The discipline of *cultural anthropology* in North America, which has oriented its research toward the diversity of human beings in different cultures and produced a large body of empirical material, has also made major advances in this field.

THREE

Anthropology in the Historical Sciences: Historical Anthropology

Whereas philosophical anthropology deals with questions of the essential nature of *Man* [*sic*], anthropology in the historical sciences investigates the elementary situations and fundamental experiences of *human beings* in the plural. While it is possible to limit the subject area of philosophical anthropology to the works of Max Scheler, Helmuth Plessner, and Arnold Gehlen, such restrictions are not possible in the case of anthropology in the historical sciences. Philosophical anthropology as a field of investigation is now by and large regarded as a closed chapter, particularly since studies that go beyond a critical discussion of the above-mentioned authors are the exception. In contrast, the turn toward anthropology in the historical sciences remains productive. Research of this kind began at roughly the same time as philosophical anthropology, with the founding of the journal *Annales* in France in 1929.[1] Over the course of only a few decades, many new studies emerged that justify calling this novel discipline a new historical science (*nouvelle histoire*). Its focus was on how human beings have changed through the ages. These studies are not oriented toward humans as a species, but toward the diversity of human life in different historical periods, investigating human feelings, experiences, thoughts, actions, wishes, and aspirations. This has led to a considerable expansion of the scope of the issues, approaches, and methods addressed by anthropology.

I begin this chapter by giving a brief outline of the turn toward the *history of mentalities* (*histoire des mentalités*) and *historical anthropology* in the French historical sciences. I then go on to describe the developments in the German-speaking world, which were strongly influenced by this French research. In conclusion, I present a short appraisal of the significance of this research for anthropology.

The *Annales* School of Historians

The *Annales* journal brought together a group of historians who, over the course of two generations, created the *"nouvelle histoire,"* which has influenced historical research in many countries, and without which the anthropological turn in the historical sciences would probably not have taken place. This applies also to Germany. The most well-known members of this group include Lucien Febvre, Marc Bloch, Fernand Braudel, Georges Duby, Jacques LeGoff, and Emmanuel Le Roy Ladurie. The aim of their work has been described as follows. First, problem-oriented, analytical history took priority over the conventional reporting of events. Second, they aspired to arrive at a history of the full spectrum of human activity, rather than focusing primarily on political history. Third, in order to achieve these two aims they needed to cooperate with other disciplines, such as geography, sociology, psychology, economics, linguistics, ethno-sociology, and so on.[2]

The research conducted by the *Annales* group is generally divided into three phases. The first phase began with the founding of the journal and lasted until the end of the Second World War. During this time the group turned against traditional political history and the history of events. Its main representatives were Lucien Febvre and Marc Bloch. In the second period, from 1945 to 1968, during which the group exerted a determining influence on the study of history in France, the group was centered around Fernand Braudel. In the third phase, from 1968 to the present day, the authors of this school have continued to have an influence on historical research in France; however, they are losing their unity as a group and therefore the coherence they previously enjoyed. Some authors are returning to sociocultural history, while others are turning to political history.

Lucien Febvre and Marc Bloch met in Strasbourg in 1920 and worked together there until moving to Paris in 1933. They were the leading members of an interdisciplinary working group that included, among others, the social psychologist Charles Blondel, whose work on historical psychology influenced Lucien Febvre. Georges Lefebvre, who specialized in the history of the French Revolution and was interested in the history of mentalities, was also teaching in Strasbourg at that time. Gabriel Le Bras, a sociologist of religion, and André Piganiol, a scholar of ancient history, also engaged in discussions with Febvre and Bloch.[3]

In 1924, Marc Bloch's *Les rois thaumaturges* was published.[4] This study examines a belief that was widespread between the Middle Ages and the eighteenth century, namely, that kings were able to cure a common skin disease by a ritual laying-on of hands (fig. 3.1). This study was important for the development of mentality research and for the turn toward anthropology in the historical sciences. First, it concentrates on notions of a miracle-working power of royalty, as a manifestation of the special power of kings. Here we see an example of "collective ideas," which are accorded substantial attention in the history of mentalities. Bloch's examination of this healing ritual specifically acknowledges the long period of time during which it was practiced. Moreover, he used comparison as a methodological approach. Systematic comparison remains one of the desiderata of historical anthropological research. Bloch's study on the culture of feudalism, which was published a few years later, also contains many new and challenging views.[5] In it, Bloch examines "forms of feeling and thinking," the "collective memory," and the medieval concept of time.

Lucien Febvre's studies on the Renaissance and the Reformation are also dedicated to an examination of collective attitudes.[6] Febvre was interested in the problem of relationships between the individual and society and between personal initiative and social necessity. Remaining true to his commitment to interdisciplinary research, problem-oriented studies, and the history of feelings, Febvre continued his work after the foundation of the *Annales* in Paris and after being appointed to a chair at the Collège de France.[7] He was fascinated to discover why Margaret of Navarre, a clever and pious noblewoman, wrote the *Heptameron*, a collection of indecent stories. He also wanted to establish to what extent the French author Rabelais believed in God. It was important for him to show why, in his opinion, atheism was impossible in the sixteenth century and why nonbelief did not belong to the "mental tools" of that time.[8] Many of Febvre's hypotheses were questioned in later case studies and need to be modified. Nevertheless, the history of mentalities owes a great deal to the innovative questions and approaches of both Febvre and Bloch.[9]

After the war, during which Marc Bloch was killed as a member of the Resistance, Lucien Febvre founded the Sixième Section of the École Pratique des Hautes Études, and served as its president. In the following years, this institute was devoted to furthering the development of

The Royal Gift of Healing

R. White sculp.

FIGURE 3.1 Sick people being brought before King Charles II of England. Reprinted from frontispiece of J. Browne, *Adenochoiradelogia: or, An anatomick-chirurgical treatise of glandules & strumaes, or Kings-evil-swellings. Together with the royal gift of healing, or cure thereof by contact or imposition of hands, performed for above 640 years by our Kings of England, continued with their admirable effects, and miraculous events; and concluded with many wonderful examples of cures by their sacred touch* (London: printed by Tho. Newcomb for Sam. Lowndes, 1684). © The British Library.

historiography in accordance with Febvre's teachings. In 1956 he was succeeded by Fernand Braudel, who had a different emphasis. This was already clear from his first three-part work, *The Mediterranean*,[10] which dealt first with the "unmoved" history of human beings in their relationships to their environments; second with the gradually changing history of the economic, social, and political structures; and finally with the rapidly changing history of events.[11] The first form of history is a kind of historical geography, which investigates the influence of landscape and the environment on human beings. The subjects of study are mountains and plains, coasts and islands, climates and transport routes. On this level, historical change is very slow. The second part is entitled "Collective Destinies and General Trends." Here the research focuses on the history of economic, state, societal, and cultural structures, which takes place on a level between the long periods of historical geography and the rapid changes of the history of events. In the first approach, history unfurls in the transitions between the generations and centuries, whereas the history of events is a dynamic history that includes many human actions, which Braudel uses the following metaphor to describe: "I remember that one night I found myself in the midst of a firework-like presentation of phosphorescent glow-worms somewhere near Bahia. Their pale lights glowed, went out lit up again, but without ever illuminating the night. That is how it is with the events of history—beyond their glow, darkness prevails."[12]

However new the integration of historical geography into historiography may have been, Braudel's work did not, as had that of his predecessors, contain references to attitudes, values, opinions, or mentalities. For example, even though he focused on the Mediterranean, he did not include any analysis of masculinity and honor, which play an important role in social relations in Mediterranean cultures, nor did he comment on the relationship between Christianity and Islam.[13] Instead, he presents a world that is determined by a lack of synchronicity between various temporal rhythms, in which many events are beyond the control of human beings, who only appear as actors on the margins. However, in this study Braudel did succeed in demonstrating the central importance of space and time, that is, of geographic, social, and individual time, which was an important contribution to historical anthropology.

Like his work on the Mediterranean, Braudel's second major work, *Civilization and Capitalism, 15th–18th Century*, also has a three-part structure. Again, the first volume, *The Structures of Everyday Life*, is devoted to the scarcely changing history of material life, and the second volume, *The Wheels of Trade*, discusses the slow transformation of historical economic structures. Volume 3, entitled *The Perspective of the World*, deals with the mechanisms of capitalism and the rapid pace of change that it brings about. The first volume describes the traditional economic structure, which lasted around four hundred years. The lengthy time-scale—the *"longue durée"*—and the global viewpoint are fundamental to his explanation of the sluggish changes. The second volume focuses on trade and the economic reality associated with it. The third volume gives a multidimensional account of the development of capitalism. According to Braudel, capitalism did not just arise from a single source, as suggested by Marx and Weber; rather, it is a heterogeneous, contradictory phenomenon that requires many theories from several different academic disciplines to explain it. As in his book on the Mediterranean, Braudel fails to mention perspectives from the history of mentalities developed by Bloch and Febvre. It was only in the third phase of the *Annales* school that these returned to the limelight. This phase began when LeGoff took over the post of section president from Braudel and later became president of the reorganized École des Hautes Études en Sciences Sociales in 1975.

Philippe Ariès's *Centuries of Childhood*, which was originally published in 1960,[14] was vital for the development of the history of mentalities and historical anthropology. According to Ariès, there was no concept of childhood in the Middle Ages. Up to the age of seven, children had no role to play, and thereafter they were treated as small adults. Childhood was first defined in France in the seventeenth century. From then on there were special articles of clothing for children, and adults also began to take more care of their children. The increase in the number of pictures of children during this period also supports the idea that it is only since then that there has been a concept of childhood as a special phase of life. Ariès's second book, *History of Death*, deals with another anthropological topic. Here he distinguishes between different attitudes toward death, ranging from the "tamed death" of the Middle Ages to the "invisible death" of the modern era, and from feelings of resigned powerlessness to making death a taboo. This work also received a great deal of attention because of the originality of its hypotheses and the wide range of material covered.

Although Ariès was initially an outsider among historians, his work on death inspired other studies of the family, sexuality, and love. The works of Jean-Louis Flandrin were to become particularly important.[15] Robert Mandrou published a historical-psychological study on modern France that included detailed sections on sickness, feelings, and mentalities.[16] Regarding the history of mentalities, Jean Delumeau's *La Peur en Occident* (*Fear in the West*) and his work on the relationship between sin and fears are particularly worthy of mention.[17]

The same can be said for Emmanuel Le Roy Ladurie's *Montaillou*, which made an important contribution to research on the Cathars, the history of French agriculture, economic village culture, and the mentality of village dwellers and their attitudes toward God and nature, time and space, and death and sexuality. This study is a microhistoric case study, inspired by ethnological methodology, and yields important conclusions on life in Occitania. In another study on the history of mentalities, *Carnival in Romans,* Ladurie uses psychological and psychoanalytical concepts to examine the attack on the common people by the upper classes during the carnival in Romans in 1580.[18]

Since the beginning of the 1960s, the research of LeGoff and Duby has been particularly important for the development of anthropological issues. In *The Birth of Purgatory*, LeGoff investigates the change in the worldview during the Middle Ages and demonstrates how attitudes toward space, time, and number changed, and how new habitual patterns of thought evolved and were passed on.[19] His interest in ethnological research is reflected in *Time, Work and Culture in the Middle Ages.*[20] Duby uses a case study (*The Three Orders*) to look at the relationship between the material and the mental in the three estates of the clergy, the nobility, and commoners. He shows that the revival of the image of a three-tier society in the early eleventh century is associated with a political program aimed at influencing mentalities.[21] Later Duby and Ariès edited a five-volume history of private life in which issues of the history of mentalities and anthropological themes feature prominently.[22]

Another area that had a great effect on changing mentalities is literacy. Furet and Ozouf studied the spread of literacy in French society from the sixteenth to the nineteenth century,[23] a process in which the history of the book is of vital significance. Their research focuses on the study of book-production trends, reading habits, and reading culture,[24] all of which have lasting effects on education.[25] Cultural phenomena and mentalities, which are often taken for granted, are themselves the result of a process of construction.[26] This is also demonstrated by Ariès's studies on the histories of childhood and death. In these works, the central issue is neither childhood nor death, but the differing conceptions of these phenomena.[27] French research into these issues, conducted in connection with the concept of the imaginary, subsequently played an important role.

This research was used to develop the history of mentalities (*histoire des mentalités*) in French historiography. There had also been some preparatory work in other countries, which was henceforth to constitute an important part of historical anthropology. These studies investigate worlds that are different from our contemporary world. They are located in the field of tension between the fascination for the historically foreign and the continuity of the familiar. In contrast to researchers of the history of ideas and cultural history, researchers of the history of mentalities employ all the same historical sources that historians of political and social history can also use. However, their goals are different. They try to use a large number of historical details to develop an overall history and an overall interpretation in which the subjective weighting of the source material plays an important role. Historical mentality can be understood as an ensemble of forms and contents of thinking and feeling that is formative for a group in a certain period and expressed in its members' actions.[28] Such ensembles are not systems that are free of contradictions. They are generalizing constructions and do not form homogeneous blocks, but exist in a dialectical relationship to each other. Since mentality research focuses on phenomena that are difficult to grasp conceptually, it uses soft concepts, which makes it vulnerable to attack. It uses the methods of historical research to reconstruct thought systems, feelings, attitudes, and behavioral schemata of groups such as villages, social strata, classes, and communities. The focus is on culture-specific patterns. The focus in the history of mentalities is less the brief time span of an event than the slowness of history, the long duration over which historical developments become common property. The aim is to develop a history of mentalities that encompasses all areas of human living and how they interweave.

One problem faced by the history of mentalities is the limited number of surviving sources. This problem is all the greater because in many historical epochs issues of mentality were not addressed in the sources that have survived, but have to be inferred. The more generalizing the statements on mentality are, the more open they are to attack from (positivist) positions that do not consider such generalizations justifiable. Thus, critics of research on mentalities have pointed out that its generalizing statements are frequently based on positions of historical philosophy, concepts and models of contemporary psychology, and contemporary everyday theories that are not subjected to critical reflection on their suitability. While no such methodologically inadmissible conclusions are to be found in the major works of mentality research, these studies are marked by tension between the limiting anthropological statements on specific situations and the goal of making a contribution to the interpretation of a specific historical epoch. Whatever one's appraisal of the significance of research on the history of mentalities, it must nonetheless be credited with having opened up the historical sciences for many new issues, concepts, and methodological procedures.

The Anthropological Turn

In Germany, the anthropological turn in the historical sciences took place in the 1980s and 1990s. One reason for this was the growing skepticism about the optimism of the 1970s, which had been associated with the hope that all of the major problems of society could be solved. The nuclear threat and the threat of environmental destruction amplified doubts about the belief that modernity would bring rapid progress in many important areas of human life. During this time, there was sustained criticism of both civilization and culture, which promoted a new interest in historical questions. In contrast to the situation in the newly evolving historical social sciences, which concentrated on the research of the nineteenth and twentieth centuries and which were greatly indebted to the works of Hans Ulrich Wehler and Jürgen Kocka,[29] in Germany, interest in anthropological topics was particularly evident within medieval studies and research on the early modern period. Studies on the transition from preindustrial to industrial society and on the history of the working classes promoted an interest in anthropological questions.[30] The focus of research gradually shifted toward an examination of the concrete conditions of daily life. This trend gained further impetus from references to Anglo-American cultural anthropology, folklore studies and the "European ethnology" that was developing.[31]

I attempt to capture these developments in three short outlines. The first is a brief description of six areas of research that deal with anthropological issues. The second is an outline of the most important research questions and approaches. Finally, I present three of the central subject areas of historical anthropology by way of example.

Areas of Research

An attempt to identify the most important areas of historical research in which anthropological issues and topics have been developed reveals at least the following six areas:[32] historical cultural research, historical demography and research on families, the historical study of everyday life, women's and gender studies, mentality research, and historical cultural anthropology.

HISTORICAL CULTURAL RESEARCH Research on historical folk culture or cultural research now attaches greater significance to anthropological themes. There has also been an associated increase in interest in the lower classes and marginal groups. Edward P. Thompson's work on plebeian culture, Peter Burke's book on European folk culture, and Robert Muchembled's study on the relationship between folk culture and the culture of the elites are all regarded as important milestones.[33] Research into the social history and social psychology of village dwellers was carried out at the Institute of Folklore (*Institut für Völkerkunde*) in Tübingen.[34] Some of the research conducted by Richard van Dülmen also belongs in this category.[35] These authors were reacting against the neglect and disregard for folk culture. The attempt to conceptualize the creation of folk culture as a productive achievement in its own right gave rise to the search for a new concept of culture that differed from bourgeois culture and could not be assigned to a single social group but would be oriented toward the comprehensive understanding of culture prevalent in ethnological research (see chap. 4).

HISTORICAL DEMOGRAPHY AND FAMILY RESEARCH Research in historical demography has also yielded contributions to anthropology. Arthur E. Imhof studied disease and mortality, investigating how the increase in life expectancy since the seventeenth century has affected attitudes to life and the strategic measures developed by the lower classes to deal with threats to their lives and the challenges of everyday living.[36] Although it is scarcely possible to use quantitative data to draw definite conclusions on the feelings, thoughts, and actions of individual human beings, these extensive empirical studies provide vital insights into changing attitudes toward life and death. In addition to other historical research on the family, Mitterauer's research on families also deserves mention. Mitterauer's earlier works focused on general family characteristics such as marriage age, marriage duration, and birth and death rates. In these studies he attempted, for example, to prove the inadequacy of reductionist models of the evolution from large families to small families.[37] His later research dealt more with family problems and the associated attitudes of family members.[38]

THE HISTORICAL STUDY OF EVERYDAY LIFE Another area of anthropological research is the study of the history of everyday life.[39] It looks at the lives of ordinary people and the subjective aspects of experiences of life.[40] This kind of research not only focuses on nutritional and dress habits and living and working conditions, but also aims to reconstruct history "from below," a history that describes the feelings, opinions, and inner lives of people. This starts from the assumption that the social structures and the everyday actions of individuals permeate each other. Everyday living is made up of repetitions and experiences that create social continuity. Many studies in this field are oriented toward specific regions or local areas and use everyday documents such as letters, diaries, autobiographies, and photos. Such studies cover a wide range of issues, including some as varied as everyday culture in the industrial age and in bourgeois society; studies on the history of everyday life in a volume edited by Hans Teuteberg and Peter Borscheid;[41] and research into everyday life in the Third Reich.[42]

WOMEN'S AND GENDER STUDIES   From the late 1970s and early 1980s onward, research including anthropological issues began to play a more prominent role in women's and gender studies.[43] The focus was no longer on "great women," but on the everyday lives of ordinary women and their roles in the family and in the working world. The studies discuss not only the social function of women, but also how women feel and act outside of their social duties. The history of the woman is conceptualized as a history of women, and the terms *woman* and *gender* are historicized, rendered concrete, and contextualized. The roles and the gendered nature of *woman* and *man* are seen as historical and cultural constructions, and their development and transformations are reconstructed. Many of these studies examine female sexuality, birth, women's work, and female forms of social intercourse, showing a high degree of interdependence between the different domains of research on women, men, and gender.

MENTALITY RESEARCH   Another important field of research in historical anthropology is the history of mentalities. *Mentalities* can be defined as the categorical forms of thinking that are removed from thinking itself, forming a kind of historical a priori, and as emotionally toned orientational devices. They are matrices that channel feeling into a recognizable, nameable form. Mentalities include cognitive, ethical, and affective dispositions.[44] The individual person can only access them with difficulty. They are unconscious, yet they structure perception, feelings, consciousness, and human action in every historical period and culture. Unlike many micro-analytic anthropological studies, research on the history of mentalities looks at wider contexts, often exceeding the bounds of traditional research.[45] Mentalities are subject to historical change, but this happens over a very long period. This is shown by studies on European mentality that examine basic human experiences in the context of the individual, family and society, sexuality and love, illness, age, communication, time and history, space, nature and the environment, and so forth in classical antiquity, the Middle Ages, and the modern era.[46] Norbert Elias's *The Civilizing Process* and Michel Foucault's *Discipline and Punish* also belong here, as do other works on the structure of the imaginary.[47] The complexity of these issues leaves these studies open to criticism, since it is always possible in any historical period to find contradictory examples that call the conclusions of the history of mentalities into question. However, it is essential to research the imaginary, as it prefigures the feelings, thoughts, and actions of human beings in the historical periods in which they live.

HISTORICAL CULTURAL ANTHROPOLOGY   The most important work in historical cultural anthropology is Wolfgang Reinhard's *Lebensformen Europas*. His approach focuses on *behavior* and *habit*, that is, the central emphases of historical behavioral research. Reinhard believes that, since the mental dimensions that regulate the behavior of members of human groups in such a way as to produce uniform behavior are referred to as *culture*,[48] this research into historical behavior can be regarded as a major contribution to historical cultural anthropology. Research into ways of life is conducted by means of a diachronic comparison of cultures. Its starting point is the human *body* in its historical forms, and it also includes *fellow human beings* and the *environment*, especially its influence on the formation of the human body and its ways of life.

The major works in this domain also include the international transdisciplinary studies on historical cultural anthropology initiated and implemented by Dietmar Kamper and Christoph Wulf under the series title Logic and Passion.[49] In contrast to the studies described above, which were carried out by historians attempting to investigate new historical phenomena in their respective contexts, the Berlin studies in historical anthropology were designed to be transdisciplinary and transnational from the start. This led to the development of different questions and topics of research. The authors working in this field were interested in doing research on historical phenomena chiefly in order to contribute to a better understanding of the present, which they understood as having its own historicity. This historicity determines the issues investigated, the perspectives taken, and the methodology employed. The distinguishing feature of this kind of historical anthropology is that it takes into consideration the links between the historicity of what is under study and the historicity of the researchers themselves.[50]

Research Questions and Approaches

If we take a closer look at what is understood as an anthropological orientation in these areas of research and at the problems it addresses and the approaches it develops, we find four important aspects: *basic life situations and basic experiences (e.g., pregnancy, death of the parents, weddings), subjectivity*, the *concept of culture*, and *case studies*.

Historical anthropology investigates elementary situations and basic experiences of being human. It studies a basic stock of patterns of thought, feeling, and behavior that is anthropologically constant (Peter Dinzelbacher);[51] basic human phenomena (Jochen Martin);[52] and elementary human behavior, experiences, and basic situations (Hans Medick).[53] Although it could be understood otherwise, these classifications are not concerned with making statements about humans in general but with gaining an understanding of the multidimensional conditions of life and the experiences of real people in their respective historical contexts. These anthropological studies investigate the multitude of ways in which the varieties of human life are expressed and presented. This diversity of phenomena is paralleled by the multidimensionality and open-endedness of anthropological definitions and research paradigms. In this research it is necessary to develop a feeling for the *difference between the historical world under investigation and the current frame of reference* of the research.[54] Since, for example, linguistic metaphors and terms have different meanings in different times and in different contexts, these differences in meaning must be taken into account. The same applies with regard to research into basic human behaviors, experiences, and fundamental situations. From the point of view of the historical sciences, the feelings, actions, and events under investigation can only be understood in terms of their historic uniqueness. It is this that lends them their dynamic nature and makes them subject to historical change.[55] Ariès, for example, demonstrated that the understanding of childhood is subject to historical change and is therefore never exactly the same in any two historical periods,[56] and that even our relationship to death changes over the centuries.

One of the main objectives of historical anthropology is to depict human beings in their uniqueness and subjectivity. As these are not people who are among the "great" male and female figures of history, a new understanding of both human history and the task of writing history is being articulated here. The studies therefore often focus on the lower classes or members of marginal groups.[57] Since reconstructing the lives of members of these groups requires describing numerous different elements of the life histories of many people, the area of study is considerably expanded to include historical contexts. The focus on the lives of "ordinary" people is often associated with an attempt to reconstruct the subjective side of their lives. Attention is centered on people who shape their lives with their feelings, thoughts, and actions. The praxis of human living is studied as a field of action. The focus is on specific, real life stories and people's ways of subjectively experiencing how they live. Different forms of individual action are identified, and contradictions and ambiguities are described. The studies investigate how people handle political and economic conditions and how individuals act in their dealings with social structures. In addition to rational behavior, other forms of human action are taken into consideration, and sensations, thoughts, and dreams become "historicizable." Subjective processes of acquisition and structuring are also thematized. The history of private life contains fascinating examples of the subjective nature of the actions of individuals and the subjective structuring of given conditions.

The study of anthropological topics and standpoints has resulted in a change in the concept of culture. In the last few decades the influence of cultural anthropology has led to the use of a new concept of culture in historical research. This is not a uniform concept; however, as a rule, culture and the values, attitudes, and actions associated with it are no longer identified with a section of society. Instead, a *broader concept of culture* is employed. Clifford Geertz defines it as follows.

- A system of meanings handed down through history that occur in a symbolic form
- A system of communicated ideas that are expressed in symbolic form
- A system that humans use to communicate, sustain, and further develop their knowledge about life and their attitudes to life[58]

In this view, culture is a symbolic system that is handed down and into which human beings grow. They can also influence and develop it by means of their actions.

Many anthropologically oriented historical research projects are *case studies* and can accordingly be assigned to the field of *microhistory*.[59] Some of them have been influenced by cultural anthropology. They focus on clearly defined spaces, periods of time, and units of action in which complex anthropological concepts and constellations are examined. It is possible to study details and address them from multiple perspectives by restricting the topic under investigation. It is also often possible to reflect on general relationships in a case study without diminishing the uniqueness and complexity of its findings. Case studies are often local or regional studies that substantiate general facts on the basis of a clearly defined set of sources. Case studies are the only way to gain an understanding of subjects' life histories, unique actions, attitudes toward life, and plans for the future. Microhistorical methodology is often associated with skepticism regarding general theories; however, this frequently has more to do with personal preferences than with the matter itself.[60] We often need general theories, however, if the historical details are to be appropriately categorized and interpreted. There are many examples of this in the history of mentalities.[61]

Topics of Research

The wide and open character of historical anthropological research makes it scarcely feasible to restrict it to only a few subject areas.[62] I therefore present only three issues to illustrate how anthropological problems can be handled in the historical sciences. First, many fundamental human experiences are directly related to the *body*.[63] However, the question is, in what representations does the body appear? There are several ways of addressing this, depending on what the researcher wishes to find out. Some recent studies have made efforts to do greater justice to the materiality of the body than was the case in earlier works on topics such as hygiene, nutrition, and fashion, for example. The trend toward the study of everyday life has also resulted in more importance being attached to the corporeal nature of everyday activities.[64] This includes studies of sexuality and birth;[65] childhood, youth and old age;[66] nutrition;[67] clothing;[68] illness;[69] dying and death;[70] and festivals, celebration, and rituals.[71] The growing interest in the subjective side of actions has increased interest in the bodily and sensory side of perception, feeling, and action. The fact that many studies focus on the questions of space and time and local and regional history has also resulted in attaching greater importance to the use of source material relating to the body.

A second complex area of elementary human experience is *religion*, a view shared by the founders of the *Annales* journal, Marc Bloch and Lucien Febvre, and embraced in the years that followed by other authors in the group. Religion involves the perception of the mortality associated with the body and the hope of overcoming it that is attached to religion. The central role that religion plays in all areas of life becomes clear in the normative anthropology of the Middle Ages. As LeGoff put it, few other epochs were as convinced of the existence of a universally valid and eternal idea of human beings as the Christian Middle Ages between the eleventh and fifteenth centuries. This society was dominated by religion, which permeated every area of social life, including the most intimate aspects, and its concept of the human being was obviously defined by religiosity.[72] For people of the Middle Ages, there was no place outside of religion. When heretics took up positions outside of the official religion, they were threatened with death and often executed. Religion also played a central role in the development of the individual, particularly after the invention of purgatory and the Last Judgment. People were held responsible for their own actions. This inevitably resulted in the individualization of feeling and actions. Magical practices and the practices of folk religion are more closely connected to church-approved religion than was long assumed to be the case.[73] Carlo Ginzburg used records left by the Inquisition to reconstruct the religious worldview of an Italian miller who lived in northern Italy in about 1600. His religious views deviated strongly from those held by the religious elite, which is important evidence of the diversity of religious experience and worldviews in the early modern period.[74]

The third major area of research on elementary situations and basic human experiences is related to the *stranger* or foreigner. This area of study sheds light on historical phenomena and constellations that had not previously received any attention. There was no uniform concept of the stranger or alien in either the Middle Ages or the early modern era. People who did not belong to the community of a home or village, even though they were from the region, were frequently regarded as strangers or foreigners. Someone who does not speak the local language and has different manners and social behaviors is always considered a foreigner. What is alien to the ruling classes becomes an issue for marginal groups and in certain historical situations. In anthropological-historical research Jews, gypsies, minstrels, and prostitutes have received particular attention as groups who do not belong. Subjects of study are the differences between the historical worlds of people who were charged with being heretics or witches and those of the church and nobility. The strategies and mechanisms used to ward off Otherness and the unknown in ecclesiastical and political contexts as well as in villages and towns are also a focus of research. New insights and findings arise from looking at known phenomena and events from the point of view of the outsider.

Some Critical Remarks on the History of Mentalities

The development of the concept of *mentality* (*mentalité*) by the École des Annales and its subsequent concentration of attention on this new approach led to intensive discussions on its strengths and weaknesses.[75] Its main characteristic is that it focuses not on individual attitudes but on unexpressed, unconscious assumptions associated with the practical rationality of everyday activities, in addition to the traditional analysis of ideas and conscious thoughts. Research on the history of mentalities is oriented more toward analyzing belief systems and the categories, metaphors, and symbols associated with them rather than toward investigating individual actions. It thus differs from the American history of ideas, German "Geistesgeschichte," and the more recent approaches of the history of concepts.[76] Epistemologically, the history of mentalities can be situated between the history of ideas and social history, which allows it to avoid having to make an infelicitous choice "between an intellectual history with the society left out and a social history with the thought left out."[77]

An example of a subject for which the concept of mentality would seem to be the only suitable approach is the medieval idea of the judgment of God, the trial by ordeal, which, while it can be criticized from the point of view of reason, cannot really be explained historically without recourse to the mentality concept. The same applies to the concept of correspondence, for example, between the seven planets, the seven metals, the seven days of the week, and so on, or to the notion of a great ladder of life, according to which it is better to be born as a human being than as an insect or a horse. The mentality approach is useful for analyzing such ideas, since it can help to render explicit and describe the modes of thinking of the people who held the views in question and thus to avoid superimposing our contemporary conceptions on their belief systems.

Despite this advantage of the concept of mentality, it is also associated with a number of problems that continue to dominate the discussion today. One danger in using the concept of mentality is that ideas that are unfamiliar and difficult to understand may be subsumed under a single, homogenizing mentality. This leads us to underestimate the heterogeneity of the collective ideas of a society at a given time point and to pay too little attention to their differences. Related to this is the problem of whether this lumping together of different views leaves room for changes that take place over time. We need a dynamic understanding of "mentality" that accounts for changes in mentality in space and over time. The question has also been raised as to how far it is possible to capture and conceptualize transitions between one mentality and another. There is a danger that mentalities will be seen as closed systems, thus undervaluing their dynamic character. And we must guard against the trap of seeing the belief systems to which the concept of mentality refers as more or less autonomous and failing to recognize how they are linked to social conditions. Finally, there is also a risk that the mentality approach is based on an evolutionistic view of history, that is, on the idea that historical development is inherently teleological. At least, in the work of Lévy-Bruhl, who was the first to use the concept of mentality, it is possible to discern an implicit historical evolutionism.[78] Lévy-Bruhl's starting point was Émile Durkheim's idea of collective representations and the differentiation between prelogical and logical mentalities. Elements of historical evolutionism are also identifiable in later work by Robert Mandrou, Jean Delumeau, and Robert Muchembled.[79]

These critical points apply to research on the history of mentalities in different ways. Peter Burke has suggested that in order to do this research and at the same time to improve the potential of the mentality approach, greater attention should be paid to interests, categories, and metaphors. It is highly surprising that in his study on the healing capacity of royal touch, Marc Bloch failed to ask what social interests were served by maintaining a belief in the supernatural powers of kings.[80] Later work by Georges Duby and LeGoff did analyze issues of social interest. There does seem to be a case for using differentiating categories and schemata in research on collective mentalities. The concept of the paradigm introduced by Thomas Kuhn can also help to achieve greater precision, which in turn should enable researchers to capture transitions from one mentality to another more exactly.[81] In any event, it is important to take into consideration the historical and dynamic nature of the categories and schemas employed. Finally, using different metaphors in the reconstruction of a mentality can be a helpful way to gain a more accurate idea of the differences that are discernible within a mentality.

Despite these criticisms, in the areas of history of cultural development, the social history of ideas, the history of the imaginary, the history of feelings, human geography, historical demography, and historical biography, the potential of research on the history of mentalities has not yet been fully exploited.

Review and Outlook

The historical sciences provide good examples of the exceptional productivity of the anthropological turn, which has led to the discovery of many new issues and focuses. These include the perceptions, feelings, and actions of people who had not previously been considered of interest for history. The focus is on their worldviews and subjectivities. This has yielded findings on the lives of people in their specific geographic areas and historical eras. Research into marginalized groups, which focuses on the special conditions that influence the experiences and actions of outsiders and strangers, has increased awareness of historical diversity. The selection of subjects and source materials has resulted in an increasing number of case studies on the uses of local and regional history. This concentration on microhistorical research has often been associated with diminished interest in general theories of interpretation of historical developments. In contrast, microhistorical research is more oriented toward the multidimensional study of phenomena that are limited in terms of space and time in order to gain insights into the complexity of historical contexts.

The history of mentalities involves another interesting methodological approach. It involves examining the collective representations on which people's perceptions, feelings, and actions are based and investigating their feelings, perceptions, and actions in specific historical situations. Long-term changes in mentalities are being investigated with a view to enhancing our understanding of the relationships between collective representations and the actions of individuals. This focus on elementary human experiences is associated with an interest in the body. Researchers explore historical phenomena and situations in which the materiality of the body and its symbolization in different contexts play a central role.[82] This focus has resulted in the discovery of many new research issues.[83] The basic principles of a historical cultural anthropology are being developed to incorporate ethnological approaches.[84]

More than ever before, anthropological research in the historical sciences needs to be transdisciplinary in order to handle the complexity of the problems and issues under scrutiny. Today, ethnology, psychology, sociology, theology, economics, and geography are all needed in the investigation of historical anthropological issues. The understanding of history as "open history" on which this research is based differs from approaches that regard history as a "history of progress" or "history of decline." Viewing history as open involves seeing historical actions as contingent, and it is thus important to be aware of their potentials and limitations.

FOUR

Cultural Anthropology

In recent years the cultural anthropological, social anthropological, and ethnological orientations in anthropology have gained substantially in importance. As a consequence of the changes in the world situation brought about by globalization, interest in research on "the foreign" has increased. As a result of their contributions to a comprehensive concept of culture and the methodology of qualitative social research, these fields of anthropology have come to have a strong influence on the humanities, the arts, and the social and cultural sciences. Their growing influence on historians, educationists, psychologists, and literary scholars is evident.

Ethnology, which came into being in the second half of the nineteenth century, is called *anthropology* in France, *social anthropology* in Great Britain, and *cultural anthropology* in the United States.[1] Before the first ethnologists started work, they had already had a number of forerunners. One of these was the Franciscan monk Bernardino de Sahagún (1499–1590), who worked as a missionary in Mexico, learned to speak Nahuatl, conducted surveys among the indigenous inhabitants of the different villages, and systematically recorded their worldviews. In the eighteenth century the great expeditions of the explorers Bougainville, Cook, and La Pérouse produced many travel diaries that provide some valuable insights into long-gone worlds. In the second half of the nineteenth century, large expeditions were carried out and extensively reported on. A broad knowledge of members of foreign cultures was thus accumulated.

Evolutionism was the first trend in cultural anthropology that re-mained influential well into the twentieth century.[2] One important au-thor at this time was Herbert Spencer (1820–1903),[3] who, influenced by Darwin, coined the phrase "survival of the fittest."[4] Even more influen-tial was Lewis Henry Morgan (1818–1881), who was one of the first to do field research among the Iroquois and later concluded from his field experience that humanity is developing from a state of wildness to one of civilization, with barbarism as an intermediate stage.[5] Edward B. Tylor (1832–1917), who developed instructions on how to write travel reports, also shared this view.[6]

In the last third of the nineteenth century there was a clear dichotomy between missionaries, administrative functionaries, and travelers, who gathered information on foreign cultures, and the "armchair ethnolo-gists," who read, arranged, and evaluated the information gathered by their informants and sometimes arrived at some fascinating insights. This was the strategy employed by James Frazer (1854–1941), who never left Europe, when he wrote the *Golden Bough*, a very large cultural anthro-pological study on the religions and customs of peoples.[7]

Under the influence of Franz Boas (1858–1942), who was born and originally trained as a natural scientist in Germany, later emigrating to the United States, the newly developing discipline of cultural anthropol-ogy underwent a permanent change.[8] During a one-year stay in northern Canada, Boas did research on the language and lifeworld of the Inuit population of that region. After settling in the United States, he later made several more trips to visit the Indians on the North American West Coast, during which he asked them about their languages and traditions and recorded their replies with the aid of an interpreter. Unlike Tylor and Frazer in Great Britain, who, influenced by the evolutionism of Darwin, Spencer, and Morgan, believed that humanity as a whole was follow-ing the same developmental course and that the degree to which this development had progressed in the different peoples varied, Boas was influenced by the historical orientation of anthropology in Germany and believed that each culture had its own special character.[9] In his view, the goal of research was to investigate what was distinctive about each culture, not the parallels between them. He felt that biological reduc-tionism, cultural parallelism, and universal standards of progress should be avoided.[10] He rejected all forms of cultural determinism and warned against overestimating generalized comparisons. These ideas on cultural relativism, according to which culture was a "closed assortment of spe-cific and unmistakable ways of life,"[11] led to the development of a position that was antithetical to evolutionism and has played an important role in the United States right up to the present.

In Germany philosophical anthropology was classified among the humanities, and in France historical anthropology was seen as a historical science, but cultural anthropology is a discipline that has developed out of a combination of different academic traditions in several countries. Cultural anthropology in the United States took a different direction from that taken in Britain, France, and Germany. Along with the work of Franz Boas and his students, conceptualizations of culture that were prevalent in the humanities in Germany exerted a substantial influence on cultural anthropology, which was just becoming established at the beginning of the twentieth century. The objective was to prevent the rapidly changing societies of North American Indians from falling into oblivion. Boas's four-field anthropology was a model for the empirical research on these cultures. It was in keeping with the times and gradually became established. Its value, however, is still a subject of debate.[12] The aim of research into these Native American cultures was to preserve them as part of American culture. To this end, the evolutionist interpretations that had predominated up to that time were abandoned in favor of an emphasis on the uniqueness and intrinsic values of these cultures.

Many important figures from a large number of different countries played important roles in the development of cultural anthropology during the twentieth century. These include Karl Marx and Friedrich Engels, with their views on the dynamics of society; Bronislaw Malinowski, with his participant observation and field research model; Alfred Radcliffe-Brown, the founder of structural functionalism; and also Raymond Firth, Edward Evan Evans-Pritchard, Meyer Fortes, and Edmund R. Leach, British social anthropologists who distanced themselves from Radcliffe-Brown. The structuralists Émile Durkheim, Marcel Mauss, and Claude Lévi-Strauss; the discourse analysis of Michel Foucault; Pierre Bourdieu's concept of habitus and practical knowledge; Jacques Derrida's work on deconstruction, and the French postmodern authors François Lyotard, Jean Baudrillard, and Paul Virilio also deserve mention.

This interdisciplinary and international exchange contributed to the great diversity of cultural anthropology, and, unlike other authors, who lament the dissolution of the boundaries between the disciplines, I see this as providing a valuable richness to the discipline. The diversity of developments in cultural anthropology in the twentieth century makes it impossible to present them here in their entirety. I therefore simply give a brief outline of those aspects that have been important in the development of a hermeneutic cultural anthropology that focuses on field research and is intended to supplement the other anthropological paradigms. I have taken a selective approach and leave many questions open. Readers who are interested in a systematic investigation of the entire discipline may consult some of the currently available monographs on cultural anthropology in the United States, social anthropology in Britain, anthropology in France, and ethnology in Germany.[13] Apart from a few exceptions, however, to date there are still no convincing studies that relate the developments in the respective countries to the development of the discipline as a whole.

Two overlapping developments remain significant, and I have chosen to present them in more detail in this chapter. The first is the controversy over the work of Boas and his students. Here it is less important whether one shares Boas's assumptions or opposes them from the standpoint of social anthropology, structuralism, Marxism, feminism, or postmodernism. Whatever one's stance with regard to his studies, many of which certainly have theoretical weaknesses, his research was the point of departure for all later approaches and research. I therefore give a brief overview of the beginnings of cultural anthropology in the cultural and intellectual history of nineteenth-century Germany and outline its structure in the first half of the twentieth century. I then summarize the role of field research in cultural anthropology and show how it is linked to culture and alterity. Although it is viewed differently in evolutionist, structuralist, Marxist, and postmodern approaches, we can regard field research as the hub of cultural anthropology that distinguishes it from all other anthropological paradigms. Only through field research can we gather the knowledge that constitutes the discipline.

The Creation of Cultural Anthropology by Boas and the Boasians

Under the influence of Charles Darwin (1809–1882) and Herbert Spencer (1820–1903), and also of Lewis Henry Morgan, who assumed that the overall development of humankind differed from one country to another, evolutionist positions had gained substantial ground. Franz Boas (1858–1942) and his students opposed these viewpoints and stressed the importance of particularism, relativism, and culture. In Boas's view, cultures are incomparable and can only be understood in their own right. He believed that anthropologists must therefore, as far as possible, bracket their own values and ideas, that is, their ethnocentric imaginaries, in their investigations of foreign cultures. The criticism of the representatives of this relativism, which Boas and his students shared despite all other differences that existed between them, was aimed at biological reductionism, universal standards of progress, forms of cultural determinism, and the overvaluing of generalizing comparisons of cultural phenomena. These ideas, which promoted the development of an understanding of culture as an ensemble of specific and distinctive lifestyles, were used to develop the perspectives of a moderate cultural relativism. In Boas's well-known article entitled "The Limitations of the Comparative Method," which he wrote in 1896, and in several of the articles in his book *The Mind of Primitive Man*, published in 1911, these aspects were specified in such a way that they still played a role in the discussion of four-field anthropology and the writing culture debate.

Franz Boas and his students distanced themselves from a strict cultural relativism just as persistently as they emphasized the relative autonomy of cultural processes. One reason for this was that Boas considered biological, archaeological, and linguistic research to be necessary, in addition to the investigation of culture. Some forms of academic investigation, particularly biological research, repeatedly produced insights into human beings that were generally applicable and to a great extent independent of culture.[14] When he took up his post at the American Museum of Natural History and Columbia University, Franz Boas found an institutional basis for his work in the United States that developed into a center of research on anthropology. This research was focused on the paradigm of culture and the relativism associated with it. Its aim was to investigate the North American Indian cultures empirically, using interviews and transcriptions. Studies of history and language were also carried out. Boas assumed that language has a constitutive influence on the development of culture and mentalities. He emphatically rejected the view that cultural progress consists of an unfolding of predetermined stages of development;[15] instead, he studied contacts between the cultures and, under the heading of diffusionism, on historical routes of the propagation of cultural forms and contents. Later, this development led to a growing interest in studying the relationship between culture and the individual. Boas believed that cultural phenomena are relatively autonomous.

The Cultural and Historical Background

Analysis of the relationship between Kantian universalism and Herder's historicism reveals that it is too simple merely to distinguish between an Enlightenment that assumes a universalist civilization (France) and one that assumes a relativist culture (Germany). Kant's philosophy and anthropology were also oriented toward a universalist Enlightenment and influenced Herder's views on history and anthropology.[16] Herder accepted Kant's emphasis on the abstract unity of humankind but also stressed the anthropological significance of historical and cultural diversity.[17] Herder's talk of "unity in diversity," that is, of a unity of humanity in the diversity of the cultures, was an expression of his attempt to link the general to the specific. This anthropological viewpoint determined Herder's idea of culture, whose particularity he saw as developing out of the language, customs, and mentalities peculiar to a people and from the effects of spirit and soul. He believed that the effects of these forces could be observed and experienced. Herder's concept of a people's soul is rooted in his pietistic upbringing. These ideas about the power of the culture-producing spirit and soul later led to the development of folklore studies.[18] They later led him to distinguish between *cultural peoples* (*Kulturvölker*) and *natural peoples* (*Naturvölker*) and correspondingly to view cultures in terms of hierarchies. His attempt to link the evolutionist view of history implicit in this distinction to an attempt to assess all cultures on the basis of their own values, ideas, and laws prevented him from overrating cultural realism.

However, Boas was not only influenced by the philosophies of Herder and Humboldt. His thoughts about a four-field anthropology and his activities in professional associations were stimulated by his studies with Bastian in Berlin in the last three decades of the nineteenth century. This period saw the founding of the Berlin Society for Anthropology, Ethnology, and Prehistory (1867),[19] the journal *Zeitschrift für Ethnologie*, which is still important today, and the Ethnological Museum of Berlin (*Museum für Völkerkunde zu Berlin*, 1873). The first director of this museum, Adolf Bastian, had traveled the world as a ship's physician and written a postdoctoral dissertation on ethnology in 1869. During the same period, social cultural ethnology became institutionalized, museum collections were founded, and some important books and travel reports were published. Among the most prominent of these works were studies by Johann Jakob Bachofen, Gustav Klemm, and Theodor Waitz, and the research of Heinrich Barth, who pioneered German research on Africa and attained international repute.[20]

The distinction drawn between *Volkskunde* (folklore studies), which were historically oriented, and *Völkerkunde* (ethnology/ethnography), which was supported by the developing imperial colonial policy, was characteristic of the trends of this period. Both were firmly anti-Darwinist.

This distinction was promoted by Herder's aforementioned differentiation between *Kulturvölker* and *Naturvölker,* according to which he credited natural peoples with a lower level of cultural achievement.[21] While Herder still used the word *culture* in the singular, Johann Christoph Adelung (1732–1806) would soon speak of "cultures," thus moving more in the direction of cultural relativism. This was also furthered by publications such as Friedrich von Schlegel's "On the Language and Wisdom of the Indians" and Friedrich Rückert's studies on Asian languages.[22] Wilhelm von Humboldt's research on language also led to the development of a historical and comparative anthropology of language *avant la lettre* (see chapter 10), which likewise had an influence on Boas's insight into the importance of language studies.

The spread of cultural relativism was also furthered by two other reservations regarding evolutionism, both of which influenced Bastian and the medical scientist Rudolf Virchow (1821–1902). These were Prussian pietism, with its rejection of an anti-creationist theory of the origin of humankind, and Prussian nationalism, which led to skepticism with regard to new theories from Britain. One of Bastian's research objectives was to compile *elementary thoughts* (*Elementargedanken*), concerning which he expressed his concept of the unity of humanity in diversity that was inspired by Herder. Bastian's research included detailed individual studies, exact descriptions, and linguistic analyses,[23] which were, however, on the whole not very systematic. Nevertheless, the theory of a link between the Enlightenment and positivism that Bastian developed in his works created a mixture that had a lasting effect on Boas's thinking.

Rudolf Virchow's extensive research on physiological and biological anthropology was also important for Boas's conceptualization of anthropology and was partly responsible for the fact that Boas continued to consider such research important for the rest of his life. One of Virchow's major research projects was a study on school statistics, for which millions of schoolchildren's skulls were measured. The object was to establish characteristics that distinguished between the races and thus to give a scientific basis to the concept of race, which was later to have such disastrous effects in German history.[24]

In sum, Boas had already started to develop his ideas on cultural anthropology while he was still studying in Germany. This applies both to his thoughts on culture and research on cultural anthropology, which were inspired by the Enlightenment and the Romantics, and to his views on the importance of language and anthropological linguistics, and on biological anthropology, with its use of methods from the natural sciences. In North America, prehistoric archaeology was included in research on North American Indians in cultural anthropology and provided data and findings that led to important insights into the habitats of the Native Americans and the relations between individual tribes.

The Boasians

Despite large differences among Boas's students, many of whom followed their own paths, it is still possible to obtain a general view of their points of departure and activities. This is best done by dividing them into three generations. The first generation includes his doctoral students up to the First World War. They worked empirically, but were more interested in a historically oriented cultural anthropology. The second generation consisted of those doctoral students who had worked with Boas in the 1920s and were most interested in the enculturation and socialization of individuals. The third generation received their training in the 1930s.

Among the first generation was Alfred Kroeber, who received his doctorate at Columbia University in 1901 and built up the anthropology department at Berkeley. He and many other first-generation Boasians accepted newly created posts in the United States. Thus, for instance, Robert Lowie also went to Berkeley, while Edward Sapir and Fay Cooper-Cole went to Chicago, Melville Herskovits to Northwestern University, Frank Speck to the University of Pennsylvania, and Alexander Goldenweiser to the New School for Social Research, where he taught Leslie White and Ruth Benedict. Although Boas focused mainly on ethnological and linguistic research at Columbia University, departments of cultural anthropology following the four-field model were set up at other universities. During this period Boas also tried to further the professionalization of cultural anthropology in cooperation with museums and within the American Anthropological Association, whose president he became in 1907, as well as by founding journals.

If we follow George Stocking's distinction between strict and rebellious Boasians,[25] we can also include Lowie, Spier, Herskovits, Wissler, and Speck in the first group. Kroeber, who developed his own approach to history, and Sapir, who founded his own linguistic approach and did more research in cultural anthropology on the role of the individual, belong to the second group. Paul Radin, who was critical of the distributional studies of many Boasians and studied the worldviews of the "primitive philosophers," also belongs in this group. His biography of a Winnebago Indian (1920) is an important contribution to the life-history method. Goldenweiser, who worked with Sapir and Radin, had a great interest in research on what is individual in cultural development.

Kroeber's "The Superorganic" (1917) and Sapir's "Culture, Genuine and Spurious" (1924) show the breadth of the research topics covered by the Boasians.[26] In his article, Kroeber postulated that cultural phenomena are to a great extent independent of organic dimensions, that is, of biology, psychology, and individual aspects. Sapir's article was not about cultural theory but about the "spiritual possessions" of individual groups. Sapir attempted to reformulate Boas's concept of a "genius of people" (*Volksgeist*) and thus to further the "cultural integration" of different forces by means of a "patterning of values."

Substantial differences and conflicts arose, and not only among the Boasians. The conflicts between Boasians and representatives of other positions of cultural anthropology were even more heated. Thus, the conflict between Boas and the representatives of the influential Washington/Cambridge Axis began to escalate. These were conflicts between evolutionist and historicist positions and between racial and cultural determinism. In this confrontation it was mainly old American WASPs and immigrants, the latter of mainly Jewish origin, who clashed. Their discussions reflected differences regarding, for example, immigration policy, views on the concept of race, nationalism, and the issue of isolationism during the First World War. Attacks on Boas increased in connection with his fundamental pacifism and his opposition to US involvement in the war, with the result that he lost his positions in the American Anthropological Association.

Following Boas's death in 1942, Kroeber took his place as probably the most influential representative of cultural anthropology. He continued to subscribe to the historical dimension of research in cultural anthropology and pursued his interests in cultural forms, pattern cohesion, and cultural creativity. He developed the cultural-area approach, which he used to expand research on cultural anthropology outside the boundaries of North America. In his research he was interested in identifying configurations of cultural growth and cultural styles. In his large "Culture Element Distribution Project," on which many of his doctoral students were working, his main objective was to investigate cultural configurations and styles. However, he stated later that this goal had not been reached and declared the project more or less a failure. After leaving Yale, Sapir also went his own way. His high hopes of cooperation with the psychologists at Yale were not fulfilled. It was during this period that the Sapir-Whorf hypothesis was developed, according to which the semantic structures of languages, and in particular their grammars, are not comparable, but their peculiar characteristics affect the ways of thinking of those who speak them and the cultures to which they belong.

In the 1920s the main feature of the second generation of Boasians was that they had more or less lost their interest in history. Their research was influenced by psychoanalysis and gestalt psychology and was collectively referred to as "the culture and personality school." The leading representatives in this phase were Ruth Benedict, Margaret Mead, and Clyde Kluckhohn.[27] Irving Hallowell, Ralph Linton, and Robert Lowie were also working in the same direction. Lowie, for example, wrote a book on the German national character (1945). Even Kroeber was influenced by this development and shifted the main emphasis of his research from area studies to cultural configurations. Mead carried out her first research, which was on puberty and cultural patterns of adolescence, on the island of Samoa in 1926 (fig. 4.1). She attempted to show that the common understanding of puberty in the United States, according to which it is characterized by a restlessness induced by hormonal and emotional upheavals, was highly culture-dependent and that puberty was both experienced and lived differently in other cultures. Controversial as some aspects of her research remain to the present day,[28] her study is important from the point of view of both content and methodology. It was one of the first studies to be based on field research and participant observation as conceptualized by Malinowski. Her focus on Indonesia, adolescence, and gender roles also opened up new subject areas in research in cultural anthropology.

The high point of the doctrine of cultural relativism was reached with Ruth Benedict's *Patterns of Culture* in 1934. Benedict believed that the best way to understand a culture is to establish its main areas of concern and how they determine the specific nature of its cultural configurations. Both she and many of her colleagues were convinced that each culture is unique and plays a central role in the education and socialization of its members. In their view, the respective mentalities and behaviors are learned in cultural processes. However, like Boas before them, these authors did not go so far as to assume that behavior is completely determined by culture. In this period a number of area studies were also carried out, the most well-known of which is Melville Herskovits's study on the cattle complex of East Africa.[29] According to the results of this study, in the cattle cultures we find nomadism, patrilineal descent, age sets, bride-wealth, an association of livestock with the ancestors, and so on.

This third generation of Boasians paid more attention to economic and conflictual dimensions, and there was a stronger focus on dissension and conflicts than in the preceding generation. The major authors of this period included Oscar Lewis, who studied the effects of the fur trade on the Blackfoot Indians; Jane Richardson, who investigated legal

FIGURE 4.1 Margaret Mead between two Samoan girls,1926. The photograph is a part of the Margaret Mead Papers and The South Pacific Ethnographic Archives of the British Library. © The British Library/The Institute of Intercultural Studies.

issues and status structures among the Kiowa; and Alexander Lesser, who looked at how cultural change is expressed in the Pawnee Ghost Dance hand game and demonstrated in his later studies that his cultural histori- cal approach could be linked to functionalist and evolutionist perspec- tives.[30] When Boas retired in 1937 and Ralph Linton, whose relations with Ruth Benedict were very strained, succeeded him at Columbia Uni- versity, a new phase of development began which was oriented more to- ward the social sciences.[31] Although Linton was interested in culture and personality issues, he addressed them differently in a series of seminars beginning in 1938, which he conducted together with the psychoanalyst Abraham Kardiner.

Following Mead's and Benedict's studies, cultural anthropology had become a recognized discipline in which many scholars showed interest. At the same time, research ceased to be restricted to the North American Indian peoples and had expanded to include Asia and Africa, a step that had occasioned considerable public interest. During Radcliffe-Brown's tenure in Chicago from 1931 to 1937, a strong orientation toward the social sciences had evolved, in combination with the urban sociology that had its roots in Chicago. For Radcliffe-Brown, there was only one model of scientific study, which must be oriented toward the natural sciences. In this paradigm the objective was less to understand cultural phenomena than to explain them. During the war Malinowski lived in the United States. He died at Yale, a few years after having accepted a chair there. Both researchers were influenced by British social anthropology, and for Malinowski, this influence was lasting. At the same time, the concept of cultural anthropology, with its focus on culture, became established in the United States. During this period this research was supported by substantial grants from the armed forces. Funding research on cultural anthropology was expected to lead to knowledge about other countries that would be more useful for political and military purposes. After the Second World War, the funding of cultural anthropology was again increased, leading to the development and diversification of many areas of applied research. Many new jobs were created for cultural anthropologists, particularly in Third World development projects.

Challenges from New Evolutionism, New Materialism, and Functionalism

In North American cultural anthropology, the moderate relativism of the Boasians had taken over from the evolutionism that had been the dominant paradigm in the nineteenth century, particularly in Britain, but now there was a dialectical movement toward the development of new approaches in which evolutionist elements were more prominent.

Initially the impetus for this development came from Leslie White and Julian Steward, who still espoused a position that was closer to cultural relativism. White, who taught in Michigan and whose students included Marshall Sahlins, Albert Spaulding, Robert Caneiro, and Lewis Binford, was decidedly against cultural determinist approaches.[32] In contrast to

White's linear evolutionism, Julian Steward developed the concept of multilinear evolutionism, intending to overcome the problematic generalizations of unilinear evolutionism, which required cultural development to be monogenetic. The objective was to grasp the multidimensionality of evolution and to develop an appropriate research methodology, integrating more exact historical analyses of cultural development as influenced by the environment.[33]

From the "materialism" of these two authors and Steward's search for explanations for social and cultural developments, it was only a small step to the Marxist-inspired approaches developed by Eric Wolf, Marshall Sahlins, and Marvin Harris at the Mundial Upheaval Society (MUS) at Columbia University, for whom evolutionary conceptualizations of history, society, and culture played a central role. Wolf's studies on peasant communities and the structures of social dominance, Sahlins's *Stone Age Economics* and his study on culture and practical reason, and Harris's publications on the origin of culture and cultural materialism should also be mentioned in this context.[34] Important as the introduction of this perspective was, its value is diminished by its reduction of culture to material production and materiality; the productive force of imaginary and symbolic factors is not taken into account.

New forms of materialism also played an important role in France. Claude Meillassoux criticized the structuralism of Lévi-Strauss because it failed to discuss the issue of exploitation and the material conditions of kinship. In Meillassoux's view, the conditions of production also determine the conditions of reproduction, through which conditions of production are integrated in societal power structures. In this process women are subordinated and kept under control, and their own perspectives are not taken into consideration.[35] Maurice Godelier's structural Marxism, which set out to investigate the relationships between the environment, technology, and society, should also be mentioned in this context.[36] The focus is on the respective relations of production that form the foundations of social and individual relationships. Culture is considered to be a dependent ideology, while the economy is seen as the productive factor in social development. Immanuel Wallerstein's contributions to the analysis of the world system, which were concerned with the relationship between colonialism and globalization, underdevelopment and development, also belong here.[37] His distinction between the center and the periphery was highly important in the attempt to grasp global capitalism and to better understand the structures of peripheral societies.

Like Marxism, Malinowski's and Radcliffe-Brown's functionalism included evolutionist elements. Radcliffe-Brown had repeatedly stressed that anthropology has two origins: one in evolutionist thought around 1870, in which Herbert Spencer had played a major role, and the other much earlier in Montesquieu's *Spirit of Laws* in the mid-eighteenth century. The sociological tradition that began with Montesquieu took the view that societies are structured and that investigating these structures is the task of science, that is, of sociology and the social sciences. Influenced by Montesquieu and Comte, Émile Durkheim, Marcel Mauss, and his students therefore analyzed the dynamics of structures of society. In these studies the historical perspective lost its central significance and gave way to the development of a present-centered, synchronic perspective. This was the starting point for Lévi-Strauss and French structuralism.

Malinowski's *Argonauts of the Western Pacific* and Radcliffe-Brown's *The Andaman Islanders* were both published in 1922 and supported the development of functionalism and structural functionalism in Britain.[38] Three levels of abstraction can be distinguished in Malinowski's theory of functionalism. On the first level, *function* refers to the effects of an institution on other institutions; that is, a function determines the relationships between institutions. On the second level, *function* is used to mean the manner in which members of a community understand their community. Finally, the word *function* also refers to the means with which institutions bring about social cohesion.[39] On the first level, the investigation focuses on how customs are linked to the rest of culture. The researcher's task is therefore to relate the different facets of social organization to each other. The starting point of Malinowski's theory of functionalism is a set of seven biological needs and their respective cultural responses. The biological needs include metabolism, reproduction, bodily movements, safety, movement, growth, and health. The following cultural responses correspond to them: food supply, kinship, shelter, protection, activities, training, and hygiene. Malinowski then developed four "instrumental imperatives": economics, social control, education, and political organization. While Malinowski's contribution to ethnographic field research is impressive, the value of his contribution to a scientific theory of culture and the theory of functionalism remains limited.[40]

As mentioned above, Radcliffe-Brown's structural functionalism was intended to be part of his *A Natural Science of Society*, the broad outlines of which he had developed in a series of lectures at the University of Chicago.[41] In these lectures he rejected the ideas of a unified social science and a science of culture. In his view, it is only possible to have a single natural science of society, whose task is to compare societies and systematically to improve the methods of comparative research. With this program Radcliffe-Brown was following on from his evolutionist predecessors and their comparative research. In *The Andaman Islanders*, he explained rituals in terms of their social functions and value for society. He was mainly interested in a synchronic view. He investigated how institutions function within a social system. According to him, a social system survives over a long period of time by developing a structure that ensures cohesion and solidarity. This structure must fulfill three functions: it must make arrangements that are suited to the physical environment; make provisions that can sustain ordered social living; and provide cultural mechanisms by which individuals collect habits and mental characteristics that render them capable of participating in community life.[42] This requires the application of social laws: "One such law, or necessary condition of continued existence, is that of a certain degree of functional consistency amongst the constituent parts of the social system. [. . .] To this law [. . .] we may add a second, [. . .] rights and duties which need to be defined in such a way that conflicts of rights can be resolved without destroying the structure. [. . .] Another sociological law is the necessity not merely for stability, definiteness and consistency in the social structure, but also for continuity."[43] The radical nature of this position led to much criticism, with the result that very few cultural anthropologists claim to be followers of Radcliffe-Brown. For example, Edward E. Evans-Pritchard opposed this emphasis on the universal character of functional-structural statements, favoring greater consideration of the historical and culturally relativistic dimension of social anthropological research. For him, social anthropology had more in common with history than with the natural sciences, and it examined societies as moral and symbolic systems and not as natural systems. Thus it is less interested in the process than the design, and it is a discipline that searches for models rather than laws, demonstrates correlations rather than conditioned reactions, and interprets rather than explains.[44] Between 1945 and 1970 a period began in Britain that could be called the "golden age" of social anthropology, during which the influence of Raymond Firth (1901–2002) at the London School of Economics, Edward Evan Evans-Pritchard (1902–1973) at Oxford, Max Gluckman (1911–1974) in Manchester, and Meyer Fortes (1906–1983) and Edmund R. Leach (1910–1989) at Cambridge was gaining strength.[45]

In France there has long been a particularly clear division between those who produced theory and those who were actively engaged in empirical research in the field. Mauss, for instance, instigated empirical field studies in the 1920s and 1930s, but did not actually conduct them himself, as did Marcel Griaule. Griaule initiated an expedition through Africa that was based on a quite different model from that used by Malinowski, but it met with little approval in the United States.[46] Marcel Mauss (1872–1950), who took Durkheim's structuralism as a starting point, developed his concept of exchange as the ultimate social action constituting society.[47] It centers on reciprocity—giving, taking, and reciprocating—and the social and symbolic orders that it initiates. Giving expresses a more active relationship to the world and other people, while taking demonstrates a more passive one. Both regulate proximity and distance and also structure belonging, respect, aggression, and enmity. Giving, taking, and reciprocating are the central actions of exchange with nature, the gods, and people. Gifts are a concrete form of imaginary and symbolic relationships. For Mauss, in the exchange of giving and taking it is possible to distinguish several structural elements—the gift, the act of giving, the receipt of the gift, the reciprocation of the gift, the different meanings attributed to giving and taking, and the effects thus achieved. Mauss considers that these structural elements are not culturally determined in any way. In his structural model, gifts are rarely unambiguous—they are usually contradictory in nature and open to many interpretations. They are used to resolve the ambivalence of the stranger and make the stranger a friend. The exchange of gifts initiates trust and consolidates goodwill and the relationships with gods, human beings, and things. Giving is a social act that usually implies the unspoken expectation that one will receive a gift in return. It is a voluntary act, but associated with it is the invitation to accept the gift and to give one in return. By giving, one gains esteem and prestige. The voluntary nature of giving is an expression of social power and strength. When a gift is accepted, something is transferred from the possession of the giver to the possession of the recipient, and this changes the relationship between them. The recipient is expected to do the same as the giver, thus removing the debt to the other. The receiver tries to become similar to the giver, to match the giver's generosity and gain the associated prestige. When the receiver becomes the giver, the balance of their relationship is restored.

Marcel Mauss's best-known successors were Claude Lévi-Strauss (1908–2009) and Louis Dumont (1911–1998),[48] who continued to develop French structuralism. Lévi-Strauss was born in Brussels and then, soon after the Nazis came to power, left Europe for São Paolo and New York. Upon his return to France, he took positions at the Centre National de la Recherche Scientifique, the Musée de l'Homme, and also the Ecole Pratique des Hautes Etudes. He was at the Collège de France from 1959 until he was made emeritus professor. His structuralism would hardly have been possible without his interest in linguistics and, in particular, his study of the works of Ferdinand de Saussure, who made a distinction between grammar (the abstract rules and constraints that allow language to function) and speech (the actual utterances that language-users produce). Whereas utterances are transmitted in time, the grammar used to make them is fixed. Using chess as an example, Saussure clarified how the general and the particular intersect each other. Here a set of rules is so closely bound up with the conditions of play for each game that no game is like another. Lévi-Strauss also saw the chess game as a model for the methodology of anthropology, whose task is to consider things out of context, research the rules that govern them, and consequently to develop a science that is largely context-free. Lévi-Strauss's starting point was linguistic structures, for which analogies can be found in almost all areas of culture.[49] This model paid little regard to history. Concepts that were important for him were binary opposition, on the basis of which structures are formed, and the notion of exchange, which he transposed to the system of marriage, the function of which he saw as to "marry out or die out," to use Tylor's famous phrase. In the taboo on incest that is important in all marriage systems, Lévi-Strauss saw a structure in which nature and society overlap. "Humans also surpass it [the taboo] through exchange, specifically marriage—a social device that actually makes them social, since it allows them to leave incest as a mythically natural state behind them."[50] Although cultures appear to be fundamentally different on the phenomenal level, in Lévi-Strauss's view the structure underlying the phenomena is the same for all cultures and also functions in the same way. Therefore it was necessary to study the universal characteristics of thinking and mentality that are evident in myth. This view has been criticized for its circularity of argument in the acceptance of the duality of deep structures and the way they manifest themselves on the surface. This circularity of argument arises because we only have concrete evidence for the surface manifestations and not for the deep structures themselves, whereas Lévi-Strauss's argument is clearly decidedly deductive. It is based on the premise that rationalist logic is important for gaining insight into things and allows no questioning of its validity.

Field Research—Participatory Observation—Ethnography

Since the beginnings of empirical research, with Boas and his students, and since Malinowski's development of the method of participant observation, field research has been at the center of cultural anthropology. Although views have differed as to the importance of field research, its central role has never been questioned. Field research as a method distinguishes cultural anthropology from other scientific areas, and today it is being adopted increasingly by other disciplines. In view of the continued development of hermeneutic methods in the 1970s and 1980s, with the "writing culture" debate and the associated "crisis of representation," which did not result in field research being abandoned, we need to assess the situation. I therefore propose to give a short résumé of the historical development and then focus on the reconsideration of central issues.

The Historical Perspective

Between 1914 and 1918 Malinowski spent a total of two years on the Trobriand Islands north of Guinea (fig. 4.2). During this time he developed the field research technique of *participant observation*. This technique restricts research in terms of space and time and examines many interdependent elements within their overall context. The main emphasis is on observation, which is not merely looking; rather, it is theory-driven. The field researchers are equipped with previous knowledge, a frame of reference provided by their training and research questions, an approach that influences their observations without determining them absolutely. First and foremost, the aim is to grasp the native's point of view, his relation to life—to realize *his* view of *his* world. This is why the researcher must always become acquainted with the culture, learn the language, and participate in the lifeworld of the indigenous population. Malinowski therefore believed he had to live among the people he was studying and follow their actions. In order not to endanger his position as an observer, however, he had to maintain a certain distance. He did not play a part in their way of living and could not become a full member of their community, even if he became increasingly familiar with the foreign world.

In his famous introduction to the *Argonauts of the Western Pacific* (1922), Malinowski differentiates between three complementary procedures, which together constitute his way of conducting field research.

- Statistical documentation of information obtained by conducting surveys and through observation, which can be used to show routines or the ways other societies are organized
- Continuous and detailed observations of people recorded in a field journal, which can be used to establish typical modes of behavior and to supplement the rather dry statistical documentation through illustrations
- Compiling a collection of typical narratives, magical formulas, and figures of speech, which give an insight into the mentalities of the people under observation.

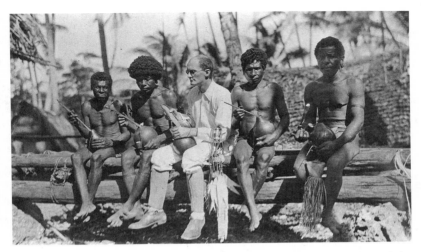

FIGURE 4.2   Bronislaw Malinowski with Trobriand Islanders in 1918. © The London School of Economics and Political Science.

These different types of information produce a multidimensional picture of the society from which to draw generalized conclusions. An important prerequisite for the success of the research is the solitude of the field researcher, who can then more easily take part in the living practices of the people being observed and overcome the prejudices inherent in her own culture.

Although participant observation overcomes the distance between the armchair ethnologists and their sources and represents a considerable advance in terms of methodology, this procedure still has many unresolved problems as a research technique. Just as in the theater the gap between the audience and the actors can never be bridged, the differences between the field researcher and people living in their everyday environment can also never be overcome. This raises the question of the extent to which we can regard the observations of the field researcher as representative. Whereas the "natives" behave and recount experiences according to their own view of the world, the ethnographer has the task of ordering the many heterogeneous observations and accounts and of interpreting them so that they are comprehensible to a member of his culture. This process of creating an ethnographic text is, to a high degree, constructive. However, the creation of such documentation is done not by the people under observation (who merely provide the raw material) but by the field researcher, who selects, organizes, and interprets the material. The field researcher thus assumes responsibility for the presentation, interpretation, and representation. This process, known as ethnographic realism, can be understood as an attempt to describe a way of life as a whole, using extensive and detailed descriptions of everyday situations that the author experienced firsthand.[51] It is assumed that there is a correlation between reality and its representation in the text, which makes it possible for the reader to obtain important information on life in other cultures. The genre suited to this is the monograph, in which one society's enclosed lifeworld is described to members of another society. This has now become the standard mode of presentation in cultural anthropology. The popularity of this genre has resulted in many individual studies about societies that have since changed dramatically, so that these studies now serve as important historical sources of information about social and cultural circumstances of the past.

In the 1980s and 1990s several methodological problems associated with the literary genre of the ethnographic monograph were discovered and discussed. The first of these relates to the way the subject under study is constructed: the writer often overlooks the unavoidable hermeneutic and communicative problems involved in the transition from the raw data to the construction and presentation of the subject of the study. The second problem is the tension between specific research and the drawing of generalized conclusions, since ethnography has the task of bridging the gap between an account derived from personal experience and impersonal social structure. It also has the task of situating the individual, the incomparable, and the incommensurable within a general frame of reference. It should reconcile the experiences and observations of the researcher, which are of necessity limited, with the requirements of the research to present a world or way of life as a whole or at least as an integral and coherent entity.[52] Third, despite their insurmountable differences, an attempt must be made to reconcile the roles of both field researcher and author.

Interpretative or reflexive ethnologists are beginning to take up these issues.[53] In their view it is the task of cultural anthropology to raise levels of knowledge of other societies by means of thorough research into the way the basic problems of life are tackled and solved in other cultures. A hermeneutic turn is needed in order to be able to understand foreign models of life and the world as required. In this view the human world has always been an interpreted world, in which meaning has to be discovered and identified. This world is created and communicated through cultural practices that form coherent systems of meaning, to which members of different lifeworlds relate through their own actions.

Ideas and meanings are communicated in the context of social acts and relationships. Cultural anthropologists attempt to reconstruct them, to read them as a text, and to deduce their objective content from what they read. The various elements of meaning are captured and portrayed in what Clifford Geertz has called a "thick description," which builds on this approach. Understanding Otherness is thus restricted to moving fragments of Otherness into the scope of one's own horizon. However, the shifts in meaning, which are sometimes considerable and occur when concepts relating to indigenous life are first decontextualized and then recontextualized, are not included in the analysis.[54]

Paul Ricoeur, to whom interpretative cultural anthropologists often refer, describes the difference between speech and the production of a text as follows: "What writing actually does fix is not the event of speaking but the 'said' of speaking, i.e., the intentional exteriorization constitutive of the couple 'event-meaning.' What we write, what we inscribe is the noema of the act of speaking, the meaning of the speech event, not the event as event."[55] In this process the effective components are the differences between the intention of the author and the meaning that she actually determines, the separation of this meaning from the dialogical situation, and the production of a text that is accessible to as many readers as possible. The cultural anthropological interpretation is only one among several possible readings of social actions, rituals, and institutions. Such interpretations are influenced not only by scientific norms and research questions, but also by the subjective conditions of individual cultural anthropologists, such as their prejudices and their psychosocial conflicts and aims, which have a marked effect on their perceptions of social reality and the manner in which they construct the ethnographic text. Despite these differences, the textual nature of cultural reality ensures the feasibility of ethnographic texts. There is no objective reality before interpretation. Culture is regarded as text.[56]

Accordingly, Clifford Geertz understands cockfighting in Bali as a form of art and an expression of Balinese culture that can be read as a "paradigmatic human event." Geertz's analysis has been criticized from various angles. One criticism is that it relates neither to a real cockfight nor to the actions and opinions of real Balinese people and that the virtuoso interpretation was purely the work of the author of the text. The cockfight and the Balinese are considered purely as a generalized whole. Geertz interprets the cockfight as a result of an inscriptive process and thereby diminishes its significance in two ways. First, he fails to clarify how he arrives at his interpretation and how he gains access to the interpretive world of the Other. Second, he does not specify how the members of a society write their own cultural text or how it develops as a sort of collective sediment of their actions and is then preserved. Geertz concentrates solely on the meaning of texts and ignores how they are produced and reproduced.[57] This gives rise to a number of problems noted and discussed by other authors, which may be summarized as follows: the "other" is not seen as a concrete person, and the actual process of gaining insight is not visible in the thick description. Despite Geertz's fundamental understanding of the problems of representation, writing, and authorship, he does not discuss the imbalance between his own scientific discourse and the speech of those to whom this discourse refers. Neither does he examine the relationship between interpretation and social practice or that between producing and conveying social structures and cultural lifeworlds. The subjectivity of the actors is reduced to their capacity for creating meaning. Their ability not only to interpret their world but also to create it is not examined. These criticisms are undoubtedly justified, and they certainly lessen the validity of Geertz's interpretation. Nevertheless this interpretation of the cockfight has made an important contribution to field research in terms of methodology, because of its "thick description" and the many layers of interpretation that result.

Although Geertz was greatly inspired by Wilhelm Dilthey, Hans-Georg Gadamer, and Paul Ricoeur and their fundamental writings on hermeneutics,[58] he always insisted on the necessity of intensive field research. For Geertz, social actions were not mere texts; reading texts simply meant drawing an analogy to the interpretation of social actions from fieldwork experience. Neither of these two modes of study was the same for him as fieldwork. Geertz was interested in many different subjects, such as political actions, rituals, and agricultural practices, and did not reduce them to their textual qualities. "Unlike the textualism derived from Derrida or Foucault, Geertz's use of the text was merely heuristic. He did not retreat from fieldwork encounters to library work or to an exclusive reliance on vignettes, pictures, media materials, and rhetoric."[59] It was important to him that his hermeneutic approach to the field should not result in the dissolution of the objects under investigation or in the degeneration of his ethnographic work into "thin" description. Geertz stayed with his interpretative method and adamantly resisted the temptation to subsume his field research under postmodern philosophical or methodological approaches.

Attempts to give the "other" more space and a voice have led to different forms of experimental ethnographic writing. These include ethno-autobiographical narratives such as Michel Leiris's *Phantom Africa* and Lévi-Strauss's *Tristes Tropiques* (Sad tropics).[60] Both focus on the ethnographic author and his experience of the foreign world. They are about the author's feelings, expectations, and disappointments, his memories and dreams, his imagination and solitude. In such works it is not the reality of the "other" that is important, but how this "other" is experienced by the author at a certain point in time. We also find subjective forms of encounters with alterity and the lifeworld of the Other as well as the realization that one cannot escape one's own culture when studying another.

Equally interesting are ethnographic biographies such as *Nisa: The Life and Words of a !Kung Woman*, which consists of fifteen interviews with Nisa, an elderly female member of the !Kung San (bushmen), conducted and transcribed by Marjorie Shostak.[61] Unlike traditional life stories, every chapter is supplemented by commentaries that refer to conversations with other !Kung women and provide the context for Nisa's subjective feelings, opinions, and experiences. The author's epilogue describes how the conversations came about and how all those involved dealt with the interview situation. This resulted in a multidimensional account of the everyday life of the !Kung San.

Another form of experimental writing is dialogue ethnography, which reports dialogues conducted between the ethnographer and the members of another culture. Successful examples of this genre, in which representatives of other cultures speak for themselves, are Vincent Crapanzano's *Tuhami: Portrait of a Moroccan* and Kevin Dwyer's *Moroccan Dialogues*.[62] In both works, the informants tell their life stories and give the reader an insight into their views of the world and their appraisals in the form of a dialogue in which the ethnologist simultaneously confronts them with the point of view of an interlocutor from another culture. Both parties confirm and correct each other in the dialogues. The viewpoint that emerges has been created by both parties in equal measure. By making the complexity of the circumstances of the dialogue completely clear and only adding their own opinions in order to call them immediately into question, authors can consciously give up their monopoly on interpretation. Their perspectives are shown to be just as culture-bound as those of their sources. The researcher's own self is reflected in the Otherness of the research subject—analysis of the Other is transformed into self-analysis.[63]

These forms of experimental ethnography are part of the efforts to turn cultural anthropology into a polyphonous discipline, its main objective being to give voice to a multiplicity of views and to give the Other the same opportunities to present and express him or herself as the cultural anthropologist.[64] The aim of such endeavors was to prevent researchers

FIGURE 4.3 African mask on black background. © Ray Massey/ Photographer`s Choice RF/ Getty Images.

from determining what is to be included and how it is depicted—like puppeteers behind the scenes, pulling the strings of the events. It was also considered undesirable for ethnologists to speak as representatives or attorneys on behalf of members of the other culture, who should have the opportunity to represent and speak for themselves. This focus on the feelings and worldviews of the subjects of study plays a vital role in qualitative research, which is becoming increasingly important in the

social sciences. Accordingly, the importance of mimetic processes in social research, in which researchers take on aspects of the people they are
studying and their lifeworlds, is also growing.[65]

Cultural anthropology now no longer assumes a reality that is divorced
from its description, nor does it continue to see ethnographic representations as inner reflections of the external world. The focus has moved to
the power aspect of interpretations and the fact that all interpretations
are contingent and open to difference and diversity. As the form and
results of interpretations are not neutral, the dialogical approaches of cultural anthropology must "negotiate" what is to be seen as "reality."[66] Due
to its contingent character, each interpretation can offer only one perspective. If the number of interpretational perspectives increases through
dialogue, this can result in multiple authorship of texts.[67] Overall, we can
say that many studies today place an increased emphasis on the representation of the "other" and the development of polyphonous research and
representation techniques in cultural anthropology.[68]

Field Research Reconsidered

The "writing culture" debate of the mid-1980s led to a discussion of some
fundamental issues of cultural anthropology. This discussion questioned
the centrality of its principal method, that is, the fieldwork experience
and the production of the ethnographic monograph that resulted.[69]
There was talk of a "crisis of representation." What was demanded was
a shift "away from the observing eye toward expressive speech (and gesture),"[70] as well as a form of experimental writing that is critical of truth
claims and includes explicit awareness of its fragmentariness. This criticism drew attention to three denials that were widespread in the research
praxis of cultural anthropology, namely, "that ethnography is a literary
genre which denies itself as such; that reliance on observation leads to a
denial of the role of the ethnographer in shaping the object/subject studied; and that ethnographers tend to deny the constructed character of
their objects and of the knowledge they produce, from the initial period
of fieldwork through to the writing of their essays and books."[71]

Moreover, the ethnographer's gaze originated in a close relationship
with colonialism, and this continued to have an effect in the postcolonial
age.[72] In this context the validity of ethnographic research, the relative
truth-value of its findings, and the possibility of comparing its results
were challenged. Criticism was directed, for example, at its concentration on premodern societies; the isolated, static, unhistorical character of

the research; and the lack of attention to processes of modernity in field research. The textualists criticized ethnographers for making a "fetish" out of fieldwork and rejected the assumption of co-residence between the subjects of research and the ethnologist as a myth. Ethnological research was even criticized as being a "metaphysics of presence," as Derrida put it. Sometimes this criticism was so extreme that it threatened to destroy the object itself in the critical process. Important as criticism is, it must not be so radical as to cause us to lose sight of the insights that can be, and have been, gained from ethnographic research. If cultural anthropology adapts to the methods used today in philosophy, philology, and history, then it will once more be in danger of becoming an armchair discipline. If that were to happen, it would take a step backwards to the stage it was at before it came under the influence of the Boasians and the followers of Malinowski and Geertz.

Unlike those who were inclined to give up the central role of field research in order to transform cultural anthropology into cultural critique, I believe that it is essential to retain ethnographic field research.[73] This is not to reject arguments in favor of broadening the spectrum of field research. Globalization phenomena such as the linking up of markets into networks, migratory movements, the flow of images in the new media, and the currents of the transnational collective imaginary are also important issues for ethnographic research today.[74] If we turn our attention toward these subjects, new data and new forms of data collection and interpretation also become important, in which categories such as fragmentariness, fictionalization, representativeness, performativity, diversity, the in-between, and experimental character play a part.

In view of the complexity of ethnographic field research, such categories are doubtless important, and yet field research is still more than this. The fact that we take them into account does not mean that questions and categories that used to be considered important but to which currently little attention is being paid are no longer worthy of our consideration. Categories from functionalist, structuralist, and interpretative approaches continue to play an important role in field research. Occasionally they are taken up again and reworked within the framework of new research questions. This is the case, for instance, in research work inspired by the writings of Karl Marx, Georg Simmel, Émile Durkheim, and Sigmund Freud. Although issues of representation and the linguistic form in which the insights of cultural anthropology are expressed are important, experiences in the field take precedence. This is where encounters with people and artifacts take place, in a way that makes ethno-

FIGURE 4.4   Sani father and two boys (8–9) watching images on laptop. © Kerstin Geier/ Getty Images.

graphic research quite different from literary studies, where reading and writing relates to texts that have already been written. In contrast with this approach ethnographers have to present their field observations, experiences, and insights by using language. In so doing they are tied to unconscious linguistic models, to their own, individual imaginary, to a collective imaginary, and also to their research practices. Approaches that do not regard field research as necessary lose a central feature of ethnography. If ethnographic research simply refers to texts and the textual nature of society and culture, then it runs the risk of turning anthropology into a textual science without, as a rule, achieving the same standard as textual sciences.

Metaphors convey meanings. This also applies to the metaphor of the text, when it is used to accentuate the symbolic structure of culture and society, and the metaphor of reading, which suggests that human cultures and societies can be read as texts. These two metaphors simultaneously reveal and conceal important relationships. Thus, in the metaphor of reading there is the danger that our relationship to the world will be expressed chiefly in words and that we will overlook the differences that exist between reading a text and what ethnographers actually experience in a foreign world. These experiences do not have the tidy character of a text that is structured for the reader. Field experiences are untidy; they are gathered in encounters with other people whose actions follow an unfamiliar logic and affect the ethnographer in some way. Experiences are contradictory and ambivalent. They are forms of participation on a physical and sensory level; they involve all the senses and not simply the ethnographer's gaze and visual observation. Tied to the sensory perceptions of the body, these experiences are initially preverbal and only very gradually lead to interpretations. They arise in the encounter with the Other and are only partly predictable.

At the center of fieldwork encounters are mimetic processes, in the course of which the ethnographer adjusts to unfamiliar surroundings. This process takes place in a body-based way, through the senses, and results in the expansion of the ethnographer's awareness into surroundings that are foreign to him. Such mimetic processes are directed toward other people and form the interactions between field researchers and their environments. As they take place, the feelings and inner worlds of other people are discovered and rendered understandable. With the aid of the imagination, a bridge is formed that allows the foreign external world to find a way into the ethnographer's own mental world of images, feelings, language, and experience. She takes an "imprint" of the external world and integrates it into her own mental world. This mimetic process results in a re-creation of the outside world, assisted by the field researcher's imagination and pictorial and linguistic imaginary. The result is a relationship to the initially foreign world of the exterior in which collective and individual aspects overlap and re-form in a new way (see chapter 7).[75]

This mimetic processing of field experiences creates a practical knowledge that is integral to field experience. In my view, labeling this knowledge as text and approaching it as something to be read fails to do it justice. As practical knowledge based on a wide variety of mimetic processes, it certainly embraces *performative* (see chapters 8 and 9),[76] *iconic* (see chapter 11),[77] and *linguistic* elements (see chapter 10),[78] which must be seen as separate although they interconnect with each other in the evaluation of field experiences. To read social reality as a text is not sufficient. The performative aspects of social action are just as important, that is, the staging and performance aspects of action, whose inclusion can also be referred to as the performative turn in the humanities. Of equal importance are the images that are produced in human acts, social spaces, and landscapes, which enter the imaginary and the feelings of ethnographers. Like the focus on the performativity of social aspects, dealing with the iconic side of "the foreign" also calls for new ways of expressing and presenting field experiences.[79] Field research takes place in the form of practices. These lead to practical knowledge, which in turn is the starting point for ethnographic knowledge.[80]

Alterity and Culture

To the extent that cultural anthropology defines itself as the study of the foreign, its field of enquiry is the Other, an area that also plays a central role in other humanities disciplines and social sciences. Thus, historians fail to do justice to the Middle Ages if they do not grasp its alterity; for instance, concepts such as the family, the state, and religion need to be understood differently in the context of the twelfth century than they are in the present. In education, too, the perception of and approach to the alterity of children play an important role. Even in literature, the aesthetic appeal of the situations and persons described often remains associated with their alterity. In cultural anthropology, the Other refers primarily to peoples who in the Western world were for a long time considered to be wild, uncivilized, or members of primitive societies.[81] In order to avoid the pejorative tone of these labels, today the terms *archaic cultures*, *pre-industrial societies*, *nonliterate cultures*, or *tribal*, *small-scale*, or *face-to-face* societies are used.[82] All refer to societies consisting of a few dozen to a few thousand individuals. Unlike the modern societies of North America and Europe, these societies place great emphasis on kinship. They are closed, have a strong sense of cohesion, and experience the difference between themselves and other ethnic groups more strongly than more open societies such as modern democracies.

For all societies, it is possible to discern a preferred site of symbolic process that is the basis for a classificatory grid that covers the entire culture. In Western societies this lies in the "institutionalization of the production process." This is what differentiates these states from the "primitive" world, where social relations, especially kinship relationships, persist as this site of symbolic distinction, and other areas of activity are determined by the kinship distinctions in operation.[83] The biological basis of kinship is the relationship between mother and child, but kinship is also a classification pattern that structures social relationships, and it is thus a suitable focus for the study of foreign cultures in cultural anthropology.[84]

Today, many people in Western cultures have difficulty in grasping the extraordinary significance of kinship in other cultures. Due to the marked differentiations in the division of labor, people in industrial societies belong to many different subworlds and subcultures in which life requires pronounced orientation skills and a high degree of flexibility. In contrast, the organization of societies on the basis of kinship seems different to us, and we find it difficult to conceptualize. Even if we can understand the structures and the principles of organization on which they are based, they remain foreign to how we view world and society. Since the world is getting smaller and cultures are closer together, experiences of difference or alterity are becoming more and more frequent. But how do we deal with them? We can try to reduce what is foreign to the familiar and thus avoid disconcerting experiences. Or we may experience alterity as an opportunity to have new experiences that broaden our own worldviews. Then we are open to them and can experience how members of other cultures and societies see the world and how they behave toward other people. In this case we experience the differentness of other societies from our own culture.

In view of the complexity of these processes, it is important but increasingly difficult to give a precise definition of culture, particularly since terms such as *recreational culture, subculture, culture industry, corporate culture, gastronomic culture, erotic culture, funeral culture*, and so forth have led to an inflationary expansion of the concept that threatens to dilute its discriminant capacity. A glance at philosophy, sociology, and ethnology will suffice to obtain an impression of the heterogeneity and complexity of the term.[85] Sartre, for example, was still grounded in a general concept of culture when he wrote, "Culture doesn't save anything or anyone, it doesn't justify. But it's a product of man: he projects himself into it, he recognizes himself in it; that critical mirror alone offers him his image."[86] Gehlen's anthropologically based concept of culture, according to which human beings are malleable "deficit beings" that are "open to the world" (*weltoffen*) and are forced to "produce themselves and their world," that is, to create culture, is similarly general. For Rehberg, the advantage of this view is that it avoids all ontologizing splits between action and thought, "society" and "culture," and can therefore contribute to the categorical foundation of a social theory that leaves such dualisms behind it for good.[87]

In cultural anthropology, too, there have been many attempts to define what we mean by the term *culture*. Back in the early 1950s, Alfred Kroeber and Clyde Kluckhohn listed more than one hundred sixty definitions of culture, which frequently did not differ much from each other.[88] But it is evident from this overview how difficult, if not impossible, it is to arrive at a coherent general definition of culture, and we must therefore content ourselves here with developing only a few dimensions of the concept. It can only be formulated more precisely in relation to a specific context and within the framework of an individual study and the issue on which it focuses.

One definition that is often quoted in cultural anthropology was formulated by Edward Tylor, who equated culture with civilization and defined it as "that complex whole which includes knowledge, belief, art, morals, law, custom, and any other capabilities and habits acquired by man as a member of society."[89] According to this definition, cultural skills are not inherited like natural aptitudes or gifts, but acquired. According to current knowledge, however, culture is no longer seen as being clearly distinguishable from nature. While human beings are by nature cultural beings and only become human by virtue of culture, cultural processes are understood to begin at the start of human evolution. They were already present in primeval humans and, interacting with nature, produced *Homo sapiens*. The use of tools and social institutions gave humans the capacity to survive and helped them to spread successfully across the globe.

A definition of culture that gives more weight to material and social conditions was developed by Malinowski: "Culture is an integral composed of partly autonomous, partly coordinated institutions. It is integrated on a series of principles such as the community of blood through procreation; the contiguity in space related to cooperation; the specialization in activities; and last, but not least, the use of power in political organization. Each culture owes its completeness and self-sufficiency to the fact that it satisfies the whole range of basic, instrumental and integrative needs."[90] In this view, culture covers both material and nonmaterial conditions, including the products of mental, social, and political activities. We must add to this various lifestyles and spheres of the imaginary. Culture forms the human body while at the same time arising from and being a product of this formation. In disruptions and innovations it produces transformation and continuity between past, present, and future. It draws boundaries between the living and the dead, the sexes and the generations, inside and outside, above and below, and develops differentiated forms of the distribution of labor. Culture is dynamic, it is practice and process; no culture is a single culture, all cultures encompass many cultures.

Clifford Geertz was thinking along the same lines when he wrote, "This circumstance makes the drawing of a line between what is natural, universal, and constant in man and what is conventional, local, and variable extraordinarily difficult. In fact, it suggests that to draw such a line

is to falsify the human situation, or at least to misrender it seriously."[91]
We do not find human beings "behind" their many different historical
and cultural manifestations, but in them. Only when we investigate social phenomena in different cultures do we discover their extraordinary
diversity and gain insight into the multifarious nature of culture. In this
view it is precisely the historical and cultural diversity that provides insight into the human species. It is "not so much the empirical commonalities in his behavior, from place to place and time to time, but rather
the mechanisms by whose agency the breadth and indeterminateness of
his inherent capacities are reduced to the narrowness and specificity of
his actual accomplishments. [. . .] Undirected by culture patterns—organized systems of significant symbols—man's behavior would be virtually
ungovernable, a mere chaos of pointless acts and exploding emotions, his
experience virtually shapeless. Culture, the accumulated totality of such
patterns, is not just an ornament of human existence but—the principal
basis for specificity and essential conditions for it."[92]

The concepts of culture differ depending on whether the emphasis
lies on the unity and oneness of culture or on the diversity of cultures.
Among the schools of thought that stress the fundamental unity of culture and strive to discover common principles of cultural development
that exist despite obvious differences, we find *diffusionism, functionalism,* and *structuralism.* To cite Kohl, "In diffusionism the main focus is
on the tangible elements of culture, while functionalism concentrates
on cultural and social institutions, and structuralism also includes the
intangible products of individual cultures."[93] In the first instance we are
concerned with theories of culture that assume that all human beings
are descended from a common source, from which the cultures have
spread. Babylon, Atlantis, and Egypt have each been seen as the well-
spring of humanity. Functionalism, according to which culture serves to
fulfill human beings' basic needs, became more influential. Malinowski,
with his definition of culture, Radcliffe-Brown, and many others belong
in this category. Structuralism, which is closely linked to the work of
Lévi-Strauss, focuses on reciprocity as the principle of organization of all
cultures, regardless of how widely they may differ.

Cultural relativism, neoevolutionism, and *cultural ecology* diverge from
this position. Influenced by Boas, Kroeber, Benedict, and Mead, cultural
relativism became highly influential (see above). It stresses the uniqueness and incomparability of each culture, which are also discernible
in Geertz's definition of culture (above). This stance reveals an anti-
colonialist attitude, which assumes that all cultures are equal and insists

that when cultures are compared, values and attitudes must always be formulated from a cultural standpoint. Cultural relativism is therefore indisputably seen as a methodological principle. "All ethnological research must do justice to the insight that our own norms, values and behaviors are culture-bound. The starting point of any attempt to gain an understanding of the realities of a foreign culture must be the relativization of our own cultural standpoint."[94] Unlike the evolutionism associated with the nineteenth-century belief in progress, the neoevolutionism of the 1950s and 1960s was based more on the idea of processes of multilinear cultural development in which developmental courses may differ, depending on the ecological conditions. This is where cultural ecology, which emphasizes the mutual dependency of the environment and cultural development, comes in.[95]

When members of different cultures encounter each other, complex processes of attraction and repulsion, suppression and assimilation take place in which violence and mimetic processes play an important role. Tzetan Todorov, Serge Gruzinski, and Stephen Greenblatt have described in detail how such processes were involved in the colonization of Mexico and Latin America.[96] They portray the Europeans as superior to the Indians in that they were better able to grasp their differentness and were therefore also better able to manipulate them in their own interest. Following their military victory, the Spaniards went to great lengths to destroy the alterity of the foreign culture and to replace it with Christian, Spanish culture. Not only were the indigenous peoples killed, with inconceivable cruelty, but the survivors' imaginary was supplanted by the ideas and images of Spanish Christianity. A mixed culture came into being whose hybrid structures and contents are still in existence and continue to develop today.

European culture has developed three strategies to limit perception of the alterity of other peoples and cultures: *logocentrism, egocentrism,* and *ethnocentrism*.[97] In the case of logocentrism, the European version of rationality (*logos*) serves to devalue other forms of rational thinking and action or simply not to see them. Egocentrism refers to the focus on the ego and its capacity for self-assertion, which is often alien to members of other cultures. Ethnocentrism refers to the forms of thinking, feeling, and action that are based on the assumption that European culture is superior to other cultures. In the subjugation of South America, the colonialism of the eighteenth and nineteenth centuries, and also the globalization of the twentieth and twenty-first centuries, these "strategies" of reducing the Other to what is in fact one's own has played a central role, even in cultural anthropological research.[98]

Insofar as cultural anthropology focuses on the study of the Other, it strives to counter processes that violate the human right to *cultural diversity*. An important strategy for raising awareness of behavior toward the Other and developing a sensitive way of dealing with the alterity of other people consists in discovering the Other in oneself. The same applies to thinking from the standpoint of the Other, a heterological way of thinking for which the experience of being alien to oneself is also essential.[99]

Since, influenced by modernity and globalization, societies and cultures that have once been studied ethnologically change fast, the spectrum of cultural anthropological research is expanding. Studies focus not only on what is alien in other societies, but on what is alien in the researcher's own culture. Influenced by the increasing speed of life, the globalization of production and markets, and the ubiquity and simultaneity of the new media, new social and cultural forms are evolving through processes in which tradition and innovation are closely interlinked. It is one of the tasks of cultural anthropology to investigate these processes. In *An Anthropology for Contemporary Worlds*, Marc Augé investigates diverse worlds in contemporary societies, looking at what we are while retaining an awareness of what we are no longer.[100] He also pursues this goal in his ethnographic studies on the Paris metro and "non-places."[101] His research focuses on everyday phenomena of contemporary life seen with the alienating eye of the ethnologist. These include the meanings, for our individual and collective identities, of places that have been shaped by culture and their value, which has evolved historically, as bearers of memories and the sacral. He distinguishes these places from "non-places" such as airports, stations, and so forth, which have no historical or cultural dimensions. These "non-places" are one result of the acceleration of time, the surfeit of events, and the inflated individualization characteristic of our times. Bound to their purposes and functions, these anonymous places are for transport, transit, and trade and are similar in that they have no relationship to their historical and cultural environments.

Today, many studies in cultural anthropology investigate modern towns and cities that are, ethnically speaking, much less homogeneous than traditional communities. Many of them are syncretistic; new cultural forms evolve in them in which it is difficult to discern which elements come from which culture. These mixtures of ethnically diverse cultures lead to *hybridity*. This is a new form of alterity to whose understanding ethnographic research can contribute. As researchers become better able to depict both the diversity and complexity as well as the alterity and polyphony of this field of investigation, cultural anthropology will become more important in this domain.

In attempts to understand these new phenomena in mixed cultures, the terms *differentiation, transgression,* and *hybrid formation* play a central role in what is foreign, what is Other, and alterity. These terms are interrelated. Their interconnectedness is obvious.[102] In processes of transcultural communication, it is important to make use of these three concepts when analyzing cultural phenomena and relations.

- The concept of *difference* is important for creating boundaries and helping to render them dynamic. It is not possible for a national, cultural, or European identity to form without differences. Thus, for example, in the processes of inclusion and exclusion that take place in rituals, differences are created that are crucial for the performative character of the rituals. The category of difference is also very important for understanding alterity. The ways in which heterogeneity and alterity are dealt with are crucial to this cultural diversity, which is created by acts of differentiation.

- When analyzing social and cultural developments, it is important to understand processes of *transgression.* Transgression consists in overstepping the limits set by rules, norms, and laws, on the one hand, and in overstepping historically created boundaries, on the other. These acts of transgression can be nonviolent, but they frequently also involve manifest structural or symbolic violence. In dealing with cultural diversity, boundaries are often transgressed, leading to the creation of something new. Transgressions change norms and rules, ways of life, and practices. They change and shift borders and create new cultural relations and constellations in the process. In order to understand these processes, we need to make a thorough analysis of their contexts, focusing on the origin of the change or innovation in question.

- In attempting to gain an understanding of our own times, it is crucial to analyze the development of new *hybrid cultural forms* by means of difference and transgression. As communication and interaction between different countries become ever closer and faster, and as economic, political, social, and cultural exchange becomes more intensive, more and more hybrid cultural forms are coming into being. Homi Bhabha first used the term *hybridization* to define cultural contacts in a nondualistic and nonessentialist way by describing them in terms of their function of creating identity by means of a "third space."[103] The third space is liminal; it is a space inbetween which emphasizes its own in-betweenness. In this liminal space, borders are subject to subversion and restructuring, and hierarchies and power relationships are altered. The crucial questions are to what extent these processes result from performative practices and how these new forms of hybridization are created. They are mixed forms in which elements belonging to different systems and contexts change their character in a mimetic process, leading to a new cultural identity. This identity is no longer constituted by distinguishing oneself from another, but in mimetically assimilating oneself to the Other.

Outlook

In cultural anthropology a number of stimuli from Europe have been taken up and developed further in an independent manner. As a result, a broad field of research has evolved that is becoming both more international and more interdisciplinary. It has also become highly diversified, and thus it is no longer possible to assume that there is a stable field of research. In the early twentieth century, cultural anthropology was defined above all by the concepts of historicity, culture, and four-field anthropology,[104] which came from Germany and were introduced and further developed by Boas and the Boasians. Soon afterwards many influences from Britain, in particular from Malinowski and Radcliffe-Brown, also contributed to the development of field research and the specific forms of American functionalism, which entered into an interesting relationship with Boasian cultural relativism, producing new research studies, for example, within the culture and personality school. After the Second World War, the tensions grew between the Marxists and the Mentalists and were still in evidence at the end of the twentieth century. In the postwar period many foreign-born anthropologists, such as Karl Polanyi, Eric Wolf, and Victor Turner, also influenced the development of cultural anthropology in the United States. There was always an interest in the work of the French sociologists, anthropologists, and philosophers such as Durkheim, Mauss, Lévi-Strauss, and, later, Foucault, Derrida, and Bourdieu. After the end of the golden age of social anthropology in Britain, whose key figures were Raymond Firth, Edward E. Evans-Pritchard, Meyer Fortes, and Edmund R. Leach, research in cultural anthropology was centered more in the United States. At the same time, other countries also continued to contribute theories and field research, and the discipline became increasingly international. This was accompanied by continued differentiation in the field, resulting in new research issues and research fields and also new forms of cooperative international research.[105]

In line with the aims of my investigation of the central paradigms of anthropology and elaboration of possible lines of development for historical cultural anthropology, I consider the following aspects to be particularly important. First, cultural anthropological research has shown clearly that it makes no sense to limit the term *culture* to literature, art, music, or theater, as is still often done today in many areas of the humanities. On the other hand, views that proceed from the premise of the *closely interwoven relationship between nature and culture* and understand social practices as elements that are constitutive of culture are productive. This view leads to many new situations and questions that have arisen in the context of globalization. A decisive factor is that enclosed cultures, which were long the subject of cultural anthropology, are gradually disappearing. Today, new forms of culture are evolving that are expanding across the world and can be found alongside traditional cultures, overlapping and intermingling with them. This overlapping, intermingling, and assimilation of global, national, regional, and local elements is leading to new forms of multiculturalism, interculturalism, and hybrid cultures, which have so far not been extensively researched.[106]

These developments are leading to many new questions as to what approach is needed to investigate "the *foreign*," which was once clearly identified in studies of enclosed tribal cultures, but is now no longer so easy to delineate. This is so even if we assume that what belongs to us and what is foreign to us always stand in relation to each other and cannot, per se, be ontologized. If what is foreign and what is our own cannot be clearly defined, then we need new concepts of cultural anthropological research in order to study the transformations, intermingling, and hybridization of cultural phenomena and situations. When we speak of a globalization of culture, what we really mean is the worldwide marketing of cultural products. Some see these developments as positive, hoping that a world society will develop that is characterized by a universal democratic culture. Others view this development more skeptically, and tend rather to expect it to result in a loss of identity, as they believe that cultural differences are necessary to maintain individuality. An analysis of the globalized culture market must take into account both the mechanisms of the market and the special nature of the cultures and the cultural goods.

Four clusters of problems can be identified in this globalization. One derives from the erosion of traditional cultures associated with global developments where there is no belief in the spread of progress. The second is the increase in the specific and heterogenic character of cultural goods and their limited distribution to certain recipients. The third cluster is linked to the question of whether, and to what extent, fragmented cultures can contribute to generating allegiances that reach beyond the confines of their own culture and thereby help to create social cohesion. Fourth, we need to investigate what influence the fragmentation of culture has on the different areas of social life and to what extent the passing on of cultural goods is negatively affected by concentrating on their production rather than on transmitting them to others. It is currently impossible to say how these issues will develop.

There can be no simple solution to these issues. What we must do above all, therefore, is investigate them systematically using cultural anthropological fieldwork. This offers the opportunity to carry out studies which, although they will be limited to specific localities, will have the advantage of being conducted in depth and will be able to do justice to the complexity of the new situations. Field research is a method that was developed in cultural anthropology and was fundamental to the evolution of the discipline. Currently it is meeting with growing approval in other social sciences and even in the humanities. It is clear that its potential for investigating these new conditions is by no means exhausted.

FIVE

Historical Cultural Anthropology

The preceding analysis of previous paradigms in anthropology reveals that the diachronic and the synchronic dimensions are constitutive of anthropology. In order to do justice to both, in what follows *anthropology* will be understood as historical cultural anthropology. As demonstrated by evolutionary research, the historical dimension is indispensable for our understanding of the evolution of the human species. In my analyses of philosophical anthropology in Germany, historical anthropology in France, and cultural anthropology in the United States, I have shown how the differences between the respective conceptualizations of anthropology are deeply rooted in the different cultures. I have also drawn attention to the fact that there are several points of contact between historical anthropology and cultural anthropology, and to the need for anthropological research to use both *diachronic* and *synchronic* perspectives. Viewing anthropological issues from both of these two perspectives opens up new ways of investigating phenomena and structures in the present. We can thus arrive at novel interpretations and improve our understanding and interpretation of human beings.

It is my view that attempts to link different anthropological perspectives in terms of content and method and to consider their historicity and culturality can be subsumed under the heading "historical cultural anthropology." Research in this branch of anthropology is being conducted at a time when the normative and obligatory character of conventional anthropology and its ability to act as an umbrella for different disciplines, and also the assumption that human history and human culture can be guided by reason and progress have been called into doubt. Thus viewed, anthropology questions widely held assumptions about social and cultural life that until recently seemed certain. It views them from a different angle and thus turns them into new subjects of research. Studies in this field are carried out on human cultures in certain areas and certain times, and on the changes that take place within them. Their aim is not to find constant or universal aspects of the human being but to emphasize the historical and cultural character of both what is under investigation and what is discovered. They are pluralistic, frequently transdisciplinary and transnational, and reflect upon both the possibilities and the limitations of their findings. Historical cultural anthropology is a focal point in the social sciences and in the humanities today.

Research in historical cultural anthropology is not a specialized academic discipline or a research field with clear boundaries. Its studies cross the boundaries of formal disciplines and attempt to create new forms of knowledge, in terms of both content and methodological approach. As employed here, the term *historical cultural anthropology* refers to diverse forms of transdisciplinary research that examine phenomena and structures of human nature without adhering to a generally accepted abstract and binding anthropological norm. After the anthropology of the "standard" human being (Western, male, abstract) had lost its normative power, anthropological research took the diversity arising from the historicity and culturality of human beings as a point of departure. The resulting anthropology is not an alternative to the philosophical and historical anthropology conducted within the historical sciences or even to that carried out as part of cultural or biological anthropology. It does not seek to advance the historical-philosophical critique of anthropology, but strives toward other findings and models of perception. It also does not see itself as a scientific discipline in its own right.

This form of anthropological research finds itself in tension between the disciplines of history and the human sciences. However, it is not simply a history of anthropology, nor is it simply history's contribution to the field of anthropology. Research into historical and cultural anthropology attempts to relate the historical and cultural aspects of its viewpoints and methods to the historical and cultural nature of what is under investigation. Thus conceived, anthropology is therefore historical and cultural in two ways: with regard to both the subject matter under examination and its methods. This creates a new dimension of complexity, insofar as the points of reference of anthropological research are constantly changing. Construction, reconstruction, and deconstruction of knowledge about human nature are all subject to these changes, so that the conviction has arisen that there is no definitive concept of the human being.

Anthropological research brings together the findings of human sciences as well as those of historical-philosophical critiques of anthropology, thereby uncovering new, paradigmatic questions for examination. It is not the objective of research in this area to find a universal theory of anthropology. This kind of research tries to understand differences and is not limited to either specific cultural areas or any particular era or eras. Its examination of its own history and culture has enabled it to leave behind both the Eurocentricity of the human sciences and a solely antiquarian interest in history and culture, and to move on to examine unsolved problems of the past and future. In the past this research has been limited to the European cultural area, but this limitation did not arise from a conscious decision. In the light of the complex process of globalization, this kind of research is likely to expand to other cultural areas.

The plan for anthropology proposed here was developed through extensive research carried out in both historical cultural and philosophical anthropology. An outline of the results of this research follows, based on a few examples. These examples are not intended to be representative of the entire domain of possible research, but to show what can be done in a field of research that is both transdisciplinary and transcultural in nature, and whose openness is seen as a strength rather than a disadvantage.

In this chapter I present the three cornerstones of my anthropological research to illustrate what is meant by the term *historical cultural anthropology*. I selected different methodological approaches to address these three areas of research. The first cornerstone is an interdisciplinary and transnational project on the subjects of logic and passion.[1] The aim of these studies, which fill several volumes, was to reconstruct some central concepts of European culture in a comprehensive, transdisciplinary, and transnational research project and thus to make a contribution to the self-interpretation of our culture and our times. Hermeneutic, phenomenological, constructive, and deconstructive methods were employed to address these issues. It was highly important for the development of this project that I had previously undertaken a critique of the critical theory of the Frankfurt School. Although all these studies clearly take a different direction from that of the Frankfurt School, their research was an important reference point for the development of the anthropological approach for this project and for critical reflection. Without Adorno's work on the *Dialectic of Enlightenment* (which he coauthored with Hork-heimer), as well as his writings on negative dialectics and aesthetic theory, and Habermas's studies on the public sphere, knowledge, and interest, it would hardly have been possible for me to understand the present. This also applies to a number of pivotal concepts that were not addressed in this research but were of major importance for their frame of reference.[2]

The second project is the comprehensive handbook on historical anthropology, *Human Beings and Their Cultures*, which covers investigations on basic human behavior and conceptualizations of the world in Germany and Europe.[3] The objective was to analyze human beings' relationships to the world, society, culture, and each other in terms of one hundred concepts relevant to cultural science and thus to contribute to the understanding of our times from an anthropological perspective. Here again, several different methods were employed. A series of studies published in *Paragrana*, an international review of anthropology, can also be added to this first phase of historical cultural anthropology.[4] These projects have been supplemented by other studies on anthropology,[5] educational anthropology,[6] and similar works in psychology and literary studies.[7]

It was through these studies that I came to realize how central mimetic processes are for the development of culture and decided to make research into mimetic processes a second cornerstone of my anthropological work.[8] In these two studies I researched mimetic processes, which form an essential part of anthropological studies.[9] The first study showed that mimesis is central to anthropology and can help us to understand and explain historical and cultural change. Its main focus was an analysis of the development of the concepts of mimesis from the time they first appeared, before Plato, to the refinements introduced by Walter Benjamin, Theodor W. Adorno, and Jacques Derrida. In the second study I went on to explore the mimetic bases of the social world, using examples of play, ritual, and gesture to show the central importance of mimetic processes in creating the social world. The historical and cultural dimensions of these processes were also analyzed. In these studies I showed that a large part of historical and cultural learning takes place in mimetic processes. This applies, for example, to the learning of the upright gait, early development of emotions, and the development of speech and the imaginary.

Thirdly, on the basis of these previous studies, I have embarked upon a broad-based ethnographic study;[10] in the twelve-year Berlin Study on Rituals and Gestures, I carried out extensive fieldwork consisting of numerous individual and collective studies, the aim of which was to demonstrate empirically the significance of rituals in child-rearing, education, and socialization. Although these studies are a large part of my basic research in anthropology, their results have been important in laying the foundations for practical social changes in the fields of child-rearing and education. Finally, in a German-Japanese study on familial happiness as performance and social action, I demonstrate that the principles and criteria of historical cultural anthropology are not limited to certain cultural areas or historical epochs and can be adapted to the analysis of other cultures and societies. This is also the result of the research I conducted over several years with Indians in India and also in the Moslem world.[11]

Logic and Passion

The title of the series of anthropological studies published with Dietmar Kamper as *Logik und Leidenschaft* (Logic and passion) refers to the tension-laden relationship between body and mind, which has been dealt with in different ways at different stages of the process of civilization. For a long time, humans were regarded as being at risk because of their inadequate physique, and it was deemed necessary to adapt and discipline the body. Today, a growing danger seems to be emanating more from our logical processes. Whereas passion is oriented toward the particular and multifarious, logic strives toward the universal. The images of the imaginary are located in between these areas. Together with Dietmar Kamper, I carried out these investigations in a mainly German-French-Italian project in order to reconstruct some of the central issues of European culture, some of which had been forced into the background, in a transdisciplinary and transnational framework. The project was carried out in the 1980s by almost two hundred researchers from more than twenty disciplines and more than ten countries. The resulting discourses were correspondingly complex. Their purpose was to elaborate a contribution to the understanding of the present and its processes of transformation by conducting a historical, cultural, and philosophical analysis of central issues.

The tension between logic and passion permeates the body and its senses. The question arises as to what role the body plays in the processes of civilization, culture, and the cultural sciences and what an examination of the body and the senses can contribute to our understanding of human nature in our times. The differences between interpretations of the body are considerable. This also applies to the senses, the relationships among them, and their role in the current era. Any attempt to understand the body and the senses will encounter contradictions, paradoxes, and antinomies. When studying this field, we are unavoidably confronted with the soul (understood as including both a spiritual level and the psyche), which is neither of a material nature like the body nor fully understandable using the instruments of logic. Instead, there is something transitory about the soul or psyche that goes beyond human beings and things and points toward religion and transcendence. Like the soul or psyche, the sacred is also not a phenomenon of the past, but is merely displaced and repressed. It defies clarity, is terrifying yet fascinating, ambivalent and paradoxical. Societal structures are created, destroyed, and transformed in its name.

The sacred manifests itself in the semblance of beauty and the fate of love. Beauty is also not clearly definable; it is elusive, fleeting, and fascinating. It is associated with the non-identical. In beauty we see the expression of the infinite in the finite. Art and love, passion and aesthetic experience, overlap. Love is the experience of the Other and thus an escape from solitude. Experiences of love can differ enormously. As expressions of both longing and satisfaction, they stimulate speech. In the course of European history, different rhetorics have developed that engender different feelings. Love is associated with sexual desire, but that is not all it is. It seeks pleasure and often leads to suffering. It aims for constancy, yet suffers from its ephemerality. It cannot keep its promise to resolve antinomies.

To experience beauty and love is to experience a time that is not the linear time that governs everyday life. These experiences are of a time condensed in a moment (*kairos*); they open up new dimensions in life. Time is one of the central conditions that constitute human life. The body and the senses, the soul and the sacred, beauty and love are manifested in time and are subject to change. The simultaneous nature of non-simultaneous events, the non-simultaneous nature of simultaneous events, and the resulting plurality of times are of particular interest. When we explore differing experiences of time, the question arises as to how language, imagination, and silence are related. What role does keeping silence play in speech and in the experience of time? We speak in the hope that we will be able to apprehend what we are talking about, but we fail. We speak out against this disappointing experience. We cannot tolerate the unavailability of the world around us and attempt to drown the noise of silence by talking.

The following section provides an introduction to the seven areas of study that were the main focus of research in historical cultural anthropology during its first ten years. Following these initial, exploratory studies, all seven became central areas of research in the field of cultural studies.

1. The return of the body and the anthropology of the senses
2. The embers of the soul
3. The sacred
4. The semblance of beauty
5. The fate of love
6. Dying time
7. Silence

The Return of the Body and the Anthropology of the Senses

As in philosophical anthropology, the body is the point of departure for research in historical cultural anthropology. Whereas the body is a major topic in cultural studies today, it was virtually ignored in the arts and social sciences during the 1960s and 1970s. The distancing from and disciplining and instrumentalization of the body as a basis for historical progress were accompanied by the suppression of mainly those aspects of the body that could not be included in the rationality and logic of the civilization process and that are now demanding more attention. On the other hand, in prosthetic medicine and bioengineering, the manipulation of the body has reached new heights. New forms of representation, fragmentation, and manipulation of the body are also being tried out in the media. The increase in psychogenic, sociogenic, and iatrogenic illnesses, the number of suicides, and the increasing use of addictive substances can all be understood as forms of resistance to these developments. The more pronounced the undesired side effects of rationalization and abstraction, the more clearly we see, in the disciplining and control of the body, a decrease in the diverse manifestations of the body and the senses. There is thus a new focus of attention on the contradictory and complex nature of the body (see chapter 6).

In the course of history, various configurations of the body have developed. In ancient Greek culture, the body was constituted as human in comparison with the bodies of the gods; as male or female, it was shaped on the basis of the difference between the sexes and the distribution of power between the genders; as a microcosm that mirrors the whole, it was seen in analogy to the macrocosm. Each configuration of the body is determined by the context in which it takes shape and is influenced by the imagination, systems of symbols and signs, and human actions.[12]

Violence plays an important role in the development of such configurations. Without violence, discipline cannot be successful. It results in the formation or deformation of the body. In some cases it takes the form of physical force, while in others it is exerted more as a symbolic or imaginary force. The aim is to reduce the number of diverse forms of the body and to establish an individual body that is both as unambiguous as possible and of use to society.[13]

To rule over people also means to rule over their bodies. We can see how this occurs in the types of human work and in the construction of gender and medical symptomatologies.[14] According to Nietzsche, human beings have never stopped short of cruelty if it gave them a place in history.[15] The resulting wounds and scars have left their mark on the history of civilization. They show that there is no such thing as the body as a natural "substance," as a "reservoir of sensibility," or a "guarantee of authenticity." Rather, these seemingly "natural" qualities of the body are as much conditioned by history and society as are its innocence, sinfulness, aesthetic relevance, and so on.

In the course of history we see the gradual development of different concepts of the body. These in turn influence how people treat their real bodies. Thus, many mechanisms of control and monitoring were involved in the creation of the working body.[16] These included the obligations of time structuring,[17] disciplining the senses, and treating the body as a machine.[18] They led to an economy of self-constraint, which required the isolation of the body, a calculated long-term view, and the toughening of the child-rearing and educational strategies of the early bourgeoisie. The sexual body is also a sociohistorical product that likewise shows the marks of ingrained violence.[19] The sexual body is a vehicle of important mechanisms of moralization and self-control. It is affected by the processes of language and imagination.[20] The body becomes the surface over which the currents of desire literally flow. The process of breaking down the sexual into images is seen at its most extreme in pornography.[21]

The physical senses have also become an issue in historical cultural anthropology.[22] They give human beings a sensory certainty of the world and of themselves, and are therefore involved in the communication of meaning. As Erwin Straus put it, the awareness of sensation—and thus sensation in general—is the experiencing of coexistence (*Mit-Sein*) unfolding in the direction of the subject and the object. In sensing, people do not have their perceptions; rather, by sensing they have themselves.[23] When we become sensorily aware of our own presence in the world through the reactions of our senses to the world, this relates our bodies and ourselves as subjects to the world and its objects. In this process human beings experience both transformation and continuity. This constitutes a prerequisite for human self-consciousness.

The ubiquity of the new media, such as television, the Internet, and cell phones, and the accelerated speed of life are bringing lasting changes to the way we handle our senses. In these processes there seems to be an increase in the cultural differentiation between the "remote" senses of the eyes and ears and the "near" senses (touch, taste, and smell), which have been marginalized and pushed more into the private sphere. The adjustments that have been made in our ways of seeing have had a particularly sustained effect on the human body and the senses as a whole. However, hearing has retained its central significance for experiencing ourselves as speakers and as part of a community. I shall use seeing and hearing as examples to illustrate the central role of the senses in this research.

Our vision projects us far beyond ourselves and can be understood as a sense that brings objects and people from outside of the body into its interior.[24] We "get an eyeful" of the world. To see is to experience alterity on the sensory surfaces of our own bodies. Sight is directed toward objects and other people, and makes a selection from the visual environment. It is a movement in which we direct our attention and focus, while at the same time turning away and excluding. Sight bridges the distance between people and objects, but simultaneously maintains distance in perception, too. It creates a "remote proximity" in which it has an affinity with processes of social abstraction. When we look, we see not only the visible, but also ourselves as viewers. It is a riddle; the body is both seeing and visible. Since they view all things, our bodies can also view themselves and can see "the other side" of their visual capacity in what they are currently seeing.[25]

As vision has become increasingly functionalized, it has become the leading sense of our culture.[26] Its controlling and self-controlling functions lead to a restriction of its versatility. The eye is supplemented with spectacles, binoculars, and microscopes, that is, with devices that show only a section of the world on which the searching eye concentrates. The result is a calculating view that becomes a tool for both creating distance and exercising power and that subjugates and establishes dominance.[27] The development of a "piercing eye" in the sciences goes hand in hand with the development of a controlling eye in social institutions. Technology and administrations create a dense network of surveillance in which the world of the visible (and with it the seeing individual) is caught.

This mode of looking, whose aim is to examine and objectify, stands in contrast to desire-driven seeing, where the eyes do not obey the will but act independently and force us to submit to their roaming. The desire of the gaze reminds the subject of its "significant dependency" (Lacan). In Bataille's *Story of the Eye*, the issue of the erotic and sexual character of the eye is developed even further than in Freud's interpretation of the *Sandman* by E. T. A. Hoffmann, which he included in his 1919 essay, *The Uncanny*, where he views the eye as a phallic symbol.[28] Bataille views the eye in different constellations—as a symbol for the vagina, the anus, and sometimes the mouth.[29] The eye symbolizes the desire for incorporation, which should help us to overcome the discontinuity of life. As a "commitment to live life to the full until we die," erotic desire shapes what we see.

Goethe presents us with another form of seeing in which human beings' claims for power and control have not prevailed over the objects, and the visible is not sacrificed to individual passions. This is his concept of visual thinking, or thoughtful observation, *"anschauendes Denken,"* which he developed in his scientific studies on nature. It plays an important role in aesthetic vision and requires viewing in as lively and formative manner as nature itself, to be able to follow its constant change or metamorphosis in creation, growth, and decay with the eye.[30] Thus the object of thoughtful observation is not to develop a vantage point from which the phenomena of nature are to be described and measured from an objective distance. Rather, the aim is to act in a lively and formative manner as nature does, to follow its growth and formation with the gaze, and to practice mimetic creation. Goethe's mimetic thinking raises objections to the reification of vision. Whether and to what extent the memory of other modes of seeing can be sustained in the face of the functionalization of vision, the development of the scrutinizing gaze, the acceleration of images, and the voracity of the eye,[31] is an open question.

The visual hypertrophy that is so typical in our present day and age raises the question as to the significance of the other senses. What is the anthropological meaning of hearing, touch, smell, and taste? Does the hypertrophy of vision force the other senses to "model themselves on vision"? If this were the case, what would be the meaning of such a development? Would the sensory diversity of earlier times be reduced, or would new perceptual habits develop? We may find some answers to this if we take a look at our hearing.

The industrial, electromechanical, and electronic revolutions led to the development of new noises that were hitherto unknown. Industrial machinery, railways, cars, airplanes, telephones, gramophones, radios, televisions, and computers all produce new worlds of sound and tone whose analysis in anthropological research promises to lead to new insights. From an ontogenetic point of view, hearing and kinesthesia are the first to develop. A fetus is already capable of responding to acoustic stimuli at four and a half months. We are in touch with the outside world through our sense of hearing before we are born. This sense enables us to hear others before we can see, smell, or touch them and to hear language before we can speak or understand it. We need to be able to hear in order to be able to understand and speak. Hearing ourselves being spoken to gives us feelings of security and belonging. Hearing is the *social sense*.[32] No community develops without its members learning to listen to each other. It is not only the words and their meanings directed toward us by other people that we perceive with our sense of hearing. In the manner in which the words are spoken, we hear more than just their meaning. We learn something about the speaker that is not expressed in the words but through speaking itself. The timbre of the voice, its tone, loudness, and articulation all convey information about the speaker to the listener.

Since hearing is also a sense that reflects back to us, we hear ourselves speak. Hearing follows speaking; it enables us to perceive ourselves as speaking, that is, to be reflective. If a word said by one person to another is heard, this is the starting point for new words for both speaker and hearer. This peculiarity of hearing gives us human beings the potential for self-perception and self-reassurance. Whenever we talk, we are also talking to ourselves. This is why hearing plays a special role in the constitution of subjectivity and sociality. Noises and voices that we hear repeatedly allow us to feel at home in our lifeworlds. Contingencies arise between the memory traces of earlier perceptions and new noises. Our hearing sense conveys external noises to our inside worlds; external worlds of sound become internal worlds. Repetition and imitation are particularly important in the development of hearing, especially in the early phases of the ontogenetic process. Ritualized, rhythmically structured, verbal repetitions stimulate our *mimetic capacities*. Speaking and understanding are learned in varying imitations.

Our hearing also enables us to experience the *three-dimensional character of space*. Whereas an object is only perceived by the eye when it is "in front" of it, the ear hears noises and sounds coming from behind the head. The human sense of hearing thus allows us to develop our feeling and awareness of space. The interaction between hearing and our sense of space is also paralleled by the morphological location of our sense of balance in the ear. We use our hearing to "locate" ourselves in space, walk upright, and maintain balance. Unlike vision, which can be focused, what we perceive with our sense of hearing is much more diffuse. We can turn our eyes away or even close them, but it is hardly possible to control the ear. The fact that the eye is easier to control than the ear is also demonstrated by the greater number of words and metaphors that relate to seeing. The sense of hearing has a middle position between vision and the contact senses, touch, taste, and smell, which are remarkably poorly represented in the Indo-Germanic languages. The transition from orality to literacy and the forms of "secondary orality" created by the new media have resulted in a fundamental change in hearing.[33]

Continuing in this direction, anthropological inquiry also examines the skin and the hand and thus the sense of touch,[34] which plays a central role in building up a sense of security, the structuring of space, connecting human beings with the world, the use of technologies, and the development of a symbolic world order.[35] We then come to taste and its relationship to food and its role in aesthetic and social judgment.[36] The nose and sense of smell lead us into the area of intimate perception of ourselves and others.[37] The contact senses seem to have been less affected by changes to the body that have occurred during the process of civilization and remain fundamental for our physical orientation in the world;[38] more research into these senses is needed.[39]

The Embers of the Soul

Anthropological research is frequently confronted with the other aspect of the body—the soul. Referred to as *psyche, anima, l'âme,* and *the soul,* it has always been a concept that has defied understanding. Thus, we talk about "the embers of the soul" because, although the soul is elusive, its traces are perceptible.[40] Historical cultural anthropology seeks to reconstruct how, over the course of European history, the soul caught light and burned brightly before the flames died down. Metaphorically, the soul both relates to human beings and reaches beyond them, to the Other. It both relates to things and transcends them. The soul is located between inanimate matter and God. It is the life force of plants, animals, and humans. As a principle of life, cause of movement, and cause of form, it is preconceptual. All attempts to locate it outside of the metaphorical or even to capture it have failed. The soul has no substance; it is immaterial. It therefore defies all scientific attempts to identify it. It is a void in human beings and nature that is impossible to fill and thus remains open and unsettling.

The soul ensures our feelings of being alive, our awareness of objects, and the non-reified nature of reason. According to Augustine, it is the soul alone, as the highest level of things in the visible universe and the lowest level of the spiritual world, that is capable of rising to God and of union with Him. Through reflection on the intelligible world of the spirit, it is able to merge with God. The word *soul* refers to human beings' spiritual inner lives: divine truth is not to be found in the outside world, but in the soul. If the soul looks down, it sees the body; if it looks up, it becomes aware of God. In the Middle Ages, as in antiquity, the soul was thought of more as a bodily entity. It was not conceived of as being an invisible spirit, but as a kind of second body. In the Middle Ages, the soul was portrayed as something visible in pictures suggesting the invisible.[41]

In the early modern period the notion of the soul took on an individualized aspect, alongside its cosmic character. The Inquisition was a major catalyst in this transformation. The soul was defined as the shaping principle that operates on both a large and small scale to bring forth the potential of our being. As the force that shapes the world, the soul was seen as immortal. Whether individual souls are immortal was a matter of debate. The religious soul was the battleground of moral struggles; Christianity censored and controlled feelings. Pastoral care became a means of controlling the individual—an instrument used to subject people to the will of the church and state. This was opposed by the Enlightenment, for which the idea of the autonomy of the human subject, promoted by reason and science, was to become characteristic. What the Middle Ages saw as the divine spark in every person now became subjective reason. The soul was conceived of as the integrational force of the individual that guaranteed the oneness of the person. Not until Kant's *Critique of Pure Reason* did the concept of the soul begin to lose its significance in philosophy.

In the Romantic period the soul once more became a central concept, this time as the other side of reason. It was examined in the context of sleep, dreams, and the unconscious. Human existence was not reduced to reason. The soul became a label for the irreducible. The unconscious was seen as holding the key to the conscious. What was conceived of as belonging together was then split and studied separately in the nineteenth century by the burgeoning disciplines of biology, psychology and psychoanalysis. Biology and psychology were oriented toward the natural sciences.[42] Freud's concept of the unconscious takes a point of reference that is inaccessible to consciousness and therefore also to science; thus its epistemological location is still a matter of unresolved debate.

The process of civilization becomes inscribed in the soul via the medium of the body.[43] An intact body is regarded as being a guarantee for an intact soul. Human identity is made up of reason, a true self, and a body. The body becomes the measure and expression of psychosocial life. The aim of human development is no longer a pure soul, but a pure body and its self-assertion. General reason and individual reason are no longer identical concepts: the lack of congruence between social structures and subjective perspectives appears insurmountable.[44] Self-realization is attained with the rediscovery of the body. The soul, which has become immanent, is only of interest in an embodied form—in the embodiment of the self in lifestyles and in the confession of feelings in intact bodies. The soul's transcendence has given way to the immanence of the body. It is only in areas such as art, literature, and theology that the transcendental nature of the soul is still to be found.[45]

The Holy or Sacred

Anyone who studies the history of the body and the soul will inevitably come up against the religious concepts of the holy and the sacred. Religious matters have recently once more become a disturbing topic.[46] There is an interest in the unexpected current topicality of religion and the spread of secular sacrality. Only a few years ago many considered these issues to be outdated. Thus the revival of interest in the "idea of the holy" has been only gradual. This phrase comes from Rudolf Otto, who describes the phenomenon of the holy as fascinating yet terrifying and therefore ambivalent.[47] For a better understanding of the sacred, one must recognize that one only experiences it as a phenomenon by adopting some kind of phenomenological attitude. If one were to adopt a different scientific attitude, for example a functionalistic, social-anthropological, or logical and analytical approach, something quite different would result. If one takes a phenomenological approach, the holy appears as a category constituted of extremes. "However complex and synthetic the idea of the holy may be, it can only be meaningfully conceptualized if one also differentiates it from something else. This is still applicable even if in prehistoric times everything may have been regarded as religion."[48]

The starting point for the examination of the subject from an anthropological viewpoint is an antithesis to Max Weber's assumption that the world has been disenchanted by science. In this view, the holy is not a thing of the past, but still remains highly topical in a displaced, hidden, repressed, and forgotten form. It needs to be rediscovered and reconstructed from its partially obliterated tracks. Disputes are therefore inevitable as the memories are revived. The terrible and fascinating character of the holy resists all attempts to identify it unequivocally. The issue to be clarified is what has become of the sacred in modernity. Whereas it once appeared that human beings had been able to liberate themselves from the sacred during the Enlightenment and that this liberation could be regarded as progress, today we are increasingly confronted with complaints that we have lost sight of the meaning of life. Such complaints are a reflection of people's suffering in a "secularized" and "unholy" reality, and evidence that humans have a strong need for hierarchy and spiritual intensity even in secular areas of life. The sacred is not a matter that can be assigned to a single discipline such as religious studies, theology, or ethnology. Rather, it is an unavoidable issue that is beyond everybody's understanding. If we are to study it nevertheless, we need to examine the following assumptions:

. The concept of the sacred, or holy, has multiple meanings and cannot be explained by a single definition. Thus, *sacer* means both "holy" and "accursed," and *taboo* means both "pure" and "dirty."
. References to the sacred are paradoxical. The sacred both fascinates and terrifies feeling (Rudolf Otto).
. Where the sacred occurs, something incommensurable is present that has to do with the regularities and ruptures in human life.
. The sacred creates order out of disorder and chaos, by means of sacrifice. It is thus inextricably linked to violence and death.

Archaic societies are based on violence and death, on continuity created from discontinuities. The disenchantment strategies of public speech, reason, and labor all work to counteract this. Modern society places its hopes in the economy rather than in sacrifices; however, as the latest wars have shown, today's society still lies under the shadow of the sacred. The difficulty is that the sacred is a topic that cannot be captured; it eludes us. It appears as the inhuman and superhuman, as something that allows violence and killing, as the fragile element in the dialectic between the sacred and the secular. The "death of God" resulted in a far-reaching reorganization of the sacred. The inner spaces of society are being transformed into smaller and medium-sized spheres of transcendence such as the socialization of the individual, the sanctification of the family, and the spread of secular sacrality, all of which are changing the face and form of the sacred.[49]

The Appearance of Beauty

It is not only the sacred that both fascinates and terrifies; beauty also has this paradoxical status. Many images from the time before the "era of art" depict the sacred as both beautiful and terrible.[50] Beauty and the sacred have another feature in common: many attempts have been made to capture beauty and to use it as a means of conveying something—good and truth in Plato's works, the greatness of God in the Middle Ages, and the perfection of human beings in the modern era. Nietzsche was the first to reverse this perspective. He viewed the radiance of beauty as mere semblance. All reality is by nature an appearance conjured up by the imagination in the form of an image and can therefore only be understood as an aesthetic phenomenon. Accordingly, the fullness of life, the self-realization of human beings beyond the mere human level, and their rise to the supra-individual level are only possible through aesthetics.

As beauty eludes capture, it awakens a desire to approach it mimetically. Mimetic processes appear to offer the option of assimilating humans to beauty rather than beauty to humans. Beauty does not exist as a physical object, and perhaps not even as an imagined image, but only in an indefinable form. Beauty is rousing; it produces pleasure, while reminding us of the fleeting nature of its appearance and the inherent temporality of human life. One aspect of beauty is its non-identical character. It lends beautiful things a face with a puzzling, indissoluble expression that troubles the imagination, sets it in motion, and triggers mimetic processes of emulation.

In antiquity beauty was seen as having another side, that of terror, madness, and death. Over the course of history, beauty may be replaced by its opposite. Ugliness, insanity, and madness have invaded art and forced out beauty. A void has resulted where memories can gather, in which the traces of beauty glimmer through. Today, it is generally only this shimmer of beauty that remains. Traces of the order and symmetry it produced in earlier centuries are still perceptible. Today, however, we have a different reality, one characterized by upheavals, deviation, and difference. It is not symmetry but asymmetry and difference that define the current era. Our world is beyond beauty and oscillates between past beauty and future terror.

In the face of the spreading aestheticization of the world and simulations that today both have in their grasp and intermesh all that is real, the appearance of appearance itself has become an issue. We can thus reflect on the shine of beauty deprived of power, which has been seen as resulting from the dialectic of the Enlightenment.[51] The ensuing link between melancholy and aesthetics can in no way be seen as an indication of the demise of culture but rather as a new key to understanding our times.

Of what does the effect of art consist? What is its relationship to reality, language, and the imagination? Is the concept of beauty still suitable for describing our aesthetic experience? From its beginnings in classical antiquity, beauty has troubled and challenged human beings—as can be seen in the contradictory interpretations and definitions; it has been attacked and battled against, has retreated and undergone metamorphoses. The history of the sublime and the development of the aesthetic perspective in the social sciences are just two examples.

Beauty does not only promise the reconciliation of differences; it also causes unforeseen upheavals that demonstrate the limits of human beings and their frailty. Medusa exemplifies the transformation of beauty into terror—a mythological transformation that ends in death. Beauty is repeatedly linked to death and thus has difficulty in wresting itself from chaos. Beauty promises perfection and freedom and has the power to subjugate those who have looked upon it with their naked eyes. It contains conundrums and contradictions and is associated with discord, ruptures, and differences. It destroys existing orders and provides the conditions for a new aesthetic, whose seismic form has resulted from a shaking of the foundations of perception which, in turn, thus pave the way for new configurations.

These configurations are emerging on the other side of beauty. They point toward aspects that were not previously associated with beauty, such as anarchy, horror, and emptiness. Venice and the aesthetic aspect of ruins have long been seen as examples of morbid beauty and of the fascination instilled in us by the other side of beauty's glister—the decline of human culture. Today the relationship between nature and history has already been disrupted to such an extent that beauty has sought refuge in artificially created memories, where it must be rediscovered and reconstructed.

Beauty can be found in shifts, displacements, distortions, and what has been repressed. The sought-after luster results in paradoxical changes in our thinking. This includes accepting outward appearances as a sign of genuine truth—giving up the usual strategy of unmasking and identifying objects by force does not mean that we also cease to think and perceive. Other movements arise in the eroticism of the veil and clothing and in the interplay between revealing and hiding. These movements create imaginary images and result in transitions from states of nonexistence to human configurations. The metonyms of desire, the signs of self-enchantment, and the material indications of nothingness are all reflected in the appearance of beauty. They affect us and bring into relief the temporality of wishes and their expression.[52]

The Fate of Love

While love is linked to sexual desire, that is not all it is.[53] It seeks pleasure and frequently ends in suffering; it seeks permanency and laments its temporality. In its urge for more life it transcends the boundaries of individuals and even brushes with death. Love seeks the Other and yet cannot tolerate it. It is an event and a non-event in one, and can only be experienced as a paradox. The more we expect from it, the more severely we are disappointed. It cannot keep its promise of reconciling differences. Separations and contradictions are final and only apparently surmountable. The more imagination and desire stimulate each other, the less we can disentangle ourselves from their enmeshment. Love becomes fate; it befalls us, whatever we may try to do to avoid it. Love is not an "object" that can be isolated and identified; but a force that, condensed and displaced, affects nearly every sphere of human culture in many varied and multifaceted ways. The erotic connotations are not always apparent. They are discernible in the following areas of life: language, images, mythology, gender, money, time, death, the "Other," beauty, self, community—ciphers for the tangled web of erotic energies.[54]

What one experiences in love and how this experience is to be understood is among the disturbing and recurrent issues in anthropology. Love is the issue in the Platonic myth of people being split into two halves; Socrates interpreted love as striving for immortality. Early Christianity focused on how love could be institutionalized in marriage. Passionate love resists this attempt at institutionalization and insists on the aspect of fate. It is not the union of the lovers but their separation that gives rise to the feeling of passion. Voluntariness and exclusivity are its prerequisites. Passionate love can never be sated. This form of love and the rhetoric that made it possible were invented at the courts of the twelfth century. Its effects are still evident today. Its focus is not so much on a real person ("Thou") as the imaginary Other, which is a metaphor for an unattainable whole. The essence of love becomes tangible when it is talked about. The manner in which it is talked about determines how it is experienced. Like love, talk of love is also boundless. Speech both conceals and contains love by searching ceaselessly for its secret, without ever grasping it or letting go of it; speech seduces with its promises without being able to be sure of fulfillment and points toward a void from which at the same time it emanates.

Love is the result of certain cultural conditions; it depends on the myths and rhetorical structures of a society and is socially controlled.

Closely linked to the sex drive, it serves the will to survive. It is a productive force that makes human beings what they are. The sexual instincts, which are inextricably interwoven with love, need to be channeled in a social manner. Love has been integrated in the comprehensive system of the bartering economy, but is not determined exclusively by social bartering processes. Every instance of passionate love also has an asocial side that is immune to the influence of society. In the family structures of today, love determines the freedom of choice—one selects one's partners and spouse. Even in the everyday processes of love, what is important is the wish to be freed from one's individuality and the constraints of isolation with the help of the other. Wishes for redemption and survival become operative and bind individual experiences to collective myths. The mythologizing of love relationships is unavoidable. The myths contain a mixture of religious, ethical, and aesthetic elements, which, while they can be brought to awareness by critical reflection on the myths, cannot be completely dissolved. Perhaps the reenchantment that is being sought in passionate love can be understood as an attempt to have the ecstatic experiences that were an institutionalized component of archaic societies.

The history of love has many hidden sides. Thus it is also necessary to examine the other history of love that is associated with madness, dreams, and the journey to the interiors of the mind, which is the story of an endless return. Both Odysseus and Christ return home, but have we not now lost, forever, the home to which we could return? This is clearly demonstrated in narcissism: the subject destroys itself because it cannot win itself.

In light of this situation we can hardly justify speaking of *one* feeling of love; we should speak of several, potentially contradictory feelings. Although the word *love* designates different feelings, depending on the historical and social context, it is often used in a way that diminishes the diversity of feelings to which it refers. From the beginning of history, love has been spoken of as both a longing and a satisfaction. In the course of historical change, different "rhetorics" of love have developed that shape people's feelings. The literature of love is an important meeting point for language and desire, where they are constantly combined anew to produce new forms.[55]

Dying Time

If the sacred or holy can be understood as an attempt by human beings to stay the course of time, then beauty and love are inextricably linked to the transience of time. There is no permanence in either beauty or love. "What then is time? If no one asks me, I know what it is. If I wish to explain it to one who asketh, I know not."[56] Who would not today feel as St. Augustine did, provided, of course, that they found the time to think about their confusion about time. In fact, the problem has become worse over the last few decades insofar as its urgency is now disproportionate to the actual experience of time. For roughly the last one hundred years, the literature on the subject of time has been punctuated with reports that it is disappearing, standing still as everywhere we preserve our heritage, and running out; it is in light of this consequence, which no one can seriously wish for, that time itself has become a central issue.[57] Karl Marx predicted that all economics would ultimately become "economics of time." The more time is brought into economic calculations, the less time there is. However, this paradox only becomes noticeable when the point of no return has been passed. The view that only the person who really has time can waste it is no longer a harmless tautology today.

Gradually, the view is becoming widely established that the time allotted to the human species, nature, and the cosmos is limited. The ecological crisis and the looming scarcity of resources are contributing to the spread of an "apocalyptic" experience of life in which the end of time would seem to be increasingly imminent. Furthermore, the natural sciences have long been confronted with the historicity of nature and the cosmos. The universe, nature, and human culture all have a beginning and will therefore have an end—perhaps many beginnings and many ends. Even events that are not regarded as historical cannot be repeated: Newton was wrong about this. There is no going back; time is irreversible. This irreversibility applies not only to human life, which is mortal, but also to nature and the cosmos, which also "age." Our growing understanding of the subject of time is paralleled by a growing awareness of how much still remains to be understood. This is the experience of natural and social scientists, historians, philosophers, and scholars of literary studies, especially when they are well-versed in the intricacies of time and its structures in our culture, nature, and the cosmos.

The differences in the way we view time in the current era suggest that the history of the cosmos, nature, and the human species should be rewritten. The old classifications of periods and eras seem arbitrary and cannot capture the complexity of today's consciousness of time. In the face of different stages of economic, social, and cultural development in different countries as well as inside a given country, greater consideration must be given to the simultaneous nature of non-simultaneous events and the non-simultaneous nature of simultaneous events. Such a view

FIGURE 5.1   William Hogarth: *Tail Piece, The Bathos*. Etched and engraved, 1764. © Leuder h.
Niemeyer—Germany. E-mail: hogarth@william-hogarth.com/; website: www.william-hogarth.com.

that takes account of the plurality of times renders the problem even
more complex, and thus a transdisciplinary approach is required.

Reflections on the "ageing" and "dying" of time have been fruitful in
two ways. On the one hand, the findings of various scientific disciplines
have been collated and made accessible to others so as to promote mutual
understanding. On the other hand, there has been progress toward understanding more about the secret laws that cause time to be "young" or
"old," abundantly available or in extremely short supply. However much
we may know about spaces, fields, areas, and even horizons, time remains
a mystery. There has been no reflection on either its nonmaterial nature
from the very beginning or its final cessation. To change this, at least on
a small scale, we need to break with the thought tradition that discon-
nects time from the rhythm of life, transferring it to the wider world of

machinery, and finally only understands it as post-history or in terms of the Apocalypse.[58]

Silence

Compared to countries of the Far East, our culture of silence is relatively undeveloped. Where such a culture is developed, it is recognized that not only conversation but also shared silence can be a uniting force. Remaining silent is an art that must be mastered. The urge to talk is often too great to be able to share silence with others. Silence is often seen as an expression of incompetence and inarticulateness. In contrast to speech, it is seen as a sign of passivity and weakness. This is evidently a narrow view resulting from cultural peculiarities. Places where silence is maintained are part of the culture of silence: temples, churches, concert halls, theater auditoriums, cinemas, and libraries. These places are home to rituals that require and exercise the art of silence: religious services, legal rituals (e.g., marriages), burials, and other similar events. Taboos, zones, and domains of silence that differ from society to society and from subculture to subculture must also be included here.[59]

What can be said, what cannot be expressed in words, and what is the role of silence in speech? We speak in the hope of being able to capture what we are talking about. But we are disappointed. We speak to counteract this disappointing experience that accompanies our speech. We cannot endure the inaccessibility of the world around us and we use speech in an attempt to stifle the dreadful voice of silence whose loudness fills the entire horizon. Again and again speech is reduced to a feeble stammering in the face of the almighty silence of the world, trying in vain to master the horror induced by the ubiquity of silence.

Silence is both the starting point and the end-point of speech—its origin and its destination.[60] It occurs as both an interruption and as a boundary, and as such can hardly be rendered in discourse. However, the demand that one should remain silent about what cannot be put into words is not the end of it. Rather, the fact that we fail to express what we want to express continually gives us the impulse to start talking anew. The dual nature of silence is revealed in a simple paradox: we feel the need to talk about silence and yet cannot talk about it as we would about other things. Speech is wrested from silence and sinks back into silence as it finishes. When we carelessly launch into speech without thinking, the result is prattle. Responsible speech is always linked to silence.

Silence is closely linked to speech, being at once an element within it and also its boundaries. There is no speech without pauses. All speech constituted in time is related to a beginning and an end—a time before and a time after. Silence is the starting point of speech, action, and creativity. The meaning of everyday talk, constantly affirmed by speaking and action, is silenced by music, art, and poetry. To experience music, art, and poetry, we need to maintain silence; not to speak becomes an art, the precondition for mimetic involvement. In the encounter with the arts, refraining from speech becomes a necessary action, a skilled activity, without which mimetic involvement would not be possible. This allows the audience to align itself with aspects of the musical, artistic, or poetic works without destroying the diversity of their meanings. Mimetic processes help us to approach the Other that reveals itself in the aesthetic experience and is shrouded by silence. Speech counteracts forgetfulness; memory opposes the silence of oblivion by anamnesis as an attempt to avoid compulsive repetition. Breaking silence seems to confer an identity on the person from whose mask speech emanates.

Silence is always also a lack of memory, the expression of forgetting and of speechless unhappiness. Silent suffering can be repressed but not erased from memory. On the contrary, the memory refuses to be quashed, repeatedly reliving the traumata in internal images. Silence is then a pool from which pour endless repetitions of our suffering. It is the masses, especially, that remain silent, and it is by remembering and speaking that one becomes an individual. Historically, women are very much part of this silent mass, their speechlessness the outward sign of an enforced silence and oppression. Today, women are raising their voices, overcoming their muteness, and have begun to have their say. In order to break their silence, they need to remember the suffering that muted them in the past. It is an expression of the exclusion through which "femininity" was produced as the Other of the male, or "man."

There is a link between silence and forgetting, which in turn is connected with secrets. We speak only for as long as our speech forms a tension with silence. Where silence is the result of forgetting, it is eloquent and requires hermeneutics to decipher it. In the process we can experience that silence as a form of existence in which things that are disparate can come together, yet where the tension between them and their ambiguity is retained. In silence, the world, speech, and discourse are reorganized; meaning is transformed, and an enigmatic complexity evolves in which speech struggles in vain and the gap between it and the world cannot be breached. Silence can only be understood through speech and through the mimetic movements.

Finally, there is also a link between silence and the relationship between life and death. Where there is no more life, there is no speech, no noise, no movement, only emptiness. Where there is no consciousness or speech, a silence develops in which autistic children and other unfortunate victims become engulfed. The limits of speech, imagination, humans, and their worlds become experienceable, but this experience no longer helps. Death silences meaning—it is the end of all hermeneutics. There are irreversible and permanent limits and interruptions, the emptiness of silence that no language can fill.

A Handbook of Historical Anthropology: Human Beings and Their Culture

The aim of the project described below was to reconstruct the current relationships between human beings and the world, and between different groups of humans, in one hundred concepts and to present these from a transdisciplinary, anthropological perspective.[61]

Sixty authors from more than a dozen disciplines were involved in the reconstruction of these central concepts of historical cultural anthropology. Here again, the methodological approaches employed range from phenomenological and historical-hermeneutic procedures to constructivist techniques. Since these methods were coordinated with each other, it was possible to achieve a high degree of methodological precision and complexity.

If humans perceive and comprehend their own creations, every perception in the human world is, by definition, self-reflective. Thus, by investigating lifeworlds and cultural environments, we can gather information that sheds light on human beings and their relationships with the world. These relationships with the world and themselves are real, symbolic, and imaginary relationships that are institutionalized in various areas of social activity and cultural practice. Different approaches are required to examine these cultural areas. For example, one area of research looks at the manner in which humans use language and the imaginary to process nature and reality in social and cultural environments; this is an area that mainly requires philosophy and the humanities.

Another important field is the empirical study of material social institutions and cultural orders, which is primarily the domain of the social sciences. Anthropological research forges links between these two fields of study. This requires the investigation of real, symbolic, and imaginary phenomena, including the forms of action communicated by media and conflict as well as their values and norms.[62] One particularly challenging task is, wherever possible, to take culture in its broad sense into account, both as the subject of investigation and as a frame of reference.

This requires an anthropological examination of the fundamental conditions of human life in the diverse, polycentric culture of today. The attempt to define today's culture and make a diagnosis of our time is conducted with an awareness of a double historicity and culturality and the contingencies associated with this. Intensive interdisciplinary cooperation does not, of course, do anything to alter the fragmentary nature of anthropological knowledge. However, it does create a basis for further research on social diversity and thus for improving our understanding of ourselves as human beings and of our culture. The anthropological study of human beings' understanding of themselves and their world, along with their historical and cultural roots, leads to findings that give us a different perspective on many of the functional relationships of everyday life. Such findings give rise to a skeptical questioning of the view of history as a history of progress and learning, the logic of the identifying concept, the scope of hermeneutics, and also the view of the monocentric subject that creates itself and the world. In turn, such skepticism leads to an awareness of the historical and cultural relativity of anthropological knowledge. However, whereas previously the provisional nature of anthropological knowledge was regarded as a deficiency, today it is viewed as an advantage. The quality of this knowledge results from the fundamentally indeterminate nature of human beings, from which, however, our openness to the Other and other kinds of knowledge also arises. It is this indeterminateness that spurs us on to look for new ways to increase the complexity and depth of anthropological knowledge.

In light of this situation, it seems worthwhile to attempt to draw up an inventory of anthropological knowledge about human beings' relationships with the world and themselves as presented in the following seven fields, around which the handbook of historical anthropology is organized: *cosmology, the world and objects, genealogy and gender, the body, the media and learning, chance and destiny*, and *culture*.[63]

COSMOLOGY   Following the departure from the normative anthropology of Christianity, Christian cosmology also became less important. Irrespective of this, even today it is still impossible to say what human beings are and how they are to understand their relationship to nature without referring to the four elements—earth, wind, fire, and water. The elements and the conservation of resources continue to play an important role in the ecological debate and the issue of sustainable global development.

The same applies to human beings' understanding of the world—we relate to nature largely through the four elements. An examination of the elements inevitably leads to questions about life itself. Plants and animals are all part of its long history, and without them a relationship between human beings and nature is inconceivable.

THE WORLD AND OBJECTS   We gradually seem to be developing a planetary awareness within which ideas about the relationship between humans and the world are undergoing a fundamental change. On the one hand, economic and cultural globalization is leading to a more uniform world, which provokes wide resistance and has made dealing with alterity one of the central issues of human coexistence.[64] In order to deal with this situation, we need a global ethic with the capacity to affect the states of societies and institutions.[65] Alongside the development of a highly fragmented global awareness, significant changes are taking place in human beings' relationships to space and time, movement and mobility, towns and houses, all of which are also resulting in lasting changes in everyday life.

GENEALOGY AND GENDER   In a time in which the individuality and subjectivity of human beings is very much the center of attention, anthropological research can add to this perspective by demonstrating how it is linked to genealogy and gender. In this view, issues of reproduction and genetics, sexuality, and relations between the generations play a major role. Human life develops within the relationships between the generations and is characterized by different family relationships.[66] This results in historically and culturally heteronymous forms in which humans perceive themselves as men and women, fathers and mothers, and parents and children, and act accordingly.

THE BODY   Here again, the focus is on the human body and its various senses, as well as the aspects of genome and brain research, which contribute to our understanding of the body. In connection with the body, we study the anthropological significance of movement, sitting, gestures, feelings, ecstasy, and obscenity. The body is seen as a riddle—its biological constitution and historical and cultural shaping pose many questions. However, it is equally apparent that the body is at the center of all of relationships between human beings and the world and themselves. This remains one of the most enduringly challenging aspects of anthropological research.

MEDIA AND LEARNING The importance of media for the human beings' perception of the world is undisputed. This can already be seen in the transition from an oral to a literate society in ancient Greece, in the late Middle Ages, and in many developing countries, where the implementation of education for all is still an important issue.[67] In addition to writing, communication media and the new media both play a special role. If we take a wider view, images, language, numbers, and signs also belong to the media that we use to structure our worlds and ourselves. Our responses to different forms of media trigger learning processes that allow us to develop our individuality and identity. We learn through actions and in processes of remembering, and also through our experiences, at school, in lessons, and at the workplace.

CHANCE AND DESTINY In contrast to constructivism, it is assumed that people have many options when they construct their views of the world and themselves; however, they experience many things that have nothing to do with their actions or their possible actions and over which they have little or no influence. These include beauty and good fortune, sickness and health, fear and violence, war and peace, evil and death. The manner in which these phenomena and events are perceived—whether as chance or as fate—depends on their respective views of the world and human beings.

CULTURE If we define culture broadly, to include all that is produced by humans, there are still a few topics that have not been conclusively dealt with and need to be addressed, including wishes and fantasy, religion, alterity, myths, utopia, secrets, play, rituals and ceremonies, and music and theater. In these areas the imagination and the imaginary play a greater role in human production than in the other sections above.

In the fields of anthropological research described above, groups of issues are investigated that are so complex as to require a transdisciplinary approach. The findings in each of these areas raise so many questions that awareness of how much is *un*known is growing (apace). The insight gained from this is that human beings are a puzzle to themselves; since their understanding is provisional and based on restricted perspectives, they are unfathomable to themselves. Thus there is no definitive concept of the human being, and there can be no such concept on principle.

For this reason, historical cultural anthropology cannot be described as a self-contained subject area; rather, it consists of issues and points of view that are shared with other subject areas. At the current state of the art, this is advantageous because it aids the discovery of new questions and topics and makes it easier to examine them from new perspectives. In this situation, the aim of the research, the choice of issues, the materials available, and the selection of methodology all play a vital role.

Mimetic Ways of World-Making

In the course of the second phase of my anthropological research, I came to realize how important mimetic processes are for the development, transmission, and future development of cultures and societies (see chapter 7). The aim of the first study in this phase was therefore to reconstruct the main elements of the development of the theory of mimesis, from its beginnings in the works of Plato and Aristotle to its later development in those of Benjamin, Adorno, and Derrida.[68] Different forms of mimetic processes can be elaborated using Wittgenstein's concept of family resemblance. A widespread view in the humanities is that mimetic processes are particularly important in aesthetics: artists are considered to mimic Nature's powers of creation (*natura naturans*) so as to be creative like Nature herself. In contrast, the results of my research show that the ability to behave mimetically is an anthropological capacity. In his development of Plato's thought, Aristotle observed that mimesis is present from early childhood and that the particular form in which it appears in human beings distinguishes them from all other living creatures. He also commented that they experience particular pleasure in mimetic processes. In these processes human beings undergo an alignment with other human beings and worlds, be they real or fictitious. More than any other philosopher, Plato emphasized the potential of mimetic processes to shape and teach human beings. He was even of the opinion that children are not able to resist them and that they must therefore be kept away from all harmful role models.

Mimetic processes are always ambivalent. On the one hand, as processes of mimicry, they can lead to an adjustment to that which is given, stagnant, or lifeless;[69] on the other, they can attract many hopes. They can result in a "vital experience" of the outside world, the Other, and self. Mimetic processes can initiate movements with responsive intentionality and provide space for what is not identical by protecting the particular against the universal. At the current stage of sociocultural development, the ambivalence of mimetic processes cannot be avoided.

The mimetic capacities of children, adolescents, and adults are closely linked to bodily processes and run counter to social tendencies toward abstraction. They create links with the outside, the world and other people, and tend to reduce the hard subject-object split and the acuity of the difference between what is and what ought to be. It's a question of grasping the "between,"[70] which is experienced in the alignment of the subject to an outside world or another person. Mimetic processes contain rational elements, but not exclusively. In mimetic processes we step outside of ourselves and align ourselves with the world; mimesis gives us an opportunity to bring the outside world into our inner worlds and to express our inner worlds. Through mimetic processes, we can come closer to objects and the Other, and we therefore need these processes in order to improve our understanding.

While modern rational thought relates to the individual, isolated, knowing subject, mimetic processes are always a matter of a web of relationships between persons. In the creation of a symbolic world through mimesis, contact is made with other worlds and their creators, and other persons are included in the subject's world. Mimetic processes are exchanges that occur between the world and human beings and always include an aspect of power. The history of mimesis is a history of conflicts about power over the creation of symbolic worlds, the power to portray oneself and others and to interpret the world in accordance with one's own ideas. Mimetic processes, especially in the fields of education and socialization, are thus an integral part of the history of power relationships. They are not merely processes of imitation, reproduction, or imprinting. On the contrary, they require individual shaping by the child, adolescent, or adult. The extent of individual difference due to differing conditions varies. Many mimetic processes are inextricably linked with processes of desiring and wishing, perception, and experience.[71]

During my systematic examination of the anthropological meanings of mimetic processes involved in the handing down and transformation of culture, it also became clear to me how important mimetic actions are in the social world. It seemed to me that a good way to demonstrate this would be to analyze play, rituals, and gesture, since these all consist of bodily movements.[72] This connection with the body and its materiality, its capacities, and presence in social situations is the starting point for my investigation of the mimetic bases of social action. Social action is first and foremost visible and concrete, and involves the materiality, appearance, and habitus of the body, as well as its bearing and social behaviors. This kind of material action elicits feelings and associations that can themselves influence interactions.

CHAPTER FIVE

Gestures, rituals, and games are extremely important in our society. Their importance derives from the fact that they do not exert any force, and individuals can also act *differently*. This makes our society different from its precursors. Both participation in rituals and the use of gestures are a matter of choice. However, irrespective of the independence and autonomy of our actions, we orient ourselves toward other worlds and other people. Here we are not faced with explicit decisions but act on the basis of a specific human capacity for managing our actions in everyday life. Such actions have dual effects: they strengthen the ego, which experiences itself as largely autonomous, while *at the same time* intensifying relationships with other worlds and other persons. They thus integrate the individual more firmly into society. In contrast to the situation in tribal societies, in our modern societies gestural, ritual, and ludic actions are to a great extent a matter of free orientation, and we do not need to think much about consenting to them. We know what is "right" for ourselves and what "suits" us. We know this because we usually reject other possibilities intuitively. We are not subject to any obligation to perform certain rituals or gestures, and when we do so, it is without constraint.

Social events such as games, rituals, and gestures never take place more than once in exactly the same way, and thus it is not possible to see them as identical in the strict sense. Their similarity lies in their variation, which is typical for mimetic acts. There is no uniform theoretical principle that would render it possible to identify them as actions of the same type. They take place in different situations and never produce exactly the same results. The reasons for these inevitable variations lie in the differences in the situations in which the actions take place, the involvement of the body, the way in which each variation evolves, and the lack of, or impossibility of, giving exact rules for their performance. But any observer is capable of seeing whether two actions are the same or not. It is as it is with signatures: everyone has a characteristic, authentic, and recognizable signature, but people never sign their names in exactly the same way. The human motor system is not capable of producing *identical* movements; however, we are able to recognize the many different signatures as versions of the *same* signature. It is no different with gait and posture—we recognize other people by the way they walk, stand, sit, and turn toward others, and yet their movements are never exactly the same. The sameness of human actions is not an *effect* of something common, that they all shared. It is produced in processes in which this common factor is formed with the aid of a network of "family resemblances," as Wittgenstein called them.[73]

Mimetic acts are replays of previous actions. Three aspects are important here: (1) The connection is not made theoretically, but with the aid of the senses, *aisthetically*. (2) Compared to the first event, or the first world, the second is removed from purpose-oriented social practices in that it does not affect them directly or alter them, but must be seen as a recreation of the first world. (3) Mimetic actions have a demonstrative and performative character; performing them produces their own aesthetic qualities.

Mimetic processes are body-based. The body unites us with the world and has the capacity to internalize society. Physically we are in the world, and we have the world in us. We incorporate social structures and form a body of practical knowledge about society. The objects of the world and other people around us are part of the self; the self is part of them. Because of its plasticity, the body mediates between the acting subject and the world. Mimetic action is not only an adjustment on the part of the individual to society; it also includes a constructive element. All social subjects produce their own worlds in agreement with the social world. While the acting subject is seen in the social sciences as being influenced, molded, and socialized by society in many ways, its main characteristic is that, as a thinking being, it receives and creates the world inside of itself. Little attention is paid to the subject's concrete actions. Other persons are also rarely conceived of as having a bodily existence; rather their actions are viewed on an abstract level—that of norms, rules, laws, exchanges, expectations, roles, and rational decisions.

Wherever we act in relation to an already existing world and simultaneously produce a world ourselves, there is a mimetic relationship between the two, as when we imitate the movement of another person, act in accordance with a model, portray something, or give bodily expression to an idea. What is important is to see that it is not simply a question of imitative actions. A performance is not a mere reproduction, following a prototype, but a *production of something of one's own*. The opposite is also true: actions that appear to emerge from the acting subject alone, also include references to other worlds. This capacity to interweave the subject and others is a basic characteristic of human beings' relationship with the world. However, the differentiation between self and others does not function as a dichotomy or delimitation between two fundamentally different, clearly separate entities. The self is, like the others, an open category, which is seen in such a way that both sides "create" each other reciprocally. Without the others there could be no self, and the self also contains, from the start, that which is outside of it. The social world also could not exist without the perceptions, appraisals, interpretations, intentions, strategies, and inner involvements of the individual selves.[74]

The Berlin Study on Rituals and Gestures

In my third research phase I am placing more emphasis on an ethnographic approach. I have begun a twelve-year ethnographic research project that follows on from my work on mimetic action in the social world. Together with my research team, I am conducting ethnographic investigations into the role of rituals and ritualization in families, schools, peer groups, and the media. At the same time I am pursuing the goal of redefining the concepts of ritual and community (*Gemeinschaft*). I have demonstrated that rituals and ritualization have a productive side without which there would be no social life. Since this project focuses on the dynamics and performativity of rituals, it can be seen as a contribution to the development of new concepts of community, ritual, and education.

The ritual processes in child-rearing, education, and socialization in the family, at school, in peer groups and in the media that I have concentrated on in my research are central fields of social life whose dynamics in an inner-city area are determined by the prevailing economic, social, and political conditions. As a result of its focus on child-rearing and education, this study has also had a practical effect: it has modified social reality. Thus, many people working in the four fields of practice have taken note of the results of this study, which to date remains unique in Germany and Europe, and used them to improve their pedagogical and social praxis. This synchronic study has thus also helped to improve our understanding of the role of rituals in child-rearing, education, and socialization.

These investigations focus on an inner-city primary school with 340 students, half of whom have German as their mother tongue, while the other half come from about twenty different non-German migration backgrounds. The school follows the principles of progressive education and is a UNESCO model school. The children chosen for the study on family rituals and ritualized practices were from this school, as were those selected for the studies on peer groups and media usage. In some cases, adolescents from outside the school were integrated into the investigation, thereby broadening its case-study character.[75] The results of this ethnographic study are extensive and I can only report them briefly in this chapter. I present only six main findings, which can be summarized as follows.

(1) Rituals and ritualization play a major role in pedagogy, education, and the socialization of school children. Rituals structure their lives and help them both to integrate into a social order and to work with it constructively. Rituals help to form links between different fields of socialization and between institutions, and facilitate social learning. The study has revealed the various forms and functions that rituals and ritualization can assume within diverse fields of socialization. Thus, the investigation of breakfast rituals, for example, has shown for the sphere of the "family" just how important this communal meal is in preparing family members for the day. Breakfast is an occasion for the family members to come together and engenders feelings of belonging and togetherness. By talking through problems likely to arise at school, the family prepares the children for school and its challenges. In these ritualized, everyday interactions between parents and children and among children themselves, *gender-related* behavior patterns are experienced, and *gender* roles are learned. Mealtime rituals are opportunities for enacting and working through differences and conflicts, the potential destructiveness of which is channeled by the social magic of ritual arrangements.[76] In addition to these everyday rituals, family celebrations and parties also create family coherence. These include Christmas celebrations, children's birthdays, religious ceremonies (e.g., confirmations), and family holidays. We have shown how the religious ritual of confirmation becomes a ritual family event through which the sacrality of the liturgy becomes extended to the family and gives rise to a new connection between faith, knowledge, and skill. Annual family holidays can also be regarded as rituals that create community through new common experiences. The suspension of everyday expectations and the resulting openness to new experiences shared by family members is characteristic of this ritual. Various family learning cultures can be identified in accordance with family style and culture. These result in the different ways that common holiday experiences are processed.

With the aid of mimetic processes, children who are participating in rituals develop a *practical knowledge* that serves as a basis for action skills in rituals and other social situations.[77] Through mimetic processes, they assign each other roles in ritual actions and embody them. As a result of the repetitive character of rituals and ritualization children recall these mental "castings" time and time again, adapting them to new situations and reassuring themselves of their communities at school and in their classes, families, and peer groups. Rituals constitute the *social memories* of such communities. They bring past events back into the present and turn them into a basis for future action. They evoke a sense of continuity for the children and convey a sense of *security* and *reliability*. By means of the goal-oriented actions that the children undertake together in rituals and ritualized practices, they work out existing differences and learn to postpone or resolve them in order to be able to act together. It has been shown that the potential for violence in groups is channeled by rituals. Rituals have a strong formative effect on children when they believe in them. If there is a "flow of emotions" among participants in a ritual, it can develop its magic. This is particularly effective if rituals clearly differentiate between the "outside" and the "inside," that is, when boundaries are drawn and sufficient scope is given to their ludic aspects. It is important to take into consideration that rituals both include and exclude, and that these processes have a potential violence that can also lead to restrictions and oppression.

(2) Due to their *performativity*, pedagogic practices such as rituals and ritualized practices work in all fields of socialization. The performativity of actions becomes apparent in the way that children behave and act either by themselves or with adults. The performative character of pedagogic and social practices is related to their *corporeality*. The investigation of rituals among primary school children has brought the *performativity of educational practice* into focus and led to a reflection on what can be termed the *pedagogy of the performative*.[78]

It is important to realize that we do not do justice to educational situations if we view them merely as texts.[79] The recent increase in emphasis on the performative in educational practice is a decisive new development. This novel approach complements ideas developed in the context of cultural anthropology by Geertz, who saw a need for "thick description" and regarded culture as a "collection of texts."[80] In contrast to the classical hermeneutical approach, we no longer assume the existence of a deeper structure of meaning contained in an educational reality that has evolved historically and must only be brought to light by the researcher. Rather, extensive discussions about the "crisis of representation" and an insight into the double historicity and culturality of all statements about cultural fields of action have shown that neither the internal perspectives of the actors nor the external perspectives of the researchers can construct the objective meaning structure that is contained in the field of child-rearing and education.[81] As a result of this shift in emphasis from the hermeneutics of educational reality to the performativity of educational practice, the focus is now less on the question of whether representations and interpretations are "real" and more on how these interpretations and representations are employed. When we are talking about the performativity of pedagogical and educational processes, the emphasis is on their enactment, their performance, and their reality-constituting character, and we investigate the relationship between physical and symbolic action. Research has focused on education and learning as processes of dramatic interaction in which bodily and vocal action overlap. The focus on the performative implies a view of educational science as a science of action and therefore also implies an interest in generating practical knowledge as a condition for educational action.

This study focuses on investigating the performativity of learning processes and interactions among children. These areas were studied as part of the four broad fields of socialization in which we looked at *how* children learn, *how* they perform their learning, and *how* this manifests itself in their interactions with other children. Our primary school studies show how children pursue their own learning programs over long periods of class time. This occurs in parallel with, and sometimes in opposition to, the official curriculum. The core of their own learning program consists in their interactions with other children, which are sought out, enacted, and performed. Here the question as to *how* boys distance themselves from girls and *how* girls distance themselves from boys has been crucial. The strong desire that most children have to make a performance out of their own actions is not only evident in their own learning programs. Scenes that show clearly how children perform themselves and their learning also emerge during class, sometimes with their teachers' support. Such situations are more likely to arise if the pupils' own initiative is encouraged in class. Whenever poietic learning occurs and is supported at school, the activities emerge from amongst the children.[82]

(3) Important parts of cultural life among primary school children take place by way of *mimetic* processes. These facilitate the incorporation of images, schemata, and the imagination of other people, social situations, events, and actions, and integrate them into a mental world of images. The children thereby acquire a practical knowledge that enables them to learn, act, live, and be together. Last but not least, the Berlin Study on Rituals and Gestures was able to prove, for all of the four fields of socialization studied, that mimetic processes are of central significance for education and learning. Large areas of cultural learning are thus mimetic. Examples of this are the acquisition of ritual and practical knowledge and of aesthetic experiences.[83] The same applies to the processing of lifeworlds and atmospheres and to the use of the new media.

The following example provides an illustration of mimetic learning. A group of girls, ages eight to twelve, had rehearsed Lou Bega's "Mambo No. 5" by reproducing a video clip of it. This was done during a project week in preparation for a performance at the school's summer party. In the song the German-African singer displays varying attitudes of court-ship and rejection toward several young women who are flirting with him. The video clip shows the attractive young women charming the singer while moving to the rhythm of the mambo. At the party, the ado-lescent girls danced in front of their fellow pupils, teachers, and parents on a stage built for such occasions. In their dance they mimicked the movements of the women in the video clip. They thus demonstrated to everyone that they were no longer children and on their way to becom-ing young women. They reenacted this passage and playfully performed it for their relatives and for their school community. In mimetic pro-cesses, the children's desire is directed toward other people whom they want to resemble. This is not unlike taking an "imprint" of these people, which is then incorporated into the mental world of images and imagi-nations by means of a mimetic process. In this way, children relate to parents, relatives, and other adults such as their teachers. They want to become like the people toward whom their desire is directed. By means of such role-model-related mimetic processes, they create themselves, developing their own individuality and uniqueness. Without modeling themselves on other people, children would not be able to develop into either individuals or social beings. The desire to become like others is often the point of departure for mimetic processes. What is decisive for the mimetic process, however, is not the wish to resemble, but the rela-tionships that the children build up with other people, which may well contain elements of distance and demarcation. Mimetic processes among pupils also take place in mixed age groups, in which younger children learn from older ones, and the development of the older ones is con-firmed by the younger ones.

Such practical knowledge that is so crucial for living together is also acquired largely by mimesis. Only by participating in social practices can children develop the competence to act autonomously. The same applies to the learning of poietic skills, that is, the ability to produce something.

Mimetic processes further polycentricity in both boys and girls. They reach levels of corporeality, sensuality, and desire at which a different set of dynamics is at work from those that dominate in the realm of con-sciousness. These include aggression, violence, and destruction, which are also roused and learned by the medium of mimetic processes. In group situations, the individual's center of control and responsibility is replaced by a group dynamic. This makes it particularly easy for destruc-tive forces to take effect. As a result of ecstatic contagion, actions become possible that an individual would not have been able to commit alone. Functioning rituals and ritualized practices can channel these dynamics in such a way that their destructiveness is contained. As our study showed, mimetic processes relate not only to other people in *face-to-face* situations, but also to places, spaces, things, imaginary actions, scenes, and issues. Institutions such as the family and school, the role-playing that is implicit in the media, and also values, attitudes, and norms are learned and embodied by children through mimetic processes.

(4) *Gestures* proved to play an important role in child-rearing and socialization. With my research team, I investigated the occurrence and use of gestures in the family, at school, in peer groups, and in the use of media, thus also trying to establish research on gestures within the educational sciences. Child-rearing, education, and socialization take place largely in bodily and sensory processes in which gestures play an important role. They are continuously and inseparably linked to speech, thought, and imagination.[84] They render internal processes visible for both their "producers," in whom they "arise," and those to whom they are addressed. They thus contribute to social interaction and social cohesion and to the education of individuals and groups. The performativity of gestures, on which these processes are based, while at the same time resulting from them, is therefore associated with the fact that gestures create community and modulate child-rearing and educational processes. Gestures have been shown to be historically and culturally shaped and learned and transformed in mimetic processes.

Gestures are performative and frequently used in rituals and ritualized activities. They have a mimetic effect. The performative nature of gestures plays a central role in the production and execution of speech. Gestures are also enacted and performed and generate something that would otherwise remain invisible. They are actions with which social reality is created and (re-)presented. Without gestures, there would be no social reality and no shared intentionality or cooperation. The human body and its substantiality and sensory aspects are displayed in gestures. Individual and collective meanings are condensed within them. Gestures are the expression of internal processes presented in an objective form, whose objectification also affects the individuals who make them, allowing them to become conscious of their inner processes. In the same process the gesture has an external effect on the person to whom it is addressed, and thus it has a reciprocal effect. For the effect to be reciprocal, the author of the gesture must be in the same communicative community as its recipient. This community can be a temporary one, but it may also be permanent and sustained over time. For gestures to be able to develop both their internal and their external effects, their authors and their recipients must believe that they share a common communicative basis, which arises through familiarity with the gestures of individual persons and groups. Within such a community, one knows what the gestures mean and how they are to be evaluated and responded to. Gestures make it possible to assess human behavior. They are part of the body language that tells the members of a community much about each other. Gestures become part of the acquired social knowledge that is important for regulating our actions.

Thus, gestures are part of the imaginary of a culture and regulate social practices. Presenting new students with a sunflower on their first day at school is one such gesture. It is perceived and understood by all students, parents, and teachers present at the ceremony and needs no interpretation. All participants at the ceremony understand this gesture, which is used to welcome the new students and wish them a "sunny" time at school. It is understood because all those present know, without being consciously aware of it, what giving someone flowers means in our culture. The basis for understanding the gesture is implicit knowledge that has been acquired in many different situations. In countries where there is no culture of giving people flowers, it may be different.

(5) With increasing globalization, *pedagogy and education in Europe have taken on an intercultural task* in which rituals and ritualization, educational and social gestures, the performativity of social practices, and mimetic forms of learning play an important role. More than ever before, pedagogy and education have become an intercultural task that needs to be elaborated in all four fields of socialization.[85] The new media and children's peer groups provide particularly good opportunities for children from European cultural backgrounds and children from various ethnic backgrounds to experience and understand alterity. At the inner-city primary school in Berlin that has been the focus of our study, there is a well-developed awareness of the need to acquire intercultural knowledge and to learn to act and build community together. Our study has revealed situations—some of which have already been analyzed—in which these relatively new conditions and forms of learning are practiced.

One example of this is how the principal of the school accords particular importance to the composition of mixed groups, which transcend the limits of age, gender, and ethnic backgrounds. The teachers regard ethnic backgrounds as a major factor of difference between the children and try to ensure that children from different backgrounds sit together in class so that they can deal with their differences. In composing the mixed groups, the principal goes against the wishes of the children, insofar as older children would prefer to be in the same groups as other older children, boys would prefer to be with other boys, girls with other girls, and children with the same ethnic backgrounds would also like to be together. The principal, however, insists that the age, gender, and cultural differences are represented and dealt with within the mixed groups. Pupils are also constantly exposed to alterity during lessons. Thus, regardless of their ethnic backgrounds, while learning about Egypt, for example, they studied various aspects of a culture that was foreign to all of them. This subject was also focused on in all lessons, from German to mathematics, art, and the natural sciences. Several weeks of concentration on this part of the curriculum were rounded off by a visit to the Egyptian Museum. During several group discussions (which space does not permit me to reproduce here), the children talked about their fascination with stories about that culture and how they enjoyed both retelling and inventing their own. They talked about how it had been fun to cut out and paint Egyptian kings and aristocrats in Styrofoam and look at how the Egyptians built their pyramids. Irrespective of their own cultural backgrounds, through this focus on alterity the children experienced freedom and the implicit opportunity to develop their own imaginations.

(6) *Ethnography and qualitative methods* are useful for investigating rituals and ritualized practices, the performativity of pedagogic practices, and mimetic and intercultural processes of education. Participant observation, video-based observation, video-performance, photo-analysis, interviews, and group discussions are among the most important research methods employed. They can be combined and complement each other. This diversity of methods is particularly suitable for obtaining complex and methodically transparent research findings. The Berlin Study on Rituals is characterized by a methodological diversity and oriented toward the methodology of reconstructive social research, especially the documentary method.[86] Due to the rule-guidedness of ritual behavior, we have also employed sequence analysis, which has contributed to the understanding of the sequential nature of ritual action. We have also employed methods used in the analysis of narratives, ethnomethodological conversation analysis, biographical research, and ethnography.[87]

Because our study has focused mainly on the investigation of pedagogical, educational, and learning processes, we have employed process-oriented procedures. Whenever we have concentrated on the *performative character* of rituals and ritualized practices and of pedagogical and social practices, methods used in *visual anthropology* and *visual ethnography* have played key roles.[88] These procedures are particularly important in the study of bodily interactions, educational and social actions, and spatial arrangements. Our research methodology has therefore not been limited to interviews and group discussions, although these have provided valuable insights into the imaginary and into children's symbolizations. In addition to participant observation, we have also made substantial use of video-based observation, photo analysis, and video performance.[89] Of the latter three procedures, video-based observation was most widely employed. In the field of research on families, in particular, it was complemented by photo analysis. For the first time in the field of pedagogy, video performances were systematically developed in the context of our study. They provided insights into the children's imaginary and its performative powers, which would not otherwise have been possible. The relationships between body and movement, enactment and performance, and image and media were central to our research. In this context, it was important to differentiate between various types of images: (1) images as a medium of pedagogy, education, and learning; (2) mental images of the imaginary that are created by ritual arrangements, pedagogic and social practices, and also in learning situations; (3) body images; and (4) images as empirical approaches to the investigated processes of pedagogy, education, and learning.

With this multifaceted, ethnographic case study centering on rituals in an inner-city school and their families, my aim was to demonstrate the role played by rituals in the rearing and education of children. I wanted to draw attention to the significance of rituals for enculturation, socialization, and education, as there is little awareness of this among parents and teachers. In the course of our ethnographic research on the staging and performing of rituals, we also developed new ways of using rituals intentionally in the above-mentioned areas. Since the study was conducted within the frame of reference of historical cultural anthropology, I also paid attention to the changes in rituals and ritualized practices in the course of the histories of industrial societies in the modern era. During this period, while there has been a rise in the use of rituals and ritual actions due to an increasing differentiation in society, they have become less publicly visible and less binding. A readiness to see ritual phenomena from a historical and cultural perspective led to the development of a special focus on the dynamics of change in rituals. From this perspective, our examination of rituals helped us to gain new insights into local urban culture and also into contemporary cultural and social developments.

Happiness in the Family

In this large study on the role of rituals and gestures in child-rearing, education, peer-group culture, and the media, I became aware of how important well-being and happiness are for human development. I therefore decided to carry out a study on happiness in the family. In an ethnographic study, we examined the staging of *happiness in the family* in Germany and Japan. In line with a long tradition in cultural anthropology, we studied Christmas in Germany and the celebration of the New Year in Japan, family rituals that offer us a window into our own and the foreign culture. Using three German-Japanese teams, we studied the ways in which three families in each culture celebrate their most important festival in such a way that their members are happy and content, identifying similarities and differences. It became clear how many different ways there are to make families happy through rituals, but it was also evident that in both countries happiness is very much linked to the quality of the social relationships. We also found some *transcultural elements* that play a role in creating happiness in families at holiday times.

Social and Cultural Elements in Happiness in the Family

The social and cultural practices involved in producing happiness are an important part of the intangible cultural heritage, and they play a substantial role in the forming, preservation, and modification of cultural identity. In the face of the homogenizing tendency of globalization, the UNESCO conventions on the Safeguarding of the Intangible Cultural Heritage (2003) and on the Protection and Promotion of the Diversity of Cultural Expressions (2005) stress the need for maintaining cultural difference and identity. Rituals are among the most important forms of the intangible cultural heritage, and family rituals, both in everyday life and on festive occasions, are central. Our study shows how they play a part in developing the family members' social and cultural identities, their togetherness and cohesiveness as a family, and thus their familial well-being and happiness. There are six structural elements that play a key role in this.

LANGUAGE AND IMAGINATION Emotions are always linked to other human characteristics. Language usually plays an important role in whether emotions of happiness exist and are felt. If a particular culture has a term for a certain aspect of happiness, then there will also be evidence of this emotion being expressed in that culture. If another culture has no such word, it will be quite hard to find there the aspect of happiness that it denotes. One example is the Japanese word *amae*, which means something like "depending on the love of another person" or "delivering oneself up to the sweetness of the other person." There is no corresponding term in the English language or in the European imaginary for this central concept in the Japanese mentality.

EMOTIONS Many feelings of happiness are engendered in social interactions. They change according to what is happening in everyday life. They are overlayered by earlier emotional experiences, and emotional dispositions are constantly being selected and adjusted in response to changing circumstances. Emotions are evaluative—they evaluate experiences, and this determines our actions. This helps us to find our bearings in the world and in our relations with other people, and also to make distinctions and grasp the meaning of social situations, actions, and contexts.

CORPOREALITY AND PERFORMATIVITY If our emphasis is on the performative character of the production of happiness, our main interest lies in understanding how people express and display the different feelings of happiness. Our focus is on the process by which being happy is staged and performed, that is, on the different ways in which it is expressed by the body.

MIMETIC PROCESSES Happy people often make others happy. One reason for this is the mimetic processes through which people take on characteristics of the Other. Just as when we laugh, our feeling is conveyed by the senses and is infectious, so, without being aware of it, we become the sounding boxes for other people's feelings of happiness, we pick up their body movements and their mimic expressions. We perceive the concrete outward expressions of happiness as they are performed and learn how happiness is staged, enacted, and also passed down to future generations in practice.

RITUALS In all human societies rituals help to intensify, control, and monitor emotions. They result in the participants relating to each other. They are of great importance for the creation of family happiness. Physical activities play an important role in creating the social emotions of closeness, affection, and trust. In the rituals of social practices, people learn to stage and perform family scenes that make themselves and others happy. Ritual action gives them the practical knowledge that they require for this to happen.

GESTURES   In rituals gestures are very important. In family rituals gestures are highly performative. Acquired mimetically, they intensify, portray, and structure the flow of emotions. Often gestures portray the meaning of a ritual in a condensed form and guide communication and interaction within the family. They render visible something that would not be apparent without them and play an important part in producing and portraying emotions of well-being and happiness.

The choice of family rituals as a stage for acting out happiness is also based on the fact (documented in many ethnographic studies of everyday life) that people hardly reflect at all on how they shape their everyday lives and their rituals, or on the suppositions, implications, and consequences thereof. One can assume that in ritual family celebrations, people are following more or less unconscious strategies for creating a happy family. Our study focused on this performative and ritual creation of family happiness. Information was gathered in the families during the festive season about how members stage and understand happiness. Along with narrative interviews and group discussions, we used the methods of participant observation, especially video-aided participant observation, which permitted us to replay important sequences and analyze them.

Transcultural Elements of Happiness in the Family

Five key transcultural elements of family happiness emerged as the main outcome of the study. In the family rituals studied in Germany and Japan the aspects of *eating, praying, giving of presents, remembering,* and *being together* have special importance for the creation of happiness in the family.

EATING   One striking similarity between German and Japanese Christmas and New Year rituals is the sharing of meals. Both in Germany and Japan, an important family celebration of this kind is unthinkable without the eating of meals. Three elements seem to be particularly important in the creation of family happiness through eating meals: (1) the symbolic aspect of the shared meal and the food served; (2) the bodily element of the establishing of a common taste; and (3) the performative aspect of how the meal is arranged and displayed.

1. *Creating community.* Often the festive meal means that family members who rarely see each other come together. By sitting down together at the same table, they show each other how important the family community is to them. In so doing, they form part of a tradition of festive meals that had various forms in the families each one of them came from and are now united in a shared form. Added to this is the conscious selection of the food to be served and the knowledge surrounding its symbolic or traditional meaning.

2. *A common taste.* Eating, drinking, and celebrating together are integral parts of Christmas and New Year festivities. They are special forms of collective sensory enjoyment and coming together as a community that produce a family habitus of taste as an interface between individual corporeality and the family bond. The ritualized sensory worlds allow us to experience treats and delicacies that we associate with security and protection. When we agree on taste, we also agree on values and meanings, sensuousness and aesthetics, the natural world and the world of culture. It is through taste, therefore, that an elementary forming of identity and the world takes place. Family happiness can be seen here as the creation of a shared world of taste; family happiness as regards taste actually comes about when individual needs have been cultivated largely within the family.

3. The *performative* aspect. Eating is essentially a social situation, as is the preparing of the meal. Often almost the entire family is involved in the shopping, preparation, and presentation of the meal situation. If a meal is to be a beautiful experience, important factors are the food, how the table is set, how the room is decorated, how the time between courses is managed, and how people talk to each other over the meal—in other words, the creation of a festive atmosphere. These qualities of atmosphere have emotional associations and are internalized and passed down to future generations. The associated sensory effects create familial convictions and attitudes.

In Germany the community that gathers to eat is above all also a community based on talking and presents, whose members constantly interrupt the meal to say something or to continue opening presents, but in Japan the community is based on being together. In both cases the festive meal points to the fact that a community can only exist if temporal and spatial limits are set that all members of the family recognize.

THE GIVING OF PRESENTS In family celebrations in both Germany and Japan the giving of presents is of central importance. Giving presents in the family is a form of exchange that preserves connections and is based on reciprocity. A present is given, it is accepted, and one is given in return. This circle of interaction intensifies the relationships between the members of the family by means of actions such as demonstrations of gratitude, touch and embraces, comments, and facial or gestural expressions of delight, all of which generate emotional closeness. This flow of similar emotions is experienced as something pleasing that brings happiness and gives the feeling of togetherness and meaningfulness. In Germany giving presents at Christmas plays a more important role than it does in the New Year celebrations in Japan, and in Germany it is therefore of greater significance for the creation of family community.

The giving of presents as an action that produces and strengthens emotional closeness is based on cultural and social traditions that the family members have acquired in mimetic processes. Ideally gifts are selflessly directed toward the other person and their wishes. They have a power to create reality that lies not only in their material value, and they play a considerable role in producing an atmosphere of family happiness. With every present, the givers give something of themselves to the other person. At the Christmas and New Year celebrations, the family members also give each other their time; they give themselves to each other and thus create their family community.

BELIEFS In both cultures the family celebrations have a religious dimension that is staged and presented symbolically and performatively in the giving of gifts. They also include ritual practices that are described here under the heading "beliefs" because they are associated with sacred elements.

Explicit religious faith is evident not only in visits to shrines or ancestral graves, or in going to church, singing sacred songs, and saying sacred prayers, but also in practices involving the family altar or the Christmas crib. A *secular form of faith* revolves around the advent calendar, Father Christmas, the good luck symbols associated with food, or the good luck wishes associated with the New Year. We also find a rather more *implicit ritual faith* in the power of the family ritual itself, which implies that the shared celebration is vital for the happiness of both the individuals and the community.

The focus is on sacred places and times, sacred writings and songs, and sacred practices. Sacred places have a specific spatial atmosphere. Various strategies are used as adjuncts to praying together to create a concentrated sacral atmosphere. These are objects (a shrine, a crib, a family altar), temporally structured appearances and absences of the sacred (the reading aloud of the Christmas story, giving presents, etc.), and, above all, shared ritual practice, which is often deeply rooted in tradition and nowadays serves as a mutual confirmation of belief. Sacred activities such as going to church or to a shrine, and rituals of prayer and song bring human beings together in communities founded on elements that are considered transcendent.

Where religion has ceased to play an important role as the basis for family ritual, religious "patches" still remain; objects, places, activities, and so forth are attributed a quasi-religious contextual meaning. In Germany Advent calendars are put up, and stories about the Christ Child and Father Christmas are told; in Japan corresponding practices are used to ensure that the community of ancestral spirits continues to support the family. In both countries the rituals are no longer conducted as strict religious ceremonies but tend to have informal structure that creates new, individualized ritual patterns. In this way religious and secular motifs become a tool bag of practices, partly ritualized and partly inconsistent, that ensure the happiness of the family community.

The belief in one's own family ritual becomes a family habitus. Its effects are more powerful because it is partially unconscious, and thus the ritual practices develop a magical atmosphere of community energies that includes every member of the family. This gives meaning and purpose to being together, creates expectations and requirements to act in a certain way, and is experienced overall as pleasurable.

REMEMBERING   As experiences involving feelings, family celebrations create lasting memories. Their meaning is strengthened performatively by annual reenactment. The festive holidays are stored in our memories as synaesthetic experiences, and because they are constantly reenacted, they contribute to our social and cultural identity. Memories are part of the rituals; it is in processes of memory that experiences, memories, and emotions are amalgamated into a meaningful whole that gives our lives a sense that is consistent with our life histories.

In this way family celebrations make a coherent picture that unites past, present, and future, lending a sense of continuity and playing a part in the handing down and evolution of cultural and family knowledge. The family becomes a community based on memories that transcend generations. Remembering together establishes a specific family identity that then acquires meaning in particular practices.

"Family knowledge" is handed down in interpretive, narrative memories from one generation to the next. When we remember, we also have the future in mind, and this confirms the family identity again and again and is used by the next generation to develop ideas about how to lead their lives. This becomes clear especially in family interviews, in which all the adults revisit their own positive childhood memories.

Memories of Christmas and the New Year celebration make concepts such as family and transcendence into concrete realities that are actually experienced. Experiences of belonging, dependability, and trust are intensified and become inscribed on the body memory as memories. Family is staged spatially as the closest social unit and shifted into a higher context that can produce happiness.

BEING TOGETHER   Family happiness consists primarily in the fact that all the family members are together and there for each other, in all openness. The ritual form that family celebrations take aims to create situations in which there is a flow of emotions between all those present, and a sense of family community comes about that makes everyone feel happy. This is true even though family members do not all participate to the same extent in the rituals of the celebration and despite the differences in family customs in Germany and Japan and also within each country.

The emotions of togetherness and belonging are produced and communicated by the senses. Families are communities of shared taste, smell, touch, hearing, and seeing. The "family taste" of the Japanese and the "traditional" German Christmas dinner are evidence of our knowledge of how important the *flavor* of the food is for the forming of family identity. During this celebration there is also a characteristic *fragrance* in each family that is superimposed on their everyday worlds of smell. There are reciprocal gestures of *touch* that express affection, intimacy, and togetherness and produce empathy and a sense of well-being. As we *listen* to the Christmas story and Christmas carols, the prayers and sacred texts in the Shinto shrines and Buddhist temples, at the family altar in the living room, or when visiting the family grave, through hearing, feeling, and experiencing, we have a familiar sense of belonging that is linked to the intimacy and happiness of early childhood. Finally, the difference between everyday life and the staging of the family day of celebration can be clearly *seen*. At this time more than any other, we have the chance to become aware of other members of our family in a leisurely way. As we do so, we make visual movements of attending to and focusing on each other that are tied to our emotions. As we see each other, each of us gets a sense of the Other.

Thus, each of the senses plays a part in giving the individual a sensory certainty about his or her family and his or her own self. The intertwining of different sensory experiences contributes to the meaning of family identity. Experiencing oneself on a sensory level as part of the family community creates a sense of well-being for the individual and, at the same time, the happiness of the family.

Review and Outlook

The range of fields of historical cultural anthropology that I have proposed covers mainly the research done in the humanities and social sciences. The relationships between these fields, in terms of content, concepts, and methods, need to be made more explicit. In exploring the associations between logic and passion in connection with the body and the senses, the soul and the divine, the beautiful, time, and silence, our goal was to investigate some central fields of European culture from a contemporary perspective and in transdisciplinary and transnational networks. The articles for the above-mentioned handbook on human beings aimed to identify the anthropological dimensions of a hundred key concepts that describe the relationship that human beings have with the world, other human beings, and themselves. In the course of my research it became evident how important mimetic processes are for the development, transformation, and passing down of cultural heritage to future generations. I also demonstrated—taking play, rituals and gestures as examples—the major role that mimetic actions play in the social world and how important they are for cultural learning and the acquisition of practical knowledge. The Berlin Study on Rituals and Gestures is a very broad-based and multifaceted ethnographic project for the empirical investigation of the role of rituals in the family, at school, and in peer groups and the media. It shows how important rituals and ritualized practices are, not only as texts, but also as enactments and performative behavior, and demonstrates their contribution to our understanding of social life. The combination of historical and cultural interpretation, philosophical construction and reflection, and qualitative ethnographic research employed in this project has opened up new possibilities for research in anthropology.

In the second part of this book I investigate some central dimensions of historical cultural anthropology that are, in view of the open nature of this anthropological research, not so much representative as simply examples. However, through these examples, I develop some important criteria and perspectives for research, focusing on the historical and cultural perspectives. The issues that I address include the human body, which is one focus of anthropology, and the potential for mimetic learning that lies in its physical attributes. This focus on the body also leads to an interest in investigating corporeal enactments and stagings, that is, the performativity of bodily behavior. I conducted some empirical studies on these complex relationships in the Berlin Study, in which I demonstrated that rituals and ritualized practices still play an important role in our "modern" societies. In order to throw some light on the individual and collective aspects of human societies from the perspective of historical cultural anthropology, in what follows I examine how language and imagination function to produce, hand down, and transform culture. Finally, starting from the assumption that the human body is the focal point of anthropology, I investigate the central importance of mortality and natality for our understanding of human existence, on both an individual and a collective level. Above all, I bring more attention to bear on the cultural and social aspects of birth.

Core Issues of Anthropology

SIX

The Body as a Challenge

Following the decline of normative anthropology, anthropological research paid more attention to the body. There is a problem here, however, insofar as the human body is not accessible as a whole but only partially. This gives rise to different forms of expression, description, and representation. A look back at history and at other cultures shows that the human body is perceived, experienced, and interpreted in very different ways. The wide range of different viewpoints that have developed illustrates the degree to which the social and cultural dissemination of body images is linked to power, the economy, and biopolitics.[1]

The paradigms of anthropology presented thus far draw on a great variety of different concepts of the body that contribute to our understanding of it although they are contradictory. The concepts of the body developed on the basis of evolutionary theory and philosophical anthropology differ from those developed by historical sciences interested in anthropological subjects, by cultural anthropology, and by historical cultural anthropology. Whereas the first two disciplines are concerned with the body as an aspect of the human species, the other three paradigms focus their attention on both historical and cultural particularity and on the differences among human bodies. After presenting the different body concepts of the paradigms of anthropology, I attempt to show in the second section of this chapter how the central areas of historical cultural anthropology are linked to the corporeality of human beings.

Paradigms of Anthropology and the Body

Research on *evolution* and *hominization* clearly illustrates the temporality and genesis of the human body, as well as its relationship to the history of life on Earth.[2] The human body is the result of an irreversible evolutionary process dating back to the beginnings of life on Earth, which is understood to have developed as a consequence of material self-organization. The human body shares its origins with all known species and genera and is related to these in varying degrees; its development is a consequence both of this relationship and of the diverging paths of development over the course of evolution. Its form and development were heavily influenced by the urge for self-preservation and the human powers of innovation, adaptation, and specialization. The evolution of the body was largely driven by genetic recombination and natural selection, as well as the subtle interdependencies between internal and external selection.

The development of vertebrates two hundred million years ago and of primates eighty million years ago was a vital precondition for the genesis of the human body. The remains of a hominid group, *Ardipithecus ramidus*, found in Aramis in Ethiopia, are approximately four and a half million years old. These hominids probably lived somewhere on the edge of the tropical rain forest, where the lines of development of the anthropoids diverged from those of the hominids. The bodily construction of the hominids formed the basis for the development of the predecessors of humankind, who moved, or rather climbed, on two legs and had a skull and brain size similar to those of the apes today. Their extremities are, however, difficult to distinguish from those of *Homo sapiens*. As our predecessors did not have any tools, they had to use their molar teeth to process food.

Whereas primeval humans developed the ability to walk upright, prehistoric humans gradually developed a tool-based culture using stones; this allowed them to adapt more flexibly to their environment and to become increasingly independent of it. This was the beginning of the omnivorous diet. In one species of prehistoric humans—*Homo habilis*—the speech centers developed in the brain, and the time during which females could conceive also increased. Not only did couple relationships evolve as a result, but also more intense social communication, and a division of labor gradually emerged between the genders and improved the rearing of the young. With the development of prehistoric human beings at the latest, culture began to exert a greater influence on the development and physique of the human body.

Early Humans (Homo erectus)

Over the course of about two million years, *Homo erectus* developed a considerably larger and superior brain. This was accompanied by the development of the precise grip of the human hand and of a tool culture. These processes led to an improvement in food procurement and a greater degree of relative independence from the environment. Hunting and the use of fire encouraged the division of labor between the sexes, the improvement of communications, and the development of communities. The upright gait, which freed the hands, and the growth of the brain allowed language and culture to develop. Various forms of migration emerged as a result.

While the Neanderthals were evolving from a late, archaic form of *Homo sapiens* in Europe, *Homo sapiens sapiens* was probably simultaneously emerging in Africa, accompanied by the development of the body of the modern human being. Although the Neanderthals had also developed powers of imagination, *Homo sapiens sapiens* was superior in nearly every respect. In relation to their body weight, modern humans have a comparatively larger brain volume and a skeleton and musculature that require less energy; they are more fertile and have a lower level of infant mortality, and they possess more highly developed cultural skills that aid survival. In addition to this, an improved ability to fashion and use tools enabled them to use the resources of their environment more efficiently. The body of *Homo sapiens sapiens* was the result of a multidimensional morphogenesis, based on the interplay of ecological, genetic, cerebral, social, and cultural factors.

This conception of the evolution of the human body, which arose from evolutionary theory, provided the basis for two central areas of research on the body that have developed over the past few decades. Each focuses on one particular aspect of the body and has attracted a great deal of public attention. These areas of research are the *genome body* of *genetics* and the *brain body* of brain research. Their significance for anthropology is summarized below.

Having established the possible combinations of the four basic components of DNA—guanine, cytosine, adenine, and thymine—and sequenced and mapped the human genome, research now tries to assign the basic sequences of DNA to physical and mental properties and to relate them to the functions of genes. If this is successful, it will be possible to decode the "original formula" of the human being. This is assumed to contain all the data on the genetic functions of physiological and psychological

167

processes of human beings. Its decoding is regarded as an opportunity for humans to raise themselves above the limitations of their nature—which had previously been regarded as inaccessible, imposed upon them by destiny—and thereby to become "their own masters."[3] It is hoped that this knowledge can be used for medical purposes—both in order to develop therapeutic procedures and also to forecast the likelihood of illness. The possibility of eugenic selection and breeding and of thus reducing human beings to the status of mere bearers of genetic information and of objects of economic interest has become apparent and is a matter of ethical and political debate. The European Council convention on bioethics and the prohibition of cloning, as well as the European Union directive on the patenting of genes were drawn up to deal with questions of bioethics and other possible consequences of this new technology.[4]

In discussions of these issues, a dichotomy between nature and culture is constructed that divorces the scientific requirements of the genome project from its social implications. As a result, evaluations of the opportunities and risks associated with genome analysis are confined to its legal and social consequences.[5] Issues associated with scientific genome analysis are classified as matters for basic research on nature and are not subject to political or ethical discussion. Only genetic engineering and reproductive technologies are subject to political control. Although this distinction calms public opinion, it cannot be sustained in fact, as is illustrated by the breeding of recombinant life forms such as the genetically moderated monkey "ANDi,"[6] who was given an additional gene that was intended to make him glow fluorescently in the dark. Attempts are made to generate embryonic stem cells by cloning. Its advocates suggest that, in the long term, these experiments have great therapeutic potential; for its opponents, they represent the unacceptable transgression of a boundary.[7] The debate surrounding these experiments on the cloning of embryonic stem cells for therapeutic purposes shows how difficult it is for politicians and scientists to prohibit or stop human activities that are technically possible. This technology allows us to intervene in our basic human biological substance and to manipulate it in such a way that *human beings will eventually be bred artificially*—despite all religious, ethical, and political misgivings. The side-effects of such developments are unforeseeable.

In contrast to the current overemphasis on genetic determinism, in *brain research* there is an insistence that genes never occur alone but are always embedded in an environment and that signals from this environment trigger the selection of genetic information and play an important role in the development from the egg to the organism. A self-organizing process takes place through which, driven by a continuous dialogue between the genome and its environmental milieu, increasingly complex structures are created.[8] It is through this process that the brain develops into an organized system distributed over a large network in which countless fragments of incoming signals are collated and processed in parallel. Although all centers of the brain interact intensively, it is still completely unclear how such a system that is organized in parallel structures can create a coherent image of the world it perceives as well as act in a purposeful manner (31–32).

However, it is certain that the development of the human brain undergoes a rapid qualitative leap after birth, as the senses are already fully formed. This leap is described as a self-organizing process. This process—the interplay between signals from the environment and the genes—is from now on determined by patterns of activity that are shaped by the environment to some degree. The nerve cells are nearly all present at birth; however, they are not all connected to each other in certain areas of the brain, especially in the cerebral cortex. Many connections only finish growing after birth, but a considerable proportion is destroyed again after only a short time. A large-scale reconstruction of the nerve connections takes place in which only around a third of the original connections are retained. This means that the formation of the functional architecture of the cerebral cortex is influenced to a great degree by sensory signals and therefore by experience (46–47). The fact that infants need to learn to see is further evidence of this. If this does not happen (e.g., in children who are born blind), it is not possible to learn to see at a later stage. First-language acquisition must also be performed within a schedule determined by the brain and the human organism.

The development of advanced cognitive abilities seems to be the result of the evolution of the cerebral cortex—a two-millimeter, folded layer that contains around forty thousand nerve cells per cubic centimeter, each of which relays information to around twenty thousand other nerve cells while receiving information from another twenty thousand. It is amazing to note that the inner organization of this structure has remained more or less unchanged over the course of evolution; thus, in terms of structure, the cerebral cortex of a mouse hardly differs from that of human beings. This affects the way we view the processes of developing new functions as, in contrast to the situation with technical systems, in the brain it is not possible to separate software and hardware. Programming for these functions is determined exclusively by the connectivity of the nerve cells. The structure of the network is the program. The algorithms that control the manner in which the cerebral cortex works have hardly changed over the course of evolution, except that more brain areas have been added. This means, first, that the processing procedures of the cerebral cortex need to be of a very general nature and, second, that the iteration of these fundamentally identical processes can create new, qualitatively different functions (64). Brain research is an interdisciplinary field of basic research. Its characteristics include recognizing that there is much of which we are still ignorant, avowing the intrinsic value of discovery, and having the courage to follow paths that lead to uncertain destinations (19). Proceeding from such a position, brain research has been able to show that subjectivity is linked to a certain developmental stage of the brain that is responsible for consciousness of the self and its communication to the outside world and that presupposes the ability to create mental models of the states of other brains or to construct a "theory of mind" (73). Basic research thus conceived helps to increase the complexity of anthropological knowledge by showing which mechanisms enable humans to acquire knowledge. First, there is evolution, which, for example, stores knowledge about the world in our genes and expresses this knowledge in the phenotype of the newly developed brain. Then there is the knowledge gained by experience during early ontogenesis, which also manifests itself in structural changes (these must incidentally be differentiated from those caused by genetic factors). Finally there is conventional knowledge acquired through learning, which can be seen in the resulting functional changes to the efficiency of already-established connections (95).

The brain is an active system that develops hypotheses and seeks solutions to problems.[9] Even when there are no external stimuli, it constantly produces highly complex and oscillating neuronal patterns. We can think of the brain as a distributively organized, highly dynamic system that organizes itself rather than subjecting its functions to a central unit of evaluation and decision making. It can be regarded as a system that develops its coordinating qualities both in the topology of its network and in the time structure of its activity patterns, a system that can express relations not only via the convergence of anatomical connections, but also through the temporal co-ordination of discharge patterns. The brain can represent content not only explicitly in highly specialized neurons, but also implicitly in dynamically associated ensembles, whereby it is continuously formulating hypotheses, based on its prior knowledge, about the world around it. It can therefore take the initiative instead of merely responding to stimuli. To this extent, the new view, according to which our brain evaluates other brains, is very much based on a constructivist position.[10]

Although many aspects of this concept of the brain are highly differentiated,[11] brain researchers frequently end up reducing the complexity of the human body exclusively to the brain. This reductionist approach becomes apparent in research into the quality of psychological and mental processes, on the one hand, and into the relationship between social subject and society, on the other. As in every area of research, any increase in knowledge raises ever new questions and uncovers areas of uncertainty that are sometimes drowned in the euphoria and publicity-seeking nature of research.

Whereas research into evolution, hominization, genetics, and the brain strives to obtain general insights into the human body, philosophical anthropology seeks to understand the particular characteristics of the human body that distinguish it from those of other animals, that is, from the bodies of the other primates, and to study the significance of these differences to further human self-understanding.[12] Plessner and Scheler both put forward a structure of life divided into different stages. Unlike plants, both animals and humans have a center that enables them to move in space. The centric position of animals and humans allows them to face an objectively structured environment and to act spontaneously. In contrast to the bodies of animals, the human body allows humans to distance themselves from the environment and to adopt an ex-centric position. This gives rise to three states of being: the human body is characterized by the mode of *having a body* in which it experiences an external world; consequently, it is also characterized by the mode of *being a body*, under which it experiences its soul and inner life. Ultimately this enables humans to take up an imaginary point of view outside of themselves, allowing them to perceive these two other modes and their interrelationship. Corresponding to this structure of the human body, the world is experienced as an outside world, an inside world, and a coexistent world [*Mitwelt*].

In contrast to this theory, Gehlen assumes that the human body is by nature deficient, and this forces human beings (handicapped by their higher powers) to act in order to overcome their deficiencies. In Gehlen's view it is largely neoteny (or the extrauterine year), reduced instinct, excess of impulses, and relief [*Entlastung*] from and openness to the world that characterize human corporeality. According to the thesis of neoteny, humans retain the fetal stage, early birth, slow bodily development, and a long childhood and adolescence. Residual instinct and excess of impulses are equally important corporeal characteristics. The hiatus between stimulus and response makes learning possible and enables humans to adapt to heterogeneous biotopes. Excess of impulses, arising from neoteny and instinct reduction, enables the broad spectrum of human behavioral patterns to develop. Because of excess of impulses, discipline and domestication are required, processes in which rituals and institutions play a central role. Relief helps to coordinate perception and motion. Behavioral patterns are practiced, become automatic, and can be performed without reflection. Habits are formed, creating continuity and liberating energy for new activities. Whereas the bodies of animals are attuned to a specific environment and have specialized organs for dealing with these habitats, the human body "has world"; that is, it can adapt to very different conditions. In Gehlen's view, the unspecialized nature of the human body enables humans to be open to the world.

Where this view of the body concentrates on the general conditions of the human body and its development, other anthropological concepts of the body concentrate on the historical and cultural nature of the human body. These concepts assume that the body changes as part of a historical and cultural process. The methods of research employed and the results produced differ accordingly.

Historical anthropology as a subdiscipline of the historical sciences examines the human body over the course of time.[13] Researchers in this field investigate how collectively held attitudes prevalent during a specific historical era can give rise to specific bodily feelings and sensations. The historical character of feeling and thinking, as well as of collective memory, becomes apparent. The conception of time in the present era differs from that of the Middle Ages, for example, in that nowadays the discrepancy between world time and individual time plays a significant role. Here world time is understood as the time horizon that the sciences have developed on the basis of the beginning of the universe and the formation of Earth. Viewed against the background of this time frame, the historical periods of human cultures and especially the human life span are infinitesimally small. This research has led to different conceptions of time that result from taking different temporal reference points as a basis. If we only lived for a month, our consciousness of time would be different again. As the concept of time alters, the experience of space also changes. Different and partially contradictory conceptions of time and space simultaneously shape life in the modern era. The historical nature of elementary situations and basic experiences and the historical character of attitudes to death, love, and work become apparent. Subjectivity appears as the result of historic and cultural processes such as adjusting, distancing, and disciplining. Even sexuality and birth, childhood, youth, old age, and clothing reveal their historical nature, clearly illustrating that the human body appears only in concrete historical forms and that its historical nature must therefore be researched if we are to understand its specific character at any historical juncture.

Whereas historical research into the body takes a diachronous view of the human body, focusing on its historical particularity, cultural anthropology has developed a synchronous perspective (see chapter 4). What applies to the historical nature of the human body applies analogously to its culturality. The heterogeneous nature of cultural influences results in the development of bodies with very different cultural characteristics; their variety and scope are irrevocable. Only by reducing alterity to what we own and know from experience can we create the impression that it is possible to transcend cultural differences without any loss of complexity. On closer examination, however, it becomes apparent that such a reduction ignores the specific features of a cultural anthropological view of the body, which can only be found by studying and illustrating alterity and corporeal difference. What is to be regarded as a cultural difference in terms of the body depends on the prerequisites of the research task and is constituted in a reciprocal relationship between the cultural frame of reference applied and the related perceptions of alterity. The task is to increase the complexity of our knowledge of the human body by identifying cultural diversity. Although the cultures of, for example, northern and southern Europe are very similar, they still display significant differences in their attitudes to the body—differences concerning every aspect of human social life.

As I attempt to trace the role of the body in cultural and social anthropology I would like to distinguish between three phases. Two books by Mary Douglas, *Purity and Danger* and *Natural Symbols*, are central to the first phase.[14] The aim of her first study was to show that the dietary rules in the Book of Leviticus can be seen as a summary of central facets of the culture of the Israelites and that these rules create a link between physical and social experiences. In other words, the body can be understood as being analogous to the social system. It is at the base of a natural symbolic system. This means that the demand to fit into society leads to a control of the bodily functions and vice versa. Social distance is expressed in terms of a distancing from one's physiological origins. This relationship between symbolic and social experience is, however, only valid within the context of a social environment, which determines how much room individuals have to maneuver. Here the body is understood as a sensitive bearer of the life force and as an organ of communication. In her second book Douglas sees the body as a "medium of expression" and in terms of "techniques of expression." The physical body represents for her a microcosm of society facing the center of power, contracting and expanding its claims in direct accordance with the increase in and redirecting of social pressures. Douglas then proceeds to distinguish between a physical and a social body, the self and society, a distinction to which she repeatedly returns.[15] She stresses the fact that this distinction is purely analytical. Even before it is born, the body of the embryo is shaped by society and culture—for instance, by the food the mother eats and the rhythms of her body—so that there simply cannot be a body that is free of social and cultural influences. This question of how to understand the human body has resulted in heated discussions about commonalities and differences between humans, animals, machines, and deities.[16]

In a second group of works, the body and the way it is formed by society became the subject of theoretical analysis. Among these, Foucault's studies are particularly important. He showed how hospitals, prisons, barracks, and schools result in the disciplining of the body and how sexuality becomes a strategy for the care of the self.[17] These analyses revealed the historical nature of the body and showed the extent to which the body is a product of social institutions and power relations. Bourdieu's sociological studies also made this clear. Many of his central concepts, such as "habitus," "practical sense," "field," and "social space," point to the importance of bodily learning.[18] For Bourdieu, habitus is a generative, basic pattern that is rooted in the body and gives rise to the development of relatively homologous schemas and forms of practice that do, however, permit contradictory and creative acts. In his study entitled *Distinction*, Bourdieu was able to show the extent to which taste, which is linked with corporeality and sensuality, is determined by habitus and functions as a habitual manifestation of social differences, and that this is what helps social actors to develop a style that will be specific to a class or section of society.[19] Mimetic, performative, and ritual processes are of central importance for the incorporation of social norms, the development of preconscious strategies of practical sense, and also for the development of taste, style, and habitus. This was also recognized by Judith Butler, who established the importance of ritual and performative processes in the forming of gender identity.[20]

These discoveries about the central significance of the body constituted a third group of studies, most of them in the field of cultural anthropology. Some of these studies involved a rethinking of the relationship between culture and self and between the body and embodiment.[21] They investigated how, in the embodiment process, subjective and intersubjective experiences are gained in which the self is created.[22] Of key importance in all these studies is the realization that the body is the existential condition for the existence of human life, and that it forms the basis from which a variety of forms of embodiment emerge.[23] Culture was seen as an artifact of practices resulting in the production of ethnographic texts whose interpretation would lead to an understanding of culture. "The body as text," "the inscription of culture on the body," "reading the body"—these were important metaphors in such attempts. However, it is an oversimplification to see the embodiments of culture as an assemblage of symbols to be read like texts. It was Merleau-Ponty who first established that the starting point of all analyses is perception. Therefore the body must no longer be understood as object but as subject.[24] Thus, culture cannot be limited to objects and representations; for in bodily perception, it is not so much that representations are created, but that perception is an existential experience that is rooted in the body.[25] We can conclude from this that "in brief, the equation is that semiotics gives us textuality in order to understand representations, phenomenology gives us embodiment in order to understand being-in-the-world."[26] These thoughts on the understanding of human corporeality are picked up and expanded in my work on cultural learning as mimetic learning and on the importance of the performativity of the body and of rituals as practices of the social framework (see chapters 7–9).

Historical anthropological research has the aim of identifying historical changes in humans' relationship to their bodies and of examining and evaluating these changes.[27] It focuses on images and concepts of the body as well as bodily practices and the use of the senses. Many of the methods and procedures used in this field are based on research performed by Norbert Elias, Michel Foucault, Max Horkheimer, and Theodor W. Adorno. These works form the basis for our attempt to analyze how the body and its senses are changing today. The aim here is to estimate what influence the acceleration of time, the ubiquity of the new media, and the greater use of computers have on human perception and on the way we relate to our bodies, and to assess what part increasing abstraction and imagination within society play in this.

In his reconstruction of the process of civilization in Europe, Norbert Elias showed that the human body is becoming increasingly disciplined.[28] The controls exercised affect eating habits, social behavior, and emotional life. Greater shame and embarrassment thresholds play a central role here. Humans are establishing a greater distance from their bodies. Modern humans are becoming increasingly distanced from each other, the world, and themselves, resulting in self-control and self-discipline, which can be employed as strategies to attain self-perfection.[29] A more extensive inner world is being developed, consisting of suscepti-bilities, feelings, moral principles, and sets of values. This development occurs through practical acts and social activities, which create examples and models. The transformation to a body exercising a greater degree of control and under the dominance of rational thinking emerges in the course of mimetic acquisition in the form of regularly repeated exercises and imitation, following guidelines and instructions, and control and correction.[30] Gradually the closed and hermetic bodies (*corpus clausum*) of modern humans emerged.

Foucault's analysis points in the same direction.[31] In contrast to Elias however, he places greater emphasis on the controlling and disciplining power of institutions in whose spaces the roles of society and individuals interlink, a process in which the activity of the body and the constructive side of the subjects play an important part. Foucault describes power as a subcutaneous body politic, which he does not see as only suppressing human beings, but also as advancing them, and "producing" them as individuals. What looks like humanization—more lenient punishments, the introduction of psychology into the penal system, understanding the culprit and the crime—is, in fact, a more subtle means of control, herald-ing a new era of civilization.[32] The aim of this is the *control, discipline*, and *standardization* of the body, its gestures, and its behavior. The exemplary development of such processes can be seen in the temporal and spatial structures of prisons, schools, and the military, where the body's ability to learn enables it to be subjected to the "microphysics of power" and to be colonized politically.

In their *Dialectic of Enlightenment*, Horkheimer and Adorno use Freud-ian theory to show that the development of rationality, Enlightenment, and emancipation during the course of civilization was not achieved without sacrifices, postulating that the history of civilization is the his-tory of the introversion of sacrifice.[33] The liberation of the human body from the perils of nature went hand in hand with its subjection to the *forces of social rationality*. The transition from the external control of the body to the establishment of a self for internal control is an irreversible process and both a gain and a loss, depending on one's vantage point. Against the background of the horrors of the Second World War, Hork-heimer and Adorno emphasized the losses involved in this transition— the change from rationality to myth, from life to death. They described the symptoms and encoded messages of a maltreated, slaughtered, and violated corpse, which could not be transformed into a body again, but must remain the cadaver it had become. These analyses show that *the body is a medium for human history and culture.* Anthropology examines the body as the location of both individual and collective cultural memory.[34] Here the self comes up against its limits, thereby experiencing the fictive character of its oneness.[35] The body is treated as a medium of expression and representation; its energies transform the world into narratives, pictures, stagings, and performances. Depending on our viewpoint, we can regard the body in terms of an inscription, expression, or representation. Sometimes it appears as a machine, sometimes as having a soul, or as a dynamic living organism with a tendency to transform and transcend itself. In the human body, the external world is transformed into the inner world, and materiality becomes imagination, and the reverse is also true—the inner world becomes the outer world, and imagination becomes materiality. Despite collective historical and cultural experiences, every human body is unique. Even in cases where the collective character of attitudes and opinions is emphasized in studies on the history of mentalities,[36] the processes of socialization and enculturation are different for every person.

Concentration on the historical and cultural constitution of the body focuses the emphasis of research on the senses and their relationships to each other. Evidence of lasting changes to the orientation of the senses and the way they are experienced can be found throughout the course of civilization. The increase in distance, control, discipline, and abstraction, as outlined above, as well as the growing significance of images presented by the media, have changed the relationships of the senses to each other. Smell, taste, and touch have been pushed back further into the private sphere, while sight has become the paramount sense of the present era. Visibility, clarity, and transparency predominate over hearing in the experience of alterity and the community. The rise of the culture of the written word and the new media have brought about a lasting change in the perception and sensation of the body.

A key role in the experience of the alterity of the body is played by the *soul* and the *sacred*, whose complex nature defies scientific understanding. Scholars of the arts and the social and cultural sciences insist that these concepts are based on circumstances and elements that have long been considered constituent parts of European culture, and that summoning up their presence prevents human life from being reduced to pure immanence. Like beauty and love, the soul and the sacred are certainly linked to the body, but they are not restricted to it; they transcend its boundaries. They form part of those areas of human experience that go beyond subjectivity and individuality in the direction of alterity.

The Body in Central Fields of Anthropology

The presence of the human body is a constant source of mystery. Although we can feel our bodies, our consciousness has only limited access to such feelings. The body can only be understood in its historical and cultural manifestations.[37] Researching these manifestations is one of the tasks of anthropology, which focuses on the corporeal aspect of the complex of phenomena under analysis and thus creates new perspectives. This can be seen, for instance, in mimetic learning as cultural learning, in the theories and practices of the performative, in rituals as practices that create community, in language in the tension between universality and particularity, and in the relationship between image and imagination, as well as in the role of death as the "Other" of life.

In classical antiquity, the processes of copying and imitation were designated as the *mimetic* processes. In the third book of Plato's *Republic*, mimesis is used as a synonym for education. When humans learn, they do so mimetically from role models. Plato sees no way of resisting the pressure to act mimetically, that is, to attempt to copy role models. For this reason, he believed it necessary to exclude bad role models from society. Aristotle also emphasized the special, mimetic gift of humans that is inextricably bound to the properties of the human body. In the tenth book of the *Republic*, Plato refines the definition of mimesis, restricting its application to the field of aesthetics and thereby creating, for the first time, the independent field of aesthetics with no commitment to truth; however, this definition simultaneously debased it. In spite of the Aristotelian objections, this depreciative view has long been associated with our conception of mimesis. This conception was only corrected after studies proved the anthropological significance of mimetic processes.[38]

This proof clearly shows that the human body forms the basis of our mimetic relations to the world around us. Mimetic processes enable us to relate to other humans and the world around them. The mimetic processes, which are bound to the body and the senses, are used by social subjects to recreate a previous world as *their own* world. In doing so, they can both create their own world and integrate themselves into society. They both contribute to society and help to shape it by using their bodies. Just as social subjects are contained within the world, they also contain the world in their bodies. The plasticity of the human body precludes humans from simply becoming subjugated to the world. Instead, it enables them to create and shape it productively. Motion plays a vital role in this. Mimetic actions create practical knowledge that is stored in the body's memory and can be updated in a variety of situations. When the body is used as an instrument, techniques are acquired that make it possible to use the body in an intentional, controlled, and functional manner.

During these processes, gestures are learned that equip us with some of the most important forms of corporeal presentation and expression. The mimetic acquisition of gesticulatory skills results in our incorporating institutional norms, social values, and power structures. These help to us to shape movements and body positions. The same applies to the acquisition of ritual knowledge, practical playing skills, and all other cultural and social areas that require practical knowledge.[39]

An analysis of cultural processes with regard to their performative character sheds new light on these processes.[40] Perception, knowledge, media, rituals, and gender can be regarded as practices of the performative, where aspects of language, the body, and aesthetics all interact. These practices are characterized by their staging aspects and performative qualities. Perception is conceived of as a sequence of related actions that create historical, cultural, and medial spaces, and during which the rhythmic interaction of time, order, movement, memory, and expectation plays an important role. Knowledge and science also have a performative side, closely linked with the fact that they are also staged and performed, which expresses the historically diverse yet irreducible indexicality of science. Media make the remotest of objects appear and become perceptible. Their performative character is revealed in the way they are used, in that area where materiality and creativity overlap, and in intermedial references. In the different kinds of media, the processes of embodiment and disembodiment assume different intensities. The corporeality of the Other and the performative way we deal with this play key roles in the ritual treatment of differences. Depending on context, ritual acts develop strategies of inclusion and exclusion, in which bodily performance and the staging of power and alterity play essential parts. The performance of the body is also central in the evolution of gender. Gender can be understood as the result of the embodiment of a specific sex, in which relationality and historicity play vital roles. In these processes, the practices of exercising power, the formation of habitus, and the subversion of standardized gender roles reveal their impact.

The performative character of rituals and ritualization plays an important role in the creation, preservation, transformation, and transfer of culture to the next generation.[41] In contrast to discourse, their corporeal side contributes enormously to their effect. Rituals result from the symbolically coded staging and performance of human bodies. The ritual arrangement creates a sense of belonging among the participants, even if its meaning is interpreted differently by each person involved. Without the physical staging and performance of rituals, neither commonality nor the social fabric would be able to develop. Rituals create continuity between the past, present, and future. Through their repetition, they also always involve the staging and performance of new things and are thus open to change in the future. They help to inscribe normative standards and values into the bodies of the ritual participants. Many rituals mark times and places of particular significance, such as seasonal changes or organized transitions from one social position or institution to another. This process is characterized by distinct phases of separation, transition, and renewed integration. During the performance of rituals, differences are worked through, orders are established and modified. Where rituals do not fulfill their function of sustaining order, violence threatens to erupt. Rituals encompass very different forms of corporeal staging and performance, ranging from liturgies and ceremonies to festive celebrations. In these forms, the ritual creation of the sacred plays an important role; here, the magic of sacred actions and spoken words is of central significance. The seemingly natural quality of rituals makes it appear as if things had always been that way and thus disguises the power structures that are being enacted. The dynamic inherent in rituals that strives for change often goes unnoticed.

The ritual side of cultural stagings and performances also illustrates the performative significance of language. Where it is a case of the relationship between body and language, the bodily prerequisites of language are of fundamental importance.[42] Humans have an innate ability to acquire language. Its origins can be traced back a hundred thousand years, and it was probably already very advanced as far back as forty thousand years ago. For the capacity of speech to develop, it was necessary for the hands to be liberated from the duties of locomotion, for vision to be freed from the task of prehension, for the brain to increase in size, the lateralization of the brain to evolve, the speech centers to form, the larynx to assume a lower position, and the vocal apparatus and hearing to develop. This general ability to evolve language resulted in the development of many different languages rather than one universal one. Although the ability to form words, syntactic constructions, and sentences is inherent in the human body and is passed on down the generations, this does not explain the diversity of words or grammatical rules of individual languages. Language must be acquired at an early age; otherwise the capacity for acquiring it is lost permanently. Brain research experiments have shown that early learning processes are required to train the capacity for learning languages. Once one language has been learned, other languages can also be acquired. If this opportunity is not seized early in life, learning a language at a later stage will no longer be possible. In articulating the sounds of speech, the human body is both active in forming sounds and passive in receiving them. When we articulate sound, the ear hears it at the same time. Touch is also experienced on two levels by humans. The structural parallel between the hand busy using a tool, and the head, which is concerned with symbolization processes, is essential for the development of the hand and language, and for the reciprocal relationship between them. Language is rooted in a physical movement of the human body—in the articulation of the vocal apparatus—resulting in the sequentiality of speech acts and the attendant articulation of thoughts. Hearing is directly related to these two forms of articulation—to the voice creating the speech and the thoughts expressed.

Imagination is also closely linked to the corporeal nature of human beings. It is possibly rooted in the "vegetative area" (Gehlen), the vital processes of the human body, and can be understood as a projection of humans' excess of impulses.[43] Whatever the case may be, humans can be regarded just as much as creatures of fantasy as creatures of language. Castoriadis viewed humans in this way when he assumed that the imaginary is a self-creating world of images, where bodily energies are interwoven with historical and social forms and contents, thus forming collective and individual meanings that change in the course of historical and cultural developments. The imaginary implants meaningful figures and configured meaning into people's imaginations, where they influence their actions. In this way, the imaginary creates a common historical and cultural world, which serves as reference point for the building of community. These imaginary meanings structure human beings' language, values, and actions, and also affect the internal structures of society and the lives of its members. The imaginary becomes the engine of the continuous self-reassurance and self-change of subjects and society. The imagination allows humans to turn the outside world into an inner one and the inner world into the outside one. The imagination makes mimetic processes and ritual arrangements possible, allows the performative to evolve, and creates community through collective images, meanings, and ritual practices. It is essential for perception and corporeal memory, passion and desire, daydreams and visions, and it creates images, sounds, smells, and tastes, as well as sensations of touch. Imagination and language, thinking and images, are inextricably linked.

One of the major themes of the imaginary is death, which threatens human beings and causes the fear and terror that religion, philosophy, literature, and science attempt to address.[44] From the point of view of evolutionary research and the theories of hominization, the body we have today would not have evolved without the deaths of innumerable prehuman, prehistoric, and early human generations. Living and dying are inseparable and can only be understood in their reciprocal relationship to one another. Temporality and mortality not only define the limits of the human body, but are also the preconditions for its evolution. Without birth and death, there would be no human body, no human species, and no individual life. In the human sciences, however, far less attention is given to the subject of birth than to that of death. This is surprising, since it is no less fundamental and baffling than death. Only since Hannah Arendt expressed her thoughts on a philosophy of natality has birth been discussed in the humanities and social sciences.[45]

Death is a threat not only to individual lives, but also to the community, for the experience, by members of society, of the pain and loss that accompany death is unavoidable. For this reason, every culture develops strategies for dealing with death. Among these, the most important are rituals for the care of the dying and those related to burial and mourning. Throughout different historical eras, the cultures of the world have produced a great many rites, myths, and images to help human beings not only to face the transition from life to death and the suffering it entails, but also to lend it form and meaning. Death remains a void, one that troubles human beings, challenges our imaginations and our thinking, and leaves us constantly ill-at-ease. As Paul Valéry wrote, "Death speaks to us in a solemn voice to tell us nothing."

SEVEN

The Mimetic Basis of Cultural Learning

Recent studies in the field of primate research have shown that although elementary mimetic learning skills exist among nonhuman primates, they are present to a particularly high degree in humans. This finding comes as no surprise to scholars of cultural studies. Aristotle was among the first to note that the ability to learn mimetically and the pleasure we take in participating in mimetic processes is a particular human gift.[1] By referring to the research on the social behavior of primates and making comparisons, specialists in the fields of developmental and cognitive psychology have recently managed to identify some of the characteristics of early human learning and to determine the special nature of mimetic learning in human infancy and early childhood. Michael Tomasello sees small children as having the ability to "identify with other persons; perceive other persons as intentional agents like the self; engage with other persons in joint attentional activities; understand many of the causal relations that hold among physical objects and events in the world; understand the communicative intentions that other persons express in gestures, linguistic symbols, and linguistic constructions; learn through role-reversal imitation to produce for others those same gestures, symbols, and constructions; and construct linguistically based object categories and event schemas."[2]

These abilities enable small children to participate in cultural processes. By taking part in enactments of the practices and skills of the social group in which they live, they are able to appropriate the cultural knowledge of the group. The skills referred to here show how learning from role models is central for the development of small children.[3] However, these processes are better conceptualized as mimetic processes. The skills of identifying with other people, of understanding them as beings that are acting intentionally, and of jointly focusing attention on something are all connected to children's mimetic desire to emulate adults and to adjust their own behavior to become similar to them. This desire to be similar to their elders motivates small children to understand causal relationships between objects of the world and the communicative intentions of other people, as expressed in gestures, symbols, and language constructions and, like them, to construct object categories and event schemas. Even nine-month-old children are capable of using their inherent mimetic skills, whereas other primates never attain such skills at any point in their lives.[4]

These insights are also confirmed by the findings of neuroscientific research in the 1990s, which proved that what distinguishes human beings from nonhuman primates is the fact that they have a special capacity to use mimetic processes to make sense of the world. This scientific paradigm attributes this capacity to the mirror neurons. An analysis of how the mirror neuron system works shows how recognition of other people, including their actions and intentions, depends on our capacity for movement. The mirror neuron system enables our brains to relate observed movements to our own capacities for movement and to recognize their significance. Without this mechanism, we would perceive the movements and behavior of other people, but we would not know their significance or what they are really doing. The mirror neuron system explains why we are able to behave not simply as individuals but also as social beings (or, to put it in more basic terms, it provides one of many possible physiological correlates for this capacity). It is partially responsible for our capacities for mimetic behavior and learning, verbal and gestural communication, and our understanding of the emotional reactions of others. The perception of a person's pain or disgust activates the same brain areas that would be activated if we were experiencing these feelings ourselves. Although these mirror neurons do exist in nonhuman primates, the system is more complex in humans. Unlike other primates, human beings are able to distinguish between transitive and intransitive locomotive actions and to choose types of actions and sequences of actions that constitute these types. They are also able to engage in actions that are not actually carried out, but merely imitated. The mirror neuron system allows us to grasp the significance of the actions of other people—not only actions in isolation, but also actions in sequence. Numer-

FIGURE 7.1   Father teaching two sons (5–7) to shave in bathroom. © Steven Puetzer/Digital Vision/Getty Images.

ous experiments have also confirmed what primate research had already demonstrated for nine-month-old children: that the system of mirror neurons processes not only observed actions but also the intention that lies behind the performance of these actions. When we see people carrying out an action, their movements have an immediate meaning for us. The same can be said for our own actions and how they are understood by other people. Experiments have shown that the qualities of the locomotive system and the mirror neuron system are necessary but not sufficient prerequisites for the capacity for mimesis. Further neuronal mechanisms are also required for processes to arise that involve more than simple repetition. Here, a mimetic adapting to become similar to the world and

FIGURE 7.2 A newborn macaque imitates tongue protrusion. The only animal in which mirror neurons have been studied individually is the macaque monkey. This picture was published by the Public Library of Science. *Source:* L. Gross, "Evolution of Neonatal Imitation," *PLoS Biol* 4, no. 9 (2006). This research article was, and may well still be, available on the website at http://www.plosbiology.org/article/info:doi/10.1371/journal.pbio.0040311. © 2006 Public Library of Science. This is an open-access article distributed under the terms of the Creative Commons Attribution License.

other people takes place.[5] These mimetic skills allow small children to take part in the cultural products and processes of their societies. Small children can thus incorporate the material and symbolic products of their cultural community, which are thus preserved and handed down to the next generation.

Mimetic processes are principally oriented toward other people. Infants and small children relate to the people with whom they live: parents, elder siblings, other relatives, and acquaintances.[6] They try to be like them, for example, by answering a smile with a smile. However, they also initiate responses in adults by using skills they have already acquired. These early exchanges also enable small children to learn feelings. They learn to evoke their own feelings toward other people and to elicit them in others. The brain develops in the course of its exchanges with the environment; that is, certain capacities are trained and endure, while others fade.[7] The cultural conditions of early life are imprinted in the brains and bodies of small children. Anyone who has not learned to see, hear, or speak at an early age can no longer acquire these skills at a later age.[8] Initially, the mimetic actions of infants and children do not allow for a separation of subject and object; this occurs only at a later stage of development. At first, the world is perceived as magical; that is, not only humans, but also objects are experienced as being alive. As rationality becomes more developed, the capacity to experience the world in this way gradually becomes less central. However, it is this capacity upon which children draw to transform the external world into images in mimetic processes and to incorporate them into their internal image-worlds.

In his autobiography, *Berlin Childhood around 1900*, Walter Benjamin illustrated how children incorporate their cultural environments in processes of assimilation.[9] In the course of these processes, children assimilate aspects of the parental home, such as the rooms, particular corners, objects, and atmospheres. They are incorporated as "imprints" of the images and stored in the child's imaginary world, where they are subsequently transformed into new images and memories that help the child gain access to other cultural worlds. Culture is handed on by means of these processes of incorporating and making sense of cultural products. The mimetic ability to transform the external material world into images, transferring them into our internal worlds of images and making them accessible to others, enables individuals to shape cultural realities.

These processes encompass not only our modes of dealing with the material products of culture, but also social relationships, forms of social activity, and the way social life is staged and performed. In particular, this involves forms of practical knowledge that are learned mimetically in body-oriented, sensory processes and enable us to act competently in

FIGURE 7.3   Heinrich Zille: Nine Berlin Boys. © Berlinsche Galerie.

institutions and organizations. Ritual knowledge is an important area of this practical social knowledge, and this is the means by which institutions become rooted in the human body, enabling us to orient ourselves in social situations. Images, schemas, and movements are learned in mimetic processes, and these render the individual capable of action. Since mimetic processes involve products of history and culture, scenes, arrangements, and performances, these processes are among the most important ways of handing down culture from one generation to the next. Without our mimetic abilities, cultural learning and "double inheritance," that is, the handing down of cultural products along with biological inheritance, which enables culture to change and develop, would not be possible.[10]

Writing—an assemblage of nonsensory similarities—elicits mimetic processes that help to bring to life what is read.[11] It is the same with other products of culture that also require a mimetic relationship for them to come alive.[12] Without such a relationship, they represent simply a cultural possibility that can only realize its full potential through processes of education and self-education, that is, independent learning and development. Such processes are particularly important in the transfer of culture from one generation to the next, since these processes require a metamorphosis to keep forms of living, knowledge, art, or technology alive. As mimetic processes are not simply methods of copying worlds that have already been symbolically interpreted but also consist in our taking and then incorporating "impressions" of these worlds, these mimetic relationships always contain creative aspects that alter the original worlds. This creates a cultural dynamism between generations and cultures that constantly gives rise to new things.[13]

To a great extent, cultural learning is mimetic learning, which is at the center of many processes of education and self-education. It is directed toward other people, social communities, and cultural heritages and ensures that they are kept alive. Mimetic learning is a sensory, body-based form of learning in which images, schemas, and movements needed to perform actions are learned. This occurs largely unconsciously, and it is this that is responsible for the lasting effects that play an important role in all areas of cultural development.[14]

Mimetic processes are also connected with the processes whereby we are overwhelmed by experiences in which our subjectivity dissolves into chaos and uncontrolled violence.[15] These processes also involve visible confrontations with power, dominance, violence, and oppression, which are part of every culture and into which the mimetic processes are repeatedly immersed. The vicious circle of violence is an example of the mimetic structure of many forms of violence.[16] However, mimetic processes are also linked to aspirations for the forms and experiences of higher levels of life, in which "living experiences" (Adorno) can be sought and found.[17] "Becoming similar" to the world in mimetic action becomes an opportunity to leave egocentrism, logocentrism, and ethnocentrism behind and to open oneself to experiences of alterity.[18]

History and Culture

A glance at the history of the concept of mimesis also reveals the cultural nature of mimetic processes. If mimesis is synonymous with education (as it was for Plato), if mimetic processes create art and poetry, and if works of poetry and art are interpreted as part of an aesthetic experience, then these processes can be said to encompass the handing down, creation, and presentation of cultural works. According to Hermann Koller, the idea and the concept of mimetic processes have their roots in dance and are therefore linked with the performative side of Greek culture.[19] Proceeding from this assumption, Koller establishes "representation" and "expression" alongside "imitation" as original aspects of mimetic processes. The term *mimesis* gained in importance when Plato used it in his *Republic*.

Today we have moved on from Koller and now believe that the term *mimesis* came to Greece from Sicily—the home of mime. Examining the etymology of the term thus yields two meanings.[20] There is no particular link between mimesis and music or dance; the link is with *mimos*. The role of the *mimos* is not to copy or to reproduce something, but to perform a burlesque, to act the clown. It relates to scenes from the everyday culture of simple people that were performed at the celebrations of the wealthy to entertain them. These scenes and performances were often ribald and disrespectful. According to this view, which is supported by a great deal of linguistic evidence, the origins of mimesis lie in cultural performative practices and have a distinctively sensuous aspect, with an emphasis on movements of the body. In the fifth century BCE, the term *mimesis* was more widespread in Ionia and Attica. In the Platonic era it had already come to be used to refer to processes of "imitation," "emulation," and "striving to be like."[21]

In Book III of the *Republic*, working on the assumption that poets in Greece played a large part in educating the next generation, Plato examines how the educational effects of literary works unfold through the mimetic processes. In Plato's view, the characters and plots created in literature are inscribed into the imagination of the young in mimetic processes. He believed that these images were so powerful that young people were unable to resist their effects. Therefore, the stories and images that were going to grip the imaginations of young people should be selected with care, and the content of some literature should be withheld from the young. The *polis* should therefore make a selection of literary stories suitable for the education of children, in order to control the mimetic processes that shape the imaginations of the young. Literary works that do not serve the aims of educating the young should be excluded from the Republic. This applies, for example, to literary works that tell of the imperfections of the gods and heroic figures. The only literary works that should be made available to youth are those from which they can learn what they need in order to fulfill their duties to the *polis*, through mimetic processes.

According to Plato, painters and poets, unlike craftsmen, do not create commodities but only the *appearances* of things. Painting and literature are not merely the artistic representation of things, but the artistic representation of things as they appear. The aim is not the representation of reality or truth, but the artistic representation of appearances as they appear. Therefore, painting and mimetic literature can, in principle, make anything that is potentially visible appear.[22] This is the mimesis that creates images and illusions, where the difference between model and depiction becomes immaterial. The aim is not true depiction or similarity, but the *appearance of what appears*.[23] Art and aesthetics constitute their own field, where the artist or poet is sovereign. Plato believed that the artist or poet did not have the ability to produce anything that truly exists, and that he was therefore free of the obligation to seek truth that must be applied in philosophy. This ascribed to the field of aesthetics a certain independence from the rigors of philosophy, with its search for truth and knowledge and its striving for the good and the beautiful. The price to be paid for this was exclusion from the ideal Republic, which would only accept art and literature that conformed to its ideas.

Aristotle also regarded art as mimesis. In particular, he viewed music as the imitation of ethos; unlike painting and sculpture, which create visible lines, music creates a clearly felt inner movement and has ethical effects. At the heart of his *Poetics* is *tragedy*, the mimesis of people in action. In tragedy, nothing is represented that has already taken place. Its themes and plots are rooted in the mythical, which is clearly not reality. The plot of a tragedy should be performed so that the audience experiences "pity" and "fear" in a mimetic process, thereby undergoing a cathartic experience and a strengthening of character.[24]

According to Aristotle, mimetic actions do not create a copy of reality whereby the difference between the model and depiction is supposed to disappear. Mimetic processes lead to simultaneous imitation and change; they strive for "beautification" and "improvement," a "creative imitation." Homer's representation of Achilles is an example of this. Even though Achilles is depicted as a short-tempered, reckless man, he still appears predominantly as an outstanding hero. In literature, the mimetic process leads to the fashioning of the possible and the general. This brings a new element in the imitation process into play, which is not part of the pure process of representation.

Cultural works of literature, painting, and music are created by the imitation of nature in mimetic processes. To understand how culture comes into being through the imitation of nature, it is necessary to define what we understand by nature. Unlike the concept of nature in the nineteenth and twentieth centuries, which reduced it to an object, for Aristotle the term *physis* denotes nature and its integral power to create life—living nature. When literature, painting, and music set out to imitate nature in a mimetic process, this does not mean simply creating a reproduction or a "naturalistic" copy of something. If one interprets the concept of nature as "living nature," which incorporates a spiritual principle, then imitating nature means something different. Literature, art, and music must imitate the creative force of nature. In this concept, imitation is no longer seen in its narrowest sense; instead something is to be portrayed that exists as an image within the poet or painter, regardless of whether this corresponds to things or persons in the outer world. Here, imitating or reproducing does not mean the production of a copy, but the creation of an image that, although it certainly relates to a particular original image, does not simply duplicate it.

Mimetic processes aim to flesh out an inner picture that the poet or painter has before his or her eyes. In the process of artistic creation something new comes into being. The original image that is used to guide the creative process gradually dissolves into the work of art, be it picture, drama, or music, which then emerges in a medium that is created in a different medium from the image in the imagination. Changes, omissions, embellishments, and so forth will occur, so that only a limited similarity is present in the work. Frequently, the original images for the pictures and drafts of the painters and poets are unknown because they either never existed or no longer exist. At the center of the artistic process is the image, which may bear a relationship to the original image, or it may simply be converted into a work of art through the artistic process. In either case, the creation of the picture involves the transformation of the original image.

What is the relationship between the original image and the image that is made of it? Is the latter created by means of the former? Or how is the relationship to be understood? When we look at Phidias's famous statue of Zeus, we may ask ourselves whether there was an image upon which this statue was based and, if so, where this could be found. As there cannot have been such an original, this image of Zeus is new. It was created through the artistic process itself—through working with the materials. Anyone who sees the statue recognizes the image, although we do not know the model for "Zeus" because it did not exist before this image was made. We can thus conclude that the work of art is an image searching for the image on which it was based—created to find its antecedent image in the human mind and thus to fulfill its destiny of becoming an image.[25] This image has no clear meaning; it is not an answer but a question that the work of art poses to its recipients, who can answer it in a variety of ways. The structure implicit in works of art creates images, contexts of meaning, and interpretations, and it is these that form the complexity and materiality of the work of art.

From this point of view, works do not become art or literature until there is an interaction between the work and the recipient.[26] This shifts the mimetic relationship to a different level. The work of art is no longer understood as an imitation of a prior image. The (decisive) process of imitation takes place between the work of art and the recipient. The aesthetic experience becomes a central factor in mimetic behavior. The work of art comprises certain content, forms, connotations, and statements, but these only come to life in the "aesthetic experience." The concept of mimesis loses some of its importance in the aesthetics of the modern age. The concept of the original creativity of man comes into conflict with an understanding of mimesis that has been reduced to imitation (*imitatio*) and results in the term becoming devalued.[27]

Mimetic processes are important for child-rearing and education, for the creation and communication of literature, art, and music, and also for the acquisition of practical social skills, as illustrated in the next section. We turn first, however, to the way mimetic processes are involved in the establishment and destruction of societies from the start. These processes permeate the social hierarchies and orders, and their effects are highly ambivalent. They help to establish social orders, and at the same time they endanger them and work toward their destruction. On the one hand, they can be contained and channeled; on the other, such as when crowds form, they threaten to trigger violence and become uncontrollable.

Awareness of the "infectious nature" of mimetic processes is the basis of an influential theory of the origins of social violence.[28] The mimetic acquisition of attitudes and behavioral patterns creates competition and rivalry between the imitators and those imitated, which can trigger violence. A contradictory situation arises—the fact that the imitators strive to acquire characteristics from those they are imitating conflicts with the fact that both parties aspire to be different and to assert their uniqueness. This paradoxical situation leads to an increase in the potential for social violence.

Actions containing great emotional intensity seem to trigger the mimetic processes to a high degree; the infectious nature of laughter, love, and violence is proverbial. In many early cultures acts of violence were answered with acts of violence. This resulted in a vicious circle of violence that increased the extent and intensity of these acts. Not infrequently, the cohesion of societies was threatened by this; their response was to use *prohibitions* and *rituals* to attempt to control the mimetically intensified violence.

In mimetic crises where violence breaks out and cannot be suppressed by the use of prohibitions and rituals, a "scapegoat" might be ritually sacrificed in order to help to end the crisis.[29] A potential victim would be selected by common agreement, designated as the scapegoat, and sacrificed. The community was bound together by "mimetic antagonism," that is, by an alliance against the victim, who had been declared the enemy. A defenseless person was usually chosen unanimously, whose death would not unleash any further violence. Although the sacrifice was itself an act of violence, it was expected to bring an end to the mimetic circle of violent acts. The community came together in solidarity in the act of violence against the victim. This action gave them, to all appearances, the opportunity to free themselves from their own inherent violence.

The crisis was ended by the following mechanism of reversal. On the one hand, the victim was made responsible for the violence inherent in society. This ascribed to the victim a power that he or she did not have; yet it still enabled the society to relieve itself of the burden of its own potential for violence. On the other hand, the victim was given the power of reconciliation, which occurred in the society after his or her death. Both cases involve processes of attribution and transference that are intended to ensure that the sacrifice will have the expected results. The return of peace was interpreted as proof that the victim was responsible for the *mimetic crisis*. This assumption was, of course, an illusion. It was not society that was suffering from the aggression of the victim, but the victim who was suffering from the violence of society. In order for this mechanism of reversal to function, it was important that people should not be aware of these two processes of transference onto the victim. If people realized the truth of what was happening, the victim would lose his or her reconciliatory, liberating powers.

Social Action and Mimetically Acquired Practical Knowledge

The capacity for social action is acquired mimetically in cultural learning processes. This has been shown in numerous studies in recent years.[30] In mimetic processes people develop skills that differ from one culture to another, in games, the exchange of gifts, and ritual behavior.[31] To act "correctly" in each situation, people need practical knowledge. This is acquired in sensory, body-orientated, mimetic learning processes in each different field of activity. The corresponding cultural characteristics of social behavior can also only be learned using mimetic approximations. Practical knowledge and social activity are shaped largely by historical and cultural factors.[32]

In a first approximation, we can regard social acts as mimetic if they meet the following conditions:

- They relate to other movements.
- They can be understood as performances or enactments of the body.
- They are independent actions that can be understood in their own terms and that relate to other actions or worlds.[33]

Thus nonmimetic actions would be mental calculation, decisions, reflex actions, or routine behavior, as well as unique acts or rule-breaking.

The relationship between social action, practical knowledge, and mimetic acquisition of knowledge is demonstrated by the following example taken from everyday contemporary culture.

A woman is about to celebrate her birthday, and her partner wants to give her a present. He wonders what she might like. Initially he does not have many ideas. It should not be something useful that she would buy herself. He rejects the idea of the fondue set she has shown him in a catalogue, which would be a present for them both rather than a birthday present, and he finds this a little too impersonal for his partner. His thoughts focus on what she would like and what would really give her pleasure. He looks through the art books in a bookshop and then through the latest novels. Then he remembers that last year she gave him an album of photographs from the early days of photography, so he decides that a book would not be the correct choice. In an antique shop he looks for a candlestick or an

THE MIMETIC BASIS OF CULTURAL LEARNING

old lamp. He likes what he finds but is still not satisfied. Then he sees a garnet ring. He remembers that she once told him that her grandmother had such a ring, which she had loved to try on when she was a little girl. Now he is certain that he has found the right present.

On the morning of her birthday he prepares a glass dish decorated with ivy leaves and fills it with water, he makes little boats from walnut shells and places a candle in each one. Next to the dish there is a birthday cake, a large bunch of roses, a bottle of champagne, and the ring, which is packed in a large box, to make it more of a surprise. Breakfast is waiting on the table, which has been elaborately set; his wife waits outside the room until he has lit all of the candles and opened the champagne. He takes her in his arms, they exchange a few words of affection, and she is delighted with the preparations and the present he selected so lovingly. They both sit down and have breakfast—taking slightly longer than usual. The day begins.

This scene shows us how a man looks for a birthday present and, after going to a good deal of trouble, finds it, and how he stages and performs the giving of the present and the small, early morning birthday party. His efforts are successful and bring great joy. Even when searching for the present, the man avoids decisions that would make the present less meaningful for his wife. He selects neither a useful nor a "joint" present; he also avoids giving her a present similar to the one she had given him recently. After a long search, he finds something that is particularly suitable for his partner and that will appeal to her individually. His sensitive selection of a present is complemented by the loving preparation of the breakfast table—candles floating amidst the leaves, roses, champagne, a birthday cake, the wrapped present, the elaborately set table, the tender words, and the embrace.

How does the man celebrating his wife's birthday know what he has to do to show her his affection and to turn his efforts into a confirmation of the emotional quality of their shared life? Nobody has given him a set of rules to follow when celebrating birthdays or giving presents. Nevertheless, the man still has a knowledge of what to do and what criteria are important when selecting the gift and setting the stage to give it. How does the recipient know what the chosen present and the early morning celebration arranged in such a manner mean, and how she is supposed to react for the breakfast to become a celebration of their togetherness? No one has ever told her what the rules are either. However, they both know their roles, what they need to do, and how they should respond to each other so that the morning becomes a celebration of their life together.

195

Such situations are only successful because all the participants have a *practical knowledge* of what they need to do, how they should respond to each other, and how they should present themselves. Their actions are derived from practical knowledge of which situations are to be performed, how and when to perform them, and how their performance and staging can meet or contradict the expectations of others. They have learned this in the many opportunities provided by everyday life, where they perceived through their own senses the way their parents prepared birthday celebrations for them, their siblings, or each other. In these earlier situations there may well not have been candles floating amidst ivy leaves or thoughts that resulted in the purchase of a garnet ring. However, there will have been other scenes involving the search for presents to delight the recipients, the loving, thoughtful attitude toward the birthday celebrant, and the joy of a shared life. There will have been other birthday scenes where, for example, siblings expressed their affection in a teasingly aggressive manner, where "Happy Birthday" was sung, and presents were given that had been expressly asked for. In spite of such differences, birthday parties resemble each other in a number of aspects. In mimetic processes inner pictures, feelings, and performative sequences arise in the participants, which serve as material from which they can fashion the scene of the giving or receiving of a present or of celebrating or being celebrated in similar situations.

Wherever someone acts in reference to an existing social practice and thereby creates a social practice, there is a mimetic relationship between the two. This occurs, for instance, when one performs a social practice such as the giving of a birthday present, or when one acts according to a social model or uses the body to express a social concept. As we have seen, this does not simply involve actions of imitation. Mimetic actions are not mere reproductions that follow a preexisting image precisely. Social practices performed in a mimetic manner lead to the creation of something individual.

Unlike the processes of mimicry, which merely require an adaptation to given conditions, mimetic processes—as we can also see in the example of the birthday present—create both similarities to *and* differences from the situations or persons to which or whom they relate. In "adapting and becoming similar" to situations experienced earlier and to worlds that bear the mark of the culture of which they are part, the subjects acquire the skills required to behave appropriately in a certain social situation. By participating in the living practices of other people, they expand their own lifeworlds and create for themselves new ways of experiencing and acting. Receptivity and activity overlap. In this process, the given world becomes interwoven with the individual experience of those who form a mimetic relationship with it. We recreate the situations and external worlds experienced earlier and, by duplicating them, turn them into our own. It is only by confronting earlier situations or external worlds that these gain their individuality. Not until this happens does our excess drive lose its indeterminate nature and become directed into individual wishes and needs. The confronting of the external world and the creation of the self occur as part of one and the same system. The external and internal worlds become increasingly similar and can only be experienced in their mutual dependency. Thus the internal and the external take on similarities and begin to correspond to each other. People make themselves similar to the outside world and change as they do so; this transformation involves the changing of their perception of the external world and of themselves.

Mimetic processes lead us to perceive similarities and create links to our social environment, and it is through experiencing this that people make sense of the world. One of the earliest human skills was to create similarities, and these can be seen clearly in phenomena that correspond in a sensory way. Similarities can occur between two faces or in processes where one person imitates the actions of another. Forms of similarity can also be found between the living and the inanimate. One of the purposes of the human body is to create and express similarities. Dance and language illustrate this clearly; in them there is no difference between representation and expression, on the one hand, and performance and behavior, on the other. They form two aspects that are not separate in the act of mimesis but inextricably linked.

The acquisition of practical knowledge in mimetic processes does not necessarily involve similarities. Similarity is nevertheless a frequent trigger for the mimetic impulse. However, creating a magical contact can also become the initial point of mimetic action.[34] A mimetic relationship is even necessary to distinguish actions from existing social practices, and it is only this that gives us the option of accepting, changing, or rejecting previous social actions.

Previous social actions are carried out for a second time in mimetic learning processes. The relationship is created not by theoretical thinking but aisthetically, through the senses. The second action differs from the first not by challenging it or altering it but by re-performing it; thus, the mimetic action has both a revelatory and a performative character, and its performance creates its own aesthetic qualities. Mimetic processes relate to social worlds already created by humankind that are either real or imaginary.

The dynamic character of social activities is connected with the practical nature of the knowledge required to enact them. As practical knowledge, it is less subject to rational controls than is analytical knowledge. This is also because practical, ritual knowledge is not a reflexive, self-aware knowledge. It only becomes this in the context of conflicts and crises, where the actions that result from it require justification. If social practice is not questioned, practical knowledge remains "semi-conscious."[35] Like habitus knowledge, it embraces images, schemas, and forms of activity that are used for the staging and bodily performance of social acts without requiring any reflection on their appropriateness. They are simply known and called upon for the staging of social practices.[36]

Human beings' residual instinct, the hiatus between stimulus and response, and also their "ex-centricity" are prerequisites of the extraordinary plasticity of humankind and the opportunities this provides for acquiring practical knowledge in mimetic processes,[37] thereby allowing social action to be conceptualized, staged, and performed. This practical knowledge also includes the body movements that are used to stage scenes of social action. Discipline and control of body movements result in a disciplined and controlled practical knowledge that is stored in the body memory and enables human beings to enact the corresponding forms of symbolic actions and scenic arrangements. Practical knowledge is based on the social forms of action and performance established in a particular culture, and is therefore a pronounced but specific knowledge, limited in terms of its historical and cultural horizons.

Imitative change and adaptation of previous worlds take place in mimetic processes. This is the innovative factor of mimetic actions.[38] Social practices are mimetic if they relate to other actions and can themselves be seen as social arrangements that constitute independent social practices and also relate to other practices. Social actions are made possible by the acquisition of practical knowledge in the course of mimetic processes. The practical knowledge necessary for social actions is not only historical and cultural but also body and ludic knowledge. It is formed in face-to-face situations and is not semantically unequivocal; it has components of the imaginary and cannot be reduced to intentionality. It incorporates an excess of meaning and is evident in the social stagings and performances of religion, politics, and everyday life.

EIGHT

Theories and Practices of the Performative

The aspect of acting, speaking, and behaving that is closely linked to the human body and has to do with staging and performing is known as *performative*. The performative view of human activity differs from reading the symbolic structures of actions as though they were texts and analyzing them hermeneutically. Focusing on the performative character of interaction adds a perspective to the world of cultural activity and behavior that reveals a fundamental difference between the staging and performing of human behavior and its interpretation. In the first case, an action takes place that requires the application of skill for its execution. In the second case, the interpretation of the action takes place after the event, and this interpretation requires hermeneutic skills. Practical knowledge is required to carry out actions; hermeneutic knowledge is required to interpret them. When focusing on the performative, one difficulty consists in detecting how the performative aspects of social and aesthetic practices actually come into being.

Three aspects were important in the development of the concept of performativity. One was developed in the field of cultural anthropology and relates to different forms of *cultural performances* (Milton Singer). The second aspect was developed in the philosophy of language, and looks at *performative utterances* (John L. Austin). The third aspect relates to the aesthetic side—*performative art*. The core of this last concept is the staging and performing of the body and its ability to portray and express itself. In these aesthetic

FIGURE 8.1   Magician's hands, gesturing. © Ryan McVay/ Photodisc/Getty Images.

performances, there is no text, as in the theater, and therefore there are quite new opportunities for the staging and performing of the body. *Performativity* is used as a derivative term that designates all these aspects and can be defined as *the combination of cultural performance, speech as action, and the (aesthetic) staging and performing of the body.*

Human activity creates *cultural performances.* According to Milton Singer, these include "particular instances of cultural organization, e.g., weddings, temple festivals, recitations, dances, musical concerts, etc."[1] In Singer's view, such performances are used to express and represent the self-image of a culture to its members and to outsiders. "For the outsider these [performances] can be conveniently taken as the most concrete observable units of the cultural structure, for each cultural performance has a limited time span, a beginning, a place and occasion of performance."[2] The term, in its pure sense, can also be applied to everyday actions. In this case, cultural performance is understood as the corporeality, staging, and event character of social actions. Social and cultural activity is more than just the realization of intentions. This additional aspect has to do with the way people fulfill their intentions by staging and performing them. The reasons behind the *modus operandi* for these actions lie in the historical and cultural circumstances, in the specific features that make up the individuality of the participants, and in the event nature of social action and practice.

Verbal utterances that are also actions are performative. Performative utterances have four features that distinguish them from other utterances.[3] The first of these is the *self-referential* character of performative utterances. They often feature the word *hereby*. In this case something is done as something is said, e.g., "I hereby christen you Louise." The second feature is the *declarative* character of such utterances. Making a statement is sufficient for it to become a reality. This is the case, for example, when an American jury states, "The defendant is guilty," which has the consequence that the accused is deemed to be guilty. Such performative utterances are frequently *linked to social institutions*. This is the case, for example, during wedding ceremonies, the conclusion of contractual negotiations, and appointments to an office. Finally, performative utterances consist of *utterances formulated in advance*, which have a repetitive or stereotypical character. If one uses the term *performative* in a broader sense, then the focus shifts to the performative character of language and thus to the relationship between body and language. In this connection, it is possible to analyze texts in terms of their performativity. How can the relationship between language and the use of the body be determined from a text? How are feelings, laughter, and gestures staged and performed?[4] How do literary genres differ in regard to their performativity, etc.?

The third aspect of the performative relates to the creative *performance*. The nature of these performances is determined by three different factors.[5]

1. The *materiality* of the performance, which is determined by the location (theater, factory, public space) and the body of the performer, its movements, and the accessories (language, music, etc.).
2. The *mediality* of the performance and how it is presented to the audience—the use of pictures, excerpts from films, or *virtual reality*.
3. The *aesthetic aspects* of the performance, which are largely determined by its event characteristics.[6] Ludic elements and spontaneous actions play an important role here, as well as the fact that there is no script to dictate proceedings.

When *performativity* is discussed in cultural studies, the factors of *cultural performance*, *language as action*, and *aesthetic aspects* of the staging and performing are considered in relation to each other. This may be done, for instance, in studies on social behavior or research into rituals and how social behavior is engendered by the performative nature of ritual actions (see chapter 9). Here the focus is on the social and cultural shaping of the body and the performative, practical knowledge stored within it. This knowledge is corporeal, ludic, and ritualistic; it is also historical and cultural. Performative knowledge evolves in *face-to-face* situations and is semantically ambiguous. It is aesthetic and evolves in mimetic processes. It also has imaginary components, contains a multiplicity of meanings, and cannot be reduced to intentionality alone. It is expressed in the performances and staging of everyday life, literature, and art.[7]

The etymology of the word *performative* goes back to the Latin *forma*, which means "form, figure, appearance and character"; the verb derived from it means "to fashion, to represent, or to form." Etymologically, the term *performativity* refers to the presentation, associated with a person's appearance, of the body in its own particular form and showing the marks of life. Performativity thus also relates to the staging and performance of the body from an etymological point of view. Each bodily expression is based on a certain staging of the body, irrespective of whether this is conscious or not. Performativity relates to the human ability to take up an "ex-centric position" (Plessner), that is, not only to *be* within our bodies but also to *have* them. We have to design ourselves and perform ourselves in different settings. In order to be able to perceive and understand ourselves, we enact ourselves. It is in this staging, and its effects on others, and their reactions to our actions that we experience ourselves. The plasticity of the human body allows for a wide spectrum of different performances, as we can see by looking at history and other cultures. The range of forms of the performative found in different fields of human life and activity is closely linked to issues of social differentiation between the genders, generations, and social classes. Who can stage and perform what, when, and how is fundamentally a question of power.

Literature, art, theater, and music are also influenced by this. In these fields, however, the focus is largely on the staging and effects of symbolic and cultural power. These areas provide a platform for the possibilities of performative behavior. If we participate as readers, spectators, or listeners, we broaden our own performative options, which usually gives rise to pleasure. In the previous chapter, I referred to these processes as mimetic. In mimetic processes it is as if an imprint is taken of the staging and performance—the performative arrangement—and this is stored in the imagination and subsequently embodied. In this way, the performance is changed in the reader's, spectator's, or listener's imagination. In art

FIGURE 8.2 Masked monks dance in a traditional *tsechu*, an annual religious festival. The *tsechu* is the most significant festival in Bhutanese Buddhism. *Tsechu* are held in honour of Guru Rimpoche and consist mostly of dances that depict the life of the Guru in twelve episodes. The dances are performed not only by monks, but also by lay people. The dance that incorporates traditionally designed colorful masks is the highlight of the festival. © Pete Ryan/ National Geographic/ Getty Images.

and culture every repetition contains novel elements. These can differ in intensity and range from minor deviations to almost completely new creations.

These components of the mimetic process, in which change and novelty are brought about, can be described as performative. Especially in open societies, the relationship between repetition and innovation tends to clearly favor the latter. Wolfgang Iser views this as a reason to use the term *performativity* to refer to this aspect of the creation of novel forms.[8] Theodor W. Adorno, Paul Ricoeur, and Gunter Gebauer and Christoph Wulf,[9] on the other hand, regard the very simultaneity of the reference to a previous world and the re-creation of this reference as being the distinctive feature of mimetic processes. Ricoeur suggests that a distinction should be made between prefigurative, configurative, and transfigurative processes—or simply Mimesis 1, Mimesis 2 and Mimesis 3. Taking Aristotle's view of literature as mimesis of action as a starting point, Mimesis 1 focuses on the references of poets, artists, and musicians to the world outside of their art, Mimesis 2 on artistic creation, and Mimesis 3 on the processing of the artistic work by the reader, viewer, spectator, or listener. By the very fact of making this distinction between the prefigurative, configurative, and transfigurative processes, Ricoeur is able to uphold the unity of the mimetic process. In his view performance is primarily a mode of articulating mimetic processes. In his *Aesthetic Theory*, Adorno also does not describe the mimetic process as merely imitating what already exists; rather, the mimetic process is an objection to what exists and creates something that did not exist before. According to Adorno, "The being-in-itself to which art works are devoted is not the imitation of something real but rather the anticipation of a being-in-itself that does not yet exist."[10] For Adorno, the peculiar characteristic of mimetic processes is that they create something new that did not exist before and yet is based on something existent. In this view also, staging and performing are seen as integral components of mimetic processes.

Performances bring something to light that cannot be objectified. This "staged unavailability" can be seen in literature, art, theater, and music "because staging allows the otherwise impossible state that one can experience one's own ability to have oneself."[11] Staging demonstrates "the extraordinary plasticity of human beings who, precisely because they do not seem to have a determinable nature, can expand into an almost unlimited range of culture-bound patternings. The impossibility of being present to ourselves becomes our possibility to play ourselves out to a fullness that knows no bounds, because no matter how vast the range, none of the possibilities will 'make us tick.'"[12] Within this structure of staging, we can see "an anthropological mode that can claim a status equal to that of knowledge and experience insofar as it allows us to conceive what knowledge and experience cannot penetrate."[13] It is the task of historical cultural anthropology to examine to what extent this anthropological structure is also valid for other periods and cultures.

Enactment and performance play central roles not only in the arts but also in social and community life. Rituals and ritualized events are good examples of this, as their enactment and performance character—their performativity—leads to the formation of communities (see chapter 9).[14] With rituals, the extent to which their staging and performance are linked to social hierarchies and issues of power is apparent. This is why many rituals are used to settle differences and questions of power.[15] Rituals blend aspects of bodily and cultural performance with linguistic, symbolic, and aesthetic features. Historical studies and analyses that compare different cultures show the diverse ways in which rituals are staged and performed.[16] Not only in ritual arrangements, but also in the staging and performing of human behavior in general, the limitations on the possibilities of performance depend on the constitution of the body, and today even that can change, thus further expanding our performative possibilities.[17]

After the *linguistic* and *iconic turns* of the 1970s and 1980s, in which it became evident that cultural action and understanding depend on language and images, the last decade of the twentieth century saw a *performative turn* in cultural sciences.[18] Here cultural behavior is viewed in terms of staging and performance. All three turns are shifts toward an *anthropological view*. The first is concerned with the dependency of human interaction and understanding on language, the second with the role played by the imaginary in the constitution of culture, and the third with the form and structure of human action focused on the human body. In the course of the three turns, there was a shift toward applying the principles of historical cultural anthropology. Furthermore, in most research on performativity, explicit attempts are being made to include the perspectives of the other two turns. This is possible because the two different aspects of performativity—performative utterance and aesthetic performance—directly relate to the performative side of language and images.[19]

The focus on performativity in cultural sciences has had a number of consequences for the methodology employed. Texts now have to be examined from the perspective of performativity. This can be done in different ways. What is most important, however, is to bring out the performative and action aspects of the texts. With images too, the aim is also to determine their performative aspects. Ethnographic and qualitative methods in the social sciences offer useful modes of exploring performative processes: participatory observation, photography, audio and video recordings, and individual and group interviews are all particularly suitable for describing and interpreting the performative dimension of the social, linguistic, and aesthetic performances of the body.[20] The following sections illustrate the importance of performativity as a perspective for cultural science research in the area of historical anthropology, using *perception, media*, and *gender constitution* as examples.[21]

Perception

On the basis of phenomenological studies that established the chiastic character of perception, perception is understood as a performative process that can be described as oscillating between the perceiving individual and the object perceived. In this process, the sensory is understood as "nothing other than a certain way of being in the world suggested to us from some point in space, and seized and acted upon by our body, provided that it is capable of doing so, so that sensation is literally a form of communion."[22] The bipolar nature of the oscillating movement of the perception process is realized in the two aspects of participation and distance; it is rhythmic and dependent on space. The bodily, medial, and historical dimensions are important for understanding this. Central to the bodily dimension is the chiastic structure, as defined by Maurice Merleau-Ponty, whereby objects and people look at each other, and the self and the world become intertwined in an intercorporeality. If one takes a wider concept of media, then the medial nature of perception and the differences created by it play an important role. For the anthropological approach, perception processes are both historical and cultural.

As Maurice Merleau-Ponty, Bernhard Waldenfels, and Gernot Böhme clearly state, space, which is not passive, but changes in relation to bodily movements, plays a central role in perception.[23] Michel de Certeau uses walking as an illustration of this: it is during the course of walking that space first becomes space.[24] This idea leads to the development of a *performative concept of space*.[25] Walking can be understood as a form of tactile perception. As anthropology and the psychology of perception have shown, spatial vision is based on scanning the shape, dimensions, and positions of three-dimensional objects. Such an overarching concept of perception can be described as a perception cycle. The perception cycle includes all of the senses and is produced by the interaction between perception and movement. The cycle cannot be split into individual stages, and it also indicates that every current perception both contains elements of past experiences and simultaneously anticipates future perceptions. Perception that is kinesthetic, multisensory, and transtemporal would seem to be central to a performative concept of space.[26] This performative space is an anthropological space. As such, it creates historically and culturally specific ways of staging and performing perception. At the same time it is created as cultural space by contemporary historical subjects. This pattern of interdependent construction can be seen in the spaces of medieval churches, in literary texts, in the spaces used for the sets of films, and in the visual spaces used in computer-generated virtual images.[27]

The space of the medieval church has a lifelong association, even today, with Christian memories of baptism, services, the Eucharist, and marriage ceremonies. What Christian believers experience today in liturgical rituals remains inextricably linked with the space of the church, which initiates these actions and in which they are performed. Christians of the Middle Ages experienced the sacred or holy in church far more intensely than Christians of today. Through experiencing the presence of the sacred, the atmosphere of the church, and the holy images, and absorbing them mimetically, Christians were able to align themselves with or become part of the space and the images and to contemplate their sinful lives. Correspondingly, it can be shown how the atmosphere and feeling of the spaces described in literature lead the reader into a fictitious world and set the scene for the unfolding action. The same applies to the spaces shown in films, in which the movement of images and the use of time play a central role. In virtual spaces, an additional interactive component comes into play that allows the user to become part of the creation of space.

Perception as a process is determined by movement and rhythm and is only "at home when in motion."[28] The performative character of perception is illustrated by aspects of the relationship between perception and rhythm. Rhythm consists of bodily motions coordinated in time and brought about by a repetition of contrasting elements. These elements often have a bipolar structure, similar to that of the heartbeat. Rhythm is not the modality of just one of the senses. As an element of time structure, it can manifest itself in different modalities, as happens in modern multimedia performances, for example. Such performances can give rise to synergetic effects that are interesting from an artistic point of view. Rhythmic phenomena are perceived psychologically and cognitively. They are recognized because they correspond to our sense of expectation and feel for regularity. The relationship between past experiences and expectations of the future plays an important role in this. We perceive rhythms by adjusting ourselves to a temporal structure of time and continuing movement. The experience of rhythm is based not only on regularity, but also on pauses and interruptions. Rhythm, as the interaction and interplay between memory, past experience, current experience, recognition, and the anticipation of something familiar, has been shown to be the basic underlying principle of every experience of performative processes.[29] Rhythms arise between the subject and the world and structure perception. In dance, for example, they not only inspire bodily movements, but also control them and discipline them. In the arts, particularly in music, but also in literature and theater, rhythms are also of central importance. Within the performative interaction of contrast and combination, they influence the creation of atmospheres and thus also aesthetic perception and experience.[30]

In general, when studying perception, it is important to explore categories of experience that have always emerged from an interaction of the senses. The more this interplay is controlled and has an internal hierarchy, the more clearly it enters our consciousness. Atmosphere, mood, ambience, rhythm, attentiveness, and so on all require a basic, coherent interaction of the senses and contribute to the definition and use of *perception* as an aesthetic phenomenon. For an approach oriented toward modalities of experience, it is important to realize that to understand perception adequately, we cannot retain our pure, clear-cut ideas of subject and object. Therefore the question of what it is that we see must always be accompanied by the questions of what is looking at us, why it is looking at us, in what manner it is looking at us, and how it deals with our looking at it. Perception is therefore action taken in relation to that which is perceived. What is it doing to us by looking at us, appealing to us, touching us, or making us bored, and why is it doing it?[31]

Media

On the assumption that a medium can be anything that is used as such, we must, on the one hand, avoid falling into a media fundamentalism that views media as the source of the creation of the world, as the point of articulation of our relationships to the world and ourselves, and as filling the void left by the erosion of the modern concept of subject.[32] On the other hand, we must also beware of going to the other extreme of media marginalism, identifying media merely as the material prerequisites for the realization of sign processes. A performative concept of media must try to steer a middle course between these two extremes and examine questions such as whether communication by means of media can be understood as both transforming and subverting what is communicated. In this process, practices of embodiment assign what is invisible or unavailable in our immediate vicinity a position in time and space by means of a sublime interaction between incorporation and excorporation. In this context, "representation" must be understood not as going beyond the normal boundaries of the senses to a sense that lies beyond, but as allowing meaning to be created out of the very process of rendering something sensory. Media are the historical grammar of our way of dealing with what is at a distance. Media abolish space, allowing the distant to appear in our local worlds. Media phenomenalize—their communication function is based on making things perceptible, on aistheticization (131–32). Since *medium* has the meanings "medium," "mediator," and "means," its role as a means is the focus of the present-day discussion, and its function as a mediator is ignored or reduced to that of a means of communication. In what follows I link the use of media to their role as mediators. Media permit us to see and to hear. The perceptive function of media is therefore fundamental: their cognitive and communicative role feeds on this aistheticization potential (132). Media make an object that is foreign to them appear. Therefore media-in-use are always hybrid forms. This hybridity becomes clearly evident in intermediality.

In the history of the media, we have hardly ever seen one medium simply being replaced by another, as is often believed. It is more productive to examine the interference and competition among different media, and the instances in which they overlap. As one medium becomes redundant, it frequently opens the way for the development of a new medium. Developments in the history of the media cannot be described as linear processes or as radical changes. Rather, historically documented situations in which media have been used reveal interferences between old and new media, which in combination transcend the functions of the individual media (141). Media can convey information and create reality. However, their inherent "waywardness" may also disturb these processes of communication and creativity. It is useful to investigate these interferences to gain a better understanding of the relationship between mediality and performativity.

In literary and artistic media configurations, boundaries between media are both drawn and transgressed. The resulting intermediality includes switches from one medium to another, combinations of media, and intermedial relationships. Creating links between one medium and another produces an illusion-generating quality that helps the recipient to recall the experiences associated with the respective "other" medium. For example, with the literary means available to them, authors of narrative texts cannot really zoom in, fade pictures into each other, or apply any of the other techniques, conventions, and rules of film. However, elements and structures of the other media system can be evoked and simulated with the means available to the medium with which one is working. In this way, the recipient has the impression of cinematic, pictorial, or musical qualities, or a general visual and acoustic atmosphere is created (143). In contrast to such cross-references between media, it is also possible to combine different forms of media as, for example, in the installations of the German sound artist Andreas Oldörp, who combines material sculptures with sound and space by creating sculptures that are also sound-producing instruments.

Multimedia installations create new opportunities for performative aesthetics. They create new ways to exhibit art by using technical media such as photographs, film, and videos, as well as the participation of the observer, thus lastingly transforming the relationships between space, perception, and performativity. In so doing, they bring about a paradigmatic shift in aesthetic experience, from an aesthetics of the work or object to a process aesthetics that must be seen as performative (151). This is illustrated by Gary Hill's *Tall Ships* installation (1992), in which video sequences are projected along a line that runs along the middle of the ceiling of a long, dark, narrow room. These images are only seen if the viewer walks through the room and triggers the video projections by means of sensors. In this case, the use of space becomes a means of creating interactions between mediality and performativity. The following three aspects are important for the relationship between the two:

"(1) the role of movements and kinesthetic processes, since, wherever they move, the positions of viewers of an installation are constantly in a direct relationship with the multimedia environment; [. . .] (2) the relationship between the viewers and large-scale audio-visual projections. Here we are concerned with the question as to what extent the viewers see themselves as part of the projection area, causing a three-dimensional effect to emerge from the two-dimensional surface which has a decisive influence on how the space is experienced; [. . .] (3) the removal of the fundamental separation of the inner and outer worlds in the experience of space, in favor of a threshold experience where the inner and outer dimensions of the perceived space permeate each other [. . .]" (157–58).

We now come to the processes of embodiment and disembodiment that occur during exposure to the old and new media. The voice and gestures have particular significance as communication media. From a performative perspective, language cannot be separated from its actual medial form. Language as we speak it is not a pure, ideal language but an interactive interweaving of language, voice, and gestures. This interdependence becomes apparent when we remind ourselves that people who speak several languages have different voices in each language. The sound of a voice is shaped by the language that one usually speaks. In addition to knowledge of grammar and vocabulary, to be able to speak a language, one also requires vocal skills, that is, a knowledge of which voice or, to be more specific, which intonations and timbres are suitable in which contexts.

Roland Barthes spoke of the "grain" of the voice in this context—a notion that conveys the role not only of the personal nuances but also of the influences on language that go beyond the personal level. As a medium of speech, the voice is not a "transparent" communicator of semantic content that can be theoretically conceptualized independently of this content. The voice does not simply communicate something that is essentially different from the voice itself. Insofar as the voice shows anything at all, what it shows contributes to the *content* of what is said and at the same time goes beyond it. This suggests a new model of communication that differs radically from the conventional transmitter-receiver model, that is, communication as making music together (163). In terms of time, the voice is always in the present; it is never neutral; it has a dynamic of its own and always communicates something about the speaker of which he or she is not fully aware. The voice, like a face, is considered one of the most distinguishing features of a person. No two voices are alike. Yet the uniqueness of the voice does not evolve in a vacuum. Voices can only develop in relation to other voices. Every voice carries the traces of other voices. When we think about the unique qualities of a voice, we also need to examine the alterity of the voice (164). Every voice contains other voices that have been absorbed into its own peculiar character in mimetic processes.[33]

Aside from the voice, gestures are also part of the old media of embodiment. They are not merely the mute accompaniments of language. There are several different types of gesture: gestures that accompany speech, gestures that are similar to words, emblematic gestures, and sign languages. Most research on gestures has focused on their expressive and appeal functions and only to a lesser extent on their illustrative function, in which they are themselves part of the message and contribute directly to its meaning. Gestures have individual and universal components, as well as elements relating to individual cultures and languages. Thus, in addition to the fact that gestures are becoming increasingly "linguistic" in character, the gesture system includes a continuum of gestures, ranging from the idiosyncratic to the conventional. On the other hand, all gestures have both idiosyncratic as well as cultural and language-specific traits.[34] Gestures are closely linked to the performative nature of human communication and the bodily performances of human beings. Like the voice, they also have a medial function: they communicate something that did not exist and was not perceivable before. From the start, performativity has played a role in the use of new media. "We are reminded of the theatre-like aspects of the computer world, the emphasis on the lack of permanence and modifiability of writing in hypertext or the performative construction of identities in Internet chat rooms, etc."[35] As a medium, the computer engenders new forms of knowledge and interaction that are not possible without it and structures them according to the conditions of its mediality. Its image-creating processes render the invisible visible. Since it came on the scene, its performative character has been a major contributing factor to the increasing awareness of the performative dimension of anthropological research.

Gender

Research on women's issues conducted in the 1960s and 1970s assumed that women were the victims of a society dominated by men, and the main objective was to rewrite the history of women. In contrast, gender research, a field that has been developing and expanding since the 1980s, focuses on the differences among women as well as on the differences among men and the relationship between gender and other categories that lend themselves to the creation of hierarchies, such as race, ethnic group, religion, class, status, sexual orientation, and disability. Gender research is no longer concerned with "women" or "men," but with investigating cultural representations and interpretations of gender differences and how these are naturalized by being related to biological phenomena.[36] Instead of assuming a polarization between man and woman or nature and culture, this research places much more emphasis on understanding gender difference as a central element in the creation of cultural meanings, and on linking these to their respective historical and cultural contexts.

In anthropology, gender is understood as being subject to historical and cultural change. Gender identity is not assigned by nature, but created by performative acts.[37] The decisive factors in its evolution are repetition, quotability, processuality, and action. *Embodiment practices* and the interrelationships within the triad *sex/gender/desire* play a major role when we consider the issues of the performativity of gender and gender identity, which are investigated using data from different historical eras and cultural contexts. From a methodological point of view, major focuses include placing concepts in a historical context, linking data analysis with existing theoretical concepts, and the subversion of gender norms.

In contrast to approaches that use discourse analysis, which build on Michel Foucault's social constructivism, in which the effects of culture on the body are viewed as resulting from knowledge and power structures, the concept of *embodiment* applied here focuses attention on three areas. One is the processuality of embodiment in the development of gender identity; another is relationality, which emphasizes the collective aspect of these processes; and the final aspect involves the historicity and culturality of real practices of embodiment. *Processuality* takes into account the fact that the embodiment of gender is a process with numerous repetitions, interruptions, and restarts, during the course of which the gender habitus is formed. Butler views the body on three levels: the body that materializes itself, that is, is subject to the discursive production of what can claim validity as the body; the body of the subject, which, as a somatic and melancholic body, imitates and thereby retains its identifications with the rejected same-sex love objects of childhood; and finally the acting body, which portrays gender identity in social interaction.[38] In this context the focus on the *relationality* of these embodiment processes directs the attention to the collective nature of the formation of gender identity. Subjects do not develop their gender alone, but in communities. The *historicity* of these embodiment processes implies that they are modifiable, that is, that different gender styles can develop.

The formative years play a very important role in the embodiment and acquisition of gender identity, and peer groups are particularly important toward the end of childhood. During the development of gender identity, values and attitudes learned in the family are adopted or rejected and replaced by new ones; movements, gestures, and postures are tried out and consolidated by repetition. Children are initiated into youth by their peers. Gender identity is also formed and reinforced by play and sports culture. Numerous sporting disciplines have a discernible gender geography with gender-specific allocations, divisions, and exclusions that are significant as expressions and modes of reinforcement of gender identity.

The second important concept in the development of gender identity is the triad of *sex, gender, and desire,* which can be understood as a heterosexual matrix and which Judith Butler uses to define a discursive dispositive consisting of the dimensions of sex, gender, and desire, which are interrelated.[39] We can gain some insight into the prevailing orders of the sexes by analyzing unsuccessful instances of enacting the heterosexual matrix. The performativity of gender behavior is particularly important in the transitional areas where new configurations of what separates male and female are formed. This is illustrated by *coming-out* stories, in which the status of being in-between is vital, or in *cross-dressing* experiences and the practice of *cross-casting* (casting a young boy in a woman's role) in theatrical performances of the early modern period. Cracks in the matrix can also be manifested by a desire that is articulated outside of this matrix, a fact to which *queer theory* has frequently drawn attention.[40] In Lacan's interpretation, "desire" has its origins in the loss of the mother as a love object and in the child's entry into a cultural system represented by language. A decisive difference between Lacan's position and that of Freud is that Freud believed that the libido can be satisfied by different objects, while in Lacan's view desire can never be satisfied, but shifts metonymically from one signifier to another. Desire is, therefore, "boundless, and the act a slave to limit" (Shakespeare, *Troilus and Cressida*).[41] These cracks in the heterosexual matrix have been looked at in examples taken from several different contexts, such as the coming-out stories of contemporary gays, the desire in male friendships described in medieval Lancelot narratives, and in the stagings of gender in Shakespeare's *As You Like It* in the early modern period.

The studies on practices of the embodiment of gender and of fractures and metamorphoses in the triad of sex, gender, and desire are prime examples of the central role that performativity plays in gender research today. Research in areas of collective practices yields new perspectives on the body as the *agent, material,* and *bearer* of gender differentiations.

NINE

The Rediscovery of Rituals

Social scientists and arts scholars have recently rediscovered rituals. This is no surprise, coming as it does after a period of sustained criticism of the chaotic complexity of the modern age and the decay and loss of social and ethical values. However, although decay and dissolution have been diagnosed and elaborated in postmodern discourses, the social order has remained relatively stable. This discrepancy needs explaining, and this is an area where research on rituals can make a contribution. Whereas the study of rituals in the context of National Socialism and the emancipation movement of the 1968 generation highlighted rigidity and violence, the current focus is more on the productive social role of rituals.[1] Rituals were long regarded simply as a means of restricting or suppressing individual freedom, but today they are once more viewed as important forms of social activity that are fundamental to the shaping of individual lifeworlds and social life. Rituals are thought to help compensate for the loss of identity, community, order, and security. Associated with this loss we find an increasing erosion of social and cultural systems and progressive individualization, while face-to-face communication is becoming increasingly rare, and virtualization is starting to permeate nearly all areas of human life.

Rituals play a central role in nearly all areas of human existence. They are indispensable in religion, politics, economy, science, families, and education. They help us to deal with difference and alterity and to create a sense of community and social relationship. They also enable us to assign meaning and structure to human relations. Rituals connect the past, present, and future. They facilitate both continuity and change, as well as experiences of transition and transcendence.² Given their significance in so many areas of social life, it is no surprise that there is no generally accepted theory of rituals, since the positions of the individual academic disciplines differ too widely. Scholars now generally agree that it makes little sense to reduce the wealth and diversity of studies on rituals to individual theories and lines of research. What is needed is rather to be aware of a wide variety of aspects and to render the complexity of the field explicit.³

The large range of theories on rituals parallels the broad spectrum of rituals. Whereas the major social rituals are clearly associated with spiritual transcendence, this association is not evident in many everyday rituals and rituals of interaction. The ritual arrangements of the latter are often combined with other everyday activities. Deciding whether a performative arrangement can be considered to be a ritual is frequently quite difficult. Defining what constitutes rituals is much more difficult in modern societies with relatively open views of the world and themselves than it is in societies with closed views, in which rituals are clearly identifiable. However, in view of the increasing social differentiation, we need to expand our concept of rituals, since it is only possible to perceive and analyze new ritual phenomena that characterize modern societies if we take a broader view. It is therefore necessary to state why each individual social phenomenon can be seen as a ritual and interpreted as such. The concept of rituals has a constructive side that can be used to analyze social processes from a particular viewpoint. The spectrum of ritual phenomena ranges from religious and political rituals through everyday rituals and includes, for example, young people's rituals of resistance, which enable them to express individuality and independence. The analysis of social phenomena as rituals or ritual arrangements gives us considerable insight into the deep structure of human social life.

All approaches to classifying rituals are faced with the fact that rituals are always the product of multidimensional processes of symbolization and construction. The phenomena studied are also more complex than the concepts and theories used to describe them. This also applies to the attempt to organize the field of *ritual studies* by types of occasion and to distinguish, for instance, the following kinds of rituals.

· Rituals of transition (birth and childhood, initiation and adolescence, marriage, death)
· Rituals of institution or taking up office (taking on new tasks and positions)

- Seasonal rituals (Christmas, birthdays, days of remembrance, national holidays)
- Rituals of intensification (eating, celebrating, love, sexuality)
- Rituals of rebellion (peace and ecological movements, rituals of youth)
- Rituals of interaction (greetings, taking leave, conflicts)[4]

Other attempts at classification are also conceivable and can provide orientation in the complex field of ritual research. It is possible to differentiate between the following types of ritual activity: *ritualization, convention, ceremony, liturgy, celebration.*[5]

The concept of *ritualization* is taken from ethology, where it is used to designate the ritual behavior of animals in the context of mating and aggressive behavior. Ritualized behavior has an initiating character and triggers the desired reactions. It gives signals and formalizes in an expressive and repetitive fashion. It reduces the ambiguity of social situations. It leads to species-specific sexual and social behavior and reduces individual sources of error. In spite of some common features shared by animals and humans, the differences between human and animal behavior are remarkable. Whereas animal behavior is mostly genetically conditioned, human behavior is subject to cultural variations.

The term *convention* is used to designate the area of ritualized everyday activity, in which every social subject learns the forms of interaction required for his or her way of life. The interactions contain practical knowledge of how we can automatically behave appropriately in any social situation, without having to think about it. Repetition and practice formalize and stylize these forms of interaction and behavior.[6]

Ceremonies, in which it is customary for large numbers of people to work together to achieve a mutual aim, are festive and celebrate the special nature of the situation. They demonstrate togetherness and are also expressions of power. Consecrations and inductions require a ceremonial marking of the new situation. National holidays and remembrance days require ceremonies as a demonstration of power and unity; these ceremonies give the political world and social institutions an opportunity to present and portray themselves.[7]

By contrast, *liturgies* are characterized by their transcendental aspects. They approach the sacred in an inquiring manner and open themselves up to it in "passive activity." Liturgies are symbolic actions that are deeply receptive, with meditative rites and contemplative practices. The participants expect to experience something that will reveal itself to them and over which they have no power. Liturgies represent the sacred and provide a feeling of security; they allow people to bring to mind, perform, repeat, and take possession of existential events.[8]

FIGURE 9.1   Praying in a Buddhist temple in Osaka. © Dr. Ingrid Kellermann.

Most *celebrations*, such as carnivals, birthdays, and weddings, also have ritual components. They are colorful and varied, and encourage spontaneity and social creativity. They accentuate the dramatic and expressive side of ritual events. They have ludic elements. They thus formalize feelings and expression. Questions as to continuity, authenticity, and origins are not asked.[9]

This classification of types of ritual action based on their appearance and effects assumes that all ritual phenomena have the same status and value. In this approach, the terms *ritual* or *ritualization* are not used as umbrella terms with a view to determining commonalities among different types of ritual phenomenon. Thus there is no way to analyze the structure of ritual phenomena with the aim of ascertaining what they have in common. Such analyses are, however, essential in comparative ritual research, which has the objective of investigating the conditions under which ritual activities are constructed and function.

Rituals serve to overcome differences and establish common interests. They create an inside and an outside world, and they include and exclude. This occurs not only on a linguistic-communicative level, but also on the bodily and material level. They channel real and potential violence and create order. The more "naturally" these processes take place, the less conscious do their social and historical aspects become, and therefore the less aware the participants are that rituals are per se always modifiable. The effects of rituals derive especially from the staging and performing of the body, whose materiality provides an additional aspect that goes beyond the symbolic meaning of the ritual and is incorporated in mimetic processes. Thus, when we take part in a ritual, the images, configurations, schemata, and sequences of ritual arrangements become established memories and imaginations and exert their effects there (see chapter 11). As these "impressions" of ritual activities are symbolically coded, their meanings are also inscribed in our bodies at the same time. Social relations and power structures play a vital role in these processes; they are enactments of our social hierarchies that, in turn, also affect the imaginary.

Historical Perspectives

If we are to understand the extraordinary significance that rituals have in the formation of society and culture, individuals, and communities, we must review the history of the development of ritual research and distinguish between the many different approaches that have been used in the attempt to grasp the complexity of this field. There are at least four different approaches. The first emphasizes the relationship between religion, rituals, and myth (James Frazer, Rudolf Otto, Mircea Eliade).[10] The second focuses on the role of rituals in understanding social structures (Émile Durkheim, Arnold van Gennep, Victor Turner).[11] The third reads rituals as texts in order to decipher the cultural and social dynamics of a society (Clifford Geertz, Marshall Sahlins).[12] Here the objective of the research is to understand the meanings of cultural symbolizations. Recent research has also used this third approach (Catherine Bell, Ronald Grimes, Victor Turner, Hans-Georg Soeffner).[13] The fourth approach is concerned with the performative aspects of rituals—the practical and bodily aspects (Stanley Tambiah, Richard Schechner, Pierre Bourdieu, Christoph Wulf).[14]

RELIGION, RITUAL, AND MYTH   The approach that focuses on the relationship between religion, the evolution of societies, and ritual grew up in the fields of theology and ethnology at the end of the nineteenth century. The key question here is whether religion has its origin in myth or in ritual. Whereas the Cambridge School of classicists tends more to assume that religion has its source in ritual, Mircea Eliade sees it as beginning in myth. James Frazer, on the other hand, believes that the first rituals were associated with religious cults and that myths were only ways of interpreting ritual practices. In work that follows Frazer's approach and also draws on the works of Jane Ellen Harrison,[15] myths and fairy tales are examined to see what traces of rituals can be found within them. On the other hand, myths can also be understood as sacred stories whose role is actually to ensure the timeless validity of ritual activities, which, in this view, are merely reenactments of cosmic myths. Both positions share the conviction that the point of both myth and ritual is to establish human life within a cosmic order and to provide it with continuity and coherence. Both positions also take the view that religion requires both mythical narratives and ritual practices in order to be embodied in our lives as we live in community with each other.

STRUCTURE AND FUNCTION The approach that centers on the social function of rituals seeks to gain an understanding in terms of their instrumentality. The purpose of rituals is to fulfill social tasks that would be extremely difficult or impossible to perform without them. Rituals structure the processes of institutions and social groups and serve to avoid conflicts or to solve them in such a way that the institutions are transformed but not destroyed. Rituals regulate social processes and thus maintain or transform relationships between various groups. According to Durkheim, they contain a set of behavioral rules that define how humans should approach the sacred, through which societies construct their images of themselves. Rituals arouse collective excitement and increased levels of activism in humans, which, in turn, cause individuals to identify with the wider community. In terms of being conducive to the transcendence of collective actions, rituals create a collective, religious self-conception in which the ritual participants are included and experience the meaning of their existence. This forms the affective basis for their identity and their relationships with other members of the community.

Arnold van Gennep's theory of the rites of passage is also implicitly functionalistic. Societies use rituals to organize transitions between places, times, states of mind, and phases of life. To help them occur smoothly, these transitions are divided into three ritual phases: "separation," "liminality," and "reincorporation." The first phase effects a detachment from the previous situation; the second phase involves the transition, including transformations and changes; in the third phase the new state that has been attained needs to be consolidated. Victor Turner's ideas build on this—he believes that rituals are part of the social dynamic by which institutions and organizations preserve, change, and renew themselves. These processes take place in the form of a "social drama" that is performed in four stages or acts. In the first act the differences and cracks in the social situation are recognized; in the second the crisis becomes conscious and escalates; in the third the ritualized coping patterns are set in motion; and, finally, in the fourth act there is either a successful reintegration or a final break. Rituals mediate between structure and antistructure, between rigid institutional structures and a state that has little structure, which Turner calls *communitas* (community). His concept of rituals as social dramas comes close to the views that highlight the performative character of rituals.

RITUAL AS TEXT   In approaching rituals as texts, scholars focus on their symbolic structure. Rituals are seen as symbolically coded actions and cultural units that need to be read and interpreted. Reading and interpreting them yields information on social relationships. These relationships are seen not so much in terms of their institutional dimensions as in terms of their semiotic and semantic aspects, as bearers of values and meanings. Rituals are understood as meaningful forms of interaction and communication in which the social element of human relationships draws on the cultural background of ritual communication. They are read as texts, and it is thus possible to create a "thick description" of a ritual activity (Geertz). This also involves understanding the subtext in which the central collective ideas of a culture come into operation and can be deciphered by means of deep hermeneutics. In the opinion of Sahlins, in Western cultures it is the institutionalization of the production of goods that plays the most prominent role. This makes them different from tribal cultures and many other cultures in which the symbolic criterion of differentiation or relationship is contained in social relationships, especially family relationships.[16]

Geertz sees culture as a "collage of texts"; thus it can be deciphered by reading symbolically structured and encoded rituals. Geertz used this approach to cultural analysis in his description and interpretation of cock fighting in Bali. Culture has such a lasting effect on humans because its concepts represent orders that are both descriptive and prescriptive. Thus rituals contain two factors that are quite distinct from each other: the *worldview*, that is, the cognitive, existential aspects of a culture; and the *disposition*, that is, the mood and motivation requirements of social acts that are specific to each culture. It is not possible to draw up a hierarchy between the worldview and the disposition to act—both are equally primordial. Symbols and ritual activities provide an image of social situations and also the stimulus for action. Experiences are processed in the symbolic systems of a culture and therefore they affect the ritual activities. In rituals the group ethos and the worldview of a culture are conveyed to the participants physically, in symbolic processes. Rituals are texts that can be read in order to gain an understanding of a culture and the actions of its members.

The three approaches described above are not mutually exclusive, but complementary. This applies in particular to the functionalistic and the hermeneutic approach, as well as to the performative approach described in the following section. Although the functionalistic approach frequently provides much information, rituals are overdetermined because of their bodily nature and cannot therefore be reduced to a simple completion of tasks. The manner in which the rituals are arranged and performed, their aesthetic form and style, cannot be captured by such an approach. Fruitful as the hermeneutic perspective may be, with its understanding of rituals as texts to be read, and instructive as it may be for the understanding of culture, its analyses cannot capture the performative character of rituals and the associated materiality of the body. On the other hand, despite the fact that these aspects are central to the performative approach, the symbolic structure of ritual and the hermeneutic approach employed to decipher it are indispensable. The same applies to the functionalistic view, without which ritual analysis is scarcely possible. Only the discussion about the relationship between rituals and myth and the focus on issues of religion and myths of creation seem to be of reduced importance for ritual research today.

Ritual and Performativity

The following section develops some central characteristics of the performative approach to ritual research, where the focus is on the staging and the practical, bodily aspect of rituals. It touches on a large body of theoretical and empirical research and demonstrates the complexity of ritual structures and activities.

(1) Rituals create *community*. Without rituals, communities would be unthinkable. Communities are formed in and by ritual activities. They are the cause, the process, and effect of rituals. The symbolic and performative content of ritual activities creates and stabilizes their identity. Rituals create social orders that all members of the community help to shape—albeit with differing levels of influence. These orders are both real and rooted in the imaginaries of the participants. They give them a

FIGURE 9.2 Ritual Christmas dinner in Berlin. © Dr. Ingrid Kellermann.

feeling of security by making the actions of other ritual participants predictable. The ritual framework creates a sense of similarity among the different actions of everyday life. It is rare for actions to occur outside of this
frame. When they do, their consequences are analyzed, or else the frame
is changed. This framing relates the actions of the ritual participants to
each other in such a way that they answer each other and thereby create
new actions in turn. Rituals are as predictable as their spontaneity and
their playful nature allow. Institutionalized and informal communities
have a collectively shared symbolic knowledge and ritualized forms of
interaction in which they perform and modify this knowledge. The repeated staging of this knowledge, which takes place in every ritual performance, is a mode of self-portrayal and a way of securing and transforming
social order. The addressing of differences from the world outside of the
group and within the group plays a major role. The group addresses the
differences within it in such a way that prevents them from endangering
the community but ensures that it will benefit. As a rule, this is done by
repeatedly staging and performing the ritual. As this is a joint activity,
the differences must be suppressed for the ritual action to be successful. If
this does not happen, and no ritual activities take place, the community

is at risk. Community evolves in ritual activities in the form of *performative community*.[17]

(2) During the *staging and performance* of rituals, a new social reality is created. This reality is not completely new, since previous versions of it have existed before; however, it has not existed in this particular form at this particular location before this particular time. Drawing on earlier rituals, every staging and performance creates a new ritual reality and a new ritual community. This ritual community can develop for the first time among the people who carry out the ritual actions, but it can also be experienced as a repetition through which the community confirms its status as such. The performance of rituals is decisive for the forming of communities. The community presents itself in the staging and style of the performance. In the ritual presentation it expresses something that cannot be portrayed in any other way. The ritual staging should therefore be seen as a "window" that provides a glimpse into the deep structure of the community and the culture that creates it. The staging and performing of rituals renders something visible that was previously invisible. What is decisive is that this occurs in the form of an action that creates a social reality that is partially independent of how it is interpreted.

The staging of rituals always includes a reference to previous ritual performances. However, this can vary greatly. In some cases the connection between old and new ritual performances is very close; in others it is very loose. However, in both cases the performance of the ritual establishes a form of continuity that is important for the effectiveness of the ritual. Often, the historical continuity stabilizes the social order of the community and legitimizes it. Continuity creates the impression that the social situation created in the ritual has always been the way it is and is therefore "natural." This frequently serves to uphold the current distribution of power and maintain social hierarchies and requires a critical analysis of the power relations.

(3) The *performative character* of rituals clearly takes effect in the staging and performance of rituals. The term *staging*, in this case, refers to the fact that rituals are enacted. Every ritual performance allows for different modes of enactment. It is very rare for rituals to be obsessive-compulsive acts that permit no deviations. In fact, this only occurs in pathological cases. The staging of rituals can take many forms. As in the case of the inauguration of the president of the United States, they may be performances that extend over a long period of time with detailed scenographies that have even been rehearsed.[18] In other cases the staging is more spontaneous and can barely be distinguished from the performance itself. Ritual templates are used in these cases; however, it is only decided

during the actual performance of the ritual how these templates are to be used. Spontaneous demonstrations are examples of rituals in which staging and performance largely coincide. However, it still makes sense to distinguish between staging and performance in these cases. Especially in such cases, the question arises as to who is staging the ritual—who is the agent or the agency of its performance? Is it a tradition, a group, a person, or the knowledge belonging to the collective imaginary, which is at the same time practical knowledge, out of which the ritual emerges?

(4) When we look at the staging and performance of rituals, the *bodies* of the participants are implicitly involved. How do these appear in a ritual? How are they enacted? What does their arrangement in the ritual tell us about the community, the individuals, and their culture? The movements and practices of bodies need to be considered.[19] How are they used to exploit the ritual space, and what rhythm do they follow? The distance between bodies and the manner in which they approach each other and distance themselves are significant. What positions do they take up? Do they stand or sit? What movements do they make when they dance? The configurations of the body are symbolically encoded and convey messages. In terms of gestures, which we can consider to be language without words, it is possible to distinguish between iconic and symbolic gestures. *Iconic gestures* are simple "pictorial" gestures with meanings that are largely independent of the knowledge of a historical time or a particular culture. Examples of such gestures are giving indications of dimensions with simple hand movements or expressing tiredness and the need for sleep by inclining the head and placing the hands together beside it. *Symbolic gestures*, on the other hand, have different meanings depending on the historical era or culture, and more precise historical and cultural knowledge is required to understand them. In all cases, the "logic" of the body, that is, its presentation and expression, plays an important role in the performance of rituals. This is especially true of the preconscious perception of bodily expressions, which forms the basis upon which the atmosphere of ritual arrangements is felt. The bodies of other people look at us before we become consciously aware of them, and in this way they determine our perception of them.[20] In order for the performance of rituals to result in community-building processes, people need to experience the flow of energies and forces between them as a physical and psychological process that takes place at the outer reaches of consciousness.[21]

(5) *Social hierarchies* and *power relations* are staged and enacted in the performances of rituals.[22] This is illustrated by the inauguration of the president of the United States.[23] This staged ritual shows that there is only one president. Demonstrating this publicly and broadcasting it to the

225

whole world on television is the task that this ritual fulfills. The staging clarifies who bears the power. In his speech, the president ostentatiously expresses the purposes for which he will use his political power. Ritual power structures are not always so easy to recognize. Judith Butler has repeatedly drawn attention to the fact that ritual repetition is one of the most effective social strategies for establishing and securing power structures.[24] Even belonging to a *gender* is tied to ritual repetitions, by which gender identities are created in the first place.[25] Issues of power that arise between the sexes and generations are also dealt with in everyday rituals at the family breakfast table—apparently incidentally, which makes them all the more effective.[26] Several things are handled simultaneously in ritual stagings and performances. Since the coherence of communities depends on their distribution of power, the control of this distribution is one of the central tasks of ritual arrangements. Balances of power are brought about irrespective of whether the associated issues are addressed directly, dealt with in passing, or expressly analyzed.

(6) Rituals are tied to time and space, and their cultural and historical conditions are experienced in these terms. Different spaces have differing effects on the structure, quality, and style of the rituals that take place within them. *Ritual spaces* differ from physical spaces. On the one hand, they create ritual stagings and performances;[27] on the other hand, rituals create ritual spaces using body movements, settings, and symbolic and indexical frames. Rituals and space are not related in terms of subject/ object or cause and effect, but interactively. Both rituals and spaces are performative. On the one hand, a decorated gymnasium provides the space for a school dance, just as a church provides the space for a confirmation ceremony. On the other hand, the school dance transforms the gymnasium into a ballroom, and the confirmation ceremony transforms the church into a living, sacred space. The intermeshing of real, virtual, symbolic, and imaginary spaces with the bodily movements of those taking part plays an important role in the development of ritual activities.

This intermeshing of real, virtual, symbolic, and imaginary spaces with bodily movements takes place in an environment shaped by historical and cultural factors. This results in an atmosphere that affects the mood of all the participants in the ritual. Actions that have already been carried out here before and for which the space is suitable are repeated as part of an attempt to adjust to the atmosphere, structure, and function of the space in which the ritual is being carried out. The participants change by mimetically recreating the conditions of the space around them. The performative effects of ritual spaces such as the church, the family living room, and the virtual space of electronic media are very different from one another and have different socializing effects.

(7) The other constituent condition of ritual activity apart from space is *time*.[28] Two complementary views are important for the manner in which humans deal with time. First, rituals play a major role in introducing children to the time structure of society. Parents attempt to adjust their children's rhythms to the time rhythms of society and thus to accustom even infants to the manner of structuring time that is the social norm. Childhood rituals are used to ensure that time becomes the main structuring influence in children's lives. Second, in our ritualized handling of time, we acquire practical knowledge that is indispensable for the staging and performance of rituals. Insofar as the management of time results from cultural learning processes, rituals play a very important part in this. Their repetitive character helps to inscribe the order of time into our bodies, which then become structured by time.

Many rituals are repeated cyclically. Their purpose is to assure us of the presence of the community and to reaffirm its order and potential for transformation. The aim of rituals is to stage continuity, timelessness, and constancy. They are oriented toward processuality and the projectivity of communities and individuals. As we structure our time in a ritualized manner, we learn to manage it as a social skill. In today's societies the ritual organization of time lends a structure to every aspect of communal life.

(8) Between the beginning and the end of a ritual, different sequences of ritual activity occur in which different kinds of actions are expected and carried out. The rule-bound nature of ritual activity is closely linked to its *sequentiality*.[29] The ritual actions follow an order that is also chronological. Periods of time are created in and by means of rituals that differ from the uniformity of everyday life and become moments of heightened intensity. This kind of intensification is due to the exceptional character of the events and is also achieved by highly condensing them and speeding them up. In many rituals, time becomes sacred time. Memory and reconnection with the past are therefore constitutive elements of religions, which, with the aid of rituals, transfer sacred content from communicative memory to cultural memory. They thereby render it accessible, so that it can be used to shape the future. In the experience of sacred time, it is not so much the length of time that counts as its intensity. On the one hand, rites of passage make it possible to experience different stages of life as phases with their own temporal dynamics;[30] on the other, they create continuity and meaning in the process of life. In the time structures

of rituals, different times often overlap, resulting in highly complex experiences of time.[31]

(9) Rituals also play an important role in the handling and processing of *difference and alterity*. We can see this in the rituals of the Moresca dances in the Middle Ages, which include, for example, ritual reenactments of the battle with the Moors and portrayals of courtly love scenes.[32] The ritual of the Moresca deals both with the foreign nature of the Moors in grotesque portrayals of battle and with the Otherness of the woman in male courtship. In both cases the task of the ritual arrangement is to come to terms with difference and alterity. Even in the multicultural contexts of modern societies, rituals are important for interactions between members of different ethnic groups. They can promote closer contact with what is foreign and the processing of differences and coexistence. School communities offer examples of both success and failures in this area,[33] and here the imaginary, symbolic, and performative elements are equally important.

(10) Rituals are essential for *religion* and *worship*,[34] regardless of whether one sees their importance in the creation and practicing of religious feelings in cult ceremonies or focuses on their capacity to create sacrality, in which society makes an image of itself. Even the inauguration ritual mentioned above has a recognizable sacred character that is manifested in the invocation of God and appeals to the nation. The magical character of ceremonies of promotion to a higher office also has many aspects in common with sacred ceremonies.[35] Even a candlelit dinner for two, where the candles on the table emphasize the special atmosphere of sharing a meal, begs the question as to whether the scene has elements borrowed from the sphere of the sacred and transferred to everyday life. The upgrading of such customs by adding sacred symbols may be connected to the far-reaching changes in attitudes toward religion and sacred matters that we are currently experiencing.[36]

As the current European *orientation toward life before death* increases, *religion* becomes invisible, *lifeworlds* become more clearly differentiated, and we are forced more and more to live in heterogeneous frames of reference, we see a waning of the influence of the more monolithic rituals that cut across different lifeworlds.[37] Such major rituals also seem to be becoming less important not only for individuals but also at the level of states, societies, and the worlds of politics and economics. They are being replaced by smaller rituals that relate to specific lifeworlds and change according to institution and context. As rituals become more domain-specific, they bring fewer people together than previously. Since most people act in several different sectors of society, they participate in different rituals and rites, some of which are only recognized as such in the respective lifeworld. These partial rituals include many leisure-time rituals that one must master with a certain degree of skill in order to be accepted by the group in question.[38] The diversification of religions and other areas that were once central to our society has resulted in rituals becoming less visible. However, the diversification of ritual activity is not associated with a fundamental loss of significance for rituals. Individuals need rituals and ritual activities more than ever in order to be able to create performative subgroups. Many rituals evolve that are only valid in a limited context but are nevertheless indispensable.[39]

(11) The *synchronous* and *diachronous* aspects of *mimetic processes* are important for the success of ritual activities.[40] During the performance of rituals, the participants refer simultaneously and directly to the actions of other participants. They do so largely by means of mimesis, using the senses, the movements of the body, and a joint orientation toward words, sounds, language, and music. A ritual can only take place as a structured whole if all actions are successfully coordinated and precisely orchestrated. Here the staging is indispensable; however, the performance itself is the decisive factor, as the ritual actions need to be exactly coordinated. Otherwise the results are farcical, and the ritual breaks down. If the interaction is to be harmonious, the ritual activities must be mimetically coordinated with each other. If this is achieved, energies can "flow" between the ritual participants, and this is experienced as intense, pleasant, and bonding. As in dance or courtship behavior, the rational control of actions also has limits in rituals. We only have the feeling that a ritual is successful if a mimetically created harmony that is beyond rational control develops between one body and another, one movement and another, and one gesture and another. These mimetic processes form the basis of the feeling of belonging to a community as well as the experience of the sacred.

Whereas the synchronous dimension of mimetic processes relates to the importance of mimetic processes in the actual conduct of rituals, the diachronous dimension relates to the historical aspects of rituals. Rituals always relate to others that have taken place before—either ones in which one has participated or ones of which one has heard. Thus the historical dimension is essential for the creation of rituals. Ritual actions include mimetic references to earlier rituals. As these references are made by mimesis, they create an "impression" of earlier performances of the ritual, which is then adapted to suit the current context. Depending on the requirements, some aspects of the ritual may be transformed in this process. Creating a mimetic link between the current world and a previous world ensures historical continuity, which legitimizes the current ritual activity, even if it differs from its predecessor. This use of mimesis to refer to or reconnect with previous performances of a ritual does not mean that it is recreated in exactly the same way every time. To make a reference by mimesis is to "adjust oneself to become similar," that is, to repeat a similar action that would not be possible if the previous ritual activity had not taken place. In some cases the result of this mimetic referencing also leads to a critical distancing from the reference point of the ritual, although this point of reference does not become superfluous. In mimetic referencing processes, the configurations and arrangements of the ritual action are updated and modified to match the context of our own activities. Mimetic constellations, staging styles, and types of movement are acquired and modified according to necessity or what the person thinks fit. The "repetition" of earlier rituals does not result in a copy of a ritual in the sense of a copy as made by a photocopier. Rather, through the inclusion of mimetically transferred and assimilated elements, something new is created in the repetition for everyone involved. The older version is merged into the new in a dialectical fashion. The ritual that has been updated by this mimetic process contains the old ritual, which has been given a new face and new clothing.[41]

(12) There is another important reason why mimetic processes play an important role in the staging and performing of ritual events: they produce the *practical knowledge* necessary for the ritual actions in question.[42] This ritual knowledge, which enables us to act competently in rituals, evolves from real or imaginary participation in ritual activities. In mimetic processes people take part in ritual actions that are corporeal and are both independent and related to other ritual acts or arrangements. In so doing, they undergo an expansion in order to accommodate the ritual practice. Thus, through mimetic referencing, they undergo a process of adjusting to the ritual activities in which corporeality and performativity play an important role. These processes incorporate ritual configurations, scenes, sequences of events, images, and behavior patterns, all of which, in other contexts, contribute to the competent execution of a ritual practice.

Rituals connect past, present, and future. They create continuity and contribute to historical and cultural change. They are not only guardians of society and culture; they also lead to social and cultural change. Neither reform nor innovation is possible without changes in rituals.[43] Rituals are not static, but *dynamic*. Since they incorporate practical knowledge that is acquired in mimetic processes, they are *social dramas*, and the performative character of these dramas changes social orders. Rituals help to channel the *potential for violence* present in every society. However, this is also an issue of *power* and the potential of power to implement or prevent social and cultural transformation.

Rituals and Gestures

Just as ritual, performativity, and mimesis have become important subjects in anthropology, in light of the recently increasing popularity of research on gestures the world over, more interest is being shown in *gestures*, especially in their function as central elements of rituals.[44] As meaningful movements of the body, gestures play an important role in culturalization, socialization, and education.[45] As bodily and symbolic productions and portrayals of intentions and emotions, they help individuals to become social beings and play a role in creating and shaping community and society. They are means of creating meaning that support subjects in their efforts to make themselves understood and to make contact with each other. Gestures express social relationships and emotions of which those who make them are often hardly aware, and they likewise do not penetrate the consciousness of those who perceive them and react to them. Gestures are an accompaniment to the spoken language and, at the same time, have a "life of their own." They can convey messages that supplement the spoken word by intensifying or relativizing individual aspects or by contradicting them. Often what is expressed and portrayed in this way is more closely connected to a speaker's emotions than what is actually said. Gestures are thus considered to be a "more reliable" expression of a person's inner life than are words, which are more consciously controlled.[46]

In rituals, a particularly important function of the gesture is as a bearer and transmitter of expression, social interaction, and meaning. Gestures are central to many rituals. Some form the focal points that contain the ritual in a condensed form. In politics, for example, the swearing in of the president is the gesture that condenses the ritual of his election. *Ritual gestures* of apology, greeting, or healing are important examples of the cultural side of gestures. What practically all cultures have in common, however different they may be, is the use of gestures in greetings.

Without the addressees being aware of it, social hierarchies are expressed in gestures. Ritual gestures in which institutional values and norms are implicit, especially, display power relationships. The fact that gestures have a strong social and cultural meaning is also supported by historical studies.[47] Gestures help to produce social continuity and to

FIGURE 9.3 Young boy praying at the table. © Garry Wade/ Digital Vision/Getty Images.

announce social change and establish it in human behavior.[48] While their configurations may not change, far-reaching changes in their meaning may take place, of which, at first sight, we are hardly aware.

Ritual gestures (e.g., of sacrifice, blessing, or forgiveness) play a central part in all religions. They are used to portray a connection with God, gods, and the cosmos that would otherwise be impossible. Gestures render religious, social, and cultural communities visible and make it possible for us to identify with them.[49] In mimetic and ritual processes, gestures create a *cultural identity* and become focal points that contain the essence of the process and are thus firmly imprinted on the memory.[50]

In whatever the conventions happen to be, the use of gestures restricts the behavioral repertoire of human possibilities by means of concrete gestural expressions that are socially, culturally, and historically determined.[51] This restriction of the gestural expressions that are culturally and historically permissible nevertheless also gives rise to a sense of social belonging and security. Familiarity with particular gestures brings with it familiarity with individuals and groups. Children and adolescents know the meaning of particular gestures that their caregivers make and how they should respond to them. Gestures make it possible to assess human behavior. They are part of the body language that gives community members a great deal of information about each other. The cultural importance of these messages lies in the very fact that they are more part of our unconscious perceptions of ourselves and others than conscious knowledge of the other person's emotions and intentions. They become part of the social knowledge that individuals acquire as they become integrated into society and that plays a large role in their ability to manage their social actions appropriately.

We can identify significant gender and class differences in the use of gestures. Some gestures are gender- or class-specific, while others are bound to social spaces, times, or institutions. Institutions such as churches, law courts, hospitals, and schools require certain gestures and apply sanctions if they are not used. As these gestures are made, the values of the institution are inscribed on the bodies of its members and those whom it serves, and these values are validated by repeat "performances." Still today, these forms of expression that are specific to a particular institution may be, for example, gestures of humility (Church), respect (law court), consideration for others (hospital), or attentiveness and involvement (school). Thus, gestures of the body have the function of engendering, expressing, and maintaining social and cultural differences. They take place in a historical and cultural context that is structured by power and is also the key to discovering their meaning.[52] They supply information about the values that are central to a society and allow us to get a glimpse of "mentality structures."

An indissoluble link between gesture, language, thinking, and imagination evolves. If we view gestures not only as "accompanying language" but also as having a specific gestural function, it becomes clear that verbal speech is by no means the only form of human communication. Human beings deploy their bodies and, when they speak, especially their hands in a variety of ways in order to communicate with each other. Hand gestures in particular can be used very differently and are important for how speakers express themselves and for the effects they have. Unlike the propositional content of discourses, gestures can express situative, pragmatic meanings and regulate an interaction. A "totality" of gesture and language arises that is of central importance for "languaging" and expresses the indissoluble link between gesture and language.[53]

Recent contributions to evolutionary research show that gestures are of central importance in the development of "shared intentionality." In particular, deictic gestures and gesticulations form the basis of human communication and cooperation. Unlike other primates, which are only able to express individual intentions, in their use of gestures human beings have the capacity, from an early age, to share their intentions with other human beings. Both phylogenetically and ontogenetically, this capacity to cooperate with others with the aid of gestures evolves even before the development of the capacity to communicate verbally. As children use gestures they develop the social capacity for joint attention and shared intentions. With this comes the ability to act together and help each other. The capacity that is developed mimetically with the use of gestures to attend to things jointly, share intentions, and act together forms the basis not only of human language and communication, but also of cultural development.[54]

Gestures are performative. They are often staged and performed within the framework of rituals and ritualizations and are mimetic in effect.[55] In gestures, the human body presents itself in its material and sensual form. Gestures condense individual and collective meanings. They are the expression of inner processes that present themselves in an objectified form. This objectification has a rebound effect on the individuals performing the gestures, so that they become aware of the processes taking place inside them. At the same time, a gesture has an effect on the person to whom it is addressed, and a condition of this reciprocal effect is that the originator of the gesture finds him or herself in a communicative community with the other addressee. This community can be spontaneous and temporary, but it can also be lasting and sustainable. For gestures to have both an inward and an outward effect, the originators and the addressees must believe in them. In this way, through familiarity with the gestures of individuals and groups, community can come about. In a community, people know what gestures mean and how to interpret and respond to them. Gestures make it possible to assess human behavior. They are part of the body language that conveys to the members of a community a good deal about each other. Gestures are absorbed into the social knowledge that individuals acquire in the course of their lives, which enables them to manage their actions appropriately.

Gestures are embodied and emergent. In other words, they are happenings, and as such they create cultural and social realities. They are more than the realization of intentions, which is evident above all in the way people use gestures to try to achieve their goals. Even if gestures are staged and performed with the same intentions, there will be considerable differences in *how* they are carried out, that is, in the way they are performed by the body. The nature and quality of social relationships is dependent on what gestures people develop, how they deploy gestures, the physical distances they keep between each other, and the postures they adopt. These characteristics convey to other people something of how it feels to live the way one does and of one's way of seeing, sensing, and experiencing the world. Despite their central significance for the effects of social actions, these elements of gestural performativity are not mentioned in many action theories. Instead, social actors are reduced to their conscious selves, and the sensual and contextual elements that condition their actions are disregarded. If we are to avoid this reductionism, we must study how gestures emerge, how they are linked to language and imagination, how they are made possible through social and cultural patterns, and how their quality as events relates to the fact that they include repetitive elements. We must ask to what extent the use of gestures is part of social and cultural action and also what role gestures and their repetition play in the formation of gender and social and ethnic identity.[56]

Gestures are means of creating meaning. They express feelings and articulate moods. They convey individual concepts and inner images. As symbolic and bodily representations, conventionalized gestures construct homologies between the collective and the individual imaginaries.[57] Neither the originators of the gestures nor those who perceive and react to them are fully aware of the emotions and moods articulated in them. This subliminal effect is an important part of the social significance of gestures.

Gestures are the expression and representation of practical knowledge grounded in the body. They cannot simply be acquired rationally from language and thought. Mimetic processes are necessary. By copying gestures and making them their own, individuals become able to make gestures appropriate to a specific scene. They are able to deploy them in different social contexts and adapt or change them as circumstances demand. Gestures are acquired mimetically; that is, they are incorporated, thus becoming part of the practical knowledge that is grounded in the body. This gestural body knowledge develops largely unconsciously and thus independently of the participants' ability to control it; for this very reason, however, it has lasting effects. This focus on the mimetic, performative, corporeal, social, ludic, and imaginative aspects of the gesture opens up new perspectives for international research on gestures and its utilization in anthropology.

TEN

Language—The Antinomy between the Universal and the Particular

Language has long been regarded as a *conditio humana*, separating humans from other creatures. This is true even though language is a comparatively recent acquisition of the species. Paleobiologists presume that human beings have been capable of using basic forms of language for between one hundred thousand and two hundred thousand years, and that our capacity for language became fully developed around thirty-five thousand years ago—around the time of the Lascaux cave paintings. Although they were not aware of this, the ancient Greeks were nevertheless correct when they designated man not according to his linguistic ability but according to his upright gait, as *an-thropos*. This characteristic is considerably older and also is an important prerequisite in the development of language. Walking upright liberated the hands from the tasks of locomotion and vision from the duties of prehension and resulted in the expansion of brain capacity, the lateralization of the brain halves, the lowering of the larynx, and the development of the voice apparatus and the brain. All of these developments had a major influence on the development of language.[1]

We are born with a general aptitude for language; however, language development is a consequence of human sociability and culture. Not one single word, not one single grammatical rule of any particular language is innate, only the general ability to form words, grammatical construc-

FIGURE 10.1 Pieter Bruegel the Elder, *The Tower of Babel*. © Kunsthistorisches Museum, Vienna.

tions, and sentences.[2] As research on the behavior of Kaspar Hauser and feral children who have grown up outside of human communities has shown, humans who have not learned to speak during childhood cannot acquire this skill at a later stage.[3] Research into the development of the brain has confirmed that the learning processes that enable us to gain language and perception skills take place in the first years after birth; if this initial opportunity is missed, it cannot be compensated for in later years.[4]

The universal language ability present in every human body has not resulted in the formation of one uniform language but in the development of a great many different languages. There are currently around six thousand languages in the world. These evolved as a result of our general aptitude for language and different geographical, cultural, and social environments. From an anthropological point of view, this gives rise to three questions. What is the relationship between the human body and the cultural learning processes that allow humans to learn a particular language that has developed over the course of history? What is the relationship between the universal aptitude for language and the many historically and culturally heterogenic languages in existence, without which there would be no speech? What is the relationship between thought and speech, as well as language, communication, and self-perception?

Body and Language

The human body has an inherent universal aptitude for human language. This aptitude, Noam Chomsky believes, means that the particular character of the different languages is of minor importance. To clarify this, Chomsky suggests that we should imagine an alien who, having arrived on Earth from Mars, observes humans talking. What does it see? Humans articulating arbitrary sounds that other humans hear and that cause them to reciprocate by creating yet more sounds. As children can understand sentences they have never heard before and can formulate sentences that have never been uttered before, Chomsky believes that the basic principles of sentence formulation—the rules of syntax—are genetically conditioned. Moreover, in the context of the development of human intelligence, language acquisition takes place as part of our coming to terms with our cultural environment and follows a timetable that is largely determined by genetics. With these two arguments, Chomsky counters behaviorism and excessive culturalism, which both assume that the human mind is a clean slate at birth, which is then filled with the aid of culture. Chomsky regards human language, that is, the ability to use syntax, as so unique that it could only be an emergent phenomenon that has no evolutionary predecessors.

In this last point, Chomsky is contradicted by authors who are otherwise wholehearted supporters of his theories. Steven Pinker, who shares Chomsky's idea of a "speech organ" with which we are born (that is, the interaction of various organs of the body that have other primary functions, such as breathing, but are used secondarily for speech production), disagrees with the assumption that language is an emergent phenomenon that is not subject to the process of selection. In his view, as speech is an organ with which we are born, it will have developed in a similar way to other human organs. To back up his argument, Pinker attempts to find proof that humans are born with a particular speech organ. To support his argument, he cites a report by language psychologist Myrna Gopnik concerning a British family in which several members are affected by *special language impairment* (SLI). "Their speech contains frequent grammatical errors, such as misuse of pronouns and of suffixes like the plural and past tense: It's a flying finches they are, She remembered when she hurts herself the other day, The neighbors phone the ambulance because the man fall off the tree, The boys eat four cookie, Carol is cry in the church."[5] These instances of language interference are not associated with limitations of general intelligence. As the language interference does not affect all members of the family and is distributed according to Mendel's law, it is possible to conclude that there is a special apparatus for speech that is specific to mankind, is inherited genetically, and is the result of evolutionary development.

As André Leroi-Gourhan has shown, the relationship between hands and words as conditioned by the structure of the human body is extremely important for the development of language. When humans began to walk upright, thus freeing the hands from their role in locomotion, this also allowed them to use their hands to grip objects. The next step was the handling of foodstuffs and then, gradually, the use and manufacture of tools. As humans began using their hands to grip objects, they no longer needed to use their mouths for this task. In the same way as the hands, once liberated, progressed to the use and manufacture of tools, the face now developed methods of symbolization, which, as they were articulated, turned into a system for producing sounds. These two developments are both part of one and the same process. "As soon as there are prehistoric tools, there is the possibility of language, for tools and language are neurologically linked and cannot be dissociated within the social structure of humankind."[6] In common with all primates, human beings also have a neuronal connection between the hand and facial organs. However, in contrast to other primates, humans, with their upright gait, can create symbols and tools. "To put it another way, humans, though they started out with the same formula as primates, can make tools as well as symbols, both of which derive from the same process, or, rather, draw upon the same basic equipment in the brain. This leads us to conclude not only that language is as characteristic for humans as are tools, but also that both are the expression of the same intrinsically human property."[7]

In addition to the genetically conditioned neuronal connection between the hand and face, there is also a structural parallel that Arnold Gehlen was the first to point out. Both touch and sound are reflexive. When touching and during the articulation of sounds the human body is both an active participant and a passive receiver. When touching an object actively, we experience it receptively, and when articulating sounds, we hear these and therefore ourselves receptively. This structural parallel enables motions of touch to be transformed into motions of sound. This structure forms the basis for a relationship between grasping and speaking and the possibility of transferring one into the other. With the invention of writing, the division of labor between the hand, which is dedicated to the operation of tools, and the face, which has the task of symbolization, eventually resulted in the uniting of symbolization and the use of tools or hands. This gave rise to a new source of imbalance in our culture. Symbolization by the hand became so dominant that the complicated accomplishment of the face was completely changed and its importance reduced. As the motion of sound was transferred to the hand (in the form of writing), the function of the hand—holding—also became dominant for language; thus the controlling organ of the hand—the eye—gained the upper hand. Since that time, "the face and ear have been used only for communication and no longer for the acquisition (*Erfassung*) of the world (prehension, cognition); as these functions have been completely taken over by the hand and the eye."[8] Literacy makes it easy to reduce language to its semantic and therefore cognitive dimension and to disregard the communicative function linked with speaking and hearing. Nevertheless, speaking with a person, in a manner that cannot be written down, is one of the fundamental possibilities of language and is part of the necessity to articulate language.

However, symbolizing in language is not only a sublimation of taking hold of food in the mouth. It is also a form of sublimation of the bodily relations *between* humans, that is, sexual relations. Language comes at the intersection between food intake and sexuality; it enables us to perceive the other person not only as an object but also as a subject. Language arose from a cognitive need, that is, the *appetitus noscendi*.[9] This aspect will also be of interest when we examine the relationship between language and thought in the next section; in this section we concentrate on the three forms of language articulation that have their basis in the anatomical structure of the human being.

The first form is *articulation with a vocal apparatus* and the production of linguistic sounds. This is an unmediated activity and motion of the human body. Without this motion of the body, which differs from culture to culture, it would not be possible to produce sounds, and without these sounds there would be no words. Vocal articulation and sequentiality are constituent elements of speaking and language. This is a point supported by Ferdinand de Saussure. According to de Saussure, the word (or the linguistic sign) is the connection of sound and content (or of sound and thought). Unlike pictorial symbols, which depict their content, audible symbols, such as the sound sequence "chair," usually have nothing in common with the content that they represent. Sequentiality, which is closely related to vocal articulation, permits the high speed and infinite qualities of speaking. This is a basic condition for the second form of articulation.

Wilhelm von Humboldt occasionally referred to this second form of articulation as "structure" (*Gliederung*). It distinguishes the character of language, and by means of this structure, the bodily and non-bodily, or cognitive, sides become an irresolvable unit. According to Humboldt, structure is the essence of language.[10] Articulation not only creates subdivision and distinctions and permits analysis, but also reassembles, connects, and synthesizes. Articulation in the narrow sense—the structure of sounds—is therefore a depiction of the logical structure of thought, despite its differing forms.[11] As the capacity to articulate is genetic, humans have this capacity even if they are incapable of producing sounds (as is the case for deaf-mutes). The Broca and Wernicke areas in the brain are responsible for grammar and vocabulary; they can control language not only as a function of producing sounds but also as expressed by other bodily movements. Thus the deaf are able to represent single concepts by forming iconic gestures that correspond to words.

The third form of articulation is inextricably linked to the first two forms: *listening to the voice that is articulating the speech and the thoughts simultaneously*. Hearing detects both the articulation of the voice and the articulation of thoughts, and even helps to create the other two forms of articulation by means of its acroamatic structure. From a macrostructural perspective, listening, in the sense of listening to others, is also an *articulus*, linking together the parts of a whole, that we call talking to each other, or dialogue.[12] For Johann Gottfried Herder, listening is in fact the pivot around which language and human rationality revolve. Through listening, the world penetrates the inner world of the human being and demands answers. These answers are formed in speaking. Language results from the interaction of the world of sound and human listening. The connection between *language* and the *voice* and *ear*, which has its basis in the structure of the human body, makes it possible for language to make unlimited use of limited means.

Language and Thought

In his short history of linguistic thought, *Mithridates in Paradise*,[13] Jürgen Trabant examines the relationship between language and thought and shows how this relationship is connected to fundamental issues of human self-understanding and how it has been defined in different ways over the course of European history. At issue here are two questions that are of exceptional importance from an anthropological point of view and also of key significance for the cultural understanding of language. The first question is whether there is a difference between thinking and speaking and, if there is, how this difference is to be understood. The other question, which is linked to the first, concerns the relationship between language and the many historically and culturally heterogenic languages in existence. A closer look at this problem clearly reveals the antinomy between universalism and particularism—this is a contradiction that also runs through other areas of anthropology.

In the story of the creation in the Old Testament, God brings the animals before Adam so that he can give them names. The resulting nomenclature did not create the world but enabled humans to take possession of it. Adam does not lose the *universal language* of paradise even when he is exiled from paradise by God as a result of the serpent's subtly phrased temptation. God only punished human beings with a *multitude of languages* after they had constructed the Tower of Babel. In the Pentecostal message in the New Testament, however, man is given the opportunity to understand the *unity of the spirit in the many tongues*.

Where the Bible emphasized the loss of the universal language of Paradise and the unity of spirit in the many tongues, in Greek philosophy, primarily in Plato's *Kratylos*, the emphasis was on the question of whether words were assigned to objects by nature (*physei*) or were assigned by humans according to a certain system (*thesei*). Socrates presents these two positions as an aporia; however, he favored the idea of the nonlingual concept, according to which knowledge is gained from the objects themselves and words are only tools.[14] This is also Aristotle's starting point, but he arrives at a different solution. He does not assume that language and knowledge of the world are inextricably linked to each other. In the Boethius translation *De interpretatione* (which was the only version of Aristotle's work available in the Middle Ages, as the original Greek text could not be found), the term used is *conceptus*.[15] This "concept" of things is formed by thinking or cognition. It is the same in all people and is communicated in every language by "arbitrarily" formed words.[16] Therefore thinking is only related to things and is independent of language. Language serves solely to communicate thoughts to others. According to Aristotle, on the one hand, we have *cognition*, which takes place without language (and is the same in all people). On the other hand, we have *communication*, and for this purpose, we have words, and these differ in different cultures. Words designate the thoughts of the soul so that we can communicate them to others. Thinking itself has nothing to do with words; it is completely independent of them. This is the same for all people, just as the objects that people perceive are the same.[17] This notion of a fundamental difference between thinking and language is a basic position that is frequently adopted throughout the history of European linguistic philosophy, for example, by Bacon, Locke, and Chomsky. This is accompanied by regret for the loss of a uniform language and the longing for a universal language for all mankind.

Latin originated in Rome and became a universal language; it was *the* language of Europe for more than fifteen hundred years. In Greek philosophy, the dispute with the sophists in the name of the search for truth was a critique of rhetoric, but rhetoric was rehabilitated in Roman culture by Cicero's *On the Ideal Orator*. This development is important because it had to do with increasing the power of rhetoric as a tool to convince others and to ensure that essential tasks were undertaken—the fulfillment of the communicative side of language.

The demand that vernacular languages should play a role equal to that of Latin in literature, science, and social life once again gave rise to issues concerning the relationship between thought and language and between a universal language and a multiplicity of languages. Greek philosophy had investigated the relationship between language and cognition, which Plato and Aristotle viewed differently, but the new aim was to demand that works compiled in the vernacular be recognized. The works of Dante, Petrarca, and Boccaccio made it difficult for Italian humanists to disregard the claims of vernacular languages to equal status. In his *De vulgari eloquentia*, which was originally written in Latin but published in the vernacular, Dante developed a theory of this new literature, with the intention of illustrating that it was comparable in terms of quality to Latin literature. He also made several important anthropological statements about languages. The language of Adam was seen as serving to praise God. In contrast to the nature of angels and animals, who do not require language because of their solely spiritual or bodily nature, the dual (bodily and spiritual) nature of humans makes language necessary. Only with the aid of language were humans considered capable of expressing their inner feelings. Dante regarded language as a positive capacity that separated human beings from other life-forms. He believed that the multiplicity of languages had been an unavoidable condition in the historical diversity of human life ever since the punitive measures imposed in Babylon, and that all humans share a general aptitude for language, which is, however, expressed in different languages. Dante's focus was on literary quality, which he maintained is also possible in the vernacular.

In spite of such insights, it took a long time for vernacular languages to establish themselves on an equal footing with Latin. In the Renaissance, most humanists (i.e. poets and intellectuals), remained faithful to Latin. This only began to change in the sixteenth century. With the spread of printing, intellectuals slowly began to turn their backs on Latin and to write in their vernacular or national languages. Courtiers and court culture helped to develop vernacular languages. Gradually scientists started to write in the vernacular—Galileo, for example, wrote *Dialogo* (1632) and *Discorsi* (1638) in Italian. In France, the centralist policies of François I were successful in establishing the French language. In 1530 the Collège des trois Langues, which was later renamed the Collège de France, was founded. In 1580, Montaigne (whose first language was actually Latin) published his *Essais* in French. In Germany, the Lutheran translation of the Bible, the rapid spread of Protestantism, and a large number of newly founded schools were the catalysts in the process of establishing High German. The countries of Europe saw a gradual erosion of Latin as the only language of intellectual reasoning and the further development of national and vernacular languages. This added new dimensions to the questions concerning, first, the relationship between the universal language and linguistic diversity and, second, that between cognition and language. Today, we are developing in the opposite direction—from a multiplicity of languages toward administrative and academic monolingualism—and many of the problems discussed at that time have once more become topical.

Francis Bacon vigorously opposed the increasing importance of vernacular languages. He was convinced that Aristotle was wrong, rejecting his view that concepts develop independently of language by means of a depiction in the soul, in a process that requires no language. He preferred to believe that the various languages develop different perspectives of things and that therefore thinking is a language-based activity. Words generally have the same task as they did in Plato's time, that is, to make distinctions in existence (*usian diakritikon*), which Bacon aptly terms "cutting into things" (*res secant*). However, words do not fulfill their tasks because they are subject to the *captus vulgi*, the *intellectus vulgaris*, that is, the (limited) understanding of the common people.[18] Words have an integral power, so that reason is not master of the words; rather, the words are masters of reason. Thus, linguistic criticism is one of the essential tasks of philosophy and science. It is therefore necessary to rid language of all "images of the market-place" (*idola fori*), fantasies, and idols, and to develop clear terms to create a worldview that is not clouded by language.

René Descartes' aim was also to achieve a "clear and secure knowledge of all that is useful for life."[19] Such knowledge is not acquired by studying books or the world outside, but only through one's own inner thoughts. For Descartes, although thinking is a wholly independent activity, speaking is connected to the body; human beings can compile their words freely and answer to everything that is said to them. Human speech, unlike that of parrots, for example, which can only mimic, is an expression of thought.[20] Despite the fact that Descartes acknowledges this function of speaking, from an anthropological point of view, he follows Aristotle in assuming that thinking is performed independently of language.

During and after the sixteenth century, Latin was slowly driven out of academia and administration and to some extent was even forced out of the Church. This resulted in the establishment of national language norms. Some of these were achieved by political means, as in France; others resulted from religious changes, as in Germany; and others were more literary in nature, as was the case in Italy. This progressive linguistic diversification in sixteenth-century Europe was accompanied by a gathering of intellectual information on the languages of the world. The positive view of the individualities of languages suggested by humanistic concepts of *idíoma* was later supported by the idea of the *génie des langues*, which lent it a pugnacious dynamic.[21]

In his attempt to clear the "fog before our eyes" that is created by words and hinders the immediacy of thought, John Locke demonstrated the arbitrariness of the meaning of words and the problems that arise from this because of the way people assign different meanings to the same words. Such differences arise not only among individuals, but also among languages. A given language does not always have a word that is equivalent to a word in another, and words that are equivalent often have different meanings when examined more closely. Words are attached to ideas and are a barrier to insight. Although there is nothing we can do to change this, we can use philosophy and science to exercise control over the way words are used. Condillac, like Locke, assumes that the human soul is a clean slate on which the personal story of an individual is recorded throughout his life. Languages are like a tree; they have a common root and then branch out. In Condillac's view, each language has its own "génie" (characteristic essence) that gives rise to the differences that lend each language its own idiosyncratic character. These "génies" are stored differently in the memory of each individual and also give a concrete form to thought, which enables progress.

Leibniz's position diverges considerably from this. Where Locke famously claimed that there is nothing in the intellect that has not previously been in our senses, Leibniz added, "except for the intellect itself."[22] Leibniz was fascinated by the diversity of languages, which he saw as an expression of the diversity of human thinking. This was a reevaluation of languages. Their diversity was no longer seen as a lamentable chaos but as part of the richness of human intellect that we must strive to understand. Humboldt was also of this opinion, and his publication *The Heterogeneity of Language and Its Influence on the Intellectual Development of Mankind* builds on this, seeing every language as a way of viewing the world and all research in this area as a way of contributing to the body of anthropological knowledge.[23]

Anthropology of Language

One of the first contributions to the anthropology of language (and therefore to anthropology itself) was made by Herder. He aimed to demonstrate that language is a condition of being human—a *conditio humana*. This train of thought was part of his efforts to counter the position of Descartes—"I think, therefore I am." Herder's idea can be summarized as "My body is present; I can feel it/myself, therefore I am." Herder used the distinctive features of the human body as the basis for a new, independent concept of anthropology.[24] This is the context in which Herder developed his linguistic-anthropological work and established the foundations for his concept of the linguistic nature of reason. In his view, the origins of human language do not lie in the animal kingdom. In the well-known opening to his *Essay on the Origins of Language*, he states that both animals and humans communicate with other beings of their species using sounds that they produce and hear. The origins of human language are to be found at the point in which humans and animals differ, in the lack of instinct in humans, our resultant deficiency, and the manner in which we compensate for this by using our capacity for reflection (*Besonnenheit*), that is, for thought and insight. And this cognitive need, which is quite different from the animal need for *communication*, creates thought, which is, at the same time, language. Language as a specific human characteristic only evolves from the semantic-cognitive relationship to the world, and according to Herder's radically new concept, *the thought is the word*.[25] The inner word is not innate but requires the world around it and acoustic stimuli in order to be articulated acoustically; however, even without these, the inner word can already be regarded as language. Herder explained this concept using sheep as an example. "The sound of bleating perceived by a human soul as the distinguishing mark of the sheep became, by virtue of this reflection, the name of the sheep even if his tongue had never tried to stammer it. He recognized the sheep by its bleating: This was a conceived sign through which the soul clearly remembered an idea—and what is that other than a word? And what is the entire human language other than a collection of such words?"[26] This quotation mentions certain characteristics that Herder saw as determining language: "name of the sheep," "sign," "word" and "human language." Thinking is language, language is thinking. This link is indissoluble. However, it was also Herder who discovered the fundamental significance of hearing for the development of language. If we were unable to hear the bleating of the sheep, the processes within us that generate language could not develop. The Other has access to our internal thought processes by means of acroamatic perception—through hearing. Hearing enables us to perceive the Other as well as ourselves and is thus the basis for the dialogical character of language. Hearing also links language to the voice. According to Humboldt, the voice and the ear create the free structure (*Gliederung*) or articulation (*Artikulation*) that is characteristic for language.

Like Herder, Humboldt also believed that language and thinking were interwoven. For Humboldt, language is the "organ" that shapes our thought;[27] "it is the constantly repeated work of the mind in its efforts to render the articulated sound capable of expressing the thought."[28] Language is the bringing forth of thought in an interweaving of body and reason. Language is not just thought; the voice is also an integral part of thought (*conceptus* and *vox*). This synthetic unit of the word and meaning is the core of the intuitive European understanding of the unit formed by speech and thinking.[29] In this way Humboldt formulates the counterposition to Aristotle's separation of thought and word (*conceptus* and *vox*), in which only the thought (*conceptus*) has a relationship to objects or things. For Humboldt, language and thought form a unit that relates to the world. Language is, however, not only the voice or mouth but also the hearing of the voice by both the speaker and the person addressed. When this other person hears and understands within herself the sound-thought (*pensée-son*), she is prompted to answer in her own words and voice, and thus this answer is heard by the person who spoke first. Language is following the thought of the Other. It is not only the synthesis of sound and thought but also the *synthesis of cognition and communication*. Humboldt sees speaking and thinking as speaking and thinking with one another.[30] This universal task of the human mind is accomplished in different historically unique languages, each of which produces a different worldview. "Thus thinking is not only dependent on language per se but also to a certain degree on each individual language."[31]

On this basis, Humboldt suggested that entire languages as well as individual issues concerning several languages should be studied. Both are modes of anthropological study that he intended to use in research on what he regarded as the "organic essence" of languages, using comparison as the principal methodological tool. Humboldt understood the unique character of comparative anthropology to consist in the fact that it approaches empirical matter speculatively, historical objects philosophically, and the actual condition of humankind from the point of view of its possible developments.[32] Anthropology should therefore be neither exclusively empirical nor solely philosophical; rather, the aim is to interweave the empirical and the philosophical, that is, to deal with a historical subject so thoroughly on a philosophical level that the properties of humankind and our true condition and potential for development become evident. To do justice to the diversity of languages and their worldviews, a philosophical approach is required that links the philosophical, the empirical, the transcendental, and the historical.

If we are to understand the nature of language, we need to examine how it is used. Only by looking at its usage can we grasp its performative character.[33] Humboldt's position was that regardless of how thoroughly and precisely one investigates languages in their "organic being," it is their usage that decides what they can become by means of this being, since the appropriate use of terms benefits and enriches the terms themselves.[34]

This is the point of departure for Wittgenstein's *Philosophical Investigations*. In this work the author distances himself from the path he took in his earlier *Tractatus logico-philosophicus*, which he followed in an attempt to build on the philosophy of Bacon, Locke, and Condillac and to free science and philosophy from the "traps" of natural language. Analytical philosophy still follows this path today. Humboldt's rudimentary concept was radicalized by Wittgenstein, for whom the meaning of words evolves through their *use*. This lifted the restriction in philosophy on apophantic speech oriented toward truth and insight. The main objective is no longer to attain a universality of thinking and insight that transcends any form of cultural relativism but to establish the manner in which language and thinking are dependent on their use. "The meaning of a word is its use in language."[35] It is constituted by the various ways it is used in speaking—Wittgenstein referred to these uses as "language games." In section 23 of *Philosophical Investigations*, Wittgenstein asks how many types of sentences there are. His answer is that there are not only statements, questions, and commands, but there are *countless* types—an infinite number of different types of everything that we call *characters*, *words*, and *sentences*. According to Wittgenstein, this diversity is not fixed and given once and for all, but new types of language and new language games can evolve, while others become dated and are forgotten. He cites the changes seen in the field of mathematics as a rough parallel. The term *language game* is intended to emphasize that speaking language is part of an activity or a way of life.[36] The diversity of usage is linked to the diversity of social practices. Thus, speaking and thinking are no longer viewed simply in terms of the philosophical search for truth and insight; rather, every utterance can become the object of philosophical reflection. Every utterance creates world and is praxis. Language is an instrument, and its concepts are also instruments.[37] The focus here is on the pragmatic, on the interactive in speech. While Humboldt was fascinated by the diversity of languages, Wittgenstein was fascinated by the diversity of language games. For Humboldt, the diversity resulted in different "worldviews"; for Wittgenstein, it resulted in different forms of action. They have in common that they view language as activity and something to use. Humboldt saw thought as created by the "work of the intellect." *Work* as referred to here differs significantly from the work in Wittgenstein's "working" language. Humboldt's *primarily semantic* focus sees language as "creating" thought, albeit as something that is always transient and the product of work jointly undertaken—in speaking with each other. "This language work is a making or creation—*poiesis*. In contrast, in a *primarily pragmatic* view, language is joint action, a *praxis*, that initially creates nothing but the cooperation itself. It is therefore *primarily* a "game" and not work—a back-and-forth, first one and then the other, as in a game of chess."[38]

We began our review of the history of concepts of language with the idea of the loss of a universal language after our banishment from Paradise and moved from there to concepts of nonlinguistic knowledge (Plato) and then to the concept of the separation of thought and knowledge from language (Aristotle). We continued with a look at differing evaluations of the increasing significance of vernacular and national languages at the start of the modern era by Bacon, Locke, and Condillac, on the one hand, and by Leibniz, Herder, and Humboldt, on the other. Today, the debate centers on positions that either, like Chomsky's, stress the importance of the genetically determined universal capacity for language, or, like Wittgenstein's, consider the use of language in an infinite number of language games to be the decisive factor in our thought and speech. To put the debate in a more global perspective, this century will see hundreds of the world's languages die out, which will lead to a reduction in the diversity of the "human mind."

Despite considerable resistance, the current development of a new universal language, which is supported by the tendencies of globalization to create uniformity, will also inevitably result in a reduction in cultural diversity.[39] The consequences are difficult to predict. What is certain is that this trend will continue to result in major changes to our understanding of ourselves as human beings.

ELEVEN

Images and Imagination

Like language, images are another major focus of anthropological and cultural studies research. The first issue to be resolved is "What is an image?"[1] Images are ever-present: in metaphors of language, in works of art, and in the new media. Images have become ubiquitous. The "image as a cultural configuration" needs to be redefined. Taking the metaphor as a link between the subject and the world, and assuming thinking to be bound up with metaphors,[2] it is necessary to reach a better understanding of the central role played by images in culture, science, and philosophy. The "discovery" of the gaze and the resulting complex exchange between objects and the eyes (which are firmly embedded in the body) open up a new understanding of the relationship between image, gaze, and body. The chiastic model of gaze interaction, where vision and view are combined, illustrates the manner in which images are created by the gaze, deposited in the memory, and reanimated by memory. In the phenomenological observations on seeing and the reading of images, seeing appears as an independent, irreplaceable cultural skill, suggesting that the image and the imagination are very much a relevant focus in cultural studies and anthropology.

Images, Bodies, Media

When we talk about images, the question arises as to whether we are referring to external or mental images. The fact that the term *image* permits both possibilities tells us something about the character of images. External images relate to mental images, and mental images relate to external images. Images are the product of the imagination, which has its roots in the vegetative aspect of the human body.[3] Hans Belting also has this in mind when he describes the body as the "location of images," deducing from this that even though the body always seeks to gain control of these self-generated images, ultimately it remains at their mercy. The images the body creates show, however, that change is the only continuity open to it. The images leave no doubt as to the essential changeability of the body. Hence they are promptly rejected if the body adopts a different stance on questions regarding the world and its own self.[4] We have only restricted access to our own images of perception and the mental images created by them. Where our eyes rest, what we shut out, and what we store in memory for the sake of remembering things are only partially dependent on our conscious self. No less important is the human desire to make other people, situations, and things part of ourselves in the form of images. Mental images control perception and determine what we see, overlook, remember, or forget. The inner flow of images determines not only which people or external objects become images because we want them to, but also which images slip into us unnoticed and become rooted there. We are at the mercy of our mental images, even though we constantly attempt to gain control of them. These images fluctuate and change along with the changes that occur in human life. Images that were once important lose their importance and are replaced by new ones. However, all images share one characteristic: people experience themselves in images and take reassurance from them.

Mental images are largely the result of external images that are brought to our attention. As the products of our culture, they also serve as the expressions of our culture, and they differ from the external images of other cultures and other historical times.[5] The collective character of these images is remodeled individually as they pass from their objectified forms in the outside world to the inside of the human body, where they are superimposed on the images already found there. Many of these images from the collective world of images are products of the (mental) images of individuals who have the opportunity of transforming these mental images into objects and forms of the outside world or of transferring them to media and disseminating them.[6] Objectified images exist with the aid of media. This applies to early cave paintings, which exist through the medium of stone.[7] The death masks of classical antiquity, which transfer the countenance of the ephemeral body to another medium that survives the mortal body, is another example of this.[8] Further examples can be seen in photography, film, and video. In a photograph, an impression of light on the human body is made on a negative, which is then transferred to photographic paper and preserved in this medium. As an image, it can relate a story that is totally different from the body from which it is derived.[9] The same applies to film and video, which are enriched by the dimension of movement. The medium of the image does not express the image but constitutes it. Without a medium, there would be no image for us to perceive or transfer to our internal world of images and incorporate there. Hans Belting refers to a dual bodily relationship within the medium of the image. The body analogy is primarily based on our perception of the media as the symbolic or virtual bodies of images. Secondly, it develops as the media are inscribed into our bodily perception, transforming it in the process. The media control our experience of our bodies through the act of observation, to the extent that we use them as models to help us practice self-perception and the externalization of our bodies.[10] This is also underscored by McLuhan's statement that "the medium is the message."[11] The media through which images are brought to us greatly determine our experience of images. As media, they influence our manner of perceiving the images they convey, regardless of the image in question. There is a qualitative difference in experiencing an image as a painted, photographic, or digital image, which is overlooked in the semiotics of images, which reduces images to icons.[12]

Time and *space* constitute further central reference points for the human perception of images. Bodies that become images lose their transitoriness as images. Ancient death masks offer an example of this too. Even the prints of photographic images suggest that the human body can overcome its temporality. The photograph offers both an opportunity to remember and the option of surviving in the community as an image. The medial character of an image means it can be stored and remain available at all times; that is, it can be perceived in a different time than that in which it was created. The same applies to space. The medial character of images makes them independent of the space in which they are created and allows them to be experienced in different spatial contexts. Images can be presented ubiquitously. The television image shows viewers at home a distant place that they can "visit" in their imagination. Where are the viewers now? Are they still at home, or are they in that place to which the camera has brought them? In spite of their independence of time and space as media, images as images do not exist independently of their context. Not only do their meanings change depending on their context, but their nature as images also changes. The medial nature of images contains information on how they are to be used, providing instructions on how the image is to be perceived. Every use of an image made possible by its mediality results in an overlapping of different times and different spaces. Three levels can be distinguished here: the time in which the image was created, the time to which its content matter refers, and the time of its perception. The same applies to space. Furthermore, the various forms of space and time relate to different historical and cultural reference points, which form the context in which images are perceived.

Ethnology provides many examples of the shifting of such reference points and the changing interpretation of images in a collective imaginary that is constantly changing.[13] Serge Gruzinski has traced processes of this kind that occurred during the colonization of Mexico and the spread of Christianity there.[14] According to his study, to make the colonization permanent, the Spanish conquerors concentrated their energy on destroying the collective imaginary of the natives and replacing it with a Christian imaginary. A lasting reconfiguration of the Indians' world of imagination occurred in complex mimetic processes; the imaginary "heathen" and Christian figures were amalgamated. The incorporation of the new features of Christian identity in the imaginary of the Indians completed the process of their subjection. Similar processes can be identified in India and Africa.[15]

The body is accessible to us in its objectifications in images, in language, and in cultural performances. Like all other forms of objectification, images are historically and culturally different forms of expression and representation of the body. The relationship of human bodies to images changes. This change, however, is often caused by medial changes. The mirror allows us to see our bodies where they are not actually present—in the glass or the metal. As in a painting, the three-dimensional body is translated into a two-dimensional surface. The mediality of photography also alters the character of an image; an imprint is taken of the body in light, which then reproduces its appearance on a flat surface.[16] If one sees the new media as prosthetic extensions of the body, as McLuhan does, even digital images enter into a relationship with the body, albeit of a very abstract kind. Generally, medial communication in the world seems to be increasing,[17] and the *mediality* of humans' relationship to the world and the inherent self-expression of the media seem to be playing an ever-greater role. Part of this development is also due to imaging processes (e.g., X-rays, electron microscopes, computer tomography), without which the natural sciences are inconceivable nowadays. We are, however, only just beginning to grasp their significance for epistemology and cultural studies.

FIGURE 11.1 Shrine in Guadalupe, Mexico. "Our Lady of Guadalupe" (also known as the "Virgin of Guadalupe") is a Roman Catholic icon of the Virgin Mary and is displayed in the Basilica of Our Lady of Guadalupe, which is among the most-visited Marian shrines in the Roman Catholic religious world. The icon of the Virgin of Guadalupe is Mexico's most popular religious and cultural image. © Jeremy Woodhouse 2008/ Photodisc/Getty Images.

In images, the presence and absence of people and objects are inextricably linked. In the same way that a body is present in the medium of a photograph, its image simultaneously refers us to the body's absence. We experience the "here-and-now" of the image through the medium in which it appears before us. But the difference between image and image medium is more complex than is apparent from this description. The image always has a mental aspect, and the medium always has a material aspect, even if in our sensory terms they both form one entity.[18] The photograph becomes an image when people look at it and bring it to life with their gaze. As they do so, the medial character of the photograph recedes into the background. This is even more the case for film and television, which draw the viewers into the world of images displayed to them in the medium. Even if viewers are basically conscious of the medial character of the images, during the process of watching, they "forget" it—the medial images connect with the viewers' own mental images and form the television and film image as an image "experienced" by the viewers. In this process the images communicated by the media are mixed with the images that the viewers remember and associate with them. Both the current television and film images, as well as the mental images, are rooted deeply in the imaginary of culture and society; this state of affairs is repeatedly "alluded to"; indeed, it is only this that lends meaning to many "current" images in the first place.[19]

In contrast to film and television images, *digital images* have a matrix that is no longer an image.[20] However, not only their character as images but also their mediality have become problematic. Digital images are created in electronic, mathematically generated processes that are only accessible to very few people but these processes also guarantee that the images can be heavily manipulated. In a synthetic image, the traditional connection between image, subject, and object is severed.[21] Even so, the synthetic image still relates to what it represents, even if the type of reference is new and different. Viewing a synthetic image requires a screen—indeed, a screen is necessary for it to become an image at all. It relates to the mental images of its viewers, overlapping and intertwining with them. The appearance of images on the screen suggests their accessibility in a clear and controllable framework. The relatively small size of the screen, the ephemeral character of the images upon it, and the standardization of view all contribute to this illusion. As moving images, synthetic images give the viewer a double illusion, that of the image and that of motion. The illusion of movement is all the easier to create, as the body of the viewer is kept motionless in a sitting position. If the increasing spread of synthetic images fosters the disappearance of belief in the representational character of images, this may result in a lasting change in attitudes toward images and their cultural use.[22]

The growing discussion of images has resulted in ever more importance being attached to the critique of images. The debate between iconodules (image worshippers) and iconoclasts (image destroyers) has a long history and continues today.[23] Images can deceive, manipulate, and trap us in a prison of the imaginary. Their credibility is being drawn into question. Especially when they excite and amaze, they provoke skeptical questions and a refusal to accept their magical effects. Images simulate the world and become simulacra that can possess people. What are the effects of the reproduction and acceleration of images—the new floods of images? Do they contribute to increasing abstraction, more distanced social behavior, and a loss of genuine living experiences? Is our addiction to images a drug with which we anaesthetize ourselves in order to escape our fear of emptiness—a *horror vacui*? Or are images losing their fascination, and is skepticism toward images and seeing growing? And will it thereby make us more aware of the importance of rediscovering the other senses and of trying to find new forms of sensory experience?

Presence, Representation, Simulation

Images are ambiguous. It is not wrong to assume that they arose long before the development of consciousness, out of the fear of death or the fear of having to die. Dietmar Kamper suspects that the purpose of the image is to cover the wound from which human beings originated. However, this cannot succeed. Every memory that screens also reminds. Therefore, every image is in principle "sexual," even if its content is deeply "religious." Therefore, according to Roland Barthes, the image can be entitled the "death of the person." Via fear, the image plays the main role in distracting us from desire. It is a substitute for the indifference we experience toward our origins. It gives us hope that our mother's voice will resonate in us through all our ambivalent experiences. It also accompanies the transition from the sacred to the banal. For, according to Kamper, the second step in overcoming fear lies in duplication: the aspiration is that the image will become lost among other images—a forlorn hope!

The image oscillates between images with a hieratic/magical character, in which the image is identical to that which it shows, and images that no longer represent anything and can only simulate. This scenario allows us to differentiate between three types:

- the image as a magical presence;
- the image as a mimetic representation; and
- the image as a technical simulation.

These types overlap in many ways. Nevertheless, it is useful to differentiate between them, as this allows us to identify differing, partially contradictory iconic features.

The Image as a Magical Presence

The images that were created in a time when images had not yet become works of art included statuettes, masks, cult images, and sacred images.[24] Among these, the images in which gods provide a magical presence (i.e., pictures of gods or idols) play a special role. Such images include representations in clay or stone of fertility goddesses from ancient cultures. Many ancient idols, statuettes, and masks insure the presence of the divine through their existence. Painted skulls and death masks perform a similar task.[25] As early as the Neolithic era, skulls were painted and used by the living for ritual communication with ancestors and the dead. Death is the fate of the community; creating painted skulls and masks is an attempt to respond to the dread of death. Making images becomes a reaction to death.

Skulls and death masks have the function of transforming a mortal head into an image, whose presence insures the presence of the dead among the living. This transformation takes place as part of death rituals, the performance of which offers the community of the living reassurance of their own selves in the face of death. As a result, the skulls and death masks assume a sacred character.

The worship of the Golden Calf described in the Old Testament involves an idol in which god and image are united, and the presence of a god is embodied and symbolized by the calf. While Moses was on Mount Sinai receiving the Ten Commandments, which expressly prohibit making an image of God or worshipping images, his people, under the leadership of his elder brother Aaron, sought to satisfy the ancient urge to worship an image. Aaron represents the image-worshipping iconodule; Moses represents the image-fighting iconoclast—the two basic positions that still apply today with regard to images. What they both share is a conviction that images are powerful, and this power grows from their ability to make present an incomprehensible and remote form of being, and to give it a presence that completely absorbs our attention. The image's power lies in its similarity; it produces a likeness of that which it portrays. From the perspective of the ritual, the Golden Calf *is the god*. Image and content fuse and become indistinguishable.[26]

In the medieval cult of relics, a small part of the body ascribed to a saint sufficed to ensure the saint's presence. "The bodies of many saints lie here," reads the sign above the collection of religious relics in Conques. The saints are present; they are not represented by their relics. They develop their healing powers for the pious at the very spot where parts of their bodies lie. The relics sanctify both the location of ritual activities and those participating in these activities. Ritual activities help to establish a relationship between the relic, as a symbolic embodiment of the saint, and the healing expected from the ritual activity. This relationship would be referred to as magical in other cultural contexts.

Many works of modern art represent nothing beyond the work of art itself; instead, the work merely creates a presence, certainly justifying comparison with early works relating to cults created before the era of art. In the works of Mark Rothko and Barnett Newman, explicit experiences of images of the sacred (or rather the numinous) are initiated, such as in the Rothko Chapel in Houston, where the colors of the pictures leave the observer in a diffuse state of suspension where "presence and diffusion" are mysteriously balanced. Newman's pictures also confront us with our own limitations and allow us to experience our powerlessness. Newman believes that this understanding of ourselves also makes it possible for us to experience the sublime. This experience is characterized by an overtaxing of the cognitive capacity by something far bigger than we can comprehend. The failure to cope with this extraordinary dimension becomes an unanticipated advantage. To this extent, Newman's pictures aim to *show nothing* (not even pure areas of color); only a pure form is to have *an effect* here and to *trigger a response* in the viewer. It transcends itself as a picture the moment that it elicits a reaction.[27]

The Image as Mimetic Representation

In Plato's philosophy, *images become appearances* of things that they themselves are not. They represent something, express something, and refer to something. For Plato, painters and poets do not produce—in the way that God produces ideas or craftsmen produce goods. They create *appearances* of objects. Painting and poetry are not restricted to the artistic representation of things but to the artistic representation of appearances, of things as they appear. The objective is not the representation of ideas or the truth, but the artistic representation of phantasms. Therefore, painting and mimetic literature can in principle allow the visible to appear.[28] What he is dealing with here are images and mimesis, which creates illusions, in which the difference between the model and its reproduction becomes unimportant. The aim is not semblance, but the *appearance of what appears*. In Plato's work, art and aesthetics constitute an area in which the artist or poet is the master. According to Plato, the master does not have the ability to produce being and is thereby relieved of the obligation to be truthful, to which philosophy is subject, and which also forms the basis of the "state." In this way, art and aesthetics become independent of the concerns of philosophy, its search for truth and knowledge, and its efforts to find the Good and Beauty. The price of achieving this goal is exclusion from the "state," as it cannot accept the willful nature of art and poetry.[29]

The artistic creative process aims to create a mental image that artists or poets have in their mind's eye. The design that inspires creative activity is gradually dissolved and realized in the image that comes into being in a medium different from that of the imagined design. In the process, changes, omissions, additions, and other differences occur, indicating that there is only a limited degree of semblance. In most cases, the models to which the images and drafts of the artists relate are unknown, as they either never existed or no longer exist. At the center of the artistic process is the image, which contains references to previous images and assumes form in a process of transformation.

The (mimetic) production of representations is one of our elementary anthropological skills. One of its central themes is the human body.[30] From the portraits of the Renaissance era to the photographs of the present day, human bodies are represented in images. Photographs portray people at important times in their lives in the form of body images. Questions of how we humans view ourselves are inextricably linked to such depictions and other forms of representation. Without images (i.e., representations) of ourselves, we are incomprehensible to ourselves. To understand the limits of the possibilities of human self-perception, it is essential to grasp the image character of such representations.

From prehistoric times onward, human beings have created images of the human body. These body images are images of human beings in just the same way that depictions of human beings are depictions of the body. In different ways, the images represent the body, which has not changed biologically over the course of history. A history of these images would be a fair reflection of the history of the human body. It is both a history of human representations and human images. Thus Hans Belting concludes that human beings are identical with the way their bodies appear. The body itself is an image, even before it has been reproduced in images.

The depiction is not what it claims to be—a *reproduction* of the body. In fact it is a *production* of a body image that is pre-given even in the self-representation of the body. The triangle *human being—body—image* is immutable if one does not wish to lose all three parameters.[31]

The Image as Technical Simulation

Today there is a tendency for everything to become an image. Even opaque bodies are transformed—they lose their physical attributes and become fleeting and transparent. The processes of abstraction produce images and icons. One encounters them everywhere; nothing appears strange or overwhelming anymore. Images cause objects and "realities" to disappear. Not only are texts handed down, we now also save and exchange huge numbers of images for the first time in human history. Photos, films, and videos become memory aids, and image memories evolve. Whereas texts previously required us to supplement them with our own imagined images, today restraints are placed on the imagination by the production and reproduction of "image texts." The number of people involved in creating images is decreasing; the number of consumers of prefabricated images that hardly challenge the imagination is growing.[32]

Images are a specific form of abstraction—their two-dimensional nature transforms space. The electronic character of television images enables ubiquity and acceleration. Such images can be distributed almost simultaneously to all regions of the world.[33] They miniaturize the world and enable it to be experienced as images. They represent a new form of commodity and are subject to economic market principles. They are themselves produced and traded, even if the objects to which they relate do not become commodities. Images are exchanged with others, are related to others, are broken up into parts and recomposed in different ways; image fragments are created that can form a new whole each time. They move and allude to each other. Their accelerated movement makes them become like each other: mimesis of speed. Due to their two-dimensional, electronic, and miniaturizing character, images are becoming increasingly similar despite their differing content. They captivate the viewer. They fascinate and terrify. They dissolve the relationships that had built up between people and objects and transfer them into a world of appearance. The world, political, and social areas of life are aestheticized. In a mimetic process images seek preexisting images to model themselves on; they are transformed into new fractal images without a frame of reference. This results in a promiscuity of images. Intoxicating games with simulacra and simulations develop: the images are highly differentiated, yet their difference implodes at the same time. The images as images are the message (McLuhan).

Images are transmitted at the speed of light. This creates a world of appearance and fascination that is removed from "reality." This world of appearance spreads and has a tendency to deprive other "worlds" of their reality content. More and more images are being produced that have only themselves as a reference point and do not relate to any form of reality. As a consequence of this, everything becomes a game of images in which anything is possible, and ethical issues lose their importance. If everything becomes a game of images, arbitrariness and randomness are unavoidable. The worlds of images thus created affect real life. Deciding what is art or life, fantasy or reality, becomes increasingly difficult. Both areas are moving ever closer together. Life becomes the preexisting image that the world of appearance models itself on, and then life models itself in turn on this image. The visual develops hypertrophically. The world becomes transparent; time is compressed as if nothing existed outside the presence of accelerated images. The images attract desire, capture it, and remove its boundaries. At the same time they escape desire, by referring to what is absent while they themselves are present. Objects and people strive to cross the boundaries and be part of the images.

Images become simulacra.[34] They relate to something, adapt themselves to it, and are products of a process of mimicry. Political debates are not conducted for their own sake, but to make them into images and distribute them on television. From its inception, a political controversy is seen in terms of the image it will become. The television images become a medium of political debate. The viewers see a simulation of a political controversy where everything is staged in a way that induces them to believe that the political debate is authentic. Everything is oriented toward its transformation into the world of appearance. Where this can be achieved, the controversy is successful. The simulation of politics creates a political impact. Simulations have a greater impact than "real" political debate.

Simulacra are in search of preexisting images, which they themselves create. Simulations become icons that affect the character of political controversies. Drawing boundaries between reality and simulacra becomes difficult; the crossing of boundaries has resulted in images overlapping and permeating each other in a new way. Mimetic processes allow the preexisting images, the images themselves, and the copies of images to interact with each other. The aim of the images is no longer to correspond to the preexisting model, but to resemble themselves. The same happens with people. The aim is to achieve an exceptional similarity of individuals with themselves, attainable as the result of productive mimesis against the background of a wide scope of differentiation in the same subject.

Mental Images

Whereas up to this point we have dealt with images produced by human beings in their role as *Homo pictor* and depicted outside their bodies in various media, we now turn to the mental images that constitute human consciousness. Human imagination transforms the exterior world into images and transports these into the human consciousness. This process begins with perceiving; we would not see any images were it not for the image-generating capacity of the imagination within us. This power gives us a fixed place in a cultural and historical order, through which our relationship to material objects and to other human beings is determined. As we align ourselves with the world, its images come into being within us. This process, in its orientation toward the world, is driven by our desire to open ourselves to the world and at the same time to appropriate it in the shape of perceptive and mnemonic images. In the majority of cases, mental images involve an overlapping of individual and collective images of the inner imaginary with images of the exterior world.

The inner image-world of a social subject is determined on the one hand by the collective imaginary of his culture, and on the other hand by the unique and unmistakable qualities of the images derived from his individual life—and finally by the mutual overlapping and interpenetration of both image-worlds. Recent biographical research in education studies has made important advances in identifying the role and function of these inner worlds of images. I would like here to distinguish seven kinds of mental images, *images as modulators of behavior, orientation images, images of desire, images of intention, mnemonic images, mimetic images, and archetypal images.*[35]

IMAGES AS MODULATORS OF BEHAVIOR The question here is whether or to what extent humans are endowed with hereditary structures of behavior. It is undisputed that the hiatus between stimulus and reaction is peculiar to humans. This fact does not, however, rule out the possibility that human behavior is influenced by hereditary mental images and behavior patterns. In recent years, ethnography has gained important insights into how "trigger images" affect basic human behavior patterns such as eating and drinking, procreation, and caring for our young.

ORIENTATION IMAGES Socialization and education transmit thousands of orientation images that enable the young to find their bearings in their lifeworlds and to lead their lives. Many of these images are extremely simple, accessible, and easy to reproduce; they are therefore socially very powerful. These images are public. They are shared by many people, who are thus "networked" through them; sharing in such image-networks gives rise to commonality and a sense of belonging and collectivity. Under the conditions of globalization, these image-networks are extended globally, beyond the boundaries of national cultures, and generate new, transnational forms of consciousness.

IMAGES OF DESIRE Structurally, images associated with urges and fantasies of wish-fulfillment are similar. In their concrete manifestations, however, they frequently differ. They are of considerable importance for guiding human actions and human dreaming. In many cases, they aim to fulfill desires, while at the same time they contain the knowledge that such fulfillment is impossible.

IMAGES OF INTENTION Whereas images of wish-fulfillment are oriented toward possession and enjoyment, images of intention are projections of energy for action. Desires modulated by the will are manifestations of an excess of drive, and human labor and culture stem from our ability to entertain such desires.

MNEMONIC IMAGES Mnemonic images (i.e., images of memory) determine a person's specific character. In part they are accessible and malleable at will; in part they elude the grasp and control of consciousness. Many are generated by perception. Some can be traced to imaginary situations. Mnemonic images overlap and interlace with new perceptions and help shape them. They are the products of a selection process, in which suppression and consciously motivated forgetting (in the sense of forgiving) play a role. Mnemonic images make up the story of a person. They are tied to the spaces and times of her life and relate to sadness and joy. They are linked to failure and success. They propel themselves to the forefront of the memory so that the past becomes present, and provide a remedy against the relentlessness of time.

MIMETIC IMAGES Plato was one of the first to point out that images as templates or (preexisting) models (*Vor-Bilder*) pose a challenge to our mimetic ability. Such preexisting images can be living persons as well as imaginary images. Plato holds that the compulsion to imitate is so strong that we cannot resist it—especially not while we are children and adolescents. Plato's conclusion is therefore to consciously make use of all images worthy of imitation for education, and to exclude all images pernicious to education. Aristotle disagrees: for him, the point is to confront the young with the unpleasant, in a controlled way, in order to enable them to withstand it. Both positions are echoed in today's debates about the effects of violence in the new media.[36]

ARCHETYPAL IMAGES For Carl Gustav Jung, archetypal images were significant for the life of the individual. He believed that all great events in life touch upon these images and make them appear within the psyche. They become conscious as such if the individual has sufficient self-awareness and perceptive power to grasp what she is experiencing, and does not merely act, that is, does not simply enact the myth and the symbol without realizing it.[37] There is no need to subscribe to the slightly dubious explanations about the development of the "collective unconscious" and the archetypes in order to recognize that each culture has generated great guiding images, great fateful images, which are capable of influencing individuals' actions through their dreams and the cultural imaginary.

The Irreducibility of Images

The irreducibility of images is vital for our understanding of them. This is an important issue in the study of images, where it is essential to avoid reducing images to discourses. As the human body is a site of images, people live in an internal world of heterogenic images that they cannot leave. Fantasy, imagination, and the mind's eye express themselves in images—the imaginary, which could not be grasped without them.[38]

Although art history has benefited from Panofsky's iconology, the limitations of his interpretational theory are clearly visible today, as its categories, which were taken from Renaissance art and are highly cognitive, are based on the reading of texts and have little feeling for the treatment of images in their essence as images.[39] On the first level of pre-iconographic interpretation, the lines and colors of a picture are understood first as objects and figures; no further knowledge is required to understand the picture. On the second iconographic level this is different. Here, for example, knowledge of the Gospels is necessary to understand the meaning of a depiction of the crucifixion of Christ. The intrinsic meaning of the image (iconology) takes us to the third level. Here the picture is to be understood as a form of expression of the concept of Christianity at the time the picture was created. This may require an in-depth study of the theological, philosophical, and political questions of the time. The aim is to do justice to the cultural and historical relevance of the picture. What is missing is the consideration of the essence of the image. The content lies in contemplation as reflection on both the essence of the image and on possibilities that are inherent only in the image itself. One can call this iconic way of viewing, which is related to the essence of the image itself, "iconics" (where *iconic* relates to *eikon* in the way *logic* relates to *logos* or *ethics* to *ethos*).[40] If images depict stories, then, under the terms of iconics, the relationship of images to language must be considered—for example, the difference between the sequentiality of a narrative and the simultaneous nature of a pictorial representation. In addition to this, we must also examine how we contemplate a picture and the different ways we appropriate and appreciate it aesthetically. Panofsky's interpretational theory flounders when faced with highly abstract pictures such as Mondrian's squares; here the development of the iconic contemplation is indispensable if we are to run through the structuring potentials that the picture contains in a creative and even open-ended way. It is this running through the configuration of valences and opposing valences contained in each picture that makes us, as viewers, conscious not only of our structuring activities but also of our own powerlessness vis-à-vis this viewing process. This takes place in the viewer's very particular experience, in which each attempt at structuring is based on one and the same phenomenon. However, none of the possible structuring activities results in the viewer fully gaining control over and mastering this experience of identity.[41] The process makes us conscious of our insurmountable lack of control with regard to the picture and opens us up to the aesthetic experience, whereby the identity of the picture, as a vicarious form of representation, cannot itself be represented by anything else.[42] Pictures or images have an inescapable intrinsic quality that constantly refers the viewer back to the nature of the image as an image. The aesthetic experience also enables us to experience alterity, which Rimbaud summarized so aptly and succinctly: *Je est un autre*. What René Char said of poetry also applies to art: the images know something about us that we do not know. They contain an element of surprise that we cannot foresee; it often defies everyday rationality, and we must confront it before the meaning of the image is revealed.

Taking both views as a basis, the mimetic treatment of pictorial art can lead to iconic experiences. Mimetic processes have the purpose of "recreating" images with the aid of vision and storing these in the inner world of images with the aid of the imagination. The recreation of images is a process of mimetic acquisition in which the images, in their essence as images, are stored in the worlds of images and memory. The mimetic processing of images has the purpose of acquiring their essence as images, which persists before, during, after, and outside of any interpretation. Once images are stored in the inner world of images,[43] they form the points of reference for interpretations that continuously change during the course of our lives. Regardless of each interpretation, the repeated mimetic treatment of images is an act of acquisition or even cognition. It involves concentration and effort in the recreation of the imaginary images and continually demands that images be refreshed in a visual encounter with the real images or their reproductions. For the mimetic encounter with images, we must abandon our control over them. The visual re-creation of their forms and colors requires the suppression of images and thoughts emerging from the inner world of the viewer; the mimetic acquisition of images requires us to retain the image while we are seeing it, to open ourselves up to its imagery, and to surrender ourselves to it. The mimetic process involves us as viewers in allowing ourselves to become similar to the image through visually recreating it, absorbing it, and augmenting our inner world of images with this image.

The mimetic acquisition of an image can be divided into two phases that blend into each other. In the first phase, the image is in front of our eyes as viewers; in the second, it has already been taken into our inner image-world. In the first phase, the most important aspect is the overcoming of mechanical vision, which sees images in the same way as other objects and pushes them to the back of the mind, categorizing them as something one has "seen before." A process of seeing that is directed toward control and orientation forms a protective barrier against being overwhelmed by images. This kind of seeing reduces the options of seeing. In acts of conscious mimetic seeing, however, the purpose is to develop the act of seeing itself. This includes spending time with the object, looking past the usual, and discovering the unusual. Seen in this way, the mimetic acquisition of images and objects can be regarded as a retarding element that aims to possess the image through being possessed by it ourselves. In the second phase the image has already become part of the inner world of images as a result of mimetic viewing. It is only at this stage that the mimetic process of "adjusting to become similar" to the image occurs. It is necessarily incomplete and can reach new levels of intensity at any time. By retaining an image absorbed in the imagination in this manner, we exercise our powers of concentration as well as the imagination. Since the image is reproduced by the imagination, there is a constant battle against the inherent urge of the image to disappear as well as against the current of interfering images emerging from the inner world of images. This activity performed by the imagination is mimetic and comes into play every time an image is created.

The Gaze upon Images—The Gaze of Images

The images of presence, of representation, and of simulation, as well as many mental images, come into being only when they or the configurations they are based on are gazed upon. But what does *to gaze* mean? There are very different types of gaze. A gaze can be modest, benevolent, impatient, evil, angry, and so forth. Gazes are linked closely with the history of the subject and of subjectivity, as well as with the history of knowledge. Power, control, and self-control find expression in them. They are evidence of our relationship to the world, to other people, and to the self. The gazes of other people constitute the social sphere, and within this category, we may distinguish intimate from public gazes. The various gazes are linked to the collective imaginary and to the conceptions of the human being. The gaze cannot be adequately described either as a beam of light that is indispensable for rendering the world visible or as a mirror that merely receives and reflects the world. The gaze is active as well as passive; it turns outward to the world and at the same time receives it. What determines this relation between activity and passivity and how it does so has been subject to controversy in the history of the gaze. Merleau-Ponty pointed out that we must assume that the world is looking at us, too, as are the images we make ourselves. In the gaze, the world and the human being intersect in a chiasm. With a gaze, people can express many things and then deny them, for the gaze is spontaneous and does not last. It makes things visible and at the same time is a form of human expression.

Many observations have been made concerning the gaze in relation to images or pictures as works of art. As Hans Belting puts it, "gazes are already in the picture before they fall upon a picture. This alone permits the use of the history of the image in support of a history of the gaze."[44]

An iconology of the gaze can therefore furnish insights into the diversity of historical and cultural image-practices. The gaze oscillates between image, body, and medium; it dwells neither in the body nor in the image but unfolds in between them; it cannot be tethered to anything or held fast; it has the choice of how to relate to the media. Images ensnare the gaze and, in our desire for images, turn the gaze itself into an object. In works of art, the primary image-practice of the body transmutes into a secondary image-practice. In gazing upon images devoid of their own life, the imagination unfolds. Gazing at a mirror or through a windowpane, we may perceive the gaze itself. "The look through the window is echoed by the computer screen, the look in the mirror by the video."[45]

In dealing with images, the mimetic gaze plays an important role. Within this gaze, as gazers, we open ourselves up to the world. By becoming one with it, we broaden our experience. We take an image from the template of the world and incorporate it into our mental image-world. As we visually retrace shapes and colors, textures and structures, these are transformed into the inner world and become part of our imaginary. In such a process, the uniqueness of the world in its historical and cultural specificity is taken in. Here it is a question of protecting world and image from hasty interpretations by which "world" is transformed into language and meaning, but at the same time done away with as "image." Rather the aim has to be to retain the insecurity, complexity, and multiplicity of meanings of the world and not to refuse to accept its ambivalence. In mimetically retracing the world, we expose ourselves to its ambivalence and also to that of images. In this process, the task is to learn "by heart" the section of the world in view or the image in view. Thus, we must close our eyes and recreate the image we have seen before our inner eye using our imagination; we must focus our attention upon it, protect it from other images introduced by the inner stream of images, and "get hold of it" by dint of our concentration and power of thought. Recreating an image in contemplation is the first step to a mimetic engagement with images; holding on to it, working upon it, making it unfold in our imagination are further steps. Reproducing an image in inner contemplation and remaining attentive to it is just as important as interpreting it.

Fantasy, Imagination, "*Einbildungskraft*": The Imaginary

The possibility of turning images of the outside world into part of our inner world and of thereby storing them in the memory and remembering them, as well as also being capable of reifying the inner world of imagination and images in the outer world of objects is a *conditio humana*. The Greeks referred to this as *fantasy*, which the Romans translated as *imagination*; Paracelsus translated it into German as *Einbildungskraft*— the power of imagination—and today, under the influence of French authors, it is frequently referred to as the *imaginary*. It is one of the most mysterious human powers; it affects all aspects of life and manifests itself in different forms. It can only be grasped through a process of concretization. It defies all attempts to identify it. Fantasy makes it possible for us to perceive images, even if the subject depicted is not present. Fantasy encompasses the possibility of inner vision and the sketching-out of future activities.

The earliest conceptual notion of *fantasy* is to be found in Plato's *Republic (Politeia)*. In the tenth book, the mimesis of the painter is defined as the imitation of something appearing as it appears (*"pros to phainomenon, os phainetai"*). Aristotle defined fantasy as an act of bringing something before the eyes, as performed by the memory artist, who selects certain images, and as a process of creating a semblance (*fantasma*).[46] In this case fantasy is the ability to make something appear. The meaning changes in Roman antiquity when *imaginatio* appears at the side of *fantasia*. Now the emphasis is no longer on making things appear; *imaginatio* relates to the active force of absorbing images, of imagining, which Paracelsus translated into German as *Einbildungskraft* (the power of imagination). Fantasy, the imagination, and *Einbildungskraft* are three terms designating the human ability to internalize external images and thus transform the outer world into an inner world, as well as to create, retain, and alter inner worlds of images of different origins and meaning.

Fantasy has a chiastic structure in which the inside and outside worlds meet. Both Maurice Merleau-Ponty and Jacques Lacan have remarked on this structure, which is so vital for perception as well as for the production of images. A concept of seeing that assumes that objects identical to themselves are faced with an initially "empty" seeing subject is inadequate. Rather, seeing involves something that we can only approximate by scanning it with our gaze. "The look [. . .] envelops, palpates, espouses the visible things. As though it were in a relation of pre-established harmony with them, as though it knew them before knowing them, it moves in its own way within its abrupt and imperious style, and yet the views taken are not desultory—I do not look at chaos, but at things—so that finally one cannot say if it is the look or if it is the things that command."[47] Such an interaction between the senses and the outside world as perceived by them takes place not only in seeing but also when touching, hearing, and, in principle, when smelling and tasting.

Human perception is not without certain prerequisites. On the one hand, we perceive the world anthropomorphically, that is, on the basis of the physiological attributes of our bodies. On the other hand, our historical-anthropological and cultural attributes also influence our perception. With the invention and spread of writing, visual perception changed in comparison to the way oral cultures see. In a similarly dramatic manner, our perception processes are being changed by new media and the accompanying accelerated processing of images. As research in Gestalt psychology has shown, fantasy has a role to play even in basic perception, in the process of complementary perception completion. The same applies to cultural frames of reference which give the perceived objects their sense and meaning in the first place. Every act of seeing is both made possible and also restricted by historical and cultural factors. As such it is contingent, changeable, and open to future developments.

If we examine the corporeal basis of fantasy, we come across Gehlen's assumption that

> in the detritus of our dreams, or in the periods of concentrated vegetative processes, in childhood, or in the contact between the sexes; in other words, wherever forces of developing life announce themselves, [. . .] [t]here are, amid ever-changing images, certain primal visions or images of the overall purpose of life, which senses within itself a tendency toward a higher form, a greater intensity of current, so to speak. An immediate vital *ideality* exists, a tendency in the *substantia vegetans* toward a higher quality or quantity (whereby it should be noted that the right to make this distinction remains questionable).[48]

Gehlen understands fantasy as a projection of excessive impulses. However, it is even possible that fantasy precedes the excess of impulses, so that the urge to live can use it to create images for its own satisfaction.[49] In Gehlen's view, fantasy is connected to the status of humans as deficient beings and to our residual instincts and the hiatus between stimulus and reaction. Therefore fantasy is related to needs, stimuli, and desire for satisfaction. However, it is not merely restricted to these. Human plasticity and openness to the world are evidence that fantasy is shaped by culture, in which it plays such a central role that the human being is "a being of imagination (*Phantasiewesen*) as well as a being of reason (*Vernunftwesen*)."[50]

Clearly, fantasy resists rational access. Even images can only be understood as a way of pinning down those elementary powers that elude us and cannot be objectified. The three most common terms used in the German language accentuate different aspects, but these differences are not absolutely clear-cut. Provisionally, we might say that *Phantasie* (fantasy) refers to the wilder side, *Imagination* (imagination) refers to the world of images, and *Einbildungskraft* (power of imagination) refers to the power or faculty by which new ideas and images are created. For fantasy, it is possible to distinguish among four different aspects that relate to different historical periods and cultural contexts. One aspect of fantasy involves the possibility of human participation in art. Another aspect is the understanding of the alterity of other cultural and human worlds, which can only be "recreated" with the aid of fantasy in a way that makes them understandable. The third aspect is the relationship between the unconscious and fantasy; in this instance, fantasy is the force that works outside of the realm of consciousness to shape the human world of images, as articulated in dreams and fantasies, in streams of desire, and in our life force. A fourth aspect is the wish and the ability to implement desires in a counterfactual manner.[51] In all four cases the aim of fantasy is to change the world, albeit in a manner that is more spontaneous, situation-based, and random than strategic.[52] Adorno summarizes the social debate on the role of fantasy in science, art, and culture thus:

It would be worthwhile to write an intellectual history of fantasy, since the latter is the actual goal of positivist prohibitions. In the eighteenth century, both in Saint-Simon's work and in d'Alembert's Discours préliminaire, fantasy along with art is included in productive labor and participates in the notion of the unleashing of the forces of production. Comte, whose sociology reveals an apologetic, static orientation, is the first enemy of both metaphysics and fantasy simultaneously. The defamation of fantasy or its relegation to a special domain, marked off by the division of labor, is the original phenomenon of the regression of the bourgeois spirit. However, it does not appear as an avoidable error of this spirit, but rather as a consequence of a fatality which instrumental reason—required by society—couples with this taboo. The fact that fantasy is only tolerated when it is reified and set in abstract opposition to reality, makes it no less of a burden to science than to art. Legitimate science and art desperately seek to redeem the mortgage that burdens them.[53]

The concepts of imagination and the power of imagination are also assigned different meanings. In the British history of ideas, Locke regards the imagination as the "power of the mind," and Hume sees it as a kind of magical faculty in the soul, which is, however, "inexplicable by the utmost efforts of human understanding."[54] Coleridge sees imagination as a human ability or faculty and distinguishes between two forms.

The primary Imagination I hold to be the living power and prime agent of all human Perception, and as a repetition in the finite mind of the eternal act of creation in the infinite I AM. The secondary I consider as an echo of the former, co-existing with the conscious will, yet still as identical with the primary in the *kind* of its agency, and differing only in *degree,* and in the *mode* of its operation. It dissolves, diffuses, dissipates, in order to re-create: or where this process is rendered impossible, yet still at all events it struggles to idealize and to unify. It is essentially *vital*, even as all objects (*as* objects) are essentially fixed and dead.[55]

Thus, imagination is seen as part of the subject in which it acts, which the subject uses to breathe vitality into the world. According to Coleridge, imagination also encompasses the ability to release and destroy connections in order to create new ones. Whereas the first form is conceived as being analogous with the force of nature—*natura naturans*, which creates everything—the second form of imagination relates to the world of things, which it destroys and rebuilds. Added to this is a third force—*fancy*, a force that creates and interlinks things and relationships. These three aspects of the capacity of imagination affect and interact with each other in a playful manner. They create images, destroy them, and combine their elements to form new images in constantly oscillating motion.

Herder believed the power of imagination to be the connection between body and soul; for Kant and Fichte it was the bridge between reason and the senses. Kant's famous formulation, that "thoughts without content are empty, concepts without intuition are blind," recognizes the power of imagination as being necessary for all conceptual cognition. However, cultural development has not adhered to this norm: empty ideas and images without concepts have become the norm, and in more and more areas of society, fiction has become reality, and reality has become fictitious. Taking a historical perspective, Vilém Flusser, in "A New Power of Imagination," differentiates between four stages of development of the power of imagination in human history: "First, man took a step back from his life-world, to imagine it. Then man stepped back from the imagination, to describe it. Then man took a step back from the linear, written critique to analyze it. And finally, owing to a new imagination, man projected synthetic images out of analysis. [. . .] But what concerns us right now in an existential sense is the [. . .] leap out of the linear into the zero-dimensional (into the realm of 'quanta')."[56]

In the French discussion of the imaginary, another concept arises, adding yet another dimension of meaning. Jean-Paul Sartre defined the imaginary as the "irrealizing" function of consciousness, within which the consciousness creates absent objects, makes them present and, in so doing, creates an imaginary relationship to its objects.[57] For Jacques Lacan, the imaginary belongs to a prelinguistic bodily condition in which the individuals are not yet aware of their limits and deficiencies.[58] According to this, the imaginary has its origins in the identification of the infant with the mother, which is so strong that it cannot imagine itself as being "different" from her. The infant is fascinated by the bodily unity of the mother. As if looking in a mirror, seeing the mother's bodily completeness, the child has a sense of its own intactness and power. However, the experience of the wholeness of the mother endangers the infant's own "completeness" and engenders an experience of its incompleteness and dependency on others. This experience of our own incompleteness and finite nature is also the origin of the sexual subject. According to Lacan, the imaginary, with its world of images, precedes the symbolic, with its world of language. Cornelius Castoriadis takes this position further and defines the relationship between the two worlds as follows:

The imagination has to use the symbolic not only to 'express' itself (this is self-evident), but to 'exist,' to pass from the virtual to anything more than this. The most elaborate delirium, just as the most secret and vaguest fantasy, are composed of 'images,' but these 'images' are there to represent something else and so to have a symbolic function. But, conversely, symbolism too presupposes an imaginary capacity. For it presupposes the capacity to see in a thing what it is not, to see it other than it is. However, to the extent that the imaginary ultimately stems from the originary faculty of positing or presenting oneself with things and relations that do not exist, in the form of representation (things and relations that are not or have never been given in perception), we shall speak of a final or *radical imaginary* as the common root of the *actual imaginary* and of the *symbolic*. This is, finally, the elementary and irreducible capacity of evoking images.[59]

TWELVE

Death and Recollection of Birth

Although the human body has now been the central concern of historical cultural anthropology for more than
twenty-five years, it remains enigmatic. One important
spectrum in which we experience its enigmatic qualities and
its inscrutability is indicated by the dynamics of *the anticipation of death and the recollection of birth*. To date, research
in the humanities, philosophy, and the social sciences has
dealt with the transience and mortality of the human body.
Death especially, as the boundary of life, has been a focus of
interest. On the other hand, birth, the other side of physical existence, has hardly received any attention at all.[1] The
situation has begun to change only recently.[2] Thus, the discussion is gaining in complexity: birth is the precondition
of death; only what has been born can die. The alternation
of birth and death permits the *creatio continua*, without
which neither the human body nor any human life could
ever have come into being. This has also been shown by
evolutionary research into the development of life, including human life. From an evolutionary point of view, the life
of one individual is not as important as the survival of the
species, and the birth and death of individuals are, in fact,
essential for the species to advance. Not individuals, but the
human species as a whole has developed. In view of this
key role of birth and death in the development of human
beings, I address the question of how cultures deal with
human temporality, transitoriness, and mortality. I intend to

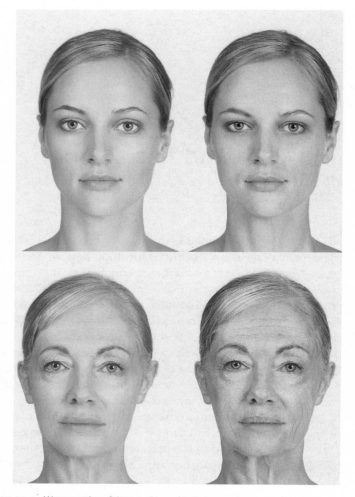

FIGURE 12.1 Woman aging. © Images Source/Getty Images.

show that the fear and dread of death occupied the imaginations even of the Neanderthals and led to the development of ideas about the afterlife. I will also show that death plays a central role in cultural studies with regard to ontogenesis. This makes it necessary to reflect on birth and the natality of the human body—which is the subject of the second section.

The Anticipation of Death

The first evidence we have of cultural responses to death dates back to the Neanderthals. *Homo sapiens* did not bury his dead simply to protect himself against the putrefaction of the corpses: he buried them in a fetal position, which suggests that the Neanderthals believed in rebirth. The discovery of traces of pollen in some of the graves, where the dead had been laid on a bed of flowers and were also covered with flowers, leads us to the same conclusion. The fact that some of the bones found were painted with ochre indicates a second burial after the corpse had decomposed. Stones were also used to protect the remains of the dead. These findings are signs that death had penetrated the world of *Homo sapiens*, and they also show that even the Neanderthals had an awareness of death and concepts of life after death. Even at this early date, death was not regarded as a final disappearance but as a transition from one state of being to another. These concepts require an awareness of present, past, and future, that is, an awareness of time.

It is with these concepts of the hereafter that the imaginary began to play a role in the human world, resulting in the development of myths and magic. By using these, people tried to protect themselves against death. Burial rites, which they used to come to terms with the trauma of death, played an important role. For *Homo sapiens*, death was an experience of loss. The dread of death made it a fixture of human life, and humans used rites and myths to attempt to overcome their fear. *Homo sapiens* started to use the imaginary to protect himself against death, mobilizing the individual and the collective imagination to counteract mortality. This resulted in an increased value being attached to individual life. When death suddenly entered conscious human life, along with it *Homo sapiens* experienced both truth and illusion, insight and myth, fear and reassurance, objective cognition, and a new subjectivity. Above all, it was an experience of ambivalence. This marked the beginning of a new development of individuality.[3]

In the Magdalenian cave paintings, we identify a further development of the imaginary and of individuality, since they mark not only the birth of art but also the birth of *Homo sapiens sapiens*.[4] These paintings are creations of the human mind and imaginary. They are the first pictorial symbols yet to be found in which new aesthetic capacities are expressed. These aesthetic skills play a fundamental role in the formation of human beings' relationship to the world around them. Many of these cave paintings are imaginary representations of animals living in the world outside, whose absence from the cave in which they were painted was transformed into a pictorial presence by these images. As representations of the outside world, these pictures are part of the human imaginary. This duplication through images created an aesthetic, man-made world in which the artistic powers of *Homo sapiens sapiens* could develop. Magic enabled humans to use the creations of their imaginary to influence the shaping of the outside world, resulting in an interchange between the inner and outer worlds, and it was not just art and language that developed in this exchange but the entirety of human culture. The playful creation of aesthetic images, which had nothing to do with fighting the challenges of daily life, and the pleasure and enjoyment derived from these images were highly significant in the development of individuality and culture. In the world of the imaginary, humans developed a relationship with themselves, thus increasing the opportunities for creating cultural diversity. The imaginary evolved in the interplay between death and rites, the production of aesthetic objects and myth, language, and magic, and with the imaginary came culture, enabling humans to find their place in the world.

Human societies and cultures are rooted in time and space, and they exist not only in spite of death; the limited life span of each individual means that communities live alongside and in opposition to death. Culture, embracing collective knowledge, practical skills, norms, rules, and so on, is passed down from one generation to the next, and in this process the concepts of death and the practices of dealing with death change.[5] Death affects not only the biological side of human life; it also poses a threat and a challenge for human culture.[6] One of the most important tasks for all cultures is to insure continuity beyond the death of individuals and generations, and this provides both the individual and the community with the opportunity to imagine and contemplate death and to come to terms with it by means of performative rituals. Each particular culture does this differently, perhaps through religious myths, stories and pictures of life after death, or a concept of an absolute end, the last of which has become more widespread due to the influence of evolution research and the natural sciences.

There are two distinct concepts of life after death. In the first case, life in the hereafter is imagined as a parallel to this life: the deceased continues to live in the same way as in this life. In the second, the deceased lives on after undergoing a metamorphosis.[7] In the first instance, life after death continues in the same form as before death. In this case, death is only partially accepted; its brutal finality is glossed over by an imaginary counterconcept, which suggests a form of immortality. In the second case, death is understood as metamorphosis. Here death is accepted, but only in its power to change and not in its power to eradicate. Both concepts recognize death as an act of violence, but, at the same time, the imaginary suggests immortality. It is precisely this suggestion that leads to a consciousness of death. In every metamorphosis, ideas of death and birth are interwoven. For the new to be created, the old must make way.

The dread of death, the grief at the burial, and the fear of the putrefaction of the corpse are all consequences of losing our individuality as a result of death. In the development of children, we can see the relationship between awareness of self and awareness of death. It is only when children become aware of themselves as persons that death begins to disconcert them, and they start to use their imaginations to address the issue of death.[8] Closely and irrevocably tied up with the awareness of individuality is the fear of death. The reverse is also true: when awareness of death is expressed, forms of individualization follow.

In spite of the dread that humans experience in the face of death, they are still able to "forget" it or deliberately endanger themselves, as if they were not afraid of it. This human peculiarity of being able to put one's life at risk is extraordinary and puzzling. It is connected with being able to overcome limits and fears, whether this be in a moment of madness, ecstasy, or passion, or in sacrificing oneself for a higher good. Risking one's life is the expression of a human ability to act that arises from our inherent plasticity, imbalance, and ex-centricity. It is this same force that makes a human being a self-determining individual and at the same time a non-predetermined microcosm that is constantly evolving and open to all of the possibilities of nature.[9] This potential to determine ourselves means that the way we approach death depends essentially on our individuality, our self-awareness, and the extent of our self-knowledge. Even suicide can be an act of self-determination and individuality.[10]

Concepts and rites of death differ according to culture and historical era.[11] In the Christian culture of Europe, rites are used for the performative expression of the sense of loss and sadness we feel when someone dies. The performative character of rituals helps to bring the mourners closer together and make them feel that they are a community of the living. Rituals of dying and burial intensify the feelings of belonging. As *rites of passage*, they allow the mourners to experience the departure and a possible passing over of the deceased into another world. Death rituals acknowledge and celebrate the life of the deceased, address the pain of "those left behind," and nurture hopes of a reunion in the hereafter.

In his research into the history of mentalities, Philippe Ariès made a much-debated attempt to differentiate between the following approaches to death in European history since the Middle Ages: tamed death (*la mort apprivoisée*), one's own death (*la mort de soi*), thy death (*la mort de toi*), and forbidden death (*la mort interdite/la mort inversée*).[12]

In the case of *tamed death*, which was typical for the Middle Ages, the dying person takes an active role. As can be seen from deathbed and mourning rituals, death is not exclusively the fate of an individual, but a test for the community. The dying person is part of a Christian community that dates back to Adam and Eve and stretches into the future to the resurrection of the dead. As death is an event that spreads dread and pain among the community of the living, it is "captured" and tamed by means of rituals, liturgy, and ceremonies. The taming is helped by the analogy between sleep and death, which raises hopes of awakening, resurrection, and eternal life in the hereafter. Although death remains a misfortune linked with suffering and sin, it can be overcome with God's help.

Between the High Middle Ages and the eighteenth century, death was increasingly experienced more as a personal fate, as *one's own death*. This way of dealing with death prevailed for a long time, reversing the traditional relationship between the Other and the self. The more highly developed the person's consciousness of her individuality, the more distanced she becomes from the community. The result is what Ariès describes as a triumph of individualism in this epoch of conversions, spectacular acts of penance, huge gifts from patrons, as well as profitable, ingenious, and daring ventures.[13] Wills too, and the expression of an individual's wishes to order her affairs, can be understood as signs of the increasing importance of individuality. Parallel to the raised profile of this life, the concept of an immortal soul also became widespread during this time.[14] The cortege was replaced by a church procession and service in the presence of the corpse. The sight of the deceased is hidden by the shroud, coffin, and catafalque and represented, if necessary, by an image. The countenance of the dead causes fear and is avoided.

In the nineteenth century a new model, *thy death*, became established. Here it was less the fate of the species or the individual that was in the foreground, but the death of another person, someone close, someone we loved, someone to whom we had a personal relationship. This development was accompanied by an increase in the importance of private life. The deathbed ritual became a staging and performance of the grief experienced by those left behind as a result of the physical separation from the deceased. Frequently, death was portrayed as a thing of beauty rather than a thing of dread. Now it was not so much fear of the hereafter, with

FIGURE 12.2 Pierre Alexandre Wille, *The Last Moments of the Beloved Wife* (1784). © Cambrai Museum, Hugo Maertens.

its images of guilt and hell, that was important, but the hope of being reunited with the person whom death had taken.

Forbidden death is the current model, where the emphasis is on the private nature and intimacy of death. The importance of the community continues to decline. Dying becomes a process to be hidden from public view, something of which to be ashamed, which thus takes place in the isolation of a hospital. Dying takes place in private, rather than within the community, so that the dying will not be a burden on families. Modern medicine spares the dying from pain. However, it also mutes the dying process. The dying are ashamed of being "defeated" by death. Issues of evil or guilt are now almost insignificant.

There are many objections to this attempt to chart the changes in concepts of death and death images and rites. In many cases these relate to the use of sources and their idealizing and generalizing interpretations. Despite this criticism, however, there is no doubt that Ariès' study of the history of death within the framework of the history of mentalities has opened up new perspectives of historical anthropological research that have inspired many additional works in this area.[15]

A radical interpretation of the relationship of modern societies to death, which is nevertheless completely compatible with the ideas described above, was developed by Jean Baudrillard. In his view, the situation that society finds itself in today is marked by a complete break with the laws of the *symbolic exchange* of life and death. Instead of turning our attention toward this exchange, all our energies are concentrated on excluding death from our lives. The aim is the accumulation of life. This results in the accumulated life being transformed into a form of "living" death. As death is only interpreted from the point of view of the living, it can only be regarded in a limited way; it is seen solely as a threat to life, which must be protected and is only understood in terms of survival. The attempt to postpone death and exclude it from our lives results in a lifeless life. The desire to survive at all costs gives rise to power. It is closely linked to the potential threat of death and decisions we make concerning life and death. All the efforts of genetic engineering to delay death and thus liberate humankind from the intense experience of the restrictions of life are geared toward survival in any form possible. The atomic threat, destruction of the environment, and depletion of resources all threaten the existence of humankind; this can be seen as a result of our desire to be ever more powerful, which is likely to implode at some point in the future. Life is staged as survival; it is simulated and becomes lost in this simulation. We create a hyper-reality in order to replace the reality of a life that has been denied the exchange with death.[16]

The ultimate consequence of this is that any social power is a power over life and death that is wielded in different manners—in some societies by sovereigns or dictators; in others by the state in a democratic framework of power-sharing. Military and police institutions are created in order to protect against death and violence. Health systems are developed and funding is given to branches of science promising to prolong survival. Huge efforts are made to postpone and "outwit" death. Human culture "is nothing more than an organized body of beliefs and rites conceived for the purpose of resisting the disintegrating power of individual and collective death."[17]

Death is a void that disconcerts humankind, and the imagination attempts to fill it by creating a multiplicity of ideas and images to gloss over the fact that we are ignorant.[18] Regardless of the number of images and metaphors the imagination creates, however, it can never really succeed in coming to terms with the void. There are forms of handling, perceiving, and reacting to death that are specific to different cultures. Humans articulate and stage their responses to the loss of another human by means of rites, myths, and images. The relationship between the individual, society, and humankind is expressed in culturally and historically defined forms and is rooted in the imaginary and the performative. Currently there are two major opposing concepts. One assumes that the deceased continue to live on in another world or that they are transformed into another form; the second maintains (in an analogous metaphysical assumption) that death is the absolute end of life. The latter has meant that there is enormous enthusiasm for the promises made by genetic engineering and the other biological sciences that death can be delayed. When viewed in a traditionally logical manner, these two concepts are mutually exclusive, and we are therefore at a loss to know what to believe. The problem consists in trying to grasp something that is essentially elusive: the definite antithesis of life and death. If there is no hereafter, then there must be only the here and now and otherwise nothingness.[19]

It is obvious that this cannot be the last word on this matter. The assumption of life after death is just as much a metaphysical statement as the assumption that everything comes to an end with the death of the individual. There is no basis of experience for either. Death is a boundary that cannot be crossed by science and philosophy. Regardless of how one confronts this boundary, death remains an issue that continues to obsess humankind. In his book *Being and Time*, Heidegger speaks of "Being-toward-death," describing it thus: "Death, as the end of Dasein, is Dasein's ownmost possibility—non-relational, certain and as such indeterminate, not to be outstripped."[20] According to this, death is unique and unrepeatable, and this uniqueness makes it a feature of individual human existence. If one assumes that the self is always *present* in a certain manner, that it is a companion of Dasein, then it is neither mortal nor immortal, then it is present—it is part of "the Other," whether we ascribe this alterity to ourselves (i.e. to our own person) or to other persons or things.[21] This self can be spoken to directly. After death this is no longer possible, and we are reduced to merely speaking about the other person.[22] If the self is present after we wake up and disappears again when we fall asleep, then is death not a "removal from the present" for the self just like falling asleep? Does Epicurus's notion still apply, according to which death concerns neither the living nor the dead? Even if this were the case, and if Pascal's aphorism that "death is easier to bear without thinking about it than the thought of death without danger"[23] holds true, the question still arises as to why death continues to occupy the thoughts of humankind. For Bahr, when thinking of death, proceeding from the unthinkable, we are faced with thinking of "nothingness starting from Nothing rather than from Being. Thinking never ceases not being able to think Nothing."[24] Thus thought cannot stop thinking what it cannot think. However, it cannot think the nothingness from the starting point of Nothing, that is, from death. As thinking needs to have something to grasp, but death is not something that can be grasped, thinking is defeated by death and the nothingness of Nothing. For the self and its existence as the companion of Dasein, this means that "the self is the only form of being with an absolute end and therefore openness to nothingness; without this openness the self could not have relationships to all that is other."[25]

The Recollection of Birth

It was Hannah Arendt who put forward a philosophy of birth, of natality, as opposed to Heidegger's "being-toward-death" or "anticipation of death," and a natology as opposed to his thanatology. This represented a change of perspective. The focus was no longer the end, but the beginning, which had repeatedly been forgotten but now became the center of attention. At first sight, birth seems quite natural and a matter of course. However, closer scrutiny reveals that it is no less enigmatic than death. Only someone who has been born can die. The body's mortality is an indication that it has been born, or of its "natality." Birth is always past. It has always already taken place. It is over once the human being has begun living in the world. For everyone, birth is the precondition of life, while death lies in an uncertain future and will only affect the living at some unknown point in the future. In contrast to death, which everybody must confront alone, in birth one is dependent on other people's cooperation and actions, especially those of one's mother. Birth, much more than death, is a social event in which a child is born into a family, into a community. Philosophical thought means not simply anticipating our death but just as fundamentally recalling our birth and natality. Unlike Hindu thought, for example, Western thought prefers being to nonbeing, and regards birth as a gift, a potential, a chance to begin. This leads to obligations of parents in relation to their children and rights of children in relation to their parents. Birth establishes a relationship which, irrespective of how well or how poorly it functions, ends only in death.

Not without reason did Socrates, himself the son of a midwife, regard philosophy as a *maieutiké techné*, a midwife's art. In the same way as a midwife assists with the bringing of new life into the world, philosophy, seen as a midwife, produces "beautiful, good and true knowledge." Like a midwife assisting pregnant women in the act of giving birth, Socrates helped young philosophers to bring forth insights. Where birth is a delivery from the mother's body, insight is a delivery from the world of appearances, of *doxa*. The maieutic, too, can only produce what has already been present in the young philosopher, who recognizes or gives birth to it. Maieutics is a form of aide-memoire for memories of prenatal knowledge, of preexistence.

Each birth is the creation of a new body. Each single instance of birth is an *imitatio creatoris*. In giving birth to a new human being, mimesis of the divine creation of man takes place. In this, humans imitate God through mimesis. Seen like this, giving birth to new life is a service—a service to God. In book 12 of *De Civitate Dei*, it is said that "*Hoc (initium) ergo ut esset, creatus est homo, ante quem nullus fuit*" (So that there be a beginning, man was created, before whom no one existed). The birth of new life continually repeats this beginning. Each return of the body means mimesis of divine creation and is therefore sacred. Both the sacred nature of man and human dignity are derived from the sacred nature of birth. Each birth can be regarded as a "being-toward-a-beginning." Each time the human body returns as an individual body, as happens in birth, there is also a new beginning to human existence. This beginning contains a potentiality that must be realized in the course of one's life. Human life comes from Nothing and hurries toward Nothing again.[26] Human existence, which is considered to begin at birth, is surrounded by Nothing before birth and Nothing after death. Human life takes place between the "nonexistence of the past" and the "nonexistence of the future." The human body, coming from the *not-yet*, moves toward the *no-more*. Having been born into life, humans leave it again in death. The return and disappearance of the body are the fundamental movements of human life.

The beginning of life in birth is at the same time the beginning of its end. Temporality and transience are the conditions of the human body. Birth and death are *compulsory*. We are not free to choose the beginning of our lives; we are likewise subject to the necessity of leaving them. When we are born, we are born into a preexisting culture that was there before we were with its historicity and culturality. Basically, we live "ex post," in retrospect in relation to the world and to ourselves, which is what makes conscience and reflection possible. This situation entails a certain kind of alienation, an unworldliness, that is essentially insurmountable. We have to resign ourselves to the compulsory nature of life, which is determined by birth and death, return and disappearance; this is the inevitable *conditio humana* of the body and its life.

From the time of birth, the body is dependent on care and nurture. The extrauterine year, the human premature birth, is the condition for learning, action, and living together. The plasticity of the human body is what makes human beings highly capable of learning. Early cultural learning is a mimetic learning that relates to something already given, which is then appropriated mimetically.[27] In this appropriation of the outside world, alterity, and society, the development of individual life takes place in intergenerational relations and social processes. At every birth a world begins. At every death, a world ends. Each human body constitutes a beginning, as though the world were being recreated each time.[28] Seen from this perspective, there cannot be a single beginning but only many beginnings. Also, since everybody has two parents, plurality is already an integral part of each individual life from the very beginning. From this it ensues that the meaning or true theodicy of birth lies in the fact that the same person does *not* return.[29] With this plurality, which is part of our constitution, we human beings become a question to ourselves—a question to which we can only ever find preliminary answers.

Only because all human beings are new beginnings can they begin anew by themselves. Their actions, tending toward the creation of these new beginnings, can thus be interpreted as a mimetic response to the fact that they themselves are new beginnings.[30] Every human being represents such a new beginning, but no one is personally responsible. Being born is the consequence of the actions of one's parents.

Nobody was asked beforehand whether they wanted to be born. Every newborn human being is an immediately evident fact that it seems hardly possible to question. This is so, even if we are not consulted about whether we want to enter existence, which is the most important question of our lives. Nevertheless, we are expected to mould ourselves in a responsible manner, turning ourselves from human beings who were born into the world without having been asked, into human beings who deal with the world and relationships with others and themselves. If we succeed, the irrevocably asymmetric relationship of responsibility between our parents and ourselves is altered to a certain extent. Being born is a painful process of emerging into the light.

This situation would appear very different to practicing Hindus, who believe that it is best for human beings not to be born at all. Birth is regarded as something compulsory from which one must try to escape. For Hindus, there is none of the Western "forgetfulness of birth" or "obsession with death." On the contrary, birth is seen as a problem. All who are born are to blame for their birth. Human beings are directly responsible for all their deeds in previous lives, which lead to their rebirth. They are to lead lives oriented toward dissolving in Nirvana without being reborn again.[31]

The alternation of birth and death makes possible the *creatio continua* of the body, the sequence of generations, and, therefore, the develop-

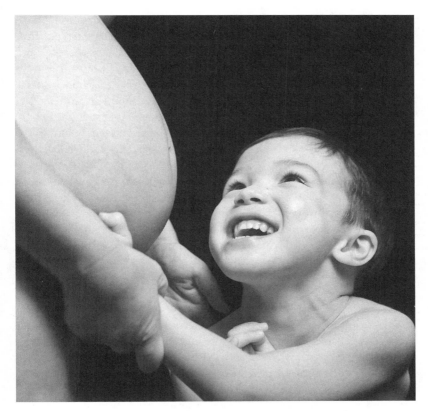

FIGURE 12.3 Pregnant mother holding boy's hands. © Russell Morales/ Flickr/ Getty Images.

ment and changes of human life. The spectrum of opinions ranges from birth being forced upon us to birth as a gift of life. In the same way as a theodicy is philosophically impossible, a biodicy, a justification of the continual return of the human body in birth, is also destined to fail.

The Rediscovery of Childbirth

In view of the recent political and public interest in childbirth, which has come about for various demographic, political, and social reasons, the aim of my investigation on how birth is experienced was to promote awareness of the significance of this aspect of life for social and family groups and for the social and cultural sciences. On the basis of selected examples, my research team and I show how couples expecting a baby, doctors and midwives in hospitals, and television portrayals deal with the subject of birth. We also reconstructed the differences between these ways of conceptualizing childbirth and the political, social, medical, and educational practices surrounding it. We employed qualitative methods (i.e., interviews, group discussions, interpretations of images and videos, and participant observation in families and obstetric institutions) to describe and analyze subjective images and practices associated with birth. At the same time, we analyzed portrayals and performances of childbirth on television and looked at how the subject is handled in the daily newspapers.

Narrative interviews were carried out with twenty couples living in Berlin to establish what significance they assigned to the event of childbirth in their narratives. In order to investigate representations of childbirth in maternity units and to determine how they affected the ideas and behavior of the couples, seventeen narrative interviews and group discussions were conducted with doctors and midwives at five hospitals. The interviews and discussions were assessed on the basis of how the health professionals experienced their communication with the parents-to-be, particularly in situations in which decisions were made. For the analyses of discourses and the media, relevant articles in leading German daily newspapers and excerpts of programs on several television channels were gathered in which childbirth, pregnancy, the family, and mother-, father- and parenthood were addressed.

We were interested in finding out *how* people visualize childbirth and the practices surrounding it in families and maternity units, as well as how the media influence the way women become mothers, men become fathers, and a couple becomes a family with one or more children. People internalize images of childbirth from medicine, psychology, the media, the social services, and education, creating a field that is becoming increasingly important for the social sciences. We demonstrated that institutional practices of preparation for childbirth, practices in obstetric units, families, and the media produce collective images and expectations of the birth process. It also became evident how the different worlds of images surrounding childbirth are dependent upon each other and how, for example, elements of subjective fantasies about medical scenarios are found in educational models and media images of childbirth in family contexts and vice versa. Finally, we also saw how the practices of institutions are shaped by the various representations of childbirth and how reflections, forms of perception, techniques, and schemes for courses of action are formed in institutional contexts.

Our study investigates how couples become families, what difficulties they encounter in the process, and how they deal with them. We show how important mental images and childbirth practices are during pregnancy, at delivery, and in the postnatal period. We also demonstrate that the birth of a child is a life-changing experience that makes a deep impression on all involved and makes mothers of women and fathers of men. As a consequence their attitudes toward each other, the relationships between them, and how they behave toward each other undergo permanent change.

The mothers and fathers to be whom we investigated were confronted with a number of real or anticipated difficulties and anxieties relating to (1) the unknowns of childbirth and the possibility that the baby may not be born healthy; (2) the impossibility of finding an optimal balance between work and the needs of the family; (3) the possibility of family breakdown, with the attendant financial and social problems; (4) the changes associated with the transition from being a couple to being a family, including restrictions on individual liberty, the increase in stresses and strains associated with parenthood, and the fear of assuming responsibility for the family; and (5) the limited number of available models of successful family life. Since the future parents have opted for a life with children, they try to address the difficulties that arise by cooperating as closely as possible. However, we also found that they were unable to solve some of these problems, which are a direct consequence of parenthood and life in a family. Some of the mothers and fathers participating in the study had already anticipated such problems during the wife's pregnancy, but they did not deter them from committing themselves to life with a child in the family. It proved that for most of the mothers and fathers who took part, the decision to have a baby was not based on rational considerations and arguments, but was more a "gut decision."

Analysis of interviews with couples and group discussions with them and their families also showed that the process of transformation from couple to family is lastingly affected by the practices of the doctors and midwives who work at maternity units and the way they conceptualize childbirth. The technologies and media employed in interactions with the health professionals exert a substantial effect on *how* the practices of pregnancy, delivery, and the postnatal period are understood by the parents-to-be. This leads many men and women to see the delivery as a medical matter and to use medical models and medical terms when they talk about it. In addition, television dramas about pregnancy and birth add to the influence of the medical discourse and its representations on the narratives of the expectant mothers and fathers. This discourse and its staging and performance in the entertainment media on television emphasize the discussion and portrayal of the uncertainties and dangers of birth, which caused marked agitation and anxiety in several of the couples interviewed. At the same time, the skill of the obstetric staff is stressed, which is seen as the only source of help when difficulties do arise.

Our results demonstrate how ways of dealing with birth arise from a combination of practices and images from several social fields interacting synergetically. They show that it is important to investigate how social practices and the ways in which they are visualized become superimposed on and interlinked with each other, if we want to understand and address them. They reveal the extent to which images and narratives are determined by the bodily practices to which they refer and how much social practices are influenced by images and narratives. Similarly, it became clear how these practices, images, and narratives determine expectations about childbirth and the course of pregnancy and how the delivery and postnatal period are experienced. However, despite the radical changes in the way the practices associated with childbirth are portrayed in images and narratives, the materiality of human practices cannot be reduced to either how they are visualized or expressed in words.

Outlook

The disappearance of the human body at death and its return at birth are the phylogenetic and ontogenetic conditions of the existence of the human body and the *creatio continua*. This is true of the process of human evolution, in which it is the disappearance of early forms of the human body that in fact results in the conditions for the body of *Homo sapiens sapiens* to evolve. In the same way, every single human being performs the actions of the return of the body at birth and of the disappearance of the body at death. It is thus rather surprising that to date historical and cultural anthropology has more or less ignored birth, although death has always been an important focus. Studying the beginning and end of every single human body at birth and death opens up new perspectives on human temporality—perspectives that need further development. For anthropologists, birth and death are the boundaries to knowledge, which they can approach in different ways but can never proceed beyond. However, it is essential that anthropology consider these boundaries.

Future Prospects:
Single Discipline and
Transdisciplinary Research

The relationships among single-discipline, interdisciplinary, and transdisciplinary research are a fundamental issue in anthropology. The anthropologist's chosen approach has far-reaching consequences on the manner in which problems are conceptualized. Anthropological research can be conducted using either single-discipline or transdisciplinary methodology. There are many examples of the success of the former approach in the fields of history, social sciences, and literature.[1] The latter approach can be seen in studies on the subjects of logic and passion, human beings and their cultures, and in several projects of the Collaborative Research Center on the subject of the performativity of cultures.[2] The quality of anthropological research does not depend on the form in which it is conducted. Some researchers have been successful in using transdisciplinary methods in their own highly specialized research fields.

While there are many different possible approaches, interdisciplinary and transdisciplinary research methods are particularly helpful for anthropology. Specialists from different fields contribute expertise deriving from a variety of scientific traditions. They contribute the findings, fundamental issues, concepts, and methodology of their own disciplines to transdisciplinary collaboration. Thus questions, concepts, and methodologies are developed that transcend individual scientific disciplines with the aim of establishing a transdisciplinary frame of reference and methodology. Where this is successful, research is then carried out that would otherwise be difficult to conduct within the scope of one specialist discipline.

Transdisciplinary research makes particularly high demands on researchers' communication skills and their ability to work with colleagues. It also requires an inquisitive mind, an interest in other fields, versatility, and openness toward new issues and viewpoints. The communication and interaction skills required of the participating researchers are complex and absolutely essential to securing the aims of transdisciplinary research.[3] Multidisciplinary research projects have the sole aim of ensuring the collaboration of individual scientific disciplines. Here participants pose questions arising in their own fields to experts in another field, in the hope that knowledge specific to this new field will provide new ways of looking at their own problems. Transdisciplinary research, on the other hand, strives to discover and investigate issues that are on the borderline of a particular discipline; such issues would be characterized not so much by the traditions of the discipline itself as by the constellations formed by various disciplines interacting. Many anthropological research projects are developed in such contexts, particularly when their subject matter does not fall within the remit of a single discipline and where the research is investigating phenomena, problems, and objects that arise both within and outside of the designated boundaries of any one scientific discipline. Examples would be topics such as the body, the senses, the soul, time, rituals, gender, and media.

This has two major consequences. On the one hand, the growth of scientific knowledge increasingly requires that it be organized clearly and transparently, and thus individual scientific disciplines are becoming more important. On the other hand, transdisciplinary anthropological research transcends boundaries. On this basis, and by applying procedures that have their basis in a particular discipline, transdisciplinary working methods are being developed that will cause lasting changes in individual disciplines. The consideration of the "foreignness" of the other disciplines is a constitutive element of transdisciplinary research.[4] This enables new themes, concepts, and methods to be developed that challenge and change established knowledge and research in the individual scientific fields. This results in increased diversity and greater complexity—the more radical the selection of subjects and methodological processes, the less predictable are the results of the research. This is the basis for the innovative character of many investigations in the field of anthropology.

Many of the subjects of anthropology are so complex that they cannot be explored sufficiently using the approaches of one discipline only. Transdisciplinary research helps to enhance the multidimensionality of what is studied, the methodological approach, and the investigation itself. In many cases, the different skills of various scientific fields can be combined to achieve the desired increase in complexity. The plurality of the scientific paradigms under consideration results in complex research that extends beyond the scope of single disciplines. If the scientific cultures from different nations also have an input into specialist disciplines and scientific paradigms, making the research transnational, there is a further layer of complexity. Transdisciplinarity, a diversity of paradigms, and transnationality are leading to an increase in the plurality and complexity of anthropological research.[5]

Complexity and Methodological Diversity

Many examples of historical cultural anthropological research are transdisciplinary, transcultural, and multi-paradigmatic, and therefore use different methods and procedures. Currently, it is not possible to designate any particular procedures of investigation as *the* methods of historical cultural anthropology. The spectrum of appropriate methods and combinations of methods is both broad and essentially open. Any attempt to restrict it would contradict the multifaceted nature and the paradigmatic openness of anthropological research. Since we can regard methodological questions as subordinate to thematic or conceptual issues, we cannot examine them outside of this context. As anthropology does not consist of a single subject area, care and consideration are required when choosing methodology.

Research using quantifying methods, such as demographic studies, can make a constructive contribution to anthropology. Because of the different theoretical basis on which their claim to validity rests, these methods require a high degree of "independence" from the specific nature of what is under investigation. By contrast, phenomenological, hermeneutic, and deconstructive methods are directly connected to the questions, subject matters, and objectives to which they are applied. These methods are of considerable importance in anthropological research and have a very wide and diverse scope. This is quite clear if we consider the variety of approaches to hermeneutics that various disciplines have developed.[6]

Hermeneutic methods have an important role to play in much anthropological research, as it is frequently necessary to interpret texts, images, and performative practices. Correspondingly, the available literature is extensive. In historical science, not only text and source criticism, but also the relationships between events, fiction, and narrative are of central importance.[7] Methods of interpretation and deconstruction are also highly productive in literary studies and educational science.[8]

In addition to the text-based methods employed in history and the humanities, hermeneutic methods are widely used in qualitative social research in the field of anthropology.[9] Although it is possible to learn how to apply these methods in general, they have to be adapted with the utmost precision to the aims, issues, and conditions of each research project. Since Malinowski's field research, these methods have become highly significant in ethnology; however, they have only recently started to gain importance in the social sciences and humanities.

In anthropological research, wonder (Greek: *thaumazein*), radical questioning, philosophical criticism, and self-criticism all play important roles. These conditions and forms of philosophical reasoning cannot be adequately described as methods.[10] They cannot be formalized, and their significance can only be gauged when they are used to examine phenomena, events, and actions. Depending on their context, these types of philosophical reflection result in differing views and insights and an increase in the complexity of anthropological research. They ensure that we continue to regard the fundamental questions about the human condition as unanswered and help us to realize that there can be no definitive concept of the human being.

Globalization and Cultural Difference

The far-reaching global changes of the last decades have had a lasting effect on the benchmarks of anthropological research. Today, studies in historical cultural anthropology examine the past and present of Western culture and societies with an awareness that, while the Western world is one of the great cultural centers of the world, it is not the only one. This awareness has consequences for the selection and treatment of themes and issues in anthropological research; it results in altered expectations and attitudes toward research findings and an openness with regard to diverging cultural and social traditions, without succumbing to normative arbitrariness. In a number of cases the basic points of reference of anthropological research have been influenced by globalization—a process that is characterized by the simultaneity of the nonsimultaneous and relates to the following areas and themes.[11]

- Transnational finance and capital markets
- The mobility of capital, and the rise in influence of neoliberal economic theory
- Company strategies and markets with global strategies of production, distribution, and cost minimization by means of outsourcing
- Research, development, and technology
- Transnational political bodies and the decline of the influence of the nation-state
- Patterns of consumption, lifestyles, and cultural styles and the tendency toward their uniformity
- Structures of perception and awareness that shape individuals and the community
- New media and tourism
- The one-world mentality

In addition, we must consider the long-ignored globalization of poverty, suffering, war, terror, exploitation, and destruction of the natural world.

These developments lead to a separation of the political from the economic as well as to a globalization of lifestyles and a rise in the importance of new communication media. These are not linear processes; they are disrupted in manifold ways and produce contradictory results. They have different objectives and decision-making structures and are organized in networks like rhizomes.[12] They do not run parallel in space or time, and they are subject to heterogeneous dynamic forces. They are multidimensional and multiregional, and they are deeply rooted in the centers of neoliberal capitalism. The dominance of a globalized economy over political life and the globalization of lifestyles due to the increasing presentation of experience as images in the new media all help to cause changes in the way we work, a decline in the influence of nation-states, and an increased permeability and homogeneity of cultures, as well as new ways and spheres of life.

Instead of a process of globalization that encourages a uniformity of the human species, we need a *reflexive, critical, and heterogeneous process of globalization*. For this, it is important to change many aspects of the way the world has been developing up to now and to insure that cultural diversity, the fascination of alterity, and the anthropological reflection of historical and cultural differences have a place in the dynamics of globalization. The role and the meaning of cultural differences and diversity and the character of current ways of living are all changed in the processes of globalization. However, they only result in ways of life becoming partially similar. Due to the contingent character of social and cultural development, unforeseen forms of syncretism and hybridity evolve.[13] These, of course, result in yet more new hybrid forms and greater cultural diversity. The historical and cultural backgrounds of these new hybrid forms and types of culture are so widely different that even if there are apparent similarities, fundamental differences remain.

The meanings of the same cultural phenomena and situations can often be understood in different ways depending upon the person responding to them. This is demonstrated by experiences of transcultural communications and transcultural learning. It is also illustrated by the differences in meaning attached to words in European languages that originated from the Latin word *natura*. The associations and connotations of the German *Natur*, English *nature*, French *nature*, or Spanish *naturaleza* differ widely, even though the cultures share a long common history. A comparison with the Japanese word for nature, *Shizen* shows even greater differences. Although the term has both descriptive and normative meanings in Japanese, its associations, emotional aspects, and atmospheric nuances are very different from those of the European variants. Different cultural backgrounds naturally result in differences in perception and experience. For example, it was Japanese primatologists who first discovered that macaque apes had a sophisticated culture and were capable of cultural learning. Japanese attitudes to community and society enabled them to notice this behavior much earlier than their European and American colleagues.[14]

In light of the *one-world mentality* that currently dominates the globalization discussion, it is imperative to highlight historical and cultural differences, even where appearances may be deceptively similar. It is this that makes it possible to communicate with the Other. If everybody were aware of the alterity in themselves and their own culture, this would open up new possibilities for understanding the alterity of other people and other cultures and for developing a way of seeing things from the point of view of the Other—a *heterological way of thinking*. The increasing awareness of differences and alterity and the recognition of cultural diversity make it possible to identify common aspects of different cultures and break down barriers between them.[15] One of the aims of globalization is a homogenous world. As a result, the ability to perceive and accept differences is essential and can even help to prevent violent conflicts. However, even acceptance of cultural diversity has its limits, which, for many people, are related to issues of human rights and global ethics. We must accept that disagreements will arise with members of other cultures, and, wherever possible, conduct such disputes without recourse to the use of force.[16] Living conditions in the twenty-first century are determined by the struggle between the uniformity of globalization and movements emphasizing cultural difference and diversity. These include the conflicts between the global and the local, the universal and the particular, tradition and modernity, the spiritual and the material, necessary competition and equal opportunities, short-term and long-term reflections, the rapid spread of knowledge, and the limited human capacity to cope with these conditions.[17]

One of the great conflicts of the future will be between globalization's intemperate consumption of the Earth's resources and the *culture of sustainability*. Sustainability aims to ensure the future of mankind by persuading societies and economic systems to use only renewable resources that can regenerate naturally. It also means reducing the consumption of nonrenewable resources, conserving biological diversity and the climate, reducing the use of land, water, and transportation enough to preclude damage to the Earth, and also preventing major technical disasters.[18]

Although the focus of anthropology is on research into history and culture, investigations in this field should not be restricted to past and current issues. They should also examine themes and problems relating to the future of humankind, including the questions and problems of a culture that has the capacity to exist in the future.

The Challenge of Transculturality

One of the tasks that confronts anthropological research today is the need to investigate the social and cultural dynamics of globalized worlds, including their historical origins. What it finds are asymmetric relations of power and exchange, and transcultural dynamics in which traditional identities are expressed in global interaction processes. *Transculturality* serves as a heuristic tool that can be used to investigate real, symbolic, and imaginary social and cultural developments in our globalized world with new methodological approaches. To achieve this objective, we need to reflect upon and reexamine the tacit assumptions of anthropological research, including its "methodological nationalism," with a view to developing new conceptualizations and methodologies for transcultural research.[19]

The dynamics of the cultural flows in our globalized world are asymmetric. Local, regional, and global studies are needed to investigate the diachronic and synchronic dimensions of the broad cultural flows. They do not simply follow a single course, but make deviations, which are then modified once more by movements in the opposite direction. Objects, meanings, and images are translated and appropriated in new environments, in the process of which new social practices, forms of knowledge, and aesthetic creations emerge. These changes can be seen in industry, politics, administration, literature, the arts, religion, and everyday life. But who produces these changes and how do they take place? Is it individuals, groups, or communities? What role do mimetic interactions play in these processes? The asymmetries that are inherent in many mimetic processes are of special interest for the development of their transcultural nature. Many can only be adequately explained if the historical dimension is taken into account. Others are identified and understood with the aid of ethnographic research. In many cases the two methodological approaches can be combined and taken as the starting point for further conceptualization and reflection.

Transcultural phenomena arise in the tension that exists between identity, alterity, and assimilation, which result from mimetic processes that lead to the translation and transformation of images, texts, and concepts. Traditional and foreign elements become mixed in these processes and create new (trans-) cultural phenomena. In view of these multilayered processes, cultures can no longer be conceived of as self-contained, linguistically homogeneous, and stable units. Cultures develop and change through interaction, circulation, and reconfiguration. They are dynamic and in relation.[20] Transculturality is a heuristic concept that confronts research with new conceptual, empirical, and methodological problems.

The relational nature of space and time plays an important role in research on transcultural phenomena. The new media, with their ubiquity and simultaneity, are also of prime importance here, since they replicate spaces and alter time structures. Contact zones with new temporospatial qualities are created within them. This effect is not limited to the new media. Transcultural spaces with their own time structures come into being at world exhibitions, in the Olympic Games, and in world championships.[21]

Various attempts have been made to describe and analyze the transcultural phenomena that are characteristic of the globalized world. Significant attention has been drawn to the osmotic or polyvalent nature of the frontiers between cultures, which enables the different cultures to develop complex internal structures by absorbing and assimilating external influences. Expressions such as *zone of contact*, *métissage*, and *hybridity* are used in an effort to describe the dynamics of cultural adaptation, translation, and production.[22] These concepts help to support self-reflection in the various disciplines and to justify the need to investigate the dynamics and constantly evolving nature of transcultural processes.

Transcultural processes become clearly evident in migratory movements, in which selective cultural processes of assimilation and translation take place, and new frames of reference are created. These processes include resistance and refusal, which interrupt or even prevent the circulation of cultural goods. This frequently leads to marginalization and displacement. These processes run counter to each other, and research needs to investigate this antagonism. For anthropological research that is oriented toward the historical, ethnographical, and philosophical exploration of our globalized world, the focus on the transcultural nature of many of the social and cultural phenomena of our times gives rise to many productive conceptual, empirical, and methodological tasks to be addressed.

Concluding Statements

Today's anthropology attempts to relate the historicity and culturality of its concepts, views, and methods to the historicity and culturality of the themes, objects, and issues that are its subject matter. Thus anthropology finds itself caught between history and the human sciences. It uses the findings of the human sciences and of anthropological criticism, based on historical and cultural philosophy, to tackle new questions on human nature. At the heart of its efforts lies a restlessness of thinking and studying that cannot be stilled. Its research is not limited to certain cultural contexts or single epochs. Reflecting the historicity and culturality of its own research enables the discipline to leave behind the Eurocentricity of the human sciences and to focus on the unresolved problems of the present and the future.

Anthropology is not a specialist discipline. Research of this kind takes place both within and across the boundaries of different scientific disciplines. The scientific basis of its investigations frequently means that research is organized in a transdisciplinary and transnational way, so that it employs a plurality of methods. These methods include historical source work, the literary science of text hermeneutics, qualitative social research, and philosophical reflection. Some investigations of anthropology cross the boundaries of different specialist disciplines but also spread into the territories of art, literature, theater, and music. Some of the central findings of this study are summarized in the following concluding statements.

(1) The history of life and the process of human evolution are the subjects of anthropological research, which must be aware of its own historicity and culturality. The evolution of life and the process of hominization are both processes that took protracted periods of time. Human evolution is understood as a multidimensional process involving the interaction of ecological, genetic, cerebral, social, and cultural factors—a process in which cultural factors began to play a role from a very early stage.

(2) Just as important as the general laws of the development of life and humankind are the specific conditions of humankind—the *human conditions*. These conditions are frequently deduced by comparing humans and animals and, most recently, also humans and machines. Humans differ from other primates in their upright gait, cerebral development, neoteny, and reduced instinct. These characteristics are supplemented by "ex-centricity," excess drive, action, facilitation (*Entlastung*), language, imagination, and openness toward the world. The special position of humans can be seen in our "natural artificiality" and "mediated immediacy."

(3) Important as these insights into humans as a species are, they neglect the historical and cultural diversity that makes humans unique. This is the point of departure for anthropological research within the field of historical science, where the focus is on examining human beings in their historical and cultural contexts. Key areas of interest in this field are how humans lived in other historical periods, the historical character of perception, feelings, and mentality, as well as the heterogeneity and discontinuity of the themes and subjects of historical research.

(4) The introduction of an ethnographic view of culture and history adds a new dimension. The alterity in one's own and other cultures and cultural diversity have become important themes. Research with synchronous perspectives relating to the present is now a common approach along with diachronous studies. Reconstructive social research involving, for instance, qualitative studies of the family, school, youth, and the media is conducted using ethnographic methods.

(5) Even where anthropological research relates to the past, its relevance for today is also important. Some studies have the express aim of contributing to the self-interpretation and self-understanding of the present. Anthropological research emphasizes the radical historicity and culturality of both the subject matter and activities of research. Some of these studies tackle issues that are either wholly or partially unsuitable for empirical research and therefore require philosophical reasoning, conceptualization, reflection, and criticism.

(6) A central theme of anthropology is the body and its various aspects. This focus also concentrates our attention on processes of increasing abstraction and imagination. The complexity of the human body means that research must clearly define which type of body is being discussed. The scope of representations and concepts of the body is wide and is, in principle, infinite. Ultimately, the concept of the body taken as a basis is that of a *corpus absconditum*, as it can only be defined within its current context, and its complexity can never be fully understood.

(7) Mimetic processes are also centered on the body. In these processes, people imitate others with the intention of emulating them and becoming like them. By relating to others in this way, humans take on similarities to other humans and thus co-create each other while preserving their uniqueness. Mimetic processes not only involve other people, but they also help us to discover the world; they relate to real environments and imaginary worlds in art and literature. During mimesis, we take an "imprint" of other people and worlds and recreate them as "our own." In this process, the outer world is merged with the inner world, providing an opportunity for cultural learning. To the extent that this cultural learning creates new knowledge in individuals and communities, creative imitation occurs in mimetic processes.

(8) The principal effect of many social and cultural actions is due to their character as stagings or performances. Their performativity encompasses three aspects: social actions as cultural performances, speaking as a performative action, and artistic performances as bodily-aesthetic actions. Cultural and social interaction is examined in terms of performative arrangements of the body. This shows that not only rituals, feelings, and learning have a performative side, but also perception, knowledge, media, and gender. Practical knowledge, acquired in mimetic processes, is required for their staging and performance.

(9) Ritual actions require knowledge acquired in mimesis. Rituals and ritualization deal with categories of difference and create communities by means of their performative character. They form bridges of continuity between the past, present, and future; they give us feelings of security and self-confidence, and channel the potential for violence. Rituals are used to organize transitions between institutions. They have ostentatious and ludic characteristics. They encompass ritualizations, conventions, liturgies, ceremonies, and celebrations, and their scope includes everyday rituals, such as greetings and farewells, rituals revolving around food and clothing, and rituals involving politics and religion. Rituals help social institutions and organizations to establish their values, tasks, and functions in the bodies of their participants and audiences.

(10) The body has an innate ability to use language, which enables every human being to form sentences. Words and the grammatical structures, however, have to be learned. Human communication is conducted in different languages, each with its own historical and cultural background. The bodily and mental aspects of every language are inextricably interwoven. We produce sound by moving our vocal cords. The connection between language and the auditory and vocal organs makes possible the unlimited use of limited means. Language is the organ that shapes our thought; it is formed through practical use as well as through the playful use of language, which has endless possibilities.

(11) Imagination is rooted in the body and bound to emotions and language. It provides continuity between the past, present, and future and between sleep, consciousness, and daydreams. Imagination transforms the outer world into the inner world and vice versa, and creates the individual and collective imaginary. Primarily, it creates images of presence, representation, and simulation, although it also employs shapes and symbols to express itself.

(12) Because the human body is a central focus of anthropology, it is natural that temporality and transitoriness, death, and birth are major anthropological themes. Without the death of individuals, humankind would not have evolved. Culture and society arise from humanity's attempts to confront death. Every historical era and every culture develop different attitudes toward death. Differences in collective mentalities emerge that influence the attitudes of individuals. Rational thought and imagination endeavor to analyze death. However, as they have to refer to something, but death is Nothing, it is inevitable that these attempts should fail.

(13) Anthropology cannot be regarded as a single discipline. Research in this field can be conducted under the auspices of one specialist discipline, or it can be organized as an inter-, multi- or transdisciplinary project. The subjects of study can often be found at the very margins of disciplines or in the areas between them, necessitating conceptual and methodological diversity and paradigmatic plurality. Many research projects in anthropology are transcultural, emphasizing the significance of historic and cultural differences and acting as a corrective measure against the tide of uniformity and homogenizing forces of globalization.

(14) Anthropological knowledge is not subject to a uniformity of methods, theories, and themes. It is transdisciplinary, transcultural, and pluralistic. Its aim is to increase the complexity of its subject matter, not to reduce it. As our knowledge of the historical and cultural aspects of human beings grows, our awareness of what remains unknown also grows.

The idea that we may be able to conquer the unknown is illusory. Human beings are only partially accessible to scientific study; overall they remain enigmatic.

(15) Anthropological criticism leads us to this conclusion, ensuring that the fundamental questions about human beings remain open despite the efforts of the human sciences to answer them. Anthropological criticism is a self-critical, reflexive understanding of anthropology that emphasizes the centrality for anthropology of human beings and that anthropological research cannot therefore be other than anthropomorphic. It attempts to comprehend the historicity and culturality of different anthropologies and thus to recognize that there cannot be a definitive concept of "the human being." Anthropology, when understood in this way, has an important role to play in our recognition that human nature, history, and culture are fundamentally open and capable of change.

Notes

PREFACE

1. The four fields are archaeology, biological anthropology, sociocultural anthropology, and linguistic anthropology.
2. See Christoph Wulf, *Anthropology of Education* (Münster: LIT Verlag, 2002).
3. On natality, see Christoph Wulf et al., *Geburt in Familie, Klinik und Medien* (Opladen, Germany: Budrich UniPress, 2008). On mortality, see Shoko Suzuki and Christoph Wulf, *Auf dem Weg des Lebens* (in preparation).
4. See Gunter Gebauer and Christoph Wulf, *Mimesis: Culture, Art, Society* (Berkeley and Los Angeles: University of California Press, 1995); Gunter Gebauer and Christoph Wulf, *Spiel, Ritual, Geste: Mimetisches Handeln in der sozialen Welt* (Reinbek, Germany: Rowohlt, 1998), and *Mimetische Weltzugänge: Soziales Handeln—Rituale und Spiele—ästhetische Produktionen* (Stuttgart: Kohlhammer, 2003).
5. See Christoph Wulf and Jörg Zirfas, eds., *Pädagogik des Performativen* (Weinheim, Germany: Beltz, 2007).
6. On language processes, see John L. Austin, *How to Do Things with Words* (Oxford: Clarendon Press, 1962). On cultural performances, see Milton Singer, ed., *Traditional India: Structure and Change* (Philadelphia: American Folklore Society, 1959). On aesthetics, see Bernd Hüppauf and Christoph Wulf, eds., *Dynamics and Performativity of Imagination: The Image between the Visible and the Invisible* (New York: Routledge, 2009).
7. See Hüppauf and Wulf, eds., *Dynamics and Performativity of Imagination*.
8. Christoph Wulf, *Anthropologie kultureller Vielfalt: Interkulturelle Bildung in Zeiten der Globalisierung* (Bielefeld, Germany: Transcript, 2006); Christoph Wulf and Christine Merkel,

eds., *Globalisierung als Herausforderung der Erziehung: Theorien, Grundlagen, Fallstudien* (Münster: Waxmann, 2002).

9. Christoph Wulf et al., *Das Glück der Familie: Ethnographische Studien in Deutschland und Japan* (Wiesbaden: Verlag Sozialwissenschaften, 2011; Japanese edition, 2012).

10. Axel Michaels and Christoph Wulf, eds., *Images of the Body in India* (London: Routledge, 2011), *Emotions in Rituals and Performances* (London: Routledge, 2012), and *Exploring the Senses: Emotions, Performativity, and Ritual* (London: Routledge, 2013).

11. See Matti Bunzl, "Boas, Foucault, and the 'Native Anthropologist': Notes toward a Neo-Boasian Anthropology," *American Anthropologist* 106, no. 3 (2004): 435–41.

INTRODUCTION

1. The term *anthropology* did not originate from classical Greek and certainly not from Aristotle. Where Aristotle speaks of *anthropologos*, he is referring to what Ross translates as "gossip." See Odo Marquard, "Anthropologie," in *Historisches Wörterbuch der Philosophie*, Bd. 1, A–C, ed. Joachim Ritter (Basel: Schwabe, 1971), 362. See also other explanations of the usage and meaning of the term on pp. 362–74.

2. See Udo Benzenhöfer and Maike Rotzoll, "Zur *Anthropologia* (1533) von Galeazzo Capella: Die früheste bislang bekannte Verwendung des Begriffs Anthropologie," *Medizinhistorisches Journal: Internationale Vierteljahresschrift für Wissenschaftsgeschichte* 26, nos. 3/4 (1991): 315–20.

3. Ullrich Langer, ed., *The Cambridge Companion to Montaigne* (Cambridge: Cambridge University Press, 2005); Michel de Montaigne, *Literary and Philosophical Essays* (New York: P. F. Collier & Son, 1910).

4. The concepts of *perfectibilité* and negative education were developed by Jean-Jacques Rousseau in *Emile*. "What are we to do to educate these odd people? Without doubt there is plenty to be done as we must prevent that something happens" (*Émile ou de l'éducation* [Paris: Bordas, 1992]).

5. Ulrich Herrmann, "Vervollkommnung des Unverbesserlichen?" in *Anthropologie nach dem Tode des Menschen*, ed. Dietmar Kamper and Christoph Wulf (Frankfurt am Main: Suhrkamp, 1994), 132–53.

6. See Immanuel Kant, *Anthropology from a Pragmatic Point of View* (New York: Cambridge University Press, 2006); Dietmar Kamper, Christoph Wulf, and Gunter Gebauer, eds., "Kants Anthropologie" (issue title), *Paragrana* 11, no. 2 (2002); Reinhard Brandt, *Kritischer Kommentar zu Kants Anthropologie in pragmatischer Hinsicht (1798)* (Hamburg: Meiner, 1999); Jean Ferrari, ed., *Kant sur l'Anthropologie: L'Année 1798; Kant et la naissance de l'anthropologie au siècle des Lumières* (Paris: Vrin, 1997); Hartmut Böhme and Gernot Böhme, *Das Andere der Vernunft: Zur Entwicklung von Rationalitätsstrukturen am Beispiel Kants* (Frankfurt am Main: Suhrkamp, 1985); Gernot Böhme,

Anthropologie in pragmatischer Hinsicht: Darmstädter Vorlesungen (Frankfurt am Main: Suhrkamp, 1985).

7. See Johann Gottfried Herder, *Philosophical Writings* (New York: Cambridge University Press, 2002); see also Herder's essays in *Treatise on the Origin of Language* (Chicago: University of Chicago Press, 1986), and *Sculpture: Some Observations on Shape and Form from Pygmalion's Creative Dream* (Chicago: University of Chicago Press, 2002). See also Wilhelm von Humboldt, "Plan einer vergleichenden Anthropologie," in *Werke in fünf Bänden*, 3rd ed., vol. 1, ed. Andreas Flitner and Klaus Giel (Darmstadt: Wissenschaftliche Buchgesellschaft, 1980), 337–75. On Boas, see Matti Bunzl, "Boas, Foucault, and the 'Native Anthropologist': Notes toward a Neo-Boasian Anthropology," *American Anthropologist* 106, no. 3 (2004): 435–41.

8. See Wolf Lepenies, *Between Literature and Science: The Rise of Sociology* (New York: Cambridge University Press, 1988).

9. See, among others, Sherry B. Ortner, "Theory in Anthropology since the Sixties," *Comparative Studies in Society and History: An International Quarterly* 26, no. 1 (1984): 126–66.

10. See Christoph Wulf and Dietmar Kamper, eds., *Logik und Leidenschaft: Erträge Historischer Anthropologie* (Berlin: Reimer, 2002).

11. Christoph Wulf, ed., *Vom Menschen: Handbuch Historische Anthropologie* (Weinheim, Germany: Beltz, 1997; 2nd ed., *Der Mensch und seine Kultur*, Cologne: Anaconda, 2010).

12. For the former, see Gunter Gebauer and Christoph Wulf, *Mimesis: Culture, Art, Society* (Berkeley and Los Angeles: University of California Press, 1995). For the latter, see Christoph Wulf, *Une anthropologie historique et culturelle: Rituels, mimésis et performativité* (Paris: Téraèdre, 2007); Gunter Gebauer and Christoph Wulf, *Spiel, Ritual, Geste: Mimetisches Handeln in der sozialen Welt* (Reinbek, Germany: Rowohlt, 1998).

13. Christoph Wulf et al., *Das Soziale als Ritual* (Opladen, Germany: Leske and Budrich, 2001); Christoph Wulf et al., *Bildung im Ritual* (Wiesbaden: Verlag für Sozialwissenschaften, 2004); Christoph Wulf et al., *Lernkulturen im Umbruch* (Wiesbaden: Verlag für Sozialwissenschaften, 2007); Christoph Wulf et al., *Ritual and Identity* (London: Tufnell Press, 2010); Christoph Wulf et al., *Die Geste in Erziehung, Bildung und Sozialisation* (Wiesbaden: Verlag für Sozialwissenschaften, 2011).

14. Christoph Wulf, Michael Göhlich, and Jörg Zirfas, eds., *Grundlagen des Performativen: Eine Einführung in die Zusammenhänge von Sprache, Macht und Handeln* (Weinheim, Germany: Juventa, 2001); Christoph Wulf and Jörg Zirfas, eds., *Pädagogik des Performativen: Theorien, Methoden, Perspektiven* (Weinheim, Germany: Beltz, 2007).

15. Bernd Hüppauf and Christoph Wulf, *Dynamics and Performativity of Imagination: The Image between the Visible and the Invisible* (New York: Routledge, 2009).

16. See Philippe Ariès, *The Hour of Our Death* (Oxford: Oxford University Press, 1991).

CHAPTER ONE

1. Ilya Prigogine, *The Molecular Theory of Solution* (New York: Interscience, 1957).
2. Steven Weinberg, *The First Three Minutes: A Modern View of the Origin of the Universe* (New York: Basic Books, 1993).
3. See Manfred Eigen's statement, quoted in Franz Mechsner, "Am Anfang war der Hyperzyklus," *Geo. Schwerpunkt Chaos und Kreativität* 2 (May 1990): 78.
4. Manfred Eigen and Ruthild Winkler-Oswatitsch, *Steps Towards Life: A Perspective on Evolution* (New York: Oxford University Press, 1992).
5. Reinhard W. Kaplan, *Der Ursprung des Lebens*, 2nd ed. (Stuttgart: Thieme, 1978); on p. 91 and in the following sections, the four stages of the development of life are defined as follows: (1) abiotic (i.e., occurring without the participation of life forms) formation of the building-block molecules, in particular for proteins and nucleic acids; (2) biotic polymerization of these modules to form macromolecules; (3) assembly of macromolecules to form larger organelle and cell-like structures (pre-cells); (4) the development of protobionts from such structures.
6. Richard E. Dickerson and Irving Geis, *Chemistry, Matter, and the Universe: An Integrated Approach to General Chemistry* (Menlo Park, CA: W. A. Benjamin, 1976).
7. William J. Schopf, ed., *Life's Origin: The Beginnings of Biological Evolution* (Berkeley and Los Angeles: University of California Press, 2002); Motoo Kimura, *The Neutral Theory of Molecular Evolution* (New York: Cambridge University Press, 1983).
8. Friedrich Cramer, *Chaos and Order: The Complex Structure of Living Systems* (Weinheim, Germany: VCH, 1993).
9. For what constitutes life, see Ernst Peter Fischer, *Die andere Bildung: Was man von den Naturwissenschaften wissen sollte*, 6th ed. (Munich: Ullstein, 2002), 214ff.
10. Franz M. Wuketits, *The Evolution of Living Systems* (Weinheim, Germany: Wiley-VCH, 2005), 88; Rupert Riedl, *Die Ordnung des Lebendigen: Systembedingungen der Evolution* (Hamburg: Parey, 1975).
11. James W. Valentine and Francisco J. Ayala, *Evolving: The Theory and Processes of Organic Evolution* (Menlo Park, CA: Benjamin, Cummings, 1979).
12. Edward Wilson, *The Diversity of Life* (Cambridge, MA: Belknap Press of Harvard University Press, 1992).
13. Ibid.
14. Charles Darwin and George Levine, *The Origin of the Species* (New York: Fine Creative Media, 2003).
15. Ernst Mayr, *Evolution: Die Entwicklung von den ersten Lebensspuren bis zum Menschen* (Heidelberg: Spektrum der Wissenschaft, 1982), 11, and *Systematics and the Origin of Species: From the Viewpoint of a Zoologist* (Cambridge, MA: Harvard University Press, 1999).

16. Jacques Monod, *Chance and Necessity: An Essay on the Natural Philosophy of Modern Biology* (New York: Vintage Books, 1971).

17. Wuketits, *Evolution of Living Systems*, 34.

18. Bernhard Rensch, *Das universale Weltbild: Evolution und Naturphilosophie* (Frankfurt am Main: Fischer, 1977), 96ff.

19. Niles Eldredge and Stephen Jay Gould, "Punctuated Equilibria: An Alternative to Phyletic Gradualism," in *Models in Paleobiology*, ed. T. J. M. Schopf (San Francisco: Freeman Cooper, 1972), 82–115.

20. Erhard Oeser, *Katastrophen: Triebkraft der Evolution* (Darmstadt: Wissenschaftliche Buchgesellschaft, 2011), 92.

21. See Marvin Harris, *The Rise of Anthropological Theory* (Walnut Creek, CA: AltaMira, 2001); Roger Keesing, *Cultural Anthropology* (New York: Holt, Rinehart & Winston, 1976).

22. Robert M. May, *Stability and Complexity in Model Ecosystems* (Princeton, NJ: Princeton University Press, 2001).

23. Wuketits, *Evolution of Living Systems*.

24. James W. Valentine, *On the Origin of Phyla* (Chicago: University of Chicago Press, 2004).

25. William S. Beck, Karel F. Liem, and George Gaylord Simpson, *Life: An Introduction to Biology* (New York: HarperCollins, 1991).

26. Richard Leakey and Roger Lewin, *Origins Reconsidered: In Search of What Makes Us Human* (New York: Doubleday, 1992).

27. *Ardipithecus* = ground ape, and *ramus* = branch/root.

28. In 2000, bones and the remains of a jawbone estimated to be approximately six million years old were found in Kenya. These became known as "Millennium Man" and have not yet been conclusively classified. According to a report in *Le Monde* dated July 12, 2002, on July 19, 2001, in Toros-Manalla in Chad, an almost complete cranium from a member of the *Sahelanthropus tchadensis* was found. It was named *Toumai*. Dated to more than six million years ago, it is twice as old as Lucy (see body of text, below). This would make Toumai one of the ancestors of the australopithecines, although its position and significance in the history of the human species is still a matter of debate. Recent years have seen several fossil discoveries that have provided new information for the difficult process of reconstructing the course of hominization. We can expect these developments to continue for many years to come.

29. Friedemann Schrenk, *Die Frühzeit des Menschen: Der Weg zum Homo sapiens*, 3rd ed. (Munich: Beck, 2001), 43. It is possible to distinguish in the main australopithecine group between *Australopithecus anamensis* (estimated to have lived 4.2–3.8 million years ago) and *Australopithecus afarensis* (3.7–2.9 million years ago). The subgroups are differentiated according to geographical distribution: Western Africa, *Australopithecus bahrelgazali* (3.5–3.2 million years ago); Northern Africa, *Australopithecus garhi* (2.5 million years ago); Southern Africa, *Australopithecus africanus* (3–2 million years ago).

Robust australopithecines (*Paranthropus*) are classified as follows: *Paranthropus aethiopicus* (2.6–2.3 million years ago); *Paranthropus boisei* (2.5–1.1 million years ago); *Paranthropus robustus* (1.8–1.3 million years ago). See Friedemann Schrenk, and Timothy G. Bromage, eds., *African Biogeography: Climate Change and Human Evolution* (New York: Oxford University Press, 1999).

30. Donald Johanson and Maitland Edey, *Lucy: The Beginnings of Humankind* (New York: Warner Books, 1981).
31. Fossils have been found in Kanapoi and Allia Bay in Kenya.
32. Schrenk, *Die Frühzeit*, 47.
33. Ibid., 49.
34. Fossils of *Homo rudolfensis* have been found in Uraha (Malawi), Chemeron, Koobi Fora (Kenya), and Omo (Ethiopia). *Homo habilis* fossils were discovered in Koobi Fora (Kenya), Olduvai (Tanzania), and Sterkfontein (South Africa).
35. Schrenk, *Die Frühzeit*, 76.
36. Leakey and Lewin, *Origins Reconsidered*.
37. Schrenk, *Die Frühzeit*, 93.
38. Edgar Morin, *The Nature of Nature* (New York: P. Lang, 1992).
39. Leakey and Lewin, *Origins Reconsidered*.
40. Schrenk, *Die Frühzeit*, 94.
41. Jean-Pierre Changeux, *The Physiology of Truth: Neuroscience and Human Knowledge* (Cambridge, MA: Belknap Press of Harvard University Press, 2004).
42. André Leroi-Gourhan, *Gesture and Speech* (Cambridge, MA: MIT Press, 1993).
43. Wolf Singer, *Der Beobachter im Gehirn* (Frankfurt am Main: Suhrkamp, 2002); Wolf Singer, *Ein neues Menschenbild? Gespräche über Hirnforschung* (Frankfurt am Main: Suhrkamp, 2003); Gerhard Roth, *Aus der Sicht des Gehirns* (Frankfurt am Main: Suhrkamp, 2003) and *Fühlen, Denken, Handeln* (Frankfurt am Main: Suhrkamp, 2001); see also Humberto Maturana and Francisco J. Varela, *The Tree of Knowledge: The Biological Roots of Human Understanding* (Boston: Shambhala, 1992).
44. Leroi-Gourhan, *Gesture and Speech*.
45. Leakey and Lewin, *Origins Reconsidered*, esp. chap. 3.
46. Schrenk, *Die Frühzeit*, 96.
47. Serge Moscovici, *Changing Conceptions of Crowd Mind and Behavior* (New York: Springer, 1986).
48. Morin, *Nature of Nature*.
49. Ulrich Kull, *Evolution des Menschen: Biologische, soziale und kulturelle Evolution* (Stuttgart: Metzler, 1979).
50. Schrenk, *Die Frühzeit*, 101.
51. Dirk Matejovski, Dietmar Kamper, and Gerd-C. Weniger, *Mythos Neandertal: Ursprung und Zeitenwende* (Frankfurt am Main: Campus, 2001).

52. Eric Trinkaus and Pat Shipman, *The Neanderthals: Of Skeletons, Scientists, and Scandal* (New York: Vintage Books, 1994).

53. See the fascinating study by Edgar Morin, which is also relevant here: *L'homme et la mort* (Paris: Éditions du Seuil, 1970).

54. Early archaic *Homo sapiens* dates from 500,000–200,000 years ago; late archaic *Homo sapiens* dates from 200,000–100,000 years ago.

55. Marie E. P. König, *Am Anfang der Kultur: Die Zeichensprache des frühen Menschen* (Frankfurt am Main: Keslein, 1981).

56. Schrenk, *Die Frühzeit*, 118.

57. Hartmut Böhme et al., eds., *Tiere: Die andere Anthropologie* (Cologne: Böhlau, 2004).

58. See, among others, Jane Goodall, *The Chimpanzees of Gombe: Patterns of Behavior* (Cambridge, MA: Belknap Press of Harvard University Press, 1986); Frans de Waal, *The Ape and the Sushi Master: Cultural Reflections by a Primatologist* (New York: Basic Books, 2001); Dominique Lestel, *Les origines animales de la culture* (Paris: Flammarion, 2001); Michael Tomasello, *The Cultural Origins of Human Cognition* (Cambridge, MA: Harvard University Press, 1999); see also chapter 7 in this book.

59. See, among others, Irenäus Eibl-Eibesfeldt, *Grundriss der vergleichenden Verhaltensforschung*, 8th ed. (Munich: Piper, 1999), and *Ethnic Conflict and Indoctrination: Altruism and Identity in Evolutionary Perspective* (New York: Berghahn Books, 1998); Eckart Voland, *Grundriss der Soziobiologie*, 2nd ed. (Heidelberg: Spectrum Akademischer Verlag, 2000).

60. See, for example, The U.S. Partnership for Education for Sustainable Development (online at http://www.uspartnership.org/main/view_archive/1; accessed March 3, 2009); and Bund-Länder-Kommission für Bildungsplanung und Forschungsförderung, *Bildung für eine nachhaltige Entwicklung: Gutachten zum Programm von Gerhard de Haan/Dorothee Harenberg* (Bund-Länder-Kommission für Bildungsplanung und Forschungsförderung: Bonn 1999).

CHAPTER TWO

1. The term *philosophical anthropology* is used in philosophy to describe the process of self-reflection, that is, human beings' attempt to grasp themselves. In this sense, philosophical anthropology is part of philosophy. In this spirit, Bernhard Groethuysen starts his *Philosophische Anthropologie* (Munich: Oldenburg, 1969) by looking at Plato and concludes it with an examination of Montaigne. This is the broad understanding of philosophical anthropology. The more specific use of the term relates mainly to the works of Scheler, Plessner, and Gehlen.

2. The works of Jakob von Uexkuell, Hans Driesch, Ludwig von Bertalanffy, Frederick J. J. Buytendijk, Louis Bolk, and Adolf Portmann were all important for philosophical anthropologists' efforts to develop their understanding

of humankind on the basis of the natural sciences. Among the influential works (given by subject area) are the following.

- Biological environmental research: Jakob von Uexkuell, *Theoretical Biology* (New York: Harcourt, Brace, 1926); Jakob von Uexkuell and Georg Kriszat, *Streifzüge durch die Umwelten von Tieren und Menschen* (1934; Frankfurt am Main: Fischer, 1970).
- Studies of self-organization and self-differentiation of the organism: Hans Driesch, *The Science and Philosophy of the Organism* (New York: AMS Press, 1979); Frederick J. J. Buytendijk, *Mensch und Tier: Ein Beitrag zur vergleichenden Psychologie* (Hamburg: Rowohlt, 1958), and *Das Menschliche: Wege zu seinem Verständnis* (Stuttgart: Köhler, 1958).
- Research on steady states and homeostasis: Ludwig von Bertalanffy, *General Systems Theory: Foundations, Development, Applications* (New York: Penguin, 1973); see also his *Theoretical Biology* (London: Oxford University Press, 1933).
- Research on neoteny: Louis Bolk, *Das Problem der Menschwerdung* (Jena, Germany: Fischer, 1926); on the "extrauterine year," see Adolf Portmann, *New Paths in Biology* (New York: Harper & Row, 1964); see also his *A Zoologist Looks at Humankind* (New York: Columbia University Press, 1990).

3. Max Scheler, *The Human Place in the Cosmos* (Evanston, IL: Northwestern University Press, 2009).

4. Max Scheler, "Späte Schriften," in *Gesammelte Schriften*, (Bern: Francke, 1976), 9–11. See also Max Scheler, *Selected Philosophical Essays* (Evanston, IL: Northwestern University Press, 1973).

5. Scheler, "Späte Schriften," 26.

6. See Gerhard Arlt, *Philosophische Anthropologie* (Stuttgart: Metzler, 2001), 98–99.

7. Johannes Flügge, *Die Entfaltung der Anschauungskraft: Ein Beitrag zur pädagogischen Anthropologie* (Heidelberg: Quelle und Meyer, 1963), 68–69; see also Christoph Wulf, "Die anthropologische Herausforderung des Offenen," *Paragrana* 10, no. 2 (2001): 11–29.

8. See, for example, Christian Bermes, Wolfhart Henckmann, and Heinz Leonardy, eds., *Vernunft und Gefühl: Schelers Phänomenologie des emotionalen Lebens* (Würzburg: Königshausen und Neumann, 2003).

9. Arlt, *Philosophische Anthropologie*, 111.

10. Helmuth Plessner, *Die Stufen des Organischen und der Mensch*, in *Gesammelte Schriften*, vol. 4 (Frankfurt am Main: Suhrkamp, 1981), chaps. 5, 6, and 7.

11. Joachim Fischer, "Exzentrische Positionalität: Plessners Grundkategorie der Philosophischen Anthropologie," *Deutsche Zeitschrift für Philosophie* 48, no. 2 (2000): 276.

12. Arlt, *Philosophische Anthropologie*, 118.

13. Plessner, *Die Stufen des Organischen*, 372–73. In the following discussion, this work is cited parenthetically by page number in the text.

14. See, for example, Felix Hammer, *Die exzentrische Position des Menschen: Methode und Grundlinien der philosophischen Anthropologie Helmuth Plessners* (Bonn: Bouvier, 1967); Axel Honneth and Hans Joas, *Social Action and Human Nature* (Cambridge: Cambridge University Press, 1988); Günther Dux, "Für eine Anthropologie in historisch-genetischer Absicht: Kritische Überlegungen zur philosophischen Anthropologie Helmuth Plessners," in *Der Prozess der Geistesgeschichte: Studien zur ontogenetischen und historischen Entwicklung des Geistes*, ed. Günther Dux and Ulrich Wenzel (Frankfurt am Main: Suhrkamp, 1994), 92–115; Hans-Peter Krüger, *Zwischen Lachen und Weinen*, vol. 1, *Das Spektrum menschlicher Phänomene* (Berlin: Akademie, 1999); Kai Haucke, *Plessner: Zur Einführung* (Hamburg: Junius, 2000); Kersten Schüssler, *Helmuth Plessner: Eine intellektuelle Biographie* (Berlin: Philo Verlagsgesellschaft, 2000); Fischer, "Exzentrische Positionalität"; Arlt, *Philosophische Anthropologie*; Stephan Pietrowicz, *Helmuth Plessner: Genese und System seines philosophisch-anthropologischen Denkens* (Freiburg: Karl Alber, 1992); Oreste Tolone, *Homo absconditus: L'antropologia filosofica di Helmuth Plessner* (Naples: Scientifiche Italiane, 2000); Christoph Dejung, *Plessner: Ein deutscher Philosoph zwischen Kaiserreich und Bonner Republik* (Zurich: Rüffer und Rub, 2003); see also the Helmuth Plessner Society, which was founded a few years ago and has a website with a wide range of information on the works of Plessner.

15. See Gunter Gebauer and Christoph Wulf, *Spiel, Ritual, Geste: Mimetisches Handeln in der sozialen Welt* (Reinbek, Germany: Rowohlt, 1998), 57.

16. Arnold Gehlen, *Anthropologische und sozialpsychologische Untersuchungen* (Reinbek, Germany: Rowohlt, 1986), 14ff. See also his *Man: His Nature and Place in the World* (New York: Columbia University Press, 1988).

17. Johann Gottfried Herder, *On the Origin of Language* (Chicago: University of Chicago Press, 1986).

18. Friedrich Nietzsche, *The Antichrist* (London: Fanfrolico Press, 1928), sec. 14.

19. A completely different concept of animals was developed in Hartmut Böhme et al., eds., *Tiere: Die andere Anthropologie* (Cologne: Böhlau, 2004); Boris Cyrulnik, ed., *Si les lions pouvaient parler: Essais sur la condition animale* (Paris: Gallimard, 1998).

20. See Dietmar Kamper and Christoph Wulf, eds., *Anthropologie nach dem Tode des Menschen* (Frankfurt am Main: Suhrkamp, 1994); see also Mary Maxwell, *Human Evolution: A Philosophical Anthropology* (New York: Columbia University Press, 1984).

21. Arlt, *Philosophische Anthropologie*, 149.

22. Cf. Bolk, *Das Problem der Menschwerdung*.

23. Cf. Gehlen, *Man*.

24. Christian Thies, *Gehlen zur Einführung* (Hamburg: Junius, 2000), 41.

25. Adolf Portmann, *Essays in Philosophical Zoology: The Living Form and the Seeing Eye* (Lewiston, NY: Edwin Mellen Press, 1990).

26. On the brain, see Wolf Singer, *Der Beobachter im Gehirn: Essays zur Hirnforschung* (Frankfurt am Main: Suhrkamp, 2002), which explains how important this early phase is for the development of the human brain; see also Gerhard Roth and Mario F. Wullimann, *Brain Evolution and Cognition* (New York: Wiley, 2001); Gerhard Roth, Wolfgang Prinz, and Sabine Maasen, *Voluntary Action: Brains, Minds, and Sociality* (New York: Oxford University Press, 2003). On human thought, see Michael Tomasello, *The Cultural Origins of Human Cognition* (Cambridge, MA: Harvard University Press, 1999), which is also an attempt to use empirical, comparative primate research to establish the specific character of small children and how they learn. See also chap. 7 on this subject.

27. See Frans de Waal, *The Ape and the Sushi Master: Cultural Reflections by a Primatologist* (New York: Basic Books, 2001); Jane van Lawick-Goodall, *My Life with the Chimpanzees* (New York: Pocket Books, 1996).

28. See Ernst Mayr, *Toward a New Philosophy of Biology: Observations of an Evolutionist* (Cambridge, MA: Belknap Press of Harvard University Press, 1988).

29. Carl Friedrich von Weizsäcker, *Der Garten des Menschlichen*, quoted in Thies, *Gehlen zur Einführung*, 76.

30. Thies, *Gehlen zur Einführung*, 76–77.

31. Gehlen, *Man*, 323–24.

32. Thies, *Gehlen zur Einführung*, 86.

33. Gehlen, *Man*, 51.

34. Arnold Gehlen, *Philosophische Anthropologie und Handlungslehre*, in *Gesamtausgabe*, vol. 4, ed. Karl-Siegbert Rehberg (Frankfurt am Main: Klostermann, 1983), 218–19.

35. In the light of other opinions that emphasize the special role of the brain in evolution, this hypothesis is very much an issue of current debate.

36. Gehlen, *Philosophische Anthropologie*, 445.

37. Konrad Lorenz, *Über tierisches und menschliches Verhalten*, vol. 2, quoted in Thies, *Gehlen zur Einführung*, 51.

38. Jakob von Uexkuell, *Umwelt und Innenwelt der Tiere* (Berlin: Springer, 1909); Jakob von Uexkuell und Georg Kriszat, *Streifzüge*.

39. See Max Horkheimer and Theodor W. Adorno, *Dialectic of Enlightenment* (New York: Seabury Press, 1972).

40. Later Pierre Bourdieu also placed this formation of attitudes and habits at the center of his theory. However, his thinking has a very different frame of reference and opposing political objectives; see Pierre Bourdieu, *Distinction: A Social Critique of the Judgment of Taste* (Cambridge, MA: Harvard University Press, 1984); Pierre Bourdieu and Alain Accardo, *The Weight of the World: Social Suffering in Contemporary Society* (Cambridge: Polity Press, 1999).

41. Gehlen, *Man*.

42. Arnold Gehlen, *Urmensch und Spätkultur: Philosophische Ergebnisse und Aussagen* (Frankfurt am Main: Athenäum, 1964), 23.

43. Arnold Gehlen, "Über kulturelle Evolutionen," in *Die Philosophie und die Frage nach dem Fortschritt*, ed. Helmut Kuhn and Franz Wiedemann (Munich: Pustet, 1964), 209; see also Francis Fukuyama, *The End of History and the Last Man* (New York: Free Press, 1992).

44. Michael Landmann, *De Homine: Man in the Mirror of His Thought* (Ann Arbor, MI: University Microfilms International, 1979); published in German as *Der Mensch im Spiegel seines Gedankens* (Freiburg: Karl Alber, 1962), and *Fundamental Anthropology* (Washington, DC: Center for Advanced Research in Phenomenology and University Press of America, 1985).

45. See also Gerold Hartung, *Das Maß des Menschen: Aporien der philosophischen Anthropologie und ihre Auflösung in der Kulturphilosophie Ernst Cassirers* (Weilerswist, Germany: Velbrueck Wissenschaft, 2003); and Jacques Poulain, *De l'homme: Éléments d'anthrobiologie philosophique du langage* (Paris: L'Harmattan, 2001).

CHAPTER THREE

1. The full version of the title is *Annales d'histoire économique et sociale*. The editorial committee included not only historians of ancient and modern history, but also the geographer Albert Demangeon, the sociologist Maurice Halbwachs, the economist Charles Rist, and the political scientist André Siegfried.

2. Peter Burke, *The French Historical Revolution: The Annales School, 1929–89* (Stanford, CA: Stanford University Press, 1990).

3. Ibid.

4. Marc Bloch, *The Royal Touch: Sacred Monarchy and Scrofula in England and France*, trans. J. E. Anderson (London: Routledge & Kegan Paul, 1973); published in French as *Les rois thaumaturges* (Paris: Gallimard, 1987).

5. Marc Bloch, *The Feudal Society* (Chicago: University of Chicago Press, 1964).

6. See Lucien Febvre, *Martin Luther: A Destiny* (New York: E. P. Dutton, 1929).

7. Marc Bloch was also recruited by the Sorbonne at roughly the same time, allowing us to see this as a relocation of the journal from the fringes of France to its center.

8. Lucien Febvre, *Le problème de l'incroyance au XIVe siècle: La religion de Rabelais* (Paris: Michel, 1968).

9. Lucien Febvre, *Combats pour l'histoire* (Paris: Colin, 1992).

10. Fernand Braudel, *The Mediterranean and the Mediterranean World in the Age of Philipp II.* (New York: Harper & Row, 1972).

11. Burke, *French Historical Revolution*.

12. Fernand Braudel, *On History* (Chicago: University of Chicago Press, 1980), 10–11.

13. In order to make up for this deficiency and in view of the current political situation, I have set up a network entitled *Philosophy and Anthropology of the Mediterranean*. With the help of the German Commission for UNESCO,

the German Ministry for Foreign Affairs, the Anna-Lindh-Foundation, the Freie Universität Berlin, and two UNESCO chairs for philosophy in Tunis and Paris, I organized five international and interdisciplinary conferences in Alexandria (on two occasions), Tunis, Casablanca, and Beirut, the results of which were published in Arabic, German, and French. To date the following eight publications have appeared: Christoph Wulf, Jacques Poulain, and Fathi Triki, eds., "Emotionen in einer transkulturellen Welt" (issue title), *Paragrana* 20, no. 2 (2011 [Beirut proceedings]); Jacques Poulain, Fathi Triki, and Christoph Wulf, eds., *La Réconstruction transculturelle de la Justice: Mondialisation, communautés et individus* (Paris: L'Harmattan, 2011 [Casablanca proceedings]); Jacques Poulain, Fathi Triki, and Christoph Wulf, eds., *Violence, Religion et Dialogue Interculturel: Perspectives euroméditerranéennes* (Paris: L'Harmattan, 2010 [Alexandria proceedings]); Christoph Wulf, Fathi Triki, and Jacques Poulain, eds., *Erziehung und Demokratie: Europäische, muslimische und arabische Länder im Dialog* (Tunis: Mediterranean Publishers, 2010 [Arabic edition,Tunis proceedings]); Christoph Wulf, Fathi Triki, and Jacques Poulain, eds., *Erziehung und Demokratie. Europäische, muslimische und arabische Länder im Dialog* (Berlin: Akademie, 2009 [Tunis proceedings]); Christoph Wulf, Jacques Poulain, and Fathi Triki, eds., *Europäische und muslimisch geprägte Länder im Dialog: Gewalt, Religion und interkulturelle Verständigung* (Wassiti, Tunisia: Sunomed, 2008 [Arabic edition, Alexandria proceedings]); Christoph Wulf, Jacques Poulain, and Fathi Triki, eds., *Die Künste im Dialog der Kulturen: Europa und seine muslimischen Nachbarn* (Berlin: Akademie, 2007 [Alexandria proceedings]); Christoph Wulf, Jacques Poulain, and Fathi Triki, eds., *Europäische und islamisch geprägte Länder im Dialog: Gewalt, Religion und interkulturelle Verständigung* (Berlin: Akademie, 2006 [Alexandria proceedings]).

14. Philippe Ariès, *Centuries of Childhood: A Social History of Family Life* (New York: Knopf, 1962); published in French as *L'enfant et la vie familiale sous l'ancien régime* (Paris: Plon, 1960).

15. Jean-Louis Flandrin, *Families in Former Times: Kinship, Household, and Sexuality* (New York: Cambridge University Press, 1979).

16. Robert Mandrou, *Introduction à la France moderne: Essai de psychologie historique (1500–1640)* (Paris: Michel, 1998); see also Georges Duby and Robert Mandrou, *A History of French Civilization* (New York: Random House, 1964).

17. Jean Delumeau, *Sin and Fear: The Emergence of a Western Guilt Culture, 13th–18th Centuries* (New York: St. Martin's Press, 1990); orig. pub. in French as *Le péché et la peur* (Paris: Fayard, 1983).

18. Emmanuel Le Roy Ladurie, *Carnival in Romans* (New York: Braziller, 1979).

19. Jacques LeGoff, *The Birth of Purgatory* (Aldershot: Scolar Press, 1990).

20. Jacques LeGoff, *Time, Work and Culture in the Middle Ages* (Chicago: University of Chicago Press, 1980); see also Jacques Le Goff, *Constructing the Past: Essays in Historical Methodology* (New York: Cambridge University Press, 1985).

21. Georges Duby, *The Three Orders: Feudal Society Imagined* (Chicago: University of Chicago Press, 1980).

22. Philippe Ariès and Georges Duby, *A History of Private Life* (Cambridge, MA: Belknap Press of Harvard University Press, 1987–1991).

23. François Furet and Jacques Ozouf, *Reading and Writing: Literacy in France from Calvin to Jules Ferry* (New York: Cambridge University Press, 1982).

24. See Robert Mandrou and Georges Duby, *A History of French Civilization* (New York: Random House, 1964); Henri-Jean Martin, *Print, Power, and People in 17th-Century France* (Methuen: Scarecrow Press, 1993), and *The French Book: Religion, Absolutism, and Readership, 1585–1715* (Baltimore, MD: Johns Hopkins University Press, 1996).

25. See Roger Chartier, *Cultural History: Between Practices and Representations* (Ithaca, NY: Cornell University Press, 1988); Stephan Sting, *Schrift, Bildung, Selbst: Eine pädagogische Geschichte der Schriftlichkeit* (Weinheim, Germany: Beltz, Deutscher Studienverlag, 1998), and "Stichwort, Literalität—Schriftlichkeit," *Zeitschrift für Erziehungswissenschaft* 6, no. 3 (2003): 317–37.

26. Chartier, *Cultural History*; Roger Chartier, ed., *The Culture of Print: Power and the Uses of Print in Early Modern Europe* (Cambridge: Polity Press, 1989); Guglielmo Cavallo and Roger Chartier, eds., *History of Reading in the West* (Amherst: University of Massachusetts Press, 1999).

27. See Michel de Certeau, *The Capture of Speech and Other Political Writings* (Minneapolis: University of Minnesota Press, 1997); Gilbert Durand, *On the Disfiguration of the Image of Man in the West* (Ipswich: Golgonooza Press, 1977); Cornelius Castoriadis, *History as Creation* (London: Solidarity, 1978); see also his *The Crisis of Culture and the State* (Minneapolis: Center for Humanistic Studies, University of Minnesota, 1987).

28. See Peter Dinzelbacher, *Europäische Mentalitätsgeschichte: Hauptthemen in Einzeldarstellungen* (Stuttgart: Kröner, 1993), XXI.

29. Hans-Ulrich Wehler, *Geschichte als Historische Sozialwissenschaft* (Frankfurt am Main: Suhrkamp, 1973) and *The German Empire, 1871–1918* (Leamington Spa, Dover: Berg, 1985); Jürgen Kocka, *Sozialgeschichte* (Göttingen: Vandenhoeck & Ruprecht, 1977), and *Geschichte und Aufklärung* (Göttingen: Vandenhoeck & Ruprecht, 1997).

30. See Peter Kriedte, Hans Medick, and Jürgen Schlumbohm, *Industrialization before Industrialization: Rural Industry in the Genesis of Capitalism* (New York: Cambridge University Press, 1982); Klaus Tenfelde, *Sozialgeschichte der Bergarbeiterschaft an der Ruhr im 19. Jahrhundert* (Bonn: Verlag Neue Gesellschaft, 1977); Franz-Josef Brüggemeier, *Leben vor Ort* (Munich: Beck, 1983); Wolfgang Ruppert, *Die Arbeiter* (Frankfurt am Main: Büchergilde Gutenberg, 1988).

31. See Hermann Bausinger, *Folk Culture in a World of Technology* (Bloomington: Indiana University Press, 1990); Helge Gerndt, *Kultur als Forschungsfeld: Über volkskundliches Denken und Arbeiten* (Munich: Münchner Vereinigung für Volkskunde, 1986); Richard van Dülmen and Nobert

Schindler, *Rebellion, Community and Custom in Early Modern Germany* (Cambridge: Cambridge University Press, 2002); Wolfgang Kaschuba, *Volkskultur zwischen feudaler und bürgerlicher Gesellschaft: Zur Geschichte eines Begriffs und seiner gesellschaftlichen Wirklichkeit* (Frankfurt am Main: Campus, 1988), and *Einführung in die europäische Ethnologie* (Munich: Beck, 1999).

32. See the interesting, wide-ranging, and noteworthy study by Gert Dressel, *Historische Anthropologie: Eine Einführung* (Vienna: Böhlau, 1996). The author attempts to provide an overview of the whole field of historical anthropology and to present its development and (relative) system along with its major topics and forms of organization. See also Richard van Dülmen, *The Society of the Enlightenment: The Rise of the Middle Class and Enlightenment Culture in Germany* (New York: St. Martin's Press, 1992).

33. Edward P. Thompson, *Plebejische Kultur und moralische Ökonomie: Aufsätze zur englischen Sozialgeschichte des 18. und 19. Jahrhunderts* (Frankfurt am Main: Ullstein, 1980), and *The Making of the English Working Class* (Harmondsworth: Penguin Books, 1968); Peter Burke, *Popular Culture in Early Modern Europe* (New York: Harper & Row, 1978); Robert Muchembled, *Popular Culture and Elite Culture in France, 1400–1750* (Baton Rouge: Louisiana State University Press, 1985).

34. Albert Ilien and Utz Jeggle, *Leben auf dem Dorf: Zur Sozialgeschichte des Dorfes und zur Sozialpsychologie seiner Bewohner* (Opladen, Germany: Westdeutscher Verlag, 1978); Wolfgang Kaschuba and Carola Lipp, *Dörfliches Überleben: Zur Geschichte materieller und sozialer Reproduktion ländlicher Gesellschaften im 19. und 20. Jahrhundert* (Tübingen: Tübinger Vereinigung für Volkskunde, 1982); Wolfgang Kaschuba, *Volkskultur in der Moderne: Probleme und Perspektiven empirischer Kulturforschung* (Reinbek, Germany: Rowohlt, 1986).

35. See van Dülmen and Schindler, *Rebellion*.

36. See Arthur E. Imhof, *Lost Worlds: How Our European Ancestors Coped with Everyday Life and Why Life Is So Hard Today* (Charlottesville: University Press of Virginia, 1996).

37. Michael Mitterauer and Reinhard Sieder, *Vom Patriarchat zur Partnerschaft: Zum Strukturwandel der Familie* (Munich: Beck, 1977); Josef Ehmer and Michael Mitterauer, eds., *Familienstruktur und Arbeitsorganisation in ländlichen Gesellschaften* (Vienna: Böhlau, 1986).

38. Michael Mitterauer, *Familie und Arbeitsteilung: Historisch-Vergleichende Studien* (Vienna: Böhlau, 1992).

39. Norbert Elias, *What Is Sociology?* (New York: Columbia University Press, 1978); Norbert Elias, *Reflections on a Life* (Cambridge: Polity Press, 1994).

40. Alf Lüdtke, ed., *The History of Everyday Life: Reconstructing Historical Experiences and Ways of Life* (Princeton, NJ: Princeton University Press, 1995).

41. See, for example, Peter Borscheid and Hans-Jürgen Teuteberg, eds., *Stadtwachstum, Industrialisierung, sozialer Wandel: Beiträge zur Erforschung der Urbanisierung im 19. und 20. Jahrhundert* (Berlin: Duncker and Humblot, 1986).

42. Detlev J. Peukert, *Jugend zwischen Krieg und Krise: Lebenswelten von Arbei-terjungen in der Weimarer Republik* (Cologne: Bund-Verlag, 1987); Lutz Niethammer, ed., *Die Jahre weiß man nicht, wo man die heute hinsetzen soll: Faschismuserfahrung im Ruhrgebiet* (Bonn: Dietz, 1986); Lutz Niethammer, *Hinterher merkt man, dass es richtig war, dass es schiefgegangen ist: Nachkriegs-erfahrungen im Ruhrgebiet* (Bonn: J. H. W. Dietz Nachfahren, 1983).

43. Claudia Honegger and Bettina Heintz, *Listen der Ohnmacht: Zur Sozialge-schichte weiblicher Widerstandsformen* (Frankfurt am Main: Europäische Ver-lagsanstalt, 1984). This volume contains contributions from many foreign female historians and has had a lasting influence on research on gender history; see also Gisela Bock, *Women in European History* (Malden, MA: Blackwell, 2001); Carola Lipp, *Medien popularer Kultur* (Frankfurt am Main: Campus, 1995); Beate Fieseler and Birgit Schulze, eds., *Frauengeschichte, gesucht—gefunden? Auskünfte zum Stand der Historischen Frauenforschung* (Cologne: Böhlau, 1991); Karin Hausen and Heide Wunder, eds., *Frauenge-schichte—Geschlechtergeschichte* (Frankfurt am Main: Campus, 1992); Rebekka Habermas, "Geschlechtergeschichte und 'anthropology of gender': Geschichte einer Begegnung," *Historische Anthropologie* 1, no. 3 (1993): 485–509.

44. Ulrich Raulff, ed., *Mentalitäten-Geschichte* (Berlin: Wagenbach, 1987), 9–10.

45. See Jacques LeGoff, *The Medieval World* (London: Collins & Brown, 1990); Aaron J. Gurjewitsch, *Das Weltbild des mittelalterlichen Menschen* (Dresden: Verlag der Kunst, 1978); Aaron Gurjevitsch, *Stimmen des Mittelalters, Fragen von heute: Mentalitäten im Dialog* (Frankfurt am Main: Campus, 1993); see also his *Medieval Popular Culture: Problems of Belief and Perception* (Cam-bridge: Cambridge University Press, 1988), and *Historical Anthropology of the Middle Ages* (Cambridge: Polity Press, 1992).

46. Dinzelbacher, *Europäische Mentalitätsgeschichte.*

47. See, for example, Durand, *Disfiguration of the Image of Man*; see also Gilbert Durand, *Introduction à la mythologie* (Paris: Albin Michel, 1996); Jean-Jacques Wuneburger, *L'imagination*, 2nd ed. (Paris: Presses Universitaires de France, 1995).

48. Wolfgang Reinhard, *Lebensformen Europas: Eine historische Kulturanthropolo-gie* (Munich: Beck, 2004), 12.

49. Christoph Wulf and Dietmar Kamper, eds., *Logik und Leidenschaft.* Erträge Historischer Anthropologie (Berlin: Reimer, 2002).

50. See discussion in chapter 5.

51. Dinzelbacher, *Europäische Mentalitätsgeschichte.*

52. Jochen Martin, "Der Wandel des Beständigen: Überlegungen zu einer histo-rischen Anthropologie," *Freiburger Universitätsblätter* 126 (1994): 42.

53. Hans Medick, "'Missionare im Ruderboot': Ethnologische Erkenntniswei-sen als Herausforderung an die Sozialgeschichte," in *Alltagsgeschichte: Zur Rekonstruktion historischer Erfahrungen und Lebensweisen*, ed. Alf Lüdtke (Frankfurt am Main, New York: Lang, 1989), 48–84.

54. See Richard J. Evans, *Fakten und Fiktionen: Über die Grundlagen historischer Erkenntnis* (Frankfurt am Main: Campus, 1998); see also Richard J. Evans, Simon Zadek, and Peter Bruzan, eds., *Building Corporate Accountability: Emerging Practices in Social and Ethical Accounting, Auditing, and Reporting* (London: Earthscan, 1999).

55. See Wolf Lepenies, "Geschichte und Anthropologie: Zur wissenschaftlichen Einschätzung eines aktuellen Disziplinkontakts," *Geschichte und Gesellschaft* 1, nos. 2–3 (1975): 325–43; Gernot Böhme, *Anthropologie in pragmatischer Hinsicht* (Frankfurt am Main: Suhrkamp, 1985), 251–65.

56. Ariès, *Centuries of Childhood*. Whereas Ariès spoke of the discovery of childhood in the seventeenth century, a few years ago there was talk of childhood disappearing.

57. See, for example, Natalie Zemon Davis, *Die wahrhaftige Geschichte von der Wiederkehr des Martin Guerre* (Berlin: Wagenbach, 1984); Norbert Schindler, *Widerspenstige Leute: Studien zur Volkskultur in der frühen Neuzeit* (Frankfurt am Main: Fischer, 1992); Hans Medick, *Weben und Überleben in Laichingen, 1650–1900: Lokalgeschichte als allgemeine Geschichte* (Göttingen: Vandenhoeck & Ruprecht, 1996); Alain Corbin, *Auf den Spuren eines Unbekannten: Ein Historiker rekonstruiert ein ganz gewöhnliches Leben* (Frankfurt am Main: Campus, 1999).

58. Clifford Geertz, "Thick Description: Toward an Interpretive Theory of Culture," in *The Interpretation of Cultures: Selected Essays* (New York: Basic Books, 1973), 3–30.

59. See, among others, Alf Lüdtke and Hans-Jürgen Goetz, "Mikro-Historie: Historische Anthropologie," in *Geschichte—ein Grundkurs*, ed. Hans-Jürgen Goetz (Reinbek, Germany: Rowohlt, 1998), 557–78; Jürgen Schlumbohm, ed., *Mikrogeschichte—Makrogeschichte: Komplementär oder inkommensurabel?* (Göttingen: Wallstein, 1998).

60. See the discussion in Schlumbohm, *Mikrogeschichte—Makrogeschichte*.

61. See also Emmanuel Le Roy Ladurie, *Montaillou: Village occitan de 1294 à 1324* (Paris: Gallimard, 1975).

62. See the explanation of this topic in Dressel, *Historische Anthropologie*, 84ff.

63. Dietmar Kamper and Christoph Wulf, eds., *Die Wiederkehr des Körpers* (Frankfurt am Main: Suhrkamp, 1982), *Der andere Körper* (Berlin: Mensch und Leben, 1984), *Das Schwinden der Sinne* (Frankfurt am Main: Suhrkamp, 1984), and *Transfigurationen des Körpers: Spuren der Gewalt in der Geschichte* (Berlin: Reimer, 1989); see also Claudia Benthien and Christoph Wulf, eds., *Körperteile: Eine kulturelle Anatomie* (Reinbek, Germany: Rowohlt, 2001); Hans Belting, Dietmar Kamper, and Martin Schulz, eds., *Quel Corps? Eine Frage der Repräsentation* (Munich: Wilhelm Fink, 2002).

64. Reinhard, *Lebensformen Europas*, esp. 43ff.

65. See, for example, Peter Gay, *The Bourgeois Experience: Victoria to Freud* (New York: Oxford University Press, 1984); Stefan Breit, *"Leichtfertigkeit" und ländliche Gesellschaft: Voreheliche Sexualität in der frühen Neuzeit* (Munich: Old-

enbourg, 1991); Beate Schuster, *Die freien Frauen: Dirnen und Frauenhäuser im 15. und 16. Jahrhundert* (Frankfurt am Main: Campus, 1995); Klaus Schreiner, ed., *Gepeinigt, begehrt, vergessen: Symbolik und Sozialbezug des Körpers im späten Mittelalter und in der frühen Neuzeit* (Munich: Fink, 1992); Daniela Erlach, Markus Reisenleitner, and Karl Vocelka, *Privatisierung der Triebe? Sexualität in der Frühen Neuzeit* (Frankfurt am Main: Lang, 1994); Sabine Kienitz, *Sexualität, Macht und Moral: Prostitution und Geschlechterbeziehungen Anfang des 19. Jahrhunderts in Württemberg* (Berlin: Akademie-Verlag, 1995).

66. See, for example, Ariès, *Centuries of Childhood*; Lloyd de Mause, *History of Childhood* (New York: Psychohistory Press, 1974); Irene Hardach-Pinke and Gerd Hardach, eds., *Kinderalltag: Deutsche Kindheiten in Selbstzeugnissen, 1700—1900* (Reinbek, Germany: Rowohlt, 1981); Peter Borscheid, *Geschichte des Alters* (Munich: Deutscher Taschenbuch Verlag, 1989).

67. Hasso Spode, *Die Macht der Trunkenheit: Kultur- und Sozialgeschichte des Alkohols in Deutschland* (Opladen, Germany: Leske and Budrich, 1993); Georges Vigarello, *Concepts of Cleanliness: Changing Attitudes in France since the Middle Ages* (New York: Cambridge University Press, 1988).

68. Neithard Bulst and Robert Jütte, eds., *Zwischen Sein und Schein: Kleidung und Identität in der ständischen Gesellschaft* (Freiburg: Karl Alber, 1993); Daniel Roche, *La culture des apparences: Une histoire du vêtement* (Paris: Fayard, 1989).

69. Elaine Scarry, *The Body in Pain: The Making and Unmaking of the World* (New York: Oxford University Press, 1985).

70. Philippe Ariès, *The Hour of Our Death* (New York: Oxford University Press, 1991); see also his *Death in America* (Philadelphia: University of Pennsylvania Press, 1975); Arthur E. Imhof, *Die gewonnenen Jahre: Von der Zunahme unserer Lebensspanne seit dreihundert Jahren oder von der Notwendigkeit einer neuen Einstellung zu Leben und Sterben; Ein historischer Essay* (Munich: Beck, 1981), and *Die Lebenszeit: Vom aufgeschobenen Tod und von der Kunst des Lebens* (Munich: Beck, 1988).

71. Gerd Althoff, "Baupläne der Rituale im Mittelalter: Zur Genese und Geschichte ritueller Verhaltensmuster," in *Die Kultur des Rituals*, ed. Christoph Wulf and Jörg Zirfas (Munich: Wilhelm Fink, 2004), 177–97.

72. LeGoff, *Medieval World*.

73. See, for example, Martin Scharfe, *Die Religion des Volkes: Kleine Kultur- und Sozialgeschichte des Pietismus* (Gütersloh, Germany: Mohn, 1980); Peter Dinzelbacher and Dieter R. Bauer, eds., *Volksreligion im hohen und späten Mittelalter* (Paderborn, Germany: Schöningh, 1990); Richard van Dülmen, ed., *Arbeit, Frömmigkeit und Eigensinn: Studien zur historischen Kulturforschung*, vol. 2 (Frankfurt am Main: Fischer, 1990); Eva Labouvie, *Zauberei und Hexenwerk: Ländlicher Hexenglaube in der frühen Neuzeit* (Frankfurt am Main: Fischer, 1993); Michael Mitterauer, *The European Family: Patriarchy to Partnership from the Middle Ages to the Present* (Chicago: University of Chicago Press, 1982).

74. Carlo Ginzburg, *The Cheese and the Worms: The Cosmos of a Sixteenth-Century Miller* (New York: Penguin Books, 1982).

75. Jacques LeGoff, "Les mentalités: Une histoire ambigue," in *Faire de l'historie*, 3 vols, ed. Jacques LeGoff and Pierre Nora (Paris: Éditions Gallimard, 1974); Raulff, *Mentalitäten-Geschichte*; Annette Riecks, *Französische Sozial- und Mentalitätsgeschichte: Ein Forschungsbericht* (Altenberge, Germany: Telos, 1989).

76. Reinhart Koselleck, *Futures Past: On the Semantics of Historical Time* (New York: Columbia University Press, 2004).

77. Peter Burke, "Strengths and Weaknesses of the History of Mentalities," *History of European Ideas* 7, no. 5 (1986): 440.

78. Lucien Lévy-Bruhl, *La mentalité primitive* (Paris: F. Alcan, 1922).

79. Robert Mandrou, *L'Europe absolutiste: Raison et raison d'État, 1649–1775* (Paris: Fayard, 1977); Robert Muchembled, *Les derniers bûchers: Un village de Flandre et ses sorcières sous Louis XIV* (Paris: Ramsay, 1981); Delumeau, *Sin and Fear.*

80. Bloch, *Les rois thaumaturges.*

81. Thomas S. Kuhn, *The Structure of Scientific Revolutions* (Chicago: University of Chicago Press, 1970).

82. See, among others, August Nitschke, *Körper in Bewegung: Gesten, Tänze und Räume im Wandel der Geschichte* (Zurich: Kreuz, 1989); Thomas Alkemeyer, *Körper, Kult und Politik: Von der "Muskelreligion" Pierre de Coubertins zur Inszenierung von Macht in den Olympischen Spielen von 1936* (Frankfurt am Main: Campus, 1996).

83. These also include rituals and the signs and gestures related to them; see Egon Flaig, *Ritualisierte Politik: Zeichen, Gesten und Herrschaft im Alten Rom* (Göttingen: Vandenhoeck & Ruprecht, 2003); Gerd Althoff, *Die Macht der Rituale: Symbolik und Herrschaft im Mittelalter* (Darmstadt: Wissenschaftliche Buchgesellschaft, 2003).

84. See Reinhard, *Lebensformen Europas.*

CHAPTER FOUR

1. Tim Ingold, ed., *Key Debates in Anthropology* (New York: Routledge, 1996), and *Companion Encyclopedia of Anthropology* (London: Routledge, 2002); Alan Barnard and Jonathan Spencer, eds., *Encyclopedia of Social and Cultural Anthropology* (London, New York: Routledge, 2002), a reference work on basic terms used in social and cultural anthropology listed in alphabetical order; see also William A. Haviland, *Cultural Anthropology*, 7th ed. (Fort Worth, TX: Harcourt Brace Jovanovich, 1993); Roger M. Keesing and Andrew J. Strathern, *Cultural Anthropology: A Contemporary Perspective*, 3rd ed. (New York: Harcourt Brace College Publishers, 1998); Jaan Valsiner, *Culture and Human Development: An Introduction* (London: Sage, 2000); and Mondher Kilani, *Introduction à l'anthropologie* (Lausanne: Éditions Payot, 1992).

2. Marvin Harris, *The Rise of Anthropological Theory: A History of Theories of Cultures*, rev. ed. (Walnut Creek, CA: AltaMira Press, 2001), see esp. 142ff.

3. Herbert Spencer, "The Development Hypothesis" (orig. pub. anonymously in *The Leader* 3 [1852]); full text available online at http://www.victorian-web.org/science/science_texts/spencer_dev_hypothesis.html (accessed June 2009).
4. Ibid., 128.
5. Lewis H. Morgan, *Ancient Society* (Cambridge, MA: Belknap Press, 1964).
6. Edward B. Tylor, *Primitive Culture: Researches into the Development of Mythology, Philosophy, Religion, Language, Art and Custom* (London: J. Murray, 1871).
7. James George Frazer, *The Golden Bough: A Study in Magic and Religion* (London: Macmillan, 1922).
8. See Franz Boas, *The Mind of Primitive Man* (New York: Macmillan, 1911), and *Race, Language, and Culture* (New York: Macmillan, 1980).
9. Harris, *Anthropological Theory*, 250ff.
10. Ibid., 295.
11. Karl-Heinz Kohl, *Ethnologie—die Wissenschaft vom kulturell Fremden: Eine Einführung* (Munich: Beck, 1993), 146.
12. See Daniel Segal and Sylvia Yanagisako, eds., *Unwrapping the Sacred Bundle: Reflections on the Disciplining of Anthropology* (Durham, NC: Duke University Press, 2005).
13. See Fredrik Barth, Andre Gingrich, Robert Parkin, and Sydel Silverman, *One Discipline, Four Ways: British, German, French and American Anthropology* (Chicago: University of Chicago Press, 2005); Alan Barnard, *History and Theory in Anthropology* (Cambridge: Cambridge University Press, 2000); Susan Carol Rogers, "Anthropology in France," *Annual Review of Anthropology* 30 (October 2001): 481–504; Richard G. Fox and Barbara J. Kind, eds., *Anthropology beyond Culture* (Oxford: Oxford University Press 2002); William Y. Adams, *The Philosophical Roots of Anthropology* (Stanford, CA: Center for the Study of Language and Information, 1998); George W. Stocking, *Observers Observed: Essays on Ethnographic Fieldwork*, History of Anthropology, 1 (Madison: University of Wisconsin Press, 1983), *Volksgeist as Method and Ethic: Essays on Boasian Ethnography and the German Anthropological Tradition*, History of Anthropology, 8 (Madison: University of Wisconsin Press, 1996), and *After Tylor: British Social Anthropology, 1888–1951* (London: Athlone Press, 1996).
14. See Clarence C. Gravlee, Russell H. Bernhard, and William R. Leonard, "Boas' Changes in Bodily Form: The Immigrant Study, Cranial Plasticity, and Boas' Physical Anthropology," *American Anthropologist* 105, no. 2 (2003): 326–32.
15. See Barth et al., *One Discipline, Four Ways*, 262.
16. See Dietmar Kamper, Christoph Wulf, and Gunter Gebauer, eds., "Kants Anthropologie" (issue title), *Paragrana* 11, no. 2 (2002).
17. John H. Zammito, *Kant, Herder and the Birth of Anthropology* (Chicago: University of Chicago Press, 2002).

18. See Manuela Fischer, Peter Bolz, and Susan Kamel, eds., *Adolf Bastian and His Universal Archives of Humanity: The Origins of German Anthropology* (Hildesheim, Germany: Olms, 2007); Klaus-Peter Köpping, *Adolf Bastian and the Psychic Unity of Mankind* (Münster: LIT Verlag, 2005); Frederick M. Barnard, *J. G. Herder on Social and Political Culture* (Cambridge: Cambridge University Press, 1969).

19. Note the similarity between the objectives of this organization and the four-field concept of Boasian anthropology.

20. Johann Jakob Bachofen, *Myth, Religion and Mother Right: Selected Writings* (Princeton, NJ: Princeton University Press, 1967); Theodor Waitz, *Introduction to Anthropology* (New York: AMS Press, 1973); Heinrich Barth, *Travels in Nigeria* (London: Oxford University Press, 1962).

21. For further details on this differentiation between *Volkskunde* and *Völkerkunde* and on present-day attempts to convert *Volkskunde* into a European ethnology that applies international standards, see Wolfgang Kaschuba, *Einführung in die europäische Ethnologie* (Munich: Beck, 2006).

22. Friedrich von Schlegel, "On the Language and Wisdom of the Indians," in *The Aesthetic and Miscellaneous Works*, trans. E. J. Millington (London: Bohn, 1860).

23. See Köpping, *Adolf Bastian.*

24. See Andrew Zimmermann, *Anthropology and Antihumanism in Imperial Germany* (Chicago: University of Chicago Press, 2001).

25. See the introduction to George W. Stocking, ed., *The Shaping of American Anthropology, 1883–1951: A Franz Boas Reader* (New York: Basic Books, 1974).

26. Alfred L. Kroeber, "The 'Superorganic,'" *American Anthropologist* 19, no. 2 (1917): 163–213; Edward Sapir, "Culture, Genuine and Spurious," *American Journal of Sociology* 29, no. 4 (1924): 401–29.

27. See Clyde Cluckhohn, "Universal Categories of Culture," in *Anthropology Today: An Encyclopaedic Inventory*, ed. Alfred L. Kroeber (Chicago: University of Chicago Press, 1953), 507–23.

28. See Derek Freeman, *Margaret Mead and Samoa: The Making and Unmaking of an Anthropological Myth* (Cambridge, MA: Harvard University Press, 1983).

29. Melville J. Herskovits, "The Cattle Complex in East Africa," *American Anthropologist* 28, nos. 1–4 (1926): 230–73; 361–88; 494–528; 633–64.

30. Oscar Lewis, *The Effects of White Contact upon Blackfoot Culture, with Special Reference to the Role of the Fur Trade* (New York: J. J. Augustin, 1942); Jane Richardson, *Law and Status among the Kiowa Indians* (New York: J. J. Augustin, 1940); Alexander Lesser, *The Pawnee Ghost Dance Hand Game: A Study of Cultural Change* (New York: Columbia University Press, 1933).

31. Ralph Linton, *The Study of Man: An Introduction* (New York: D. Appleton-Century, 1936).

32. Leslie White, *The Science of Culture: A Study of Man and Civilisation* (New York: Grove Press, 1949).

33. Julian H. Steward, ed., *Handbook of the South American Indians*, Bureau of American Ethnology, Bulletin 143, vols. 1–6 (Washington, DC: Smithsonian Institution, 1946–1959); Julian H. Steward, *Theory of Culture Change: The Methodology of Multilinear Evolution* (Urbana: University of Illinois Press, 1955).

34. Eric Wolf, *Peasants* (Englewood Cliffs, NJ: Prentice Hall, 1966), and *Envisioning Power Ideologies of Dominance and Crisis* (Berkeley and Los Angeles: University of California Press, 1999); Marshall Sahlins, *Stone Age Economics* (Chicago: Aldine, 1973), and *Culture and Practical Reason* (Chicago: University of Chicago Press, 1976); Marvin Harris, *Cannibals and Kings: The Origins of Culture* (New York: Random House, 1977), and *Cultural Materialism: The Struggle for a Science of Culture* (New York: Thomas Crowell, 1979).

35. Claude Meillassoux, *Maidens, Meal and Money: Capitalism and the Domestic Community* (Cambridge: Cambridge University Press, 1981); see also Henrietta L. Moore, *Feminism and Anthropology* (Cambridge: Polity Press, 1988).

36. Maurice Godelier, *Perspectives in Marxist Anthropology* (Cambridge: Cambridge University Press, 1977), and *The Enigma of the Gift* (Cambridge: Polity Press, 1999).

37. Immanuel Wallerstein, *The Modern World System*, 3 vols. (New York: Academic Press, 1974–1989); important in this context are Maurice Bloch, *Marxism and Anthropology: The History of a Relationship* (Oxford: Oxford University Press, 1983); Dominique Legros, "Chance, Necessity, and Mode of Production: A Marxist Critique of Cultural Evolutionism," *American Anthropologist* 79 (1977): 26–41.

38. Bronislaw K. Malinowski, *Argonauts of the Western Pacific* (London: Routledge, 1922); Alfred R. Radcliffe-Brown, *The Andaman Islanders* (Cambridge: Cambridge University Press, 1922).

39. See Phyllis Kaberry, "Malinowski's Contribution to Field-work Methods and the Writing of Ethnography," in *Man and Culture: An Evaluation of the Work of Bronislaw Malinowski*, ed. Raymond Firth (London: Routledge and Kegan Paul, 1957), 71–91.

40. Bronislaw K. Malinowski, *A Scientific Theory of Culture, and Other Essays* (Chapel Hill: University of North Carolina Press, 1944).

41. Alfred R. Radcliffe-Brown, *A Natural Science of Society* (Glencoe, IL: The Free Press, 1957).

42. Alfred R. Radcliffe-Brown, "Introduction," in *African Systems of Kinship and Marriage*, ed. Alfred R. Radcliffe-Brown and Daryll Forde (London: Oxford University Press, 1950), 9; and "On the Concept of Function in Social Science," *American Anthropologist* 37 no. 3 (1935): 394–402.

43. Alfred R. Radcliffe-Brown, *Structure and Function in Primitive Society: Essays and Addresses*, 6th ed. (London: Oxford University Press, 1965), 43ff.

44. Edward E. Evans-Pritchard, *Social Anthropology*, 7th ed. (London: Cohen & West, 1967), 60ff.; see also his *Theories of Primitive Religion* (Oxford: Oxford University Press, 1985).

45. See Frederik Barth, "Britain and the Commonwealth," in Barth et al., *One Discipline, Four Ways*, 3–57.

46. See Marcel Griaule, *Méthode de l'éthnographie* (Paris: Presses Universitaires de France, 1957), and *Conversations with Ogotemmêli: An Introduction to Dogon Religious Ideas* (Oxford: Oxford University Press for the International African Institute, 1965; orig. pub. 1948); see also Marcel Granet, *The Religion of the Chinese People* (Oxford: Blackwell, 1975).

47. Marcel Mauss, *Sociology and Psychology: Essays* (London: Routledge, 1979), and *Techniques, Technology, and Civilisation* (New York: Durkheim Press/Berghahn Books, 2006); Gunter Gebauer and Christoph Wulf, *Spiel, Ritual, Geste: Mimetisches Handeln in der sozialen Welt* (Reinbek, Germany: Rowohlt, 1998), 160–61; Godelier, *Enigma of the Gift*.

48. See Claude Lévi-Strauss, *The Elementary Structures of Kinship* (Boston: Beacon Press, 1969), *Structural Anthropology* (New York: Basic Books, 1999), *The Savage Mind* (London: Weidenfeld & Nicolson, 1966), and *Tristes tropiques* (New York: Penguin Books, 1992); Louis Dumont, *Homo Hierarchicus: The Caste System and Its Implications* (Chicago: University of Chicago Press, 1980), and *Essays on Individualism: Modern Ideology in Anthropological Perspective* (Chicago: University of Chicago Press, 1992).

49. Lévi-Strauss, *Elementary Structures of Kinship*; see also Edmund R. Leach, *Lévi-Strauss* (Glasgow: Fontana/Collins, 1970); Jean Poullon and Pierre Maranda, eds., *Echanges et communications: Mélanges offerts à Claude Lévi-Strauss à l'occasion de son 60ème anniversaire*, 2 vols., Studies in General Anthropology, 5 (The Hague: Mouton, 1970).

50. Robert Parkin, "The French-Speaking Countries," in Barth et al., *One Discipline, Four Ways*, 212.

51. See Eberhard Berg and Martin Fuchs, "Phänomenologie der Differenz: Reflexionsstufen ethnographischer Repräsentation," in *Kultur, soziale Praxis, Text: Die Krise der ethnographischen Repräsentation*, ed. Eberhard Berg and Martin Fuchs (Frankfurt am Main: Suhrkamp, 1993), 39; see also George E. Marcus and Drick Cushman, "Ethnographies as Texts," *Annual Review of Anthropology* 11 (1982): 25–69.

52. See Berg and Fuchs, "Phänomenologie der Differenz," 42.

53. See James Clifford and George E. Marcus, eds., *Writing Culture: The Poetics and Politics of Ethnography* (Berkeley and Los Angeles: University of California Press, 1986); David R. Hiley, James F. Bohman, and Richard Shusterman, eds., *The Interpretative Turn: Philosophy, Science, Culture* (Ithaca, NY: Cornell University Press, 1991); George E. Marcus, *Re-Reading Cultural Anthropology* (Durham, NC: Duke University Press, 1992).

54. Berg and Fuchs, "Phänomenologie der Differenz," 50–51.

55. Paul Ricoeur, *Interpretation Theory, Discourse and the Surplus of Meaning* (Fort Worth: Texas Christian University Press, 1976), 21; see also his *Hermeneutics and the Human Sciences: Essays on Language, Action and Interpretation*

(New York: Cambridge University Press, 1981), and *From Text to Action* (Evanston, IL: Northwestern University Press, 1991).

56. See James Clifford, *The Predicament of Culture: Twentieth-Century Ethnography, Literature, and Art* (Cambridge, MA: Harvard University Press, 1988).

57. See Clifford Geertz, "Deep Play: Notes on the Balinese Cockfight," in *Interpretation of Cultures: Selected Essays* (New York: Basic Books, 1973), 412–53; Berg and Fuchs, "Phänomenologie der Differenz," 60; see also Martin Fuchs, *Topics in the Calculus of Variations* (Braunschweig: Vieweg, 1994).

58. Wilhelm Dilthey, *Introduction to the Human Sciences: An Attempt to Lay a Foundation for the Study of Society and History* (Detroit, MI: Wayne State University Press, 1988), and *Hermeneutics and the Study of History* (Princeton, NJ: Princeton University Press, 1996); Hans-Georg Gadamer, *Truth and Method* (London: Continuum, 2004); Paul Ricoeur, *Time and Narrative*, 3 vols. (Chicago: University of Chicago Press, 1984–1988).

59. John Borneman and Abdellah Hammoudi, eds., *Being There: The Fieldwork Encounter and the Making of Truth* (Berkeley and Los Angeles: University of California Press, 2009), 15.

60. Michel Leiris, *African Art* (New York: Golden Press, 1968); Lévi-Strauss, *Tristes tropiques*.

61. Marjorie Shostak, *Nisa: The Life and Words of a !Kung Woman* (London: Earthscan, 1990).

62. Vincent Crapanzano, *Tuhami: Portrait of a Moroccan* (Chicago: University of Chicago Press, 1980); Kevin Dwyer, *Moroccan Dialogues: Anthropology in Question* (Baltimore, MD: Johns Hopkins University Press, 1982).

63. See Karl-Heinz Kohl, *Ethnologie—die Wissenschaft vom kulturell Fremden: Eine Einführung* (Munich: Beck, 1993), 125.

64. For more on the idea that "the Other speaks back" see Frantz Fanon, *The Wretched of the Earth* (New York: Grove Press, 2004); Johannes Fabian, *Time and the Other: How Anthropology Makes Its Object* (New York: Columbia University Press, 1983); Edward W. Said, *Orientalism* (New York: Pantheon, 1978).

65. See Gunter Gebauer and Christoph Wulf, *Mimesis: Art, Culture, Society* (Berkeley and Los Angeles: University of California Press, 1995); Christoph Wulf, *Anthropology of Education* (Münster: LIT Verlag, 2002), and "Mimesis," in *Hauptbegriffe qualitativer Sozialforschung*, ed. Ralf Bohnsack, Winfried Marotzki, and Michael Meuser (Opladen, Germany: Leske and Budrich, 2003), 117–19; Christoph Wulf, "Mimesis und performatives Handeln," in *Grundlagen des Performativen: Eine Einführung in die Zusammenhänge von Sprache, Macht und Handeln*, ed. Christoph Wulf, Michael Göhlich, and Jörg Zirfas (Weinheim, Germany: Juventa, 2001), 253–72.

66. See Clifford, *Predicament of Culture*.

67. For these reasons, qualitative research is often conducted in teams.

68. One such procedure used in qualitative research is the group discussion, in which a polyphony is usually attained, as every member or many members of the group express their opinions; this procedure is also particularly suited to gaining an insight into the imaginary and imaginations of a group.

69. See Clifford and Marcus, *Writing Culture*; George E. Marcus and Michael M. J. Fischer, eds., *Anthropology as Cultural Critique: An Experimental Moment in Human Sciences* (Chicago: University of Chicago Press, 1986).

70. James Clifford, "Introduction: Partial Truth," in Clifford and Marcus, *Writing Culture*, 26.

71. Borneman and Hammoudi, *Being There*, 2.

72. See, among many others, Said, *Orientalism*.

73. See George E. Marcus, "Contemporary Problems of Ethnography in the Modern World System," in Clifford and Marcus, *Writing Culture*, 165–93.

74. See Arjun Appadurai, "Disjunction and Difference in the Global Cultural Economy," *Public Culture* 2, no. 2 (1990): 1–24.

75. See Gebauer and Wulf, *Mimesis*; Gebauer and Wulf, *Spiel, Ritual, Geste* (French edition: *Jeux, Rituels, Gestes: Les fondements mimétiques de l'action sociale* [Paris: Anthropos, 2004]).

76. See Wulf, Göhlich, and Zirfas, *Grundlagen des Performativen*; Christoph Wulf and Jörg Zirfas, eds., *Pädagogik des Performativen* (Weinheim, Germany: Beltz, 2007).

77. See Christoph Wulf and Jörg Zirfas, *Ikonologie des Performativen* (Munich: Wilhelm Fink, 2005).

78. Charles L. Briggs, "Linguistic Magic Bullets in the Making of a Modernist Anthropology," *American Anthropologist* 104, no. 2 (2002): 481–98; Jürgen Trabant, *Mithridates im Paradies: Kleine Geschichte des Sprachdenkens* (Munich: Beck, 2003).

79. See Bernd Hüppauf and Christoph Wulf, eds., *Dynamics and Performativity of Imagination: The Image between the Visible and the Invisible* (New York: Routledge, 2009).

80. Christoph Wulf, "Praxis," in *Theorizing Rituals: Issues, Topics, Approaches, Concepts*, ed. Jens Kreinath, Jan Snoek, and Michael Stausberg (Leiden: Brill, 2006), 395–411.

81. Klaus E. Müller and Alfred K. Treml, eds., *Wie man zum Wilden wird: Ethnopädagogische Quellentexte aus vier Jahrhunderten* (Berlin: Reimer, 2002).

82. Kohl, *Ethnologie*, 17ff.

83. Marshall D. Sahlins, *Islands of History* (Chicago: University of Chicago Press, 1985).

84. See Claude Lévi-Strauss, *Structural Anthropology* (New York: Basic Books, 1963).

85. See, for example, Mike Featherstone, *Undoing Culture: Globalisation, Postmodernism and Identity* (London: Sage, 1995); John Hutchinson and Anthony D. Smith, eds., *Ethnicity* (Oxford: Oxford University Press, 1996);

Ralf Konersmann, ed., *Kulturphilosophie* (Leipzig: Reclam, 1996); Akhil Gupta and James Ferguson, eds., *Culture, Power, Place: Explorations in Critical Anthropology* (Durham, NC: Duke University Press, 1997); Michael Herzfeld, *Cultural Intimacy: Social Poetics in the Nation-State* (New York: Routledge, 2005); Ralf Konersmann, ed., *Kulturkritik: Reflexionen in der veränderten Welt* (Leipzig: Reclam, 2001).

86. Jean-Paul Sartre, *The Words* (New York: George Braziller, 1964).

87. Karl-Siegbert Rehberg, "Zurück zur Kultur? Arnold Gehlens anthropologische Grundlegung der Kulturwissenschaften," in Helmut Brackert and Fritz Wefelmeyer, eds., *Kultur: Bestimmungen im 20. Jahrhundert* (Frankfurt am Main: Suhrkamp, 1990), 301.

88. Alfred L. Kroeber and Clyde Kluckhohn, *Culture: A Critical Review of Concepts and Definitions*, Papers of the Peabody Museum of American Archaeology and Ethnology, 47 (Cambridge, MA: Harvard University Press, 1952).

89. Edward B. Tylor, *Primitive Culture* (New York: Harper, 1958), 1.

90. Bronislaw Malinowski, *A Scientific Theory of Culture, and Other Essays* (Chapel Hill: University of North Carolina Press, 2002; orig. pub. 1944), 40.

91. Clifford Geertz, "The Impact of the Concept of Culture on the Concept of Man," in Geertz, *Interpretation of Cultures*, 36.

92. Ibid., 45 and 46–47.

93. Kohl, *Ethnologie*, 132.

94. Ibid., 150.

95. See, for example, Julian Hayes Steward, "Cultural Ecology," in *Encyclopedia of the Social Sciences*, ed. David L. Sills, vol. 4 (New York: Macmillan, 1968), 337–44; Roy A. Rappaport subscribes to the view that culture is environment-related in *Pigs for the Ancestors: Ritual in the Ecology of a New Guinea People* (New Haven, CT: Yale University Press, 1968); Marvin Harris argues in favor of a more materialistic position in *Cultural Anthropology* (New York: Harper & Row, 1983).

96. See Tzvetan Todorov, *The Conquest of America: The Question of the Other* (Norman: University of Oklahoma Press, 1999), and *On Human Diversity: Nationalism, Racism, and Exoticism in French Thought* (Cambridge, MA: Harvard University Press, 1993); Serge Gruzinski, *The Conquest of Mexico: The Incorporation of Indian Societies into the Western World, 16th–18th Centuries* (Cambridge: Polity Press, 1993), *Images at War: Mexico from Columbus to Blade Runner (1492–2019)* (Durham, NC: Duke University Press, 2001), and *La pensée métisse* (Paris: Fayard, 1999); Stephen Greenblatt, *Marvelous Possessions: The Wonder of the New World* (Chicago: University of Chicago Press, 1992).

97. See Bernhard Waldenfels, *The Question of the Other* (Albany: State University of New York Press; Hong Kong: Chinese University Press, 2007); Gebauer and Wulf, *Spiel, Ritual, Geste*, chap. 7, "Der Andere."

98. See Jean Baudrillard and Marc Guillaume, *Figures de l'altérité* (Paris: Éd. Descartes, 1993); Umberto Curi and Bruna Giacomini, eds., *Xenos: Filosofia*

dello straniero (Padova: Poligrafo, 2002); Herfried Münkler, ed., *Die Heraus-forderung durch das Fremde* (Berlin: Akademie Verlag, 1998).

99. See Wulf, *Anthropology of Education.*

100. Marc Augé, *An Anthropology for Contemporaneous Worlds* (Stanford, CA: Stanford University Press, 1999).

101. Marc Augé, *In the Metro* (Minneapolis: University of Minnesota Press, 2002), and *Non-Places: Introduction to an Anthropology of Supermodernity* (London: Verso, 2008).

102. See Katrin Audehm and Hans Rudolf Velten, eds., *Transgression—Hybridisie-rung—Differenzierung: Zur Performativität von Grenzen in Sprache, Kultur und Gesellschaft* (Freiburg: Rombach, 2007).

103. Homi K. Bhabha, *The Location of Culture* (London: Routledge, 1998), 36ff.

104. Today, while many departments profess their adherence to the unity of four-field anthropology on their websites, few of them actually practice it, Emory's being one of the main ones to do so. This is a true reflection of anthropology's extraordinary differentiation and diversity, which makes it appear almost pointless to try to uphold the idea of a clearly structured unity within the discipline. This became particularly evident following the exodus of most of the biological anthropologists occasioned by the reorga-nization of the American Anthropological Association in the early 1980s. Nevertheless, the discussions on anthropology as a four-field discipline are still important, as they encourage its proponents to reflect upon issues of the identity of the discipline. See James M. Calcagno, "Keeping Biological Anthropology in Anthropology, and Anthropology in Biology," *American Anthropologist* 105, no. 1 (2003): 6–15.

105. See Robert Borofsky, ed., *Assessing Cultural Anthropology* (New York: McGraw-Hill, 1994).

106. "'Anthropologists Are Talking' About Anthropology After Globalization," *Ethnos* 72, no. 1 (2007): 102–26 (a talk by Eric Hirsch, Bruce Kapferer, and Emily Martin).

CHAPTER FIVE

1. Christoph Wulf and Dietmar Kamper, eds., *Logik und Leidenschaft: Erträge Historischer Anthropologie* (Berlin: Reimer, 2002).

2. These concepts include, for example, enlightenment, emancipation, rei-fication, critique, society, communication, and the relationship between theory and practice. See Christoph Wulf, *Educational Science: Hermeneutics, Empirical Research, Critical Theory* (Münster: Waxmann, 2003); Dietmar Kamper, *Geschichte und menschliche Natur: Die Tragweite gegenwärtiger An-thropologie-Kritik* (Munich: Hanser, 1973). Regarding the Frankfurt School see, for example, Max Horkheimer and Theodor W. Adorno, *The Dialectic of Enlightenment: Philosophical Fragments* (Stanford, CA: Stanford University Press, 2002); Theodor W. Adorno, *Negative Dialectics* (London: Routledge,

1990); Jürgen Habermas, *The Structural Transformation of the Public Sphere: An Inquiry into Bourgeois Society* (Cambridge, MA: MIT Press, 1989), and *Theory and Practice* (Boston: Beacon Press, 1993); Herbert Marcuse, *One-Dimensional Man: Studies in the Ideology of Advanced Industrial Society* (London: Routledge, 1991). Gadamer's work on hermeneutics is also important in this context; see Hans-Georg Gadamer, *Truth and Method* (New York: Crossroad, 1989).

3. Christoph Wulf, ed., *Vom Menschen: Handbuch Historische Anthropologie* (Weinheim, Germany: Beltz, 1997), 2nd ed., *Der Mensch und seine Kultur* (Cologne: Anaconda, 2010).

4. The issues of *Paragrana* contain articles on the following subjects in which the epistemological bases of historical anthropology are further developed. All of the following are titles of entire issues: "Emotionen in einer transkulturellen Welt," 20, no. 2 (2011); "Töten: Affekte, Akte und Formen," 20, no. 1 (2011); "Kontaktzonen," 19, no. 2 (2010); "Emotion—Bewegung—Körper," 19, no. 1 (2010); "Handlung und Leidenschaft," 18, no. 2 (2009); "The Body in India," 18, no. 1 (2009); "Das menschliche Leben," 17, no. 2 (2008); "Medien—Körper—Imagination," 17, no. 1 (2008); "Klanganthropologie," 16, no. 2 (2007); "Muße," 16, no. 1 (2007); "Sprachen ästhetischer Erfahrung," 15, no. 2 (2006); "Performanz des Rechts," 15, no. 1 (2006); "Körpermaschinen—Maschinenkörper," 15, no. 2 (2005); "Historische Anthropologie der Sprache," 14, no. 1 (2005); "Rausch, Sucht, Ekstase," 14, no. 2 (2004); "Praktiken des Performativen," 13, no. 1 (2004); "Rituelle Welten," 12, nos. 1–2 (2003); "Kants Anthropologie," 11, no. 2 (2002); "[(v)er]SPIEL[en]," 11, no. 1 (2002); "Horizontverschiebung—Umzug ins Offene?" 10, no. 2 (2001); "Theorien des Performativen," 10, no. 1 (2001); "Inszenierungen des Erinnerns," 9, no. 2 (2000); "Metaphern des Unmöglichen," 9, no. 1 (2000); "Idiosynkrasien," 8, no. 2 (1999); "Askese," 8, no. 1 (1999); "Jenseits," 7, no. 2 (1998); "Kulturen des Performativen," 7, no. 1 (1998); "Der Mann," 6, no. 2 (1997); "Selbstfremdheit," 6, no. 1 (1997); "Leben als Arbeit?" 5, no. 2 (1996); "Die Elemente in der Kunst," 5, no. 1 (1996); "Mimesis—Poiesis—Autopoiesis," 4, no. 2 (1995); "Aisthesis," 4, no. 1 (1995); "Europa: Raumschiff oder Zeitenfloß," 3, no. 2 (1994); "Does Culture Matter?" 3, no. 1 (1994); "Das Ohr als Erkenntnisorgan," 2, nos. 1–2 (1993); "Miniatur," 1, no. 1 (1992).

5. See the following books published by the Interdisciplinary Centre for Historical Anthropology at the Free University of Berlin in the Historische Anthropologie series (Berlin: Reimer Verlag [year follows each title]): Ursula Baatz and Wolfgang Müller-Funk, eds., *Vom Ernst des Spiels* (1993); Wilhelm Berger, Klaus Ratschiller, and Hubert Wank, *Flucht und Kontrolle* (1996); Marie-Anne Berr, *Technik und Körper* (1991); Elke Dauk, *Denken als Ethos und Methode* (1989); Marcel Dobberstein, *Musik und Mensch* (2000); Gunter Gebauer, ed., *Körper- und Einbildungskraft* (1988); Frithjof Hager, ed., *Körper-Denken* (1996); Susanne Hauser, *Der Blick auf die Stadt* (1990); Birgit Hoppe,

Körper und Geschlecht (1991); Dietmar Kamper and Christoph Wulf, eds., *Die erloschene Seele* (1988), *Transfigurationen des Körpers* (1989), and *Schweigen* (1992); Ae-Ryung Kim, *Metapher und Mimesis* (2002); Jutta Anna Kleber, *Krebstabu und Krebsschuld* (2003); Eugen König, *Körper, Wissen, Macht* (1989); Dieter Lenzen, ed., *Melancholie als Lebensform* (1989); Dieter Lenzen, ed., *Verbotene Wünsche* (1991); Birke Mersmann, *Was bleibt vom Heldentum?* (1995); Marianne Mischke, *Der Umgang mit dem Tod* (1996); Eckhard Neumann, *Funktionshistorische Anthropologie der ästhetischen Produktivität* (1996); Heide Nixdorff, ed., *Das textile Medium als Phänomen der Grenze—Begrenzung—Entgrenzung* (1999); Fanny Rostek-Lühmann, *Der Kinderfänger von Hameln* (1995); Doris Schuhmacher-Chilla, *Ästhetische Sozialisation und Erziehung* (1995); Manuel Simon, *Heilige Hexe Mutter* (1993); Michael Sonntag, *Die Seele als Politikum* (1988); Angela Sterken, *Enthüllung der Helvetia* (1998); Stephan Sting, *Der Mythos des Fortschreitens* (1991); Annette M. Stross, *Ich-Identität* (1991); Gerburg Treusch-Dieter, Wolfgang Pircher, and Herbert Hrachovec, eds., *Denkzettel Antike* (1989); Klaus Vogel, *Der Wilde unter den Künstlern* (1991); Rainer Wannicke, *Sartres Flaubert* (1990); Klaus-Michael Wimmer, *Der Andere und die Sprache* (1988); Jörg Zirfas, *Präsenz und Ewigkeit* (1993).

6. See the following books in the series entitled Pädagogische Anthropologie founded by Christoph Wulf and published by the Pädagogische Anthropologie Commission of the German Society of Educational Science in the educational anthropology series: Meike Sophia Baader, Johannes Bilstein, and Christoph Wulf, eds., *Die Kultur der Freundschaft* (2008); Johannes Bilstein, Gisela Miller-Kipp, and Christoph Wulf, eds., *Transformationen der Zeit* (1999); Johannes Bilstein, Matthias Winzen, and Christoph Wulf, eds., *Spiel* (2004); Bernhard Dieckmann, Stephan Sting, and Jörg Zirfas, eds., *Gedächtnis und Bildung* (1998); Michael Göhlich, *System, Handeln, Lernen unterstützen* (2001); Eckart Liebau and Christoph Wulf, eds., *Generation* (1996); Eckart Liebau, Gisela Miller-Kipp, and Christoph Wulf, eds., *Metamorphosen des Raums* (1999); Eckart Liebau, Doris Schuhmacher-Chilla, and Christoph Wulf, eds., *Anthropologie Pädagogischer Institutionen* (2001); Eckart Liebau, Helga Peskoller, and Christoph Wulf, eds., *Natur* (2003); Christoph Lüth and Christoph Wulf, eds., *Vervollkommnung durch Arbeit und Bildung?* (1997); Klaus Mollenhauer and Christoph Wulf, eds., *Aisthesis/Ästhetik: Zwischen Wahrnehmung und Bewusstsein* (1996); Gerd Schäfer and Christoph Wulf, eds., *Bild—Bilder—Bildung* (1999); Stephan Sting, *Schrift, Bildung und Selbst* (1998); Christoph Wulf, ed., *Anthropologisches Denken in der Pädagogik 1750–1850* (1996); Christoph Wulf, Hildegard Macha, and Eckart Liebau, eds., *Formen des Religiösen* (2004); Christoph Wulf, Hildegard Macha, and Eckart Liebau, eds., *Anthropologie und Pädagogik des Spiels* (2005); Jörg Zirfas, *Die Lehre der Ethik* (1999); see also the following by other publishers: Johannes Bilstein and Reinhard Uhle, eds., *Liebe: Zur Anthropologie einer Grundbedingung pädagogischen Handelns* (Oberhausen: Athena, 2007); Christoph

Wulf, Anja Hänsch, and Micha Brumlik, eds., *Das Imaginäre der Geburt* (Munich: Wilhelm Fink, 2008); Johannes Bilstein, ed., *Anthropologie der Sinne* (Opladen, Germany: Budrich, 2011); Meike Sophia Baader, Johannes Bilstein, and Toni Tholen, eds., *Erziehung, Bildung und Geschlecht: Männlichkeit im Fokus der Gender-Studies* (Wiesbaden: Verlag für Sozialwissenschaften, 2012).

7. For a good overview of this topic, see Claudia Benthien, "Historische Anthropologie. Neuere Deutsche Literatur," in *Germanistik als Kulturwissenschaft: Eine Einführung in neue Theoriekonzepte*, ed. Claudia Benthien and Hans Rudolf Velten (Reinbek, Germany: Rowohlt, 2002), 56–82; see also Werner Röcke, "Historische Anthropologie: Ältere deutsche Literatur," in *Germanistik als Kulturwissenschaft: Eine Einführung in neue Theoriekonzepte*, ed. Claudia Benthien and Hans Rudolf Velten (Reinbek, Germany: Rowohlt, 2002), 35–55; Hans Jürgen Schings, ed., *Der ganze Mensch: Anthropologie und Literatur im 18. Jahrhundert* (Stuttgart: Metzler, 1994); Wolfgang Riedel, "Anthropologie und Literatur in der deutschen Spätaufklärung: Skizze einer Forschungslandschaft," special issue, *Internationales Archiv für Sozialgeschichte der deutschen Literatur* 6, no. 3 (1994): 93–157; Jürgen Schläger, ed., "The Anthropological Turn in Literary Studies," *Yearbook of Research in English and American Literature* 12 (Tübingen: Narr, 1996); Fernando Poyatos, ed., *Literary Anthropology: A New Interdisciplinary Approach to People, Signs and Literature* (Philadelphia, PA: J. Benjamins, 1988); Gaston Bachelard, *Earth and Reveries of Will: An Essay on the Imagination of Matter* (Dallas, TX: Dallas Institute of Humanities and Culture, 2002), and *The Dialectic of Duration* (Manchester: Clinamen, 2000).

8. This subject is discussed in detail in chapter 7.

9. See Gunter Gebauer and Christoph Wulf, *Mimesis: Culture, Art, Society* (Berkeley and Los Angeles: University of California Press, 1995); Gunter Gebauer and Christoph Wulf, *Spiel, Ritual, Geste: Mimetisches Handeln in der sozialen Welt* (Reinbek, Germany: Rowohlt, 1998).

10. See Christoph Wulf et al., *Das Soziale als Ritual: Zur performativen Bildung von Gemeinschaften* (Opladen, Germany: Leske and Budrich, 2001); Christoph Wulf et al., *Bildung im Ritual: Schule, Familie, Jugend, Medien* (Wiesbaden: Verlag für Sozialwissenschaften, 2004); Christoph Wulf et al., *Lernkulturen im Umbruch: Rituelle Praktiken in Schule, Medien, Familie und Jugend* (Wiesbaden: Verlag für Sozialwissenschaften, 2007); Christoph Wulf et al., *Ritual and Identity: The Staging and Performing of Rituals in the Lives of Young People* (London: Tufnell Press, 2010); Christoph Wulf et al., *Die Geste in Erziehung, Bildung und Sozialisation: Ethnographische Feldstudien* (Wiesbaden: Verlag für Sozialwissenschaften, 2011). This study could also be seen as an ethnographic study in the field of European ethnology, which has recently become more firmly established as a research domain in its own right. In this context, many studies have been based theoretically and methodologically on previous work carried out on folklore and ethnology.

These studies have a pronounced historical dimension and are thus hardly distinguishable from studies on historical anthropology. However, many recent studies conducted in the field of European ethnology do not have this distinguishing feature. Like my Berlin Study on Rituals, they are oriented more toward the burgeoning new international research paradigm of cultural and social anthropology. The assignment of these studies to European ethnology can only be justified on the basis of their focus on the geographic region of Europe. They do not apparently differ fundamentally from research done within the Society for the Anthropology of Europe or the European Anthropological Association. For a general outline of European ethnology, see Wolfgang Kaschuba, *Einführung in die Europäische Ethnologie*, 3rd ed. (Munich: Beck, 2006).

11. Christoph Wulf, Shoko Suzuki, Jörg Zirfas, Ingrid Kellermann, Yoshitaka Inoue, Fumo Ono, and Nanae Takenaka, *Das Glück der Familie: Ethnographische Studien in Deutschland und Japan* (Wiesbaden: Verlag für Sozialwissenschaften, 2011; Japanese edition, 2012); Axel Michaels and Christoph Wulf, eds., *Images of the Body in India* (London: Routledge, 2011), *Emotions in Rituals and Performances* (London: Routledge, 2012), and *Exploring the Senses: Emotions, Performativity, and Ritual* (London: Routledge, 2013).

12. See Gert Mattenklott, *Der übersinnliche Leib* (Reinbek, Germany: Rowohlt, 1982).

13. See Rudolf zur Lippe, *Am eigenen Leibe: Zur Ökonomie des Lebens* (Frankfurt am Main: Syndikat, 1978).

14. See Dieter Lenzen, *Krankheit als Erfindung: Medizinische Eingriffe in die Kultur* (Frankfurt am Main: Suhrkamp, 1991).

15. See Kamper and Wulf, *Transfigurationen des Körpers.*

16. See Lüth and Wulf, *Vervollkommnung durch Arbeit und Bildung?* and "Leben als Arbeit?" (issue title), *Paragrana* 5, no. 2 (1996).

17. See Bilstein, Miller-Kipp, and Wulf, *Transformationen der Zeit.*

18. See Peter Köpping, Bettina Papenburg, and Christoph Wulf, eds., "Körpermaschinen—Maschinenkörper: Mediale Transformationen" (issue title), *Paragrana* 14, no. 2 (2005).

19. See Christoph Wulf, ed., *Lust und Liebe: Wandlungen der Sexualität* (Munich: Piper, 1985).

20. See "Aisthesis" (issue title), *Paragrana* 4, no. 1 (1995); "Mimesis, Poiesis, Autopoiesis" (issue title), *Paragrana* 4, no. 2 (1995); Mollenhauer and Wulf, *Aisthesis/Ästhetik*; Schäfer and Wulf, *Bild—Bilder—Bildung.*

21. Wulf, *Lust und Liebe.*

22. See Michel Serres, *The Five Senses: A Philosophy of Mingled Bodies* (London: Continuum, 2009); Robert Jütte, *A History of the Senses: From Antiquity to Cyberspace* (Cambridge: Polity Press, 2005).

23. Erwin Straus, *Vom Sinn der Sinne: Ein Beitrag zur Grundlegung der Psychologie* (Berlin: Springer, 1935), 272. See also Erwin Straus, *The Primary World of*

Senses: A Vindication of Sensory Experience (New York: Free Press of Glencoe, 1963).

24. Johann Gottfried Herder, "Über den Ursprung der Sprache," in *Werke*, Bd. II, *Herder und die Anthropologie der Aufklärung* (Munich: Hanser, 1987), 251–399, 299. See also Johann Gottfried Herder, *On the Origin of Language* (Chicago: University of Chicago Press, 1986).

25. Maurice Merleau-Ponty, *The Essential Writings of Merleau-Ponty* (New York: Harcourt, Brace & World, 1969), and *Phenomenology of Perception* (London: Routledge, 2002).

26. David C. Lindberg, *Studies in the History of Medieval Optics* (London: Variorum Reprints, 1983); see also Jean Starobinski, *The Living Eye* (Cambridge, MA: Harvard University Press, 1989).

27. See Michel Foucault, *Discipline and Punish: The Birth of the Prison* (New York: Pantheon Books, 1977), and *The Birth of the Clinic: An Archaeology of Medical Perception* (New York: Vintage Books, 1994).

28. Sigmund Freud, *The Uncanny* (New York: Penguin Books, 2003).

29. Georges Bataille, *Story of the Eye* (New York: Urizen Books, 1977), and *Erotism: Death and Sensuality* (San Francisco: City Lights Books, 1986).

30. "When something has acquired a form it metamorphoses immediately to a new one. If we wish to arrive at some living perception of nature we ourselves must remain as quick and flexible as nature and follow the example she gives" (Johann Wolfgang von Goethe, "Morphologie," in Johann Wolfgang von Goethe, *Scientific Studies*, ed. and trans. Douglas Miller (Princeton, NJ: Princeton University Press, 1995).

31. See Gert Mattenklott, "Das gefräßige Auge," in Dietmar Kamper and Christoph Wulf, eds., *Die Wiederkehr des Körpers* (Frankfurt am Main: Suhrkamp, 1982), 224–40.

32. See "Das Ohr als Erkenntnisorgan" (issue title), *Paragrana* 2, no. 1 (1993).

33. See Eric A. Havelock, *Origins of Western Literacy* (Toronto: Ontario Institute for Studies in Education, 1976), and *The Literate Revolution in Greece and Its Cultural Consequences* (Princeton, NJ: Princeton University Press, 1982); Jack Goody, *The Logic of Writing and the Organisation of Society* (Cambridge: Cambridge University Press, 1986), and *The Interface between the Written and the Oral* (Cambridge: Cambridge University Press, 1987); Walter J. Ong, *Rhetoric, Romance, and Technology: Studies in the Interaction of Expression and Culture* (Ithaca, NY: Cornell University Press, 1971), and *Orality and Literacy: The Technologizing of the Word* (London: Routledge, 2002).

34. See Claudia Benthien, *Skin: On the Cultural Border between Self and the World* (New York: Columbia University Press, 2002).

35. See Gunter Gebauer, "Hand," in Wulf, *Vom Menschen*, 479–88.

36. See Gert Mattenklott, "Mund," in Wulf, *Vom Menschen*, 471–78.

37. See Alain Corbin, *Historien du sensible: Entretiens avec Gilles Heuré* (Paris: Découverte, 2000); Gert Mattenklott, "Nase," in Wulf, *Vom Menschen*,

464–70; Jürgen Raab, *Soziologie des Geruchs: Über die soziale Konstruktion olfaktorischer Wahrnehmung* (Constance: Konstanzer Universitätsverlag, 2001).

38. See Madalina Diaconu, *Tasten, Riechen, Schmecken: Eine Ästhetik der anästhesierten Sinne* (Würzburg: Könighausen und Neumann, 2005); Constance Classen, David Howes, and Anthony Synnott, eds., *Aroma: The Cultural History of Smell* (London: Routledge, 1994); Constance Classen, *The Color of Angels: Cosmology, Gender and the Aesthetic Imagination* (London: Routledge, 1998); Michael Bull and Les Back, eds., *The Auditory Culture Reader* (Oxford: Berg, 2003); Constance Classen, ed., *The Book of Touch* (Oxford: Berg, 2005); Jim Drobnick, ed., *The Smell Culture Reader* (Oxford: Berg, 2006).

39. I have continued to work on problems relating to an anthropology of the senses in various contexts. Of the numerous studies undertaken, I mention just a few: Mollenhauer and Wulf, eds., *Aisthesis/Ästhetik*; Holger Schulze and Christoph Wulf, eds., "Klanganthropologie" (issue title), *Paragrana* 16, no. 2 (2007); Michaels and Wulf, *Exploring the Senses: Emotions, Performativity, and Rituals* (London: Routledge, 2013); Bilstein, *Anthropologie der Sinne*.

40. See Kamper and Wulf, *Die erloschene Seele*; see also Wulf and Kamper, *Logik und Leidenschaft*, esp. chap. 2.

41. See Gerd Jüttemann, Michael Sonntag, and Christoph Wulf, eds., *Die Seele: Ihre Geschichte im Abendland* (Göttingen: Vandenhoeck and Ruprecht, 2005).

42. See Sonntag, *Die Seele als Politikum*; Michael Sonntag, "Die Seele und das Wissen vom Lebenden: Zur Entstehung der Biologie im 19. Jahrhundert," in Jüttemann, Sonntag, and Wulf, *Die Seele*, 293–318.

43. Michel Serres, *Hermes: Literature, Science, Philosophy* (Baltimore, MD: Johns Hopkins University Press, 1982), and *Hominescence* (Paris: Pommier, 2001).

44. See Michael Sonntag, *"Das Verborgene des Herzens": Zur Geschichte der Individualität* (Reinbek, Germany: Rowohlt, 1999).

45. Although there are substantial differences between the terms *soul* and *emotion*, they do converge at a number of points; see Christoph Wulf et al., eds., "Emotionen in einer transkulturellen Welt" (issue title), *Paragrana* 20, no. 2 (2011); Ute Frevert and Christoph Wulf, eds., "Die Bildung der Gefühle," special issue, *Zeitschrift für Erziehungswissenschaft* no. 17 (2012).

46. See, for example, Anne Hohner, Ronald Kurt, and Jo Reichertz, eds., *Diesseitsreligion: Zur Deutung der Bedeutung moderner Kultur* (Constance: Konstanzer Universitätsverlag, 1999); Thomas Luckmann, *The Invisible Religion: The Problem of Religion in Modern Society* (New York: Macmillan, 1967); Michael Mitterauer, *The European Family: Patriarchy to Partnership from the Middle Ages to the Present* (Chicago: University of Chicago Press, 1982); Niklas Luhmann, *Religious Dogmatics and the Evolution of Societies* (New York: E. Mellen Press, 1984); Hans-Georg Soeffner, *The Order of Rituals: The Interpretation of Everyday Life* (New Brunswick, NJ: Transaction, 1997); Alois Hahn, *Konstruktionen des Selbst, der Welt und der Geschichte: Aufsätze zur Kultursoziologie* (Frankfurt am Main: Suhrkamp, 2000); Jacques Derrida and Gianni

Vattimo, eds., *Die Religion* (Frankfurt am Main: Suhrkamp, 2001); Wulf, Macha, and Liebau, *Formen des Religiösen.*

47. See Rudolf Otto, *The Idea of the Holy: An Inquiry into the Non-Rational Factor in the Idea of the Divine and Its Relation to the Rational* (New York: Oxford University Press, 1958).

48. Carsten Colpe, "Die wissenschaftliche Beschäftigung mit 'Dem Heiligen' und 'Das Heilige' heute," in Wulf and Kamper, *Logik und Leidenschaft*, 429–30.

49. See Dietmar Kamper and Christoph Wulf, eds., *Das Heilige: Seine Spur in der Moderne*, 2nd ed. (Frankfurt am Main: Athenaeum, 1997); Wulf and Kamper, *Logik und Leidenschaft*, esp. chap. 3. I have also worked on questions relating to the sacred elsewhere; see Wulf, Macha, and Liebau, *Formen des Religiösen*; Christoph Wulf, Jacques Poulain, and Fathi Triki, eds., *Europäische und islamisch geprägte Länder im Dialog: Gewalt, Religion und interkulturelle Verständigung* (Berlin: Akademie, 2006).

50. See Hans Belting, *Likeness and Presence: History of the Image Before the Era of Art* (Chicago: University of Chicago Press, 1994).

51. Max Horkheimer and Theodor W. Adorno, *Dialectic of Enlightenment*, trans. Edmund Jephcott (Stanford, CA: Stanford University Press, 2002), 26.

52. See Dietmar Kamper and Christoph Wulf, eds., *Der Schein des Schönen* (Göttingen: Steidl, 1988); see also Wulf and Kamper, *Logik und Leidenschaft*, esp. chap. 4; "Aisthesis" (issue title), *Paragrana* 4, no. 1 (1995); Mollenhauer and Wulf, *Aisthesis/Ästhetik*. I have also continued to work on questions relating to beauty and aesthetics; see Christoph Wulf, Dietmar Kamper, and Hans Ulrich Gumbrecht, eds., *Ethik der Ästhetik* (Berlin: Akademie, 1994); Schäfer and Wulf, *Bild—Bilder—Bildung.*

53. See Luhmann, Niklas, *Love as Passion: The Codification of Intimacy* (Stanford, CA: Stanford University Press, 1998).

54. Dietmar Kamper and Christoph Wulf, eds., *Das Schicksal der Liebe* (Weinheim, Germany: Quadriga, 1988); Wulf and Kamper, *Logik und Leidenschaft*, esp. chap. 4.

55. See Wulf, *Lust und Liebe.*

56. *The Confessions of St. Augustine*, bk. 11, 397.

57. See Dietmar Kamper and Christoph Wulf, eds., *Die sterbende Zeit: 20 Diagnosen* (Darmstadt: Luchterhand, 1987); Wulf and Kamper, *Logik und Leidenschaft*, esp. chap. 5; Reinhart Koselleck, *Futures Past: On the Semantics of Future Time* (New York: Columbia University Press, 2004); Martin Heidegger, *Basic Writings: From "Being and Time" (1927) to "The Task of Thinking" (1964)* (San Francisco: Harper, 1993); Ilya Prigogine, *The Molecular Theory of Solutions* (New York: Interscience, 1957); Paul Virilio, *Speed and Politics: An Essay on Dromology* (New York: Columbia University Press, 1986); Rudolf Wendorff, *Zeit und Kultur: Geschichte des Zeitbewusstseins in Europa* (Opladen, Germany: Leske and Budrich, 1980); Norbert Elias, *Über die Zeit: Arbeiten zur Wissenssoziologie*, 2 vols. (Frankfurt am Main:

Suhrkamp, 1984); Bastian van Fraassen, *An Introduction to the Philosophy of Time and Space* (New York: Columbia University Press, 1985); Hans Blumenberg, *The Legitimacy of the Modern Age* (Cambridge, MA: MIT Press, 1983); Philippe Ariès, *Le temps de l'histoire* (Paris: Éditions du Seuil, 1986); Gilles Deleuze, *Cinema* (Minneapolis: University of Minnesota Press, 1989); see also Gilles Deleuze, *L'image-temps* (Paris: Éditions de Minuit, 1985); Friedrich Kramer, *Der Zeitbaum: Grundlagen einer allgemeinen Zeittheorie* (Frankfurt am Main: Insel, 1993); Wolfgang Kaempfer, *Die Zeit des Menschen: Das Doppelspiel der Zeit im Spektrum der menschlichen Erfahrung* (Frankfurt am Main: Insel, 1994); Bilstein, Miller-Kipp, and Wulf, *Transformationen der Zeit*.

58. For research on the connection between time and space in child-rearing, education, and socialization, see Bilstein, Miller-Kipp, and Wulf, *Transformationen der Zeit*; Eckart Liebau, Gisela Miller-Kipp, and Christoph Wulf, eds., *Metamorphosen des Raums* (Weinheim, Germany: Deutscher Studienverlag, 1999).

59. See Dietmar Kamper and Christoph Wulf, eds., *Schweigen: Unterbrechung und Grenze der menschlichen Wirklichkeit* (Berlin: Reimer, 1992); see also Wulf and Kamper, *Logik und Leidenschaft*, esp. chap. 5.

60. See Christian L. Hart Nibbrig, *Rhetorik des Schweigens: Versuch über den Schatten literarischer Rede* (Frankfurt am Main: Suhrkamp, 1981).

61. See Wulf, ed., *Vom Menschen*, and 2nd ed., *Der Mensch und seine Kultur* (Cologne: Anaconda, 2010).

62. See Hartmut Böhme, Peter Matussek, and Lothar Müller, *Orientierung Kulturwissenschaft: Was sie kann, was sie will*, 2nd ed. (Reinbek, Germany: Rowohlt, 2002), 104; in this context, see also Friedrich Kittler, *Eine Kulturgeschichte der Kulturwissenschaft* (Munich: Wilhelm Fink, 2000).

63. Wulf, *Vom Menschen*.

64. See Christoph Wulf and Christine Merkel, eds., *Globalisierung als Herausforderung der Erziehung: Theorien, Grundlagen, Fallstudien* (Münster: Waxmann, 2002); Christoph Wulf, *Anthropologie kultureller Vielfalt: Interkulturelle Bildung in Zeiten der Globalisierung* (Bielefeld, Germany: Transcript, 2006).

65. See Emmanuel Lévinas, *Entre nous, essais sur le penser à l'autre* (Paris: Bernard Grasset, 1991), see also his *Outside the Subject* (Stanford, CA: Stanford University Press, 1994), and *Time and the Other and Additional Essays* (Pittsburgh, PA: Duquesne University Press, 1987); Zirfas, *Die Lehre der Ethik*.

66. See Liebau and Wulf, *Generation*.

67. UNESCO, *Education for All: Is the World on Track?* (Paris: UNESCO, 2002), and *Gender and Education for All: The Leap to Equality* (Paris: UNESCO, 2003).

68. See Gunter Gebauer and Christoph Wulf, *Mimesis: Culture, Art, Society* (Berkeley and Los Angeles: University of California Press, 1995).

69. See Horkheimer and Adorno, *Dialectic of Enlightenment*.

70. See Jacques Derrida, *La Dissémination* (Chicago: University of Chicago Press, 1972).

71. René Girard, *Violence and the Sacred* (Baltimore, MD: Johns Hopkins University Press, 1977), and *The Scapegoat* (Baltimore, MD: Johns Hopkins University Press, 1986).

72. See Gunter Gebauer and Christoph Wulf, *Spiel, Ritual, Geste: Mimetisches Handeln in der sozialen Welt* (Reinbek, Germany: Rowohlt, 1998).

73. Ludwig Wittgenstein, "Philosophische Untersuchungen," in *Schriften*, vol. 1 (Frankfurt am Main: Suhrkamp, 1960).

74. Ibid.

75. See Christoph Wulf et al., *Das Soziale als Ritual* (Opladen, Germany: Leske and Budrich, 2001); Christoph Wulf et al., *Bildung im Ritual* (Wiesbaden: Verlag für Sozialwissenschaften, 2004); Christoph Wulf et al., *Lernkulturen im Umbruch* (Wiesbaden: Verlag für Sozialwissenschaften, 2007).

76. See Kathrin Audehm, *Erziehung bei Tisch* (Bielefeld, Germany: Transcript, 2007).

77. Christoph Wulf, "Praxis," in *Theorizing Rituals: Issues, Topics, Approaches, Concepts*, ed. Jens Kreinath, Jan Snoek, and Michael Stausberg (Leiden: Brill, 2006), 395–411.

78. See Christoph Wulf, Michael Göhlich, and Jörg Zirfas, eds., *Grundlagen des Performativen: Eine Einführung in die Zusammenhänge von Sprache, Macht und Handeln* (Weinheim, Germany: Juventa, 2001); Christoph Wulf and Jörg Zirfas, eds., *Pädagogik des Performativen* (Weinheim, Germany: Beltz, 2007).

79. Wulf, *Educational Science*.

80. Clifford Geertz, *The Interpretation of Cultures: Selected Essays* (New York: Basic Books, 1973).

81. On the "crisis of representation," see Eberhard Berg and Martin Fuchs, *Kultur, soziale Praxis, Text: Die Krise der ethnographischen Repräsentation* (Frankfurt am Main: Suhrkamp, 1993).

82. See Shoko Suzuki and Christoph Wulf, eds., *Mimesis, Poiesis, Performativity in Education* (Münster: Waxmann, 2007).

83. See Wulf, "Praxis," and Bernd Hüppauf and Christoph Wulf, eds., *Dynamics and Performativity of Imagination: The Image between the Visible and the Invisible* (New York: Routledge, 2009); see also Yaso Imai and Christoph Wulf, eds., *Concepts of Aesthetic Education* (Münster: Waxmann, 2007).

84. Christoph Wulf and Erika Fischer-Lichte, eds., *Gesten* (München: Wilhelm Fink, 2010).

85. See Wulf, *Anthropologie kultureller Vielfalt*.

86. See Ralf Bohnsack, *Rekonstruktive Sozialforschung: Einführung in qualitative Methoden* (Opladen, Germany: Leske and Budrich, 2003).

87. See, respectively, Ulrich Oevermann, "Die Methode der Fallrekonstruktion in der Grundlagenforschung sowie der klinischen und pädagogischen Praxis," in *Die Fallrekonstruktion*, ed. Klaus Kraimer (Frankfurt am Main: Suhrkamp, 2000), 58–156; Fritz Schütze, "Biographieforschung und narratives Interview," *Neue Praxis* 3, no. 3 (1983): 283–93; Thomas S. Eberle,

"Ethnomethodologische Konversationsanalyse," in *Sozialwissenschaftliche Hermeneutik*, ed. Ronald Hitzler and Anne Honer (Opladen, Germany: Leske and Budrich, 1997), 245–80; Heinz-Hermann Krüger and Winfried Marotzki, eds., *Handbuch erziehungswissenschaftliche Biographieforschung* (Opladen, Germany: Leske and Budrich, 1998); Berg and Fuchs, *Kultur, Soziale Praxis, Text*; Jürgen Zinnecker, "Pädagogische Ethnographie," *Zeitschrift für Erziehungswissenschaft* 3, no. 3 (2000): 381–400.

88. See Christoph Wulf and Jörg Zirfas, eds., *Ikonologie des Performativen* (Munich: Wilhelm Fink, 2005); Hüppauf and Wulf, *Dynamics and Performativity of Imagination*.

89. See, respectively, Monika Wagner-Willi, "Videointerpretation als mehrdimensionale Mikroanalyse am Beispiel schulischer Alltagsszenen," *Zeitschrift für quantitative Bildungs-, Beratungs- und Sozialforschung* 5, no. 1 (2004): 49–66; Iris Nentwig-Gesemann, "Der Familienurlaub: Rituelle Praxis, Differenzbearbeitung und Lernprozesse," in Wulf et al., *Lernkulturen im Umbruch*, 220–52; see also Ulrike Pilarczyk and Ulrike Mietzner, *Das reflektierte Bild: Die seriell-ikonografische Fotoanalyse in den Erziehungs- und Sozialwissenschaften* (Bad Heilbrunn: Klinkhardt, 2005); Constanze Bausch and Stefan Sting, "Rituelle Medieninszenierungen in Peergroups," in Wulf et al., *Das Soziale als Ritual*, 249–323; Constanze Bausch, *Verkörperte Medien: Die soziale Macht televisueller Inszenierungen* (Bielefeld: Transcript, 2006).

CHAPTER SIX

1. On the history and the theory of the body, see, among others, Michel Bernard, *Der menschliche Körper und seine gesellschaftliche Bedeutung: Phänomen, Phantasma, Mythos* (Wiesbaden: Limpert, 1980); Claudia Gehrke, ed., *Ich habe einen Körper* (Munich: Matthes und Seitz, 1981); Dietmar Kamper and Christoph Wulf, eds., *Die Wiederkehr des Körpers* (Frankfurt am Main: Suhrkamp, 1982), *Der andere Körper* (Berlin: Mensch und Leben, 1984), and *Das Schwinden der Sinne* (Frankfurt am Main: Suhrkamp, 1984); Elaine Scarry, *The Body in Pain: The Making and Unmaking of the World* (New York: Oxford University Press, 1985); Dietmar Kamper and Christoph Wulf, eds., *Transfigurationen des Körpers: Spuren der Gewalt in der Geschichte* (Berlin: Reimer, 1989); Barbara Duden, *The Woman Beneath the Skin: A Doctor's Patients in Eighteenth-Century Germany* (Cambridge, MA: Harvard University Press, 1991); Michel Feher, ed., *Fragments for a History of the Human Body*, 3 vols. (New York: Zone, 1989); Barbara M. Stafford, *Body Criticism: Imaging the Unseen in Enlightenment Art and Medicine* (Cambridge, MA: MIT Press, 1991); Bruno Huisman and François Ribes, *Les Philosophes et le corps* (Paris: Dunos, 1992); Chris Shilling, *The Body and Social Theory* (London: Sage, 1993); Thomas Alkemeyer, *Körper, Kult und Politik: Von der "Muskelreligion" Pierre de Coubertins zur Inszenierung von Macht in den Olympischen Spielen 1936* (Frankfurt am Main: Campus, 1996); Mike Featherstone, Mike

Hepworth, and Bryan S. Turner, eds., *The Body: Social Process and Cultural Theory* (London: Sage, 1991); Pasi Falk, *The Consuming Body* (London: Sage, 1994); Paul Virilio, *The Virilio Reader* (New York: Columbia University Press, 2004); Judith Butler, *Bodies That Matter: On the Discursive Limits of "Sex"* (New York: Routledge, 1993); Sue Scott and David Morgan, *Body Matters: Essays on the Sociology of the Body* (London: Falmer Press, 1993); Frithjof Hager, ed., *Körper Denken* (Berlin: Reimer, 1996); Florian Rötzer, ed., "Die Zukunft des Körpers," *Kunstforum International* (annual) 132 (1995), and 133 (1996); Andrew J. Strathern, *Body Thoughts* (Ann Arbor: University of Michigan Press, 1996); Elisabeth List and Erwin Fiala, eds., *Leib. Maschine. Bild. Körperdiskurse der Moderne und Postmoderne* (Vienna: Passagen, 1997); Umberto Galimberti, *Les raisons du corps* (Paris: Grasset, 1998); Claudia Benthien, *Skin: On the Cultural Border between Self and the World* (New York: Columbia University Press, 2002); David LeBreton, *Anthropologie du corps et modernité* (Paris: Presses Universitaires de France, 2000); Gilles Boëtsch and Dominique Chevé, eds., *Le corps dans tous ses états: Regards anthropologiques* (Paris: CNRS Éditions, 2000); Claudia Benthien and Christoph Wulf, eds., *Körperteile: Eine kulturelle Anatomie* (Reinbek, Germany: Rowohlt, 2001); Hans Belting, Dietmar Kamper, and Martin Schulz, eds., *Quel Corps? Eine Frage der Repräsentation* (Munich: Wilhelm Fink, 2002); Ludger Schwarte and Christoph Wulf, eds., *Körper und Recht: Anthropologische Dimensionen der Rechtsphilosophie* (Munich: Wilhelm Fink, 2003); Alain Corbin, Jean-Jacques Courtine, and Georges Vigarello, eds., *Histoire du corps*, vols. 1–3 (Paris: Éditions du Seuil, 2005); Bernard Andrieu, ed., *Le dictionnaire du corps en sciences humaines et sociales* (Paris: CNRS Éditions, 2005); Michela Marzano, ed., *Dictionnaire du corps* (Paris: Presses Universitaires de France, 2007).

2. See chapter 1 and also Franz M. Wuketits, *The Evolution of Living Systems* (Weinheim, Germany: Wiley-VCH, 2005); Friedemann Schrenk, *African Biogeography, Climate Change and Human Evolution* (New York: Oxford University Press, 1999); André Leroi-Gourhan, *Gesture and Speech* (Cambridge, MA: MIT Press, 1993); Edgar Morin, *Le paradigme perdu: La nature humaine* (Paris: Éditions du Seuil, 1973).

3. See Andreas Loesch, *Genomprojekt und Moderne: Soziologische Analysen des bioethischen Diskurses* (Frankfurt am Main: Campus, 2001), 12.

4. See Kurt Bayertz, *The Concept of Moral Consensus: The Case of Technological Interventions in Human Reproduction* (Dordrecht: Kluwer Academic, 1994).

5. Loesch, *Genomprojekt*, 17.

6. This is an abbreviation for "inserted DNA," spelled backwards.

7. Regarding these facts and their criticism, see Hartmut Wewetzer, "Des Menschen Tun," *Der Tagesspiegel*, February 14, 2004, 2.

8. See Wolf Singer, *Der Beobachter im Gehirn: Essays zur Hirnforschung* (Frankfurt am Main: Suhrkamp, 2002), 44–45. In the following paragraphs, this work is cited parenthetically in the text by page number.

9. See Gerhard Roth and M. F. Wullimann, eds., *Brain Evolution and Cognition* (New York: Wiley, 2001); Sabine Maasen, Wolfgang Prinz, and Gerhard Roth, eds., *Voluntary Action: Brains, Minds, and Sociality* (New York: Oxford University Press, 2003).

10. Singer, *Der Beobachter im Gehirn*, 111.

11. See Peter Gold and Andreas K. Engel, eds., *Der Mensch in der Perspektive der Kognitionswissenschaften* (Frankfurt am Main: Suhrkamp, 1998); Bernhard Andrieu, *La chair du cerveau: Phénoménologie et biologie de la cognition* (Paris: Mons, 2002).

12. See chapter 2 and Max Scheler, *The Human Place in the Cosmos* (Evanston, IL: Northwestern University Press, 2009); Helmuth Plessner, *Die Stufen des Organischen und der Mensch*, in H. Plessner, *Gesammelte Schriften*, vol. 4 (Frankfurt am Main: Suhrkamp, 1981); Arnold Gehlen, *Man: His Nature and Place in the World* (New York: Columbia University Press, 1988).

13. See chapter 3 and also Peter Burke, *Economy and Society in Early Modern Europe: Essays from Annales* (London: Routledge, 1972); Gert Dressel, *Historische Anthropologie: Eine Einführung* (Vienna: Böhlau, 1996); Richard van Dülmen, *Historische Anthropologie: Entwicklung, Probleme, Aufgaben* (Cologne: Böhlau, 2000).

14. Mary Douglas, *Purity and Danger: An Analysis of Concepts of Pollution and Taboo* (London: Routledge, 2005), and *Natural Symbols: Explorations in Cosmology* (London: Routledge, 2003).

15. See John Blacking, ed., *The Anthropology of the Body* (London: Academic Press, 1977); Nancy Scheper-Hughes and Margaret Lock, "The Mindful Body: A Prolegomenon to Future Work in Medical Anthropology," *Medical Anthropology Quarterly* 1, no. 1 (1987): 6–41. Here the authors distinguish between an individual body, communicating individual experiences; a body as a symbol of nature, society, and culture; and then also a political body that represents control and regulation.

16. See Feher, *Fragments for a History of the Human Body*; Donna Haraway, *Simians, Cyborgs, and Women: The Reinvention of Nature* (New York: Routledge, 1991).

17. See Michel Foucault, *The Birth of the Clinic: An Archaeology of Medical Perception* (New York: Vintage, 1973), *Discipline and Punish: The Birth of the Prison* (New York: Pantheon Books, 1977), and *The Care of the Self* (New York: Vintage, 1978).

18. Pierre Bourdieu, *Outline of a Theory of Practice* (Cambridge: Polity Press, 1977), and *The Logic of Practice* (Stanford, CA: Stanford University Press, 1990); Gunter Gebauer and Christoph Wulf, eds., *Praxis und Ästhetik: Neue Perspektiven im Denken Pierre Bourdieus* (Frankfurt am Main: Suhrkamp, 1993). This book was inspired by an international conference entitled "The Relationship between Body, Sensuality, and Theory," held jointly with Pierre Bourdieu. It also contains several of his contributions on the subject.

19. See Pierre Bourdieu, *Distinction* (Cambridge, MA: Harvard University Press, 1984).
20. Butler, *Bodies That Matter.*
21. See George Lakoff and Mark Johnson, *Philosophy in the Flesh: The Embodied Mind and Its Challenges to Western Thought* (New York: Basic Books, 1999).
22. See Terence Turner, "Social Body and Embodied Subject: Bodiliness, Subjectivity, and Sociality among the Kayapo," *Cultural Anthropology* 10, no. 2 (1995): 143–70.
23. See Thomas J. Csordas, "Embodiment as a Paradigm for Anthropology," *Ethos* 18, no. 1 (1990): 5–47, and "The Body's Career in Anthropology," in *Anthropology Theory Today*, ed. Henrietta L. Moore (Cambridge: Polity Press, 1999), 172–205; for very different ideas of the human body, see Axel Michaels and Christoph Wulf, eds., *Images of the Body in India* (London: Routledge, 2011).
24. See Maurice Merleau-Ponty, *Phenomenology of Perception* (London: Routledge, 1994), and *The Visible and the Invisible* (Evanston, IL: Northwestern University Press, 1968), 130–35.
25. A search of Dissertation Abstracts Online on "anthropology and body and embodiment" shows the popularity of this particular line of research. In the 1990s there were 75 dissertations on this subject area; in the 1980s, 40; and in the 1970s, almost none (Online Computer Library Center, 2001, Inc. Dissertation Abstracts International, electronic data base, http:// www .oclc.org). It is no surprise, then, if we inquire about the extent to which this approach of anthropological research on the central position of the body is also valid for non-Western cultures. See Murphy Halliburton, "Rethinking Anthropological Studies of the Body: Manas and Bodham in Kerala," *American Anthropologist* 104, no. 4 (2002): 1123–34.
26. Csordas, "Body's Career in Anthropology," 184. See also Kim Knibbe and Peter Versteeg, "Assessing Phenomenology in Anthropology," *Critique of Anthropology* 28, no. 1 (2008): 47–62.
27. See chapter 5 and Christoph Wulf, ed., *Der Mensch und seine Kultur: Hundert Beiträge* (Cologne: Anaconda, 2010); Christoph Wulf and Dietmar Kamper, eds., *Logik und Leidenschaft: Erträge Historischer Anthropologie* (Berlin: Reimer, 2002); Christoph Wulf, *Anthropology of Education* (Münster: LIT Verlag, 2002); Dietmar Kamper and Christoph Wulf, eds., *Anthropologie nach dem Tode des Menschen: Vervollkommnung und Unverbesserlichkeit* (Frankfurt am Main: Suhrkamp, 1994); Gunter Gebauer et al., *Historische Anthropologie: Zum Problem der Humanwissenschaften heute oder Versuche einer Neubegründung* (Reinbek, Germany: Rowohlt, 1989).
28. Norbert Elias, *The Civilizing Process* (New York: Urizen Books, 1978).
29. See Ulrich Herrmann, "Vervollkommnung des Unverbesserlichen?" in Kamper and Wulf, *Anthropologie nach dem Tode des Menschen*, 132–53.

30. See Gunter Gebauer and Christoph Wulf, *Spiel, Ritual, Geste: Mimetisches Handeln in der sozialen Welt* (Reinbek, Germany: Rowohlt, 1998), 41.

31. Michel Foucault, *Madness and Civilization: A History of Insanity in the Age of Reason* (New York: Vintage Books, 1973), *The Order of Things: An Archaeology of the Human Sciences* (New York: Pantheon Books, 1971), and *Discipline and Punish*.

32. See Dietmar Kamper, "Tod des Körpers—Leben der Sprache," in Gebauer et al., *Historische Anthropologie*, 49–82, 62.

33. Max Horkheimer and Theodor W. Adorno, *Dialectic of Enlightenment* (Stanford, CA: Stanford University Press, 2002).

34. See Maurice Halbwachs, *The Collective Memory* (New York: Harper & Row, 1980); Jan Assmann, *Religion and Cultural Memory: Ten Studies* (Stanford, CA: Stanford University Press, 2006); Bernhard Dieckmann, Stephan Sting and Jörg Zirfas, eds., *Gedächtnis und Bildung: Pädagogisch-anthropologische Zusammenhänge* (Weinheim, Germany: Beltz, 1998); Harald Weinrich, *Lethe: Kunst und Kritik des Vergessens*, 3rd ed. (Munich: Beck, 2000).

35. The problematic area of individuality is one of the central issues of historical anthropology, especially in the field of educational science; this area requires further research. A good overview of this subject can be found in Käte Meyer-Drawe, "Individuum," in Wulf, *Der Mensch und seine Kultur*, 698–708; see also Remo Bodei, *Destini personali: L'età della colonizzazione delle coscienze* (Milano: Feltrinelli, 2002); Michael Sonntag, *"Das Verborgene des Herzens": Zur Geschichte der Individualität* (Reinbek, Germany: Rowohlt, 1999); Käte Meyer-Drawe, *Illusionen von Autonomie: Diesseits von Ohnmacht und Allmacht des Ich* (Munich: Wilhelm Fink, 1990); Paul Veyne, Jean-Pierre Vernant, Louis Dumont, Paul Ricoeur, Françoise Dolto, Francisco Varela, and Gérard Percheron, *Sur L'individu* (Paris: Éditions du Seuil, 1987); Luis Dumont, *Essays on Individualism: Modern Ideology in Anthropological Perspective* (Chicago: University of Chicago Press, 1992); Hans Joas, *G. H. Mead: A Contemporary Re-examination of His Thought* (Cambridge, MA: MIT Press, 1997), and *The Genesis of Values* (Chicago: University of Chicago Press, 2000).

36. See Christina von Braun, *Versuch über den Schwindel: Religion, Schrift, Bild, Geschlecht* (Zurich: Pendo, 2001); Remo Bodei, *Logics of Delusion* (Aurora: Davies Group, 2006); Remo Bodei, Giuseppe Cantillo, Alessandro Ferrara, Vanna Gessa Kurotschka, and Sebastiano Maffettone, eds., *Ricostruzione Della Soggettività* (Naples: Liguori Editore, 2004).

37. See Susanne K. Langer, *Philosophy in a New Key: A Study in the Symbolism of Reason, Rite and Art* (New York: Penguin Books, 1948).

38. See chapter 7 and also Gunter Gebauer and Christoph Wulf, *Mimesis: Culture, Art, Society* (Berkeley and Los Angeles: University of California Press, 1995); Gebauer and Wulf, *Spiel, Ritual, Geste*; Gunter Gebauer and Christoph Wulf, *Mimetische Weltzugänge: Soziales Handeln—Rituale und Spiele—ästhetische Produktionen* (Stuttgart: Kohlhammer, 2003); Christoph Wulf, *Zur Genese des Sozialen: Mimesis, Performativität, Ritual* (Bielefeld, Germany: Transcript, 2006).

39. Christoph Wulf, "Praxis," in *Theorizing Rituals: Issues, Topics, Approaches, Concepts*, ed. Jens Kreinath, Jan Snoek, and Michael Stausberg (Leiden: Brill, 2006), 395–411.

40. See chapter 8 and also Christoph Wulf, Michael Göhlich, and Jörg Zirfas, eds., *Grundlagen des Performativen: Eine Einführung in die Zusammenhänge von Sprache, Macht und Handeln* (Weinheim, Germany: Juventa, 2001); Erika Fischer-Lichte and Christoph Wulf, eds., "Theorien des Performativen" (issue title), *Paragrana* 10, no. 1 (2001); Uwe Wirth, ed., *Performanz: Zwischen Sprachphilosophie und Kulturwissenschaften* (Frankfurt am Main: Suhrkamp, 2002); Erika Fischer-Lichte and Christoph Wulf, eds., "Praktiken des Performativen" (issue title), *Paragrana* 13, no. 1 (2004); Christoph Wulf and Jörg Zirfas, eds., *Pädagogik des Performativen* (Weinheim, Germany: Beltz, 2007); Gabriele Brandstetter and Christoph Wulf, eds., *Tanz als Anthropologie* (Munich: Wilhelm Fink, 2007).

41. See chapter 9 and also Christoph Wulf et al., *Das Soziale als Ritual: Zur performativen Bildung von Gemeinschaften* (Opladen, Germany: Leske and Budrich, 2001); Christoph Wulf and Jörg Zirfas, eds., "Rituelle Welten" (issue title), *Paragrana* 12, nos. 1–2 (2003); Christoph Wulf and Jörg Zirfas, eds., "Innovation und Ritual: Jugend, Geschlecht, Schule," special issue, *Zeitschrift für Erziehungswissenschaft* 7, no. 2 (2004); Christoph Wulf et al., *Bildung im Ritual: Schule, Familie, Jugend, Medien* (Wiesbaden: Verlag für Sozialwissenschaften, 2004).

42. See chapter 10 and especially Jürgen Trabant, *Artikulationen: Historische Anthropologie der Sprache* (Frankfurt am Main: Suhrkamp, 1998), and *Mithridates im Paradies: Kleine Geschichte des Sprachdenkens* (Munich: Beck, 2003); Jürgen Trabant and Achim Eschbach, *History of Semiotics* (Philadelphia, PA: J. Benjamins, 1983); Jürgen Trabant, *New Essays on the Origin of Language* (New York: De Gruyter Mouton, 2001); Wilhelm von Humboldt, *Essays on Language* (New York: Lang, 1997), and *Gesammelte Schriften*, vol. 4 (Berlin: B. Behr, 1905); Noam Chomsky, *Knowledge of Language: Its Nature, Origin, and Use* (New York: Praeger, 1986).

43. See chapter 11 and especially Bernd Hüppauf and Christoph Wulf, eds., *Dynamics and Performativity of Imagination: The Image between the Visible and the Invisible* (New York: Routledge, 2009); Hans Belting, *Bild-Anthropologie: Entwürfe für eine Bildwissenschaft* (Munich: Wilhelm Fink, 2001); Gerd Schäfer and Christoph Wulf, eds., *Bild—Bilder—Bildung* (Weinheim, Germany: Beltz, Deutscher Studienverlag, 1999); Wolfgang Iser, *The Fictive and the Imaginary: Charting Literary Anthropology* (Baltimore, MD: Johns Hopkins University Press, 1993); Cornelius Castoriadis, *The Imaginary Institution of Society* (Cambridge, MA: MIT Press, 1987).

44. See chapter 12 and also Hans-Dieter Bahr, *Den Tod denken* (Munich: Wilhelm Fink, 2002); Constantin von Barloewen, ed., *Der Tod in den Weltkulturen und Weltreligionen* (Frankfurt am Main: Insel, 2000); Thomas Macho, *Todesmetaphern: Zur Logik der Grenzerfahrung* (Frankfurt am Main:

Suhrkamp, 1987); Jean Baudrillard, *Symbolic Exchange and Death* (London: Sage, 1993); Christina von Braun and Christoph Wulf, eds., *Mythen des Blutes* (Frankfurt am Main: Campus, 2007).

45. See chapter 12 and also Hannah Arendt, *Vita activa oder vom tätigen Leben* (Munich: Piper, 1981); Peter Sloterdijk, *Zur Welt kommen—Zur Sprache kommen: Frankfurter Vorlesungen* (Frankfurt am Main: Suhrkamp, 1988); Christoph Wulf et al., *Geburt in Familie, Klinik und Medien: Eine qualitative Untersuchung* (Opladen, Germany: Budrich Unipress, 2008); Christoph Wulf, Anja Hänsch, and Micha Brumlik, eds., *Das Imaginäre der Geburt* (Munich: Wilhelm Fink, 2008).

CHAPTER SEVEN

1. Aristotle, *Poetics* (London: Dent, 1963).
2. Michael Tomasello, *The Cultural Origins of Human Cognition* (Cambridge, MA: Harvard University Press, 1999), 161.
3. See Albert Bandura, *Self Efficacy: The Exercise of Control* (New York: W. H. Freeman, 1997).
4. See Frans de Waal, *The Ape and the Sushi Master: Cultural Reflections by a Primatologist* (New York: Basic Books, Perseus Books Group, 2001); Dominique Lestel, *Les origines animales de la culture* (Paris: Flammarion, 2001).
5. See Giacomo Rizzolatti and Corrado Sinigaglia, *Mirrors in the Brain: How Our Minds Share Actions and Emotions* (Oxford: Oxford University Press, 2008); Marco Jacoboni, *Mirroring People* (New York: Farrar, Straus, and Giroux, 2008).
6. Martin Dornes, *Der kompetente Säugling: Die präverbale Entwicklung des Menschen* (Frankfurt am Main: Fischer, 1996).
7. See Wolf Singer, *Der Beobachter im Gehirn* (Frankfurt am Main: Suhrkamp, 2001).
8. See Jean-Pierre Changeux, *The Physiology of Truth: Neuroscience and Human Knowledge* (Cambridge, MA: Belknap Press of Harvard University Press, 2004).
9. Walter Benjamin, *Berlin Childhood around 1900* (Cambridge, MA: Belknap Press of Harvard University Press, 2006); Sigrid Weigel, *Entstellte Ähnlichkeit: Walter Benjamins theoretische Schreibweise* (Frankfurt am Main: Fischer, 1997).
10. See Hartmut Böhme, Peter Matussek, and Lothar Müller, *Orientierung Kulturwissenschaft: Was sie kann, was sie will* (Reinbek, Germany: Rowohlt, 2000); Alfred Schäfer and Michael Wimmer, eds., *Identifikation und Repräsentation* (Opladen, Germany: Leske and Budrich, 1999).
11. See Walter Benjamin, "Über das mimetische Vermögen," in W. Benjamin, *Gesammelte Schriften*, vol. 2, bk. 1 (Frankfurt am Main: Suhrkamp, 1980), 210ff., and "Lehre vom Ähnlichen," in W. Benjamin, *Gesammelte Schriften*, vol. 2, bk. 1 (Frankfurt am Main: Suhrkamp, 1980), 204–10; see also Walter

Benjamin, *Selected Writings* (Cambridge, MA: Belknap Press of Harvard University Press, 1996–2003).

12. See Ae-Ryung Kim, *Metapher und Mimesis: Über das hermeneutische Lesen des geschriebenen Textes* (Berlin: Reimer, 2002); Hans Blumenberg, *Die Lesbarkeit der Welt* (Frankfurt am Main: Suhrkamp, 1988); see also Josiane Boulad-Ayoub, *Mimes et Parades: L'activité symbolique dans la vie sociale* (Paris: L'Harmattan, 1995); Kendall L. Walton, *Mimesis as Make-Believe: On the Foundations of the Representational Arts* (Cambridge, MA: Harvard University Press, 1990).

13. See Nelson Goodman, *Ways of Worldmaking* (Indianapolis, IN: Hackett, 1978).

14. See Gunter Gebauer and Christoph Wulf, *Mimesis: Culture, Art, Society* (Berkeley and Los Angeles: University of California Press, 1995), *Spiel, Ritual, Geste: Mimetisches Handeln in der sozialen Welt* (Reinbek, Germany: Rowohlt, 1998), and *Mimetische Weltzugänge* (Stuttgart: Kohlhammer, 2003); Christoph Wulf, *Anthropology of Education* (Münster: LIT Verlag, 2002); Christoph Wulf, *Zur Genese des Sozialen: Mimesis, Ritual, Performativität* (Bielefeld, Germany: Transcript, 2005).

15. See Elias Canetti, *Crowds and Power* (London: Gollancz, 1962).

16. See René Girard, *Violence and the Sacred* (Baltimore, MD: Johns Hopkins University Press, 1977), *Things Hidden since the Foundation of the World* (Stanford, CA: Stanford University Press, 1987), and *The Girard Reader* (New York: Crossroad, 1996).

17. Theodor W. Adorno, *Aesthetic Theory* (London: Continuum, 2004).

18. Bernhard Waldenfels, *The Question of the Other* (Albany: State University of New York Press, 2007).

19. Hermann Koller, *Die Mimesis in der Antike: Nachahmung, Darstellung, Ausdruck* (Bern: Francke, 1954).

20. See Gerald F. Else, "Imitation in the 5th Century," *Classical Philology* 53, no. 2 (1958): 73–90; Göran Soerbom, *Mimesis and Art: Studies in the Origin and Early Development of an Aesthetic Vocabulary* (Uppsala: Appelbohm, 1966).

21. On the role of the Thespian in the present and in recent history, see Martina Leeker, *Mime, Mimesis und Technologie* (Munich: Wilhelm Fink, 1995).

22. Plato, *Republic* (New York: Basic Books, 1968), 598a.

23. See Ulrike Zimbrich, *Mimesis bei Platon: Untersuchungen zu Wortgebrauch, Theorie der dichterischen Darstellung und zur dialogischen Gestaltung bis zur Politeia* (Berlin: Peter Lang, 1984).

24. See Paul Ricoeur, *Time and Narrative*, 3 vols. (Chicago: University of Chicago Press, 1984–1988).

25. See Viktor Zuckerkandl, "Mimesis," *Merkur* 12, no. 121 (1958): 233.

26. See Wolfgang Iser, *The Act of Reading: A Theory of Aesthetic Response* (Baltimore, MD: Johns Hopkins University Press, 1978).

27. See Sylviane Agacinski, Jacques Derrida, Sarah Kofman, Philippe Lacoue-Labarthe, Jean-Luc Nancy, and Bernard Pautrat, *Mimesis des articulations* (Paris: Aubier-Flammarion, 1975).

28. Girard, *Violence and the Sacred*.

29. See Girard, *Girard Reader*.

30. See Gebauer and Wulf, *Spiel, Ritual, Geste*, and *Mimetische Weltzugänge*; Christoph Wulf et al., *Ritual and Identity: The Staging and Performing of Rituals in the Lives of Young People* (London: Tufnell Press, 2010); Christoph Wulf et al., *Bildung im Ritual: Schule, Familie, Jugend, Medien* (Opladen, Germany: Leske and Budrich, 2004); Christoph Wulf et al., *Lernkulturen im Umbruch* (Wiesbaden: Verlag für Sozialwissenschaften, 2007); Wulf, *Zur Genese des Sozialen*.

31. See Michael T. Taussig, *Mimesis and Alterity: A Particular History of the Senses* (New York: Routledge, 1993).

32. Pierre Bourdieu was also convinced that practical knowledge is cultural knowledge and is acquired mimetically; see his *The Logic of Practice*, trans. Richard Nice (Stanford, CA: Stanford University Press, 1990).

33. Gebauer and Wulf, *Spiel, Ritual, Geste*, 11–12.

34. See James G. Frazer, *The Golden Bough* (London: Macmillan, 1940).

35. Christoph Wulf, "Praxis," in *Theorizing Rituals. Issues, Topics, Approaches, Concepts*, ed. Jens Kreinath, Jan Snoek, and Michael Stausberg (Leiden: Brill, 2006), 395–411.

36. See Beate Krais and Gunter Gebauer, *Habitus* (Bielefeld, Germany: Transcript, 2002).

37. On ex-centricity, see Helmuth Plessner, "Ausdruck der menschlichen Natur," in H. Plessner, *Gesammelte Schriften*, vol. 7 (Frankfurt am Main: Suhrkamp, 1982), 391–98.

38. Christoph Wulf and Jörg Zirfas, eds., "Innovation und Ritual," special issue, *Zeitschrift für Erziehungswissenschaft* 7, no. 2 (2004).

CHAPTER EIGHT

1. Milton Singer, *Traditional India: Structure and Change* (Philadelphia, PA: American Folklore Society, 1959), xiii.

2. Ibid.

3. Ulrike Bohle and Ekkehard König, "Zum Begriff des Performativen in der Sprachwissenschaft," *Paragrana* 10, no. 1 (2001): 13–34; see also Sybille Krämer and Marco Stahlhut, "Das 'Performative' als Thema der Sprach- und Kulturphilosophie," *Paragrana* 10, no. 1 (2001): 35–64.

4. See, respectively, Jutta Eming, Ingrid Kasten, Elke Koch, and Andrea Sieber, "Emotionalität und Performativität in der Literatur des Mittelalters," *Paragrana* 10, no. 1 (2001): 215–33; Hans-Jürgen Bachorski, Werner Röcke, Hans Rudolf Velten, and Frank Wittchow, "Performativität und Lachkultur in Mittelalter und früher Neuzeit," *Paragrana* 10, no. 1 (2001): 157–90; Horst

Wenzel and Christina Lechtermann, "Repräsentation und Kinästhetik: Teilhabe am Text oder die Verlebendigung der Worte," *Paragrana* 10, no. 1 (2001): 191–213.

5. See Erika Fischer-Lichte and Jens Roselt, "Attraktion des Augenblicks: Aufführung, Performance, performativ und Performativität als theaterwissenschaftliche Begriffe," *Paragrana* 10, no. 1 (2001): 237–53.

6. See Lea Vergine, *Body Art and Performance: The Body as Language* (Milan: Skira, 2000).

7. Christoph Wulf, Michael Göhlich, and Jörg Zirfas, eds., *Grundlagen des Performativen: Eine Einführung in die Zusammenhänge von Sprache, Macht und Handeln* (Weinheim, Germany: Juventa, 2001), 13; see also Christoph Wulf and Jörg Zirfas, eds., *Die Pädagogik des Performativen* (Weinheim, Germany: Beltz, 2007).

8. Wolfgang Iser, *The Fictive and the Imaginary: Charting Literary Anthropology* (Baltimore, MD: Johns Hopkins University Press, 1993).

9. Theodor W. Adorno, *Ästhetische Theorie* (Frankfurt am Main: Suhrkamp, 1970); Paul Ricoeur, *Time and Narrative*, 3 vols. (Chicago: University of Chicago Press, 1984–1988); Gunter Gebauer and Christoph Wulf, *Mimesis: Culture, Art, Society* (Berkeley and Los Angeles: University of California Press, 1995).

10. Adorno, *Ästhetische Theorie*, 121; Theodor W. Adorno, *Aesthetic Theory*, trans. Robert Huttot-Kentor (Minneapolis: University of Minnesota Press, 1997).

11. Iser, *The Fictive and the Imaginary*, 297.

12. Ibid., 297.

13. Ibid., 299.

14. Christoph Wulf et al., *Das Soziale als Ritual: Zur performativen Bildung von Gemeinschaften* (Opladen, Germany: Leske and Budrich, 2001); English ed.: *Ritual and Identity: The Staging and Performing of Rituals in the Lives of Young People* (London: Tufnell Press, 2010). Christoph Wulf et al., *Bildung im Ritual: Schule, Familie, Jugend, Medien* (Wiesbaden: Verlag für Sozialwissenschaften, 2004); Christoph Wulf et al., *Lernkulturen im Umbruch: Rituelle Praktiken in Schule, Medien, Familie und Jugend* (Wiesbaden: Verlag für Sozialwissenschaften, 2007).

15. See Working Group on Ritual, "Differenz und Alterität im Ritual: Eine interdisziplinäre Fallstudie," *Paragrana* 13, no. 1 (2004): 187–249.

16. See Christoph Wulf and Jörg Zirfas, eds., *Die Kultur des Rituals: Inszenierungen, Praktiken, Symbole* (Munich: Wilhelm Fink, 2004); Christoph Wulf and Jörg Zirfas, eds., "Rituelle Welten" (issue title), *Paragrana* 12, nos. 1–2 (2003); Christoph Wulf and Jörg Zirfas, eds., "Innovation und Ritual: Jugend, Gesellschaft, Schule," special issue, *Zeitschrift für Erziehungswissenschaft* 7, no. 2 (2004); Adam Kendon, *Gesture: Visible Action as Utterance* (Cambridge: Cambridge University Press, 2004).

17. See Dietmar Kamper and Christoph Wulf, eds., "Metaphern des Unmöglichen" (issue title), *Paragrana* 9, no. 1 (2000).

18. On the linguistic turn, see, for example, Jürgen Trabant, *Artikulationen: Historische Anthropologie der Sprache* (Frankfurt am Main: Suhrkamp, 1998), and *Mithridates im Paradies: Kleine Geschichte des Sprachdenkens* (Munich: Beck, 2003); Jürgen Trabant and Achim Eschbach, *History of Semiotics* (Amsterdam: J. Benjamins, 1983); Jürgen Trabant and Sean Ward, eds., *New Essays on the Origin of Language* (Hawthorne, NY: De Gruyter Mouton, 2001). On the iconic turn, see chapter 11; see also Hans Belting, *An Anthropology of Images: Picture—Medium—Body* (Princeton, NJ: Princeton University Press, 2011). On the performative turn, see the publications of a special research project entitled "Kulturen des Performativen" (Cultures of the performative) carried out at the Free University of Berlin, especially Erika Fischer-Lichte and Christoph Wulf, eds., "Theorien des Performativen" (issue title), *Paragrana* 10, no. 1 (2001), and "Praktiken des Performativen" (issue title), *Paragrana* 13, no. 1 (2004).

19. On the second aspect, see, among others, Christoph Wulf and Jörg Zirfas, eds., *Ikonologie des Performativen* (Munich: Wilhelm Fink, 2005).

20. Norman K. Denzin and Yvonna S. Lincoln, eds., *Handbook of Qualitative Research* (Thousand Oaks: Sage, 1994); Uwe Flick, *An Introduction to Qualitative Research* (London: Sage, 1998); Barbara Friebertshäuser and Annedore Prengel, eds., *Handbuch qualitative Forschungsmethoden in der Erziehungswissenschaft* (Munich: Juventa, 2009); Ralf Bohnsack, *Rekonstruktive Sozialforschung: Einführung in qualitative Methoden* (Opladen, Germany: Leske and Budrich, 2003).

21. See the research project of the five interdisciplinary working groups at The Collaborative Research Center entitled "Kulturen des Performativen" (Cultures of performativity), published in *Paragrana* 13, no. 1 (2004).

22. Maurice Merleau-Ponty, *Phenomenology of Perception: An Introduction*, trans. Colin Smith (London: Routledge, 2002), 246.

23. Maurice Merleau-Ponty, *The Visible and the Invisible* (Evanston, IL: Northwestern University Press, 1968); see also Gunter Gebauer and Christoph Wulf, *Spiel, Ritual, Geste: Mimetisches Handeln in der sozialen Welt* (Reinbek, Germany: Rowohlt, 1998), 58; Bernhard Waldenfels, *Sinnesschwellen: Studien zur Phänomenologie des Fremden* (Frankfurt am Main: Suhrkamp, 1999), and *Das leibliche Selbst: Vorlesungen zur Phänomenologie des Leibes* (Frankfurt am Main: Suhrkamp, 2000); see also his *The Question of the Other* (Albany: State University of New York Press, 2007), and *Order in the Twilight* (Athens: University of Ohio Press, 1996); Gernot Böhme, *Ästhetik: Vorlesungen über Ästhetik als allgemeine Wahrnehmungslehre* (Munich: Wilhelm Fink, 2001); see also Martin Seel, *Ästhetik des Erscheinens* (Munich, Wilhelm Fink, 2000); Erika Fischer-Lichte, *Performative Aesthetics* (New York: Routledge, 2008).

24. Michael de Certeau, *The Practice of Everyday Life*, trans. Steven Rendell (Berkeley and Los Angeles: University of California Press, 1984), esp. 99ff.

25. See Horst Wenzel, "'*Wan die vrumen liute sint / und suln sîn spiegel dem kint*': Zur kinästhetischen Wahrnehmung von Schrift und Bild im 'Welschen

Gast' des Thomasin von Zerclaere," in *Kunst der Bewegung: Kinästhetische Wahrnehmung und Probehandeln in virtuellen Welten*, ed. Christina Lechtermann and Carsten Morsch (Berlin: Lang, 2004), 181–215.

26. Working Group on Perception and Performativity, "Perception and Performativity" *Paragrana* 13, no. 1 (2004): 15–80, 27–28.
27. Ibid., 31–32.
28. Waldenfels, *Sinnesschwellen*, 64.
29. Working Group on Perception, "Perception and Performativity," 51.
30. See Katharina Mueller and Gisa Aschersleben, eds., *Rhythmus: Ein interdisziplinäres Handbuch* (Bern: Huber, 2000).
31. Working Group on Perception, "Perception and Performativity, "65–66.
32. Working Group on Media, "Über das Zusammenspiel von 'Medialität' und 'Performativität,'" *Paragrana* 13, no. 1 (2004): 129–85, 131.
33. See Reinhard Meyer-Kalkus, *Stimme und Sprechkünste im 20. Jahrhundert* (Berlin: Akademie, 2001).
34. Working Group on Media, "Über das Zusammenspiel von 'Medialität' und 'Performativität,'" 167; see also Gebauer and Wulf, *Spiel, Ritual, Geste*, 80ff.
35. Working Group on Media, "Über das Zusammenspiel von 'Medialität' und 'Performativität,'" 169.
36. Working Group on Gender, "Begehrende Körper und verkörpertes Begehren: Interdisziplinäre Studien zu Performativität und 'gender,'" *Paragrana* 13, no. 1 (2004): 251–309, 251.
37. Judith Butler, *Gender Trouble: Feminism and the Subversion of Identity* (New York: Routledge, 1990), and *Excitable Speech: A Politics of the Performative* (New York: Routledge, 1997).
38. Working Group on Gender, 259.
39. Ibid., 280; see also Butler, *Gender Trouble*.
40. See also Wolfgang Hegener, "Aufstieg und Fall schwuler Identität: Ansätze zur Dekonstruktion der Kategorie Sexualität," *Zeitschrift für Sexualforschung* 6 (1993): 132–50.
41. Working Group on Gender, "Begehrende Körper und verkörpertes Begehren," 284.

CHAPTER NINE

1. See Hans-Georg Soeffner, *The Order of Rituals: The Interpretation of Everyday Life* (New Brunswick, NJ: Transaction, 1997); Claude Rivière, *Les rites profanes* (Paris: Presses Universitaires de France, 1995); Catherine M. Bell, *Ritual: Perspectives and Dimensions* (New York: Oxford University Press, 1997); Monique Segré, ed., *Mythes, rites, symboles dans la société contemporaine* (Paris: Éd. L'Harmattan, 1997); Gunter Gebauer and Christoph Wulf, *Spiel, Ritual, Geste: Mimetisches Handeln in der sozialen Welt* (Reinbek, Germany: Rowohlt, 1998); Alfred Schäfer and Michael Wimmer, *Rituale und Ritualisierungen* (Opladen, Germany: Leske and Budrich, 1998); Andréa Belliger and David J. Krieger,

eds., *Ritualtheorien* (Opladen, Germany: Westdeutscher Verlag, 1998); Herbert Willems and Martin Jurga, eds., *Inszenierungsgesellschaft: Ein einführendes Handbuch* (Opladen, Germany: Westdeutscher Verlag, 1998); Corina Caduff and Joanna Pfaff-Czarnecka, eds., *Rituale heute* (Berlin: Reimer, 1999); Klaus-Peter Köpping and Ursula Rao, eds., *Im Rausch des Rituals* (Hamburg: LIT Verlag, 2000); Christoph Wulf et al., *Ritual and Identity: The Staging and Performing of Rituals in the Lives of Young People* (London: Tufnell Press, 2010); Christoph Wulf, Michael Göhlich, and Jörg Zirfas, eds., *Grundlagen des Performativen: Eine Einführung in die Zusammenhänge von Sprache, Macht und Handeln* (Weinheim, Germany: Juventa, 2001); Christoph Wulf and Jörg Zirfas, eds., "Rituelle Welten" (issue title), *Paragrana* 12, nos. 1–2 (2003); Christoph Wulf et al., *Bildung im Ritual: Schule, Familie, Medien, Jugend* (Wiesbaden: Verlag für Sozialwissenschaften, 2004); Christoph Wulf et. al., *Lernkulturen im Umbruch: Rituelle Praktiken in Schule, Medien, Familie und Jugendkultur* (Wiesbaden: Verlag für Sozialwissenschaften, 2007); Christoph Wulf and Jörg Zirfas, eds., *Die Kultur des Rituals: Inszenierungen, Praktiken, Symbole* (Munich: Wilhelm Fink, 2004); Christoph Wulf and Jörg Zirfas, eds., "Innovation und Ritual," special issue, *Zeitschrift für Erziehungswissenschaft* 7, no. 2 (2004).

2. See the chapter on rituals in Christoph Wulf and Jörg Zirfas, eds., "Rituelle Welten" (issue title), *Paragrana* 12, nos. 1–2 (2003): 187–249.

3. Wulf et al., *Ritual and Identity*; Wulf et al., *Bildung im Ritual*; Wulf et al., *Lernkulturen im Umbruch*.

4. Gebauer and Wulf, *Spiel, Ritual, Geste*, 130.

5. Ibid., 135ff.; see also Ronald L. Grimes, *Research in Ritual Studies* (Methuen, MA: Scarecrow Press, 1985).

6. Wulf et al., *Ritual and Identity*.

7. David I. Kertzer, *Ritual, Politics and Power* (New Haven, CT: Yale University Press, 1988).

8. Dietmar Kamper and Christoph Wulf, eds., *Das Heilige: Seine Spur in der Moderne*, 2nd ed. (Frankfurt am Main: Athenaeum, 1997).

9. Wulf et al., *Bildung im Ritual*, 23ff.

10. James George Frazer, *The Golden Bough: A Study in Magic and Religion* (London: Macmillan, 1940); Rudolf Otto, *The Idea of the Holy: An Inquiry into the Non-Rational Factor in the Idea of the Divine and Its Relation to the Rational* (New York: Oxford University Press, 1970); Mircea Eliade, *The Sacred and the Profane* (New York: Harcourt, Brace & World, 1959).

11. Émile Durkheim, *The Elementary Forms of Religious Life* (New York: Free Press, 1995); Arnold van Gennep, *The Rites of Passage* (London: Routledge & Paul, 1960); Victor Turner, *On the Edge of the Bush: Anthropology as Experience*, ed. Edith L. B. Turner (Tucson: University of Arizona Press, 1985), *The Ritual Process: Structure and Anti-Structure* (New York: Aldine de Gruyter, 1995), and *From Ritual to Theatre: The Human Seriousness of Play* (New York: Performing Arts Journal Publications, 1982).

12. Clifford Geertz, *The Interpretation of Cultures* (New York: Basic Books, 1973), and *Local Knowledge* (New York: Basic Books, 1983); Marshall David Sahlins, *Culture and Practical Reason* (Chicago: University of Chicago Press, 1976), and *Historical Metaphors and Mythical Realities* (Chicago: University of Chicago Press, 1981).

13. Catherine M. Bell, *Ritual Theory, Ritual Practice* (New York: Oxford University Press, 1992), and *Ritual*; Ronald L. Grimes, *Beginnings in Ritual Studies* (Columbia: University of South Carolina Press, 1995), and *Research in Ritual Studies*; Victor Turner, *Drama, Fields, and Metaphors* (Ithaca, NY: Cornell University Press, 1974); Soeffner, *Order of Rituals*.

14. Stanley J. Tambiah, "A Performative Approach to Ritual," *Proceedings of the British Academy* vol. 65 (1979), 113–69; Richard Schechner, *Essays on Performance Theory, 1970–1976* (New York: Drama Books Specialists, 1977); Pierre Bourdieu, *Outline of a Theory of Practice* (Cambridge: Cambridge University Press, 1977); Wulf et al., *Ritual and Identity*; Wulf, Göhlich, and Zirfas, *Grundlagen des Performativen*; Erika Fischer-Lichte and Christoph Wulf, eds., "Theorien des Performativen" (issue title), *Paragrana* 10, no. 1 (2001); Wulf et al., *Bildung im Ritual*; Erika Fischer-Lichte and Christoph Wulf, eds., "Praktiken des Performativen" (issue title), *Paragrana* 13, no. 1 (2004).

15. Jane Ellen Harrison, *Themis: A Study of the Social Origins of Greek Religion* (New Hyde Park, NY: University Books, 1962).

16. Marshall David Sahlins, *Islands of History* (Chicago: University of Chicago Press, 1985).

17. Wulf et al., *Ritual and Identity*; Wulf et al., *Bildung im Ritual*; Wulf et al., *Lernkulturen im Umbruch*.

18. Christoph Wulf, "Ritual, Macht und Performanz: Die Inauguration des amerikanischen Präsidenten," in Wulf and Zirfas, *Kultur des Rituals*, 49–61.

19. See Mary Douglas, *Purity and Danger: An Analysis of Concepts of Pollution and Taboo* (London: Routledge, 2005), and *Rules and Meanings: The Anthropology of Everyday Knowledge* (Harmondsworth, UK: Penguin Education, 1973).

20. Georges Didi-Huberman, *Ce que nous voyons, ce qui nous regarde* (Paris: Éditions de Minuit, 1992).

21. Mihalyi Csikszentmihalyi, *Flow: The Psychology of Optimal Experience* (New York: Harper & Row, 1990).

22. Christoph Wulf, "Ritual und Recht: Performatives Handeln und mimetisches Wissen," in *Körper und Recht: Anthropologische Dimensionen der Rechtsphilosophie*, ed. Ludger Schwarte and Christoph Wulf (Munich: Wilhelm Fink, 2003), 27–49.

23. Wulf, "Ritual, Macht und Performanz."

24. Judith Butler, *Gender Trouble: Feminism and the Subversion of Identity* (New York: Routledge, 1990), and *Excitable Speech: A Politics of the Performative* (New York: Routledge, 1997).

25. Working Group on Gender, "Begehrende Körper und verkörpertes Begehren," *Paragrana* 13, no. 1 (2004): 251–309.

26. Kathrin Audehm and Jörg Zirfas, "Familie als ritueller Lebensraum," in *Das Soziale als Ritual*, ed. Wulf et al., 37–116.

27. See Eckart Liebau, Gisela Miller-Kipp, and Christoph Wulf, eds., *Metamorphosen des Raums* (Weinheim, Germany: Beltz, Deutscher Studienverlag, 1999).

28. Christoph Wulf, "Zeit und Ritual," in *Transformationen der Zeit: Erziehungswissenschaftliche Studien zur Chronotopologie*, ed. Johannes Bilstein, Gisela Miller-Kipp, and Christoph Wulf (Weinheim, Germany: Beltz, Deutscher Studienverlag, 1999), 112–22.

29. See Erving Goffman, *Frame Analysis: An Essay on the Organization of Experience* (New York: Harper & Row, 1974).

30. Birgit Althans, "Fehlende Übergangsrituale im Islam—die produktive Leerstelle des Anderen," in *Bildung im Ritual*, ed. Wulf et al., 241–68.

31. Wulf, "Zeit und Ritual."

32. Working Group on Ritual, "Differenz und Alterität im Ritual," *Paragrana* 13, no. 1 (2004): 187–249.

33. See Wulf et al., *Bildung im Ritual*.

34. Christoph Wulf, "Religion und Ritual," in *Formen des Religiösen: Pädagogisch-anthropologische Annäherungen*, ed. Christoph Wulf, Hildegard Macha, and Eckart Liebau (Weinheim, Germany: Beltz, Deutscher Studienverlag, 2004), 115–25.

35. Pierre Bourdieu, "Les rites comme des actes d'institution," *Actes de la Recherche en Sciences Sociales* 43 (June 1982): 58–63; Kathrin Audehm, "Die Macht der Sprache: Performative Magie bei Pierre Bourdieu," in Wulf, Göhlich, and Zirfas, eds., *Grundlagen des Performativen*, 101–28.

36. See Christoph Wulf, Hildegard Macha, and Eckart Liebau, eds., *Formen des Religiösen: Pädagogisch-anthropologische Annäherungen* (Weinheim, Germany: Beltz, Deutscher Studienverlag, 2004).

37. Anne Honer, Ronald Kurt, and Jo Reichertz, eds., *Diesseitsreligion: Zur Deutung der Bedeutung moderner Kultur* (Constance: Konstanzer Universitätsverlag, 1999); Hans-Georg Soeffner, *Gesellschaft ohne Baldachin: Über die Labilität von Ordnungskonstruktionen* (Weilerswist, Germany: Velbrück Wissenschaft, 2000).

38. See the contributions in Thomas Alkemeyer, Bernhard Boschert, Gunter Gebauer, and Robert Schmidt, eds., *Aufs Spiel gesetzte Körper* (Constance: Konstanzer Universitätsverlag, 2003).

39. Wulf, Macha, and Liebau, *Formen des Religiösen*.

40. Christoph Wulf, "Mimesis und performatives Handeln," in Wulf, Göhlich, and Zirfas, eds., *Grundlagen des Performativen*, 253–72.

41. Ibid.

42. Christoph Wulf, "Praxis," in *Theorizing Rituals: Issues, Topics, Approaches, Concepts*, ed. Jens Kreinath, Jan Snoek, and Michael Stausberg (Leiden: Brill, 2006), 395–411.

43. Wulf and Zirfas, *Ritual und Innovation*.

44. Christoph Wulf and Erika Fischer-Lichte, eds., *Gesten: Inszenierung, Aufführung, Praxis* (Munich: Wilhelm Fink, 2010); Adam Kendon, *Gesture: Visible Action as Utterance* (Cambridge: Cambridge University Press, 2004); David McNeill, *Hand and Mind: What Gestures Reveal about Thought* (Chicago: University of Chicago Press, 1992), and *Gesture and Thought* (Chicago: University of Chicago Press, 2005).

45. Vilém Flusser, *Gesten: Versuch einer Phänomenologie* (Düsseldorf: Bollmann, 1991); Giorgio Agamben, "Noten zur Geste," in *Mittel ohne Zweck: Noten zur Politik*, ed. Giorgio Agamben (Berlin: Diaphanes, 2001), 53–62.

46. Christoph Wulf, "Der mimetische und performative Charakter von Gesten: Perspektiven für eine sozialwissenschaftliche Gestenforschung," in *Paragrana* 19, no. 1 (2010): 283–97.

47. Jean-Claude Schmitt, *La raison des gestes dans l'Occident médiéval* (Paris: Gallimard, 1990).

48. In his book *Bodytalk: A World Guide to Gestures* (London: Cape, 1994), Desmond Morris shows a collection of six hundred different gestures, arranged according to the body part that is most important for the gesture.

49. Marcel Jousse, *Anthropologie du geste*, 3 vols. (Paris: Gallimard, 1974–1978).

50. Gunter Gebauer and Christoph Wulf, *Spiel, Ritual, Geste: Mimetisches Handeln in der sozialen Welt* (Reinbek, Germany: Rowohlt, 1998), esp. chap. 3 on gestures.

51. See David Berrington, *Action Is Eloquence: Shakespeare's Language of Gesture* (Cambridge, MA: Harvard University Press, 1984); Jean Starobinski, *Gute Gaben, Schlimme Gaben: Die Ambivalenz sozialer Gesten* (Frankfurt am Main: Fischer, 1994).

52. See Jan Bremmer and Herrman Roodenburg, eds., *A Cultural History of Gesture* (Ithaca, NY: Cornell University Press, 1992).

53. See David McNeill, *Gesture and Thought*.

54. Michael Tomasello, *Origins of Human Communication* (Cambridge, MA: MIT Press, 2008).

55. Christoph Wulf et al., *Die Geste in Erziehung, Bildung und Sozialisation: Ethnografische Feldstudien* (Wiesbaden: Verlag für Sozialwissenschaften, 2011).

56. See Adam Kendon, *Gesture*.

57. Geneviève Calbris, *The Semiotics of French Gestures* (Bloomington: Indiana University Press, 1990).

CHAPTER TEN

1. See André Leroi-Gourhan, *Gesture and Speech* (Cambridge, MA: MIT Press, 1993); Philip Lieberman, *Uniquely Human: The Evolution of Speech, Thought, and Selfless Behavior* (Cambridge, MA: Harvard University Press, 1991); Jürgen Trabant and Achim Eschbach, eds., *History of Semiotics* (Amsterdam: J. Benjamins, 1983).

2. Jürgen Trabant, *Artikulationen: Historische Anthropologie der Sprache* (Frankfurt am Main: Suhrkamp, 1998), 16.
3. See Jochen Hörisch, ed., *"Ich möchte ein solcher werden wie . . ."*: *Materialien zur Sprachlosigkeit des Kaspar Hauser* (Frankfurt am Main: Suhrkamp, 1979); Jochen Hörisch, *Heads or Tails: The Poetics of Money* (Detroit, MI: Wayne State University Press, 2000).
4. See Wolf Singer, *Der Beobachter im Gehirn: Essays zur Hirnforschung* (Frankfurt am Main: Suhrkamp, 2002). The loss of these early learning skills applies not only to speaking but also to the human abilities of perception. If humans who were born blind develop the ability, physiologically, to see after many years, they still cannot actually see, as the early learning processes that are a prerequisite for sight have not taken place in the brain.
5. Steven Pinker, *The Language Instinct: The New Science of Language and Mind* (New York: W. Morrow, 1994), 49.
6. Leroi-Gourhan, *Gesture and Speech*, 114.
7. Ibid., 113.
8. Trabant, *Artikulationen*, 111.
9. Ibid., 112.
10. "Die Gliederung ist aber gerade das Wesen der Sprache; es ist nichts in ihr, das nicht Theil und Ganzes seyn könnte, die Wirkung ihres beständigen Geschäfts beruht auf der Leichtigkeit, Genauigkeit und Uebereinstimmung ihrer Trennungen und Zusammensetzungen. Der Begriff der Gliederung ist ihre logische Function, so wie die des Denkens selbst" (Wilhelm von Humboldt, *Gesammelte Schriften*, vol. 5 [Berlin: De Gruyter, 1906]), 122.
11. Trabant, *Artikulationen*, 83.
12. Ibid., 87.
13. Jürgen Trabant, *Mithridates im Paradies: Kleine Geschichte des Sprachdenkens* (Munich: Beck, 2003).
14. "didaskalikon organon kai diakritikon tes usias"—thus the word can be regarded as a tool of teaching that distinguishes between beings in the same way that a shuttle separates the threads of a loom: see Plato, *Kratylos* 388b, quoted in Trabant, *Mithridates*, 28.
15. "ta en te psyche pathemata," quoted in Trabant, *Mithridates*, 30.
16. "secundum placitum"; Greek *kata syntheken*, quoted in Trabant, *Mithridates*, 31.
17. Trabant, *Mithridates*, 30.
18. Ibid., 124.
19. "connaissance claire et assurée de tout ce qui est utile à la vie" (René Descartes, *Discours de la méthode pour bien conduire sa raison et chercher la vérité dans les sciences*, bk. 1, par. 6 [Paris: Vrin, 1960]), 35; see also René Descartes, *A Discourse on Method* (New York: Washington Square Press, 1965).

20. See Descartes, *Discourse on Method*, 96: "car les pies et les perroquets peuvent proférer des paroles ainsi que nous et toutefois ne peuvent parler ainsi que nous, c'est-à-dire en témoignant qu'ils pensent ce qu'ils disent."

21. Trabant, *Mithridates*, 155.

22. "Nihil est in intellectu quod prius non fuerit in sensibus" (Locke); "nisi intellectus ipse" (Leibniz), quoted in Trabant, *Mithridates*, 178.

23. Wilhelm von Humboldt, *On Language: On the Diversity of Human Language Construction and Its Influence on the Mental Development of the Human Species* (New York: Cambridge University Press, 1999).

24. See also Hans Rüdiger Müller, *Ästhesiologie der Bildung: Bildungstheoretische Rückblicke auf die Anthropologie der Sinne im 18. Jahrhundert* (Würzburg: Königshausen und Neumann, 1998).

25. Trabant, *Mithridates*, 221.

26. Johann Gottfried Herder, *On the Origin of Language*, trans. John H. Moran and Alexander Gode (Chicago: University of Chicago Press, 1986), 117. Originally published in German as "Abhandlung über den Ursprung der Sprache" in *Herder und die Anthropologie der Aufklärung*, vol. 2 of *Werke* (Munich: Hanser, 1978), 251–399.

27. Wilhelm von Humboldt, *Essays on Language* (New York: Lang, 1997), and *Gesammelte Schriften*, vol. 7 (Berlin: De Gruyter, 1905), 53.

28. Von Humboldt, *Gesammelte Schriften*, vol. 7, 46.

29. See Trabant, *Mithridates*, 263.

30. Ibid., 264.

31. Wilhelm von Humboldt, *Gesammelte Schriften*, vol. 4 (Berlin: B. Behr, 1905), 21.

32. Wilhelm von Humboldt, "Plan einer vergleichenden Anthropologie," in *Schriften zur Anthropologie und Geschichte: Werke in fünf Bänden*, vol. 1, ed. Andreas Flitner and Klaus Giel (Darmstadt: Wissenschaftliche Buchgesellschaft, 1960), 352–53.

33. See chapter 8; see also Michel de Certeau, *The Practice of Everyday Life* (Berkeley and Los Angeles: University of California Press, 1984), and *The Certeau Reader* (Oxford: Blackwell, 2000).

34. Wilhelm von Humboldt, *Gesammelte Schriften*, vol. 3, *Über das vergleichende Sprachstudium in Beziehung auf die verschiedenen Epochen der Sprachentwicklung* (Berlin: Reimer, 1843), 251. See also his "On the Comparative Study of Language and Its Relation to the Different Periods of Language Development," in *Essays on Language*, ed. T. Harden and D. Farrelly (Frankfurt am Main: Peter Lang, 1997), 1–22.

35. Ludwig Wittgenstein, *Philosophical Investigations: The English Text of the Third Edition* (New York: Macmillan, 1973), sec. 43.

36. Ibid., sec. 23.

37. Ibid., sec. 569.

38. Trabant, *Mithridates*, 313.

39. See Anselm Haverkamp, ed., *Die Sprache der Anderen* (Frankfurt am Main: Suhrkamp, 1997); Brigitte Joste and Jürgen Trabant eds., *Fremdes in fremden*

Sprachen (Munich: Wilhelm Fink, 2001); Christoph Wulf and Christine Merkel, eds., *Globalisierung als Herausforderung der Erziehung: Theorien, Grundlagen, Fallstudien* (Münster: Waxmann, 2002).

CHAPTER ELEVEN

1. See Volker Bohn, ed., *Bildlichkeit: Internationale Beiträge zur Poetik* (Frankfurt am Main: Suhrkamp, 1990); Georges Didi-Huberman, *Devant l'image: Question posée aux fins d'une histoire de l'art* (Paris: Éditions de Minuit, 1990), and (English edition) *Confronting Images: Questioning the Ends of a Certain History of Art* (University Park: Pennsylvania State University Press, 2005); Louis Marin, *Des pouvoirs de l'image* (Paris: Éditions du Seuil, 1993), *On Representation* (Stanford, CA: Stanford University Press, 2001), and *Cross-Readings* (Atlantic Highlands, NJ: Humanities Press, 1998); Régis Debray, *Vie et mort de l'image: Une histoire du regard en Occident* (Paris: Gallimard, 1992), and *Transmitting Culture* (New York: Columbia University Press, 2000); Gottfried Boehm, ed., *Was ist ein Bild?* (Munich: Wilhelm Fink, 1994); Martin Jay, *Downcast Eyes: The Denigration of Vision in Twentieth-Century French Thought* (Berkeley and Los Angeles: University of California Press, 1993); Marie-José Mondzain, *Image, Icon, Economy: The Byzantine Origins of the Contemporary Imaginary* (Stanford, CA: Stanford University Press, 2005), *L'image peut-elle tuer?* (Paris: Éditions du Seuil, 2002), and *Le commerce des regards* (Paris: Éditions du Seuil, 2003); Barbara Stafford, *Visual Analogy: Consciousness of the Art of Connecting* (Cambridge, MA: MIT Press, 1999); Alfred Schäfer and Michael Wimmer, eds., *Identifikation und Repräsentation* (Opladen, Germany: Leske and Budrich, 1999); Gerd Schäfer und Christoph Wulf, eds., *Bild–Bilder–Bildung* (Weinheim, Germany: Beltz, Deutscher Studienverlag, 1999); Laurent Gervereau, *Les images qui mentent: Histoire du visuel au XXe siècle* (Paris: Éditions du Seuil, 2000); Hans Belting and Dietmar Kamper, eds., *Der zweite Blick: Bildgeschichte und Bildreflexion* (Munich: Wilhelm Fink, 2000); Mike Sandbothe, *Pragmatische Medienphilosophie: Grundlegung einer neuen Disziplin im Zeitalter des Internet* (Weilerswist, Germany: Velbrück Wissenschaft, 2001); Annette Keck and Nicolas Pethes, eds., *Mediale Anatomien: Menschenbilder als Medien* (Bielefeld, Germany: Transcript, 2001); Hans Belting, *Bild-Anthropologie: Entwürfe für eine Bildwissenschaft* (Munich: Wilhelm Fink, 2001); Bernd Hüppauf and Christoph Wulf, eds., *Dynamics and Performativity of Imagination: The Image between the Visible and the Invisible* (New York: Routledge, 2009).
2. See, among others, Sheldon Sacks, *On Metaphor* (Chicago: University of Chicago Press, 1979); Paul Ricoeur, *La métaphore vive* (Paris: Éditions du Seuil, 1975).
3. I use the term *imagination* in this context to mean the power of the imagination, fantasy, and the imaginary.
4. Belting, *Bild-Anthropologie*, 12.

5. Jean-Claude Schmitt, *Le corps des images: Essais sur la culture visuelle au moyen âge* (Paris: Gallimard, 2002); see also his *Ghosts in the Middle Ages: The Living and the Dead in Medieval Society* (Chicago: University of Chicago Press, 1998).

6. See André Leroi-Gourhan, *Gesture and Speech* (Cambridge, MA: MIT Press, 1993).

7. See Emmanuel Anati, *Höhlenmalerei: Die Bilderwelt der prähistorischen Felskunst* (Zurich: Benziger, 1997).

8. See Hartmut Böhme, "Der Wettstreit der Medien im Andenken der Toten," in *Der zweite Blick*, ed. Belting and Kamper, 23–42.

9. On the theory and history of photography, see Ulrike Pilarczyk and Ulrike Mietzner, *Das reflektierte Bild: Die seriell-ikonografische Fotoanalyse in den Erziehungs- und Sozialwissenschaften* (Bad Heilbrunn: Julius Klinckhardt, 2005).

10. Belting, *Bild-Anthropologie*, 13–14.

11. Marshall McLuhan, *The Gutenberg Galaxy: The Making of Typographic Man* (London: Routledge & Kegan Paul, 1962), and *Understanding Media: The Extensions of Man* (London: Routledge, 2001).

12. On media discourse, see, among others, Friedrich A. Kittler, *Discourse Networks, 1800/1900* (Stanford, CA: Stanford University Press, 1990), and *Gramophone, Film, Typewriter* (Stanford, CA: Stanford University Press, 1999); Derrick de Kerckhove, *The Alphabet and the Brain: The Lateralization of Writing* (Berlin: Springer, 1988), and *The Skin of Culture: Investigating the New Electronic Reality* (Toronto: Somerville House, 1995); Werner Faulstich, *Das Medium als Kult: Von den Anfängen bis zur Spätantike (8. Jahrhundert)* (Göttingen: Vandenhoeck & Ruprecht, 1997), and *Medien zwischen Herrschaft und Revolte: Die Medienkultur der frühen Neuzeit (1400–1700)* (Göttingen: Vandenhoeck & Ruprecht, 1998); Stefan Münker and Alexander Rösler, eds., *Mythos Internet* (Frankfurt am Main: Suhrkamp, 1997); Dominique Wolton, ed., *Penser la communication* (Paris: Flammarion, 1997), and *Internet et après: Une théorie critique des nouveaux médias* (Paris: Flammarion, 1999); Gordon Graham, *The Internet* (London: Routledge, 1999); Karl Ludwig Pfeiffer, *Das Mediale und das Imaginäre: Dimensionen kulturanthropologischer Medientheorie* (Frankfurt am Main: Suhrkamp, 1999); Elisabeth von Samsonow and Eric Alliez, eds., *Telenoia: Kritik der virtuellen Bilder* (Vienna: Turia und Kant, 1999); Stefan Münker, Alexander Roesler, and Mike Sandbothe, eds., *Medienphilosophie: Beiträge zur Klärung eines Begriffs* (Frankfurt am Main: Suhrkamp, 2003); Régis Debray, *Einführung in die Mediologie* (Bern: Haupt, 2003).

13. On this subject, see Marc Augé, *An Anthropology for Contemporaneous Worlds* (Stanford, CA: Stanford University Press, 1999), and *The War of Dreams: Exercises in Ethno-Fiction* (London: Pluto Press, 1999).

14. Serge Gruzinski, *Images at War: Mexico from Columbus to Blade Runner (1492–2019)* (Durham, NC: Duke University Press, 2001).

15. See Fritz Kramer, *The Red Fez: Art and Spirit Possession in Africa* (London: Verso, 1993).

16. See Roland Barthes, *Camera Lucida: Reflections on Photography* (New York: Hill and Wang, 1981).
17. See Susan Sontag, *On Photography* (New York: Farrar, Straus and Giroux, 1977), 153ff.
18. Belting, *Bild-Anthropologie*, 29.
19. Siegfried Zielinski, *Audiovisionen: Kino und Fernsehen als Zwischenspiele in der Geschichte* (Reinbek, Germany: Rowohlt, 1989).
20. On this subject, see, among others, Manfred Weffender, ed., *Cyberspace: Ausflüge in visuelle Wirklichkeiten* (Reinbek, Germany: Rowohlt, 1991); Howard Rheingold, *Virtual Reality* (New York: Summit Books, 1991); Florian Roetzer and Peter Weibel, eds., *Cyberspace: Zum weltlichen Gesamtkunstwerk* (Munich: Boer, 1993); Chris Hables Gray, ed., *The Cyborg Handbook* (New York: Routledge, 1995); Nicholas Mirzoeff, ed., *The Visual Culture Reader* (London: Routledge, 2002).
21. Eric Alliez, quoted in Belting, *Bild-Anthropologie*, 39.
22. See Roetzer and Weibel, *Cyberspace*; Wolfgang Müller-Funk and Hans U. Reck, eds., *Inszenierte Imagination: Beiträge zu einer historischen Anthropologie der Medien* (Vienna: Springer, 1996); Manfred Faßler, ed., *Alle möglichen Welten: Virtuelle Realität—Wahrnehmung—Ethik der Kommunikation* (Munich: Wilhelm Fink, 1999); Academy of Media Arts, Cologne, *Lab: Jahrbuch für Künste und Apparate* (Cologne: König, 2000); Manfred Faßler, *Lab: Goodbye, Dear Pigeons* (Cologne: König, 2002).
23. See, among others, Bruno Latour and Peter Weibel, eds., *Iconoclash: Beyond the Image Wars in Science, Religion, and Art* (Karlsruhe: Zentrum für Kunst und Medientechnologie, 2002).
24. Hans Belting focused on these in *Likeness and Presence: A History of the Image Before the Era of Art* (Chicago: University of Chicago Press, 1994). However, he only investigated the cult image since the end of antiquity, which is always based on representation. Images that create the magical presence of gods are designated idols or icons.
25. Belting, *Bild-Anthropologie*, 143–88.
26. Gottfried Boehm, "Die Bilderfrage," in Boehm, ed., *Was ist ein Bild?* (Munich: Wilhelm Fink, 1994), 330.
27. Boehm, "Die Bilderfrage", 343.
28. Plato, *Republic* (New York: Basic Books, 1968), 598a.
29. Gunter Gebauer and Christoph Wulf, eds., *Mimesis: Culture, Art, Society* (Berkeley and Los Angeles: University of California Press, 1995).
30. See Arthur C. Danto, *Encounters and Reflections: Art in the Historical Present* (New York: Farrar, Straus and Giroux, 1990), and *The Body/Body Problem: Selected Essays* (Berkeley and Los Angeles: University of California Press, 1999).
31. Belting, *Bild-Anthropologie*, 89.
32. See Jean Baudrillard and Marc Guillaume, *Radical Alterity* (Los Angeles: Semiotext(e), 2008).

33. See Paul Virilio, *Polar Inertia* (London: Sage, 2000), *War and Cinema: The Logistics of Perception* (London: Verso, 1989), and *Fluchtgeschwindigkeit* (Munich: Hanser, 1996).

34. See the following by Jean Baudrillard: *Simulations* (New York: Semiotext(e), 1983); *L'autre*; *The Transparency of Evil: Essays on Extreme Phenomena* (London: Verso, 1993); *The System of Objects* (London: Verso, 2005); *The Illusion of the End* (Cambridge: Polity Press, 1994); and *The Perfect Crime* (London: Verso, 1996).

35. See Johannes Flügge, *Die Entfaltung der Anschauungskraft* (Heidelberg: Quelle & Meyer, 1963).

36. Gebauer and Wulf, *Mimesis*; Gunter Gebauer and Christoph Wulf, *Spiel, Ritual, Geste: Mimetisches Handeln in der sozialen Welt* (Reinbek, Germany: Rowohlt, 1998); Christoph Wulf, *Zur Genese des Sozialen: Mimesis, Ritual, Performativität* (Bielefeld, Germany: Transcript, 2005).

37. Carl Gustav Jung, *Psychologische Typen* (Zurich: Rascher, 1968), 311.

38. See Dieter Henrich, ed., *Theorien der Kunst* (Frankfurt am Main: Suhrkamp, 1982).

39. See Erwin Panofsky, *Studies in Iconology, Humanistic Themes in the Art of Renaissance* (New York: Harper and Row, 1962); *Meaning in the Visual Arts* (Chicago: University of Chicago Press, 1982); Mitchell also uses the concept of iconology. In contrast to Panofsky, he does not want to interpret images as texts but to differentiate between them; see William J. T. Mitchell, *Picture Theory: Essays on Verbal and Visual Representation* (Chicago: University of Chicago Press, 1994).

40. Max Imdahl, "Ikonik: Bilder und ihre Anschauung," in Boehm, *Was ist ein Bild?*, 300–24, 308; see also Max Imdahl, "Introduction," in *Who's Afraid of Red, Yellow and Blue III*, by Barnett Newman (Stuttgart: Reclam, 1971).

41. Imdahl, "Ikonik," 318.

42. Ibid., 319.

43. Terms such as *inner image world*, *taking on aspects of an image*, and other similar ideas are metaphorical.

44. Hans Belting, "Der Blick im Bild: Zu einer Ikonologie des Blicks," in *Bild und Einbildungskraft*, ed. Bernd Hüppauf and Christoph Wulf (Munich: Fink, 2006), 121.

45. Ibid., 123.

46. Aristotle, *De anima*, 3.3: "*pro homaton gar esti ti poiesasthai*"—"[imagination] is producing something for the eyes."

47. Maurice Merleau-Ponty, *The Visible and the Invisible*, ed. Claude Lefort, trans. Alphonso Lingis (Evanston, IL: Northwestern University Press, 1968), 133.

48. Arnold Gehlen, *Man: His Nature and Place in the World* (New York: Columbia University Press, 1988), 316.

49. Flügge, *Die Entfaltung der Anschauungskraft*, 93.

50. Gehlen, *Man*, 309.

51. Dietmar Kamper, "Wunsch," in *Der Mensch und seine Kultur*, ed. Christoph Wulf (Cologne: Anaconda, 2010), 997–1006.

52. See Wolfgang Iser, *The Fictive and the Imaginary: Charting Literary Anthropology* (Baltimore, MD: J. Hopkins University Press, 1993).

53. Theodor W. Adorno, "Introduction," in *The Positivist Dispute in German Sociology*, trans. Glyn Adey and David Frisby (London: Heinemann Educational Books, 1976), 51; German edition: *Der Positivismusstreit in der deutschen Soziologie* (Neuwied: Luchterhand, 1969), 62–63.

54. David Hume, *A Treatise of Human Nature* (London: Penguin Classics, 1986), 71; John Locke, *Essay Concerning Human Understanding* (Indianapolis, IN: Hackett, 1996).

55. Samuel Taylor Coleridge, *Biographia literaria; or, Biographical Sketches of my Literary Life and Opinions* (New York: Wiley and Puttnam, 1847), 378.

56. Vilém Flusser, *Writings*, trans. Erik Eisel (Minneapolis: University of Minnesota Press, 2002), 116; German version: "Eine neue Einbildungskraft," in *Bildlichkeit*, ed. Volker Bohn (Frankfurt am Main: Suhrkamp, 1999), 115–26, 125–26.

57. Jean-Paul Sartre, *The Imaginary: A Phenomenological Psychology of the Imagination* (London: Routledge, 2004).

58. Jacques Lacan, "The Mirror Stage as Formative of the Function of the *I* as Revealed in Psychoanalytic Experience," paper delivered at the sixteenth International Congress of Psychoanalysis, Zürich, July 17, 1949; in Jacques Lacan, *Écrits: A Selection*, trans. Alan Sheridan (New York: W. W. Norton, 1977), 1–7; see also his "What Is a Picture?" in *The Visual Culture Reader*, ed. Nicholas Mirzoeff (London: Routledge, 2002), 126–28.

59. Cornelius Castoriadis, *The Imaginary Institution of Society*, trans. Kathleen Blamey (Cambridge, MA: MIT Press, 1987), 127.

CHAPTER TWELVE

1. See Hannah Arendt, *Der Liebesbegriff bei Augustin: Versuch einer philosophischen Interpretation*, ed. Ludger Lütkehaus (Berlin: Philo, 2003), and *Denktagebuch*, ed. Ursula Lutz and Ingeborg Nordmann. 2 vols. (Munich: Piper, 2002).

2. See Peter Sloterdijk, *Zur Welt kommen—Zur Sprache kommen* (Frankfurt am Main: Suhrkamp, 1988); Artur Boelderl, *Von Geburts wegen: Unterwegs zu einer philosophischen Natologie* (Würzburg: Königshausen und Neumann, 2007); Christoph Wulf et al., *Geburt in Familie, Klinik, Medien* (Opladen, Germany: Budrich UniPress, 2008); Christoph Wulf, Anja Hänsch, and Micha Brumlik, eds., *Das Imaginäre der Geburt* (Munich: Wilhelm Fink, 2008).

3. See Edgar Morin, *L'humanité* (Paris: Éditions du Seuil, 2001); see also his *The Nature of Nature* (New York: P. Lang, 1992).

4. See Emmanuel Anati, *Höhlenmalerei: Die Bilderwelt der prähistorischen Felskunst* (Zurich: Benziger, 1997).

5. See the following historical studies: Claude Sutto, ed., *Sentiment de la mort au moyen-âge* (Lousanne: Éditions Payot Lousanne, 1979); Philippe Ariès, *Western Attitudes toward Death: From the Middle Ages to the Present*, trans. Patricia M. Ranum (Baltimore, MD: Johns Hopkins University Press, 1975); Michel Ragon, *L'espace de la mort: Essai sur l'architecture, la décoration et l'urbanisme funéraires* (Paris: A. Michel, 1981); Michel Vovelle, *La mort et l'Occident: De 1300 à nos jours* (Paris: Gallimard, 1983), see also his *Ideologies and Mentalities* (Chicago: University of Chicago Press, 1990); for a more contemporary focus, see Werner Fuchs, *Todesbilder in der modernen Gesellschaft* (Frankfurt am Main: Suhrkamp, 1973).

6. See Alois Hahn, "Tod und Sterben in soziologischer Sicht," in *Tod, Jenseits und Identität: Perspektiven einer kulturwissenschaftlichen Thanatologie*, ed. Jan Assmann and Rolf Trauzettel (Freiburg: Alber, 2002), 55–89.

7. See Constantin von Barloewen, *Der Tod in den Weltkulturen und Weltreligionen* (Frankfurt am Main: Insel, 2000); Zeno Bianu, *Les réligions et la mort* (Paris: Éditions Ramsay, 1981); Marc de Smedt and Bruno Lagrange, eds., *La mort est une autre naissance* (Paris: Seghers, 1979); see also the following contribution to the science and the art of dying: Christiane Montandon and Alain Montandon, eds., *Savoir mourir* (Paris: L'Harmattan, 1993).

8. On children's handling of the concept of death, see Ginette Raimbault, *Kinder sprechen vom Tod: Klinische Probleme der Trauer* (Frankfurt am Main: Suhrkamp, 1980).

9. Edgar Morin, *L'homme et la mort* (Paris: Éditions du Seuil, 1970), 101.

10. See Jörn Ahrens, *Selbstmord: Die Geste des illegitimen Todes* (Munich: Wilhelm Fink, 2001); Jean Améry, *Hand an sich legen: Diskurs über den Freitod* (Stuttgart: Klett-Cotta, 1976).

11. See Jean Guiart, *Les hommes et la mort: Rituels funéraires à travers le monde* (Paris: Musée de l'Homme, 1979); Jean-Pierre Bayard, *Le sens caché des rites mortuaires* (Paris: Éditions Dangles, 1993).

12. Philippe Ariès, *Geschichte des Todes* (Munich: Hanser, 1980); see also his *L'histoire de la mort* (Paris: Éditions du Seuil, 1978).

13. Ariès, *Geschichte des Todes.*

14. See Gerd Jüttemann, Michael Sonntag, and Christoph Wulf, eds., *Die Seele: Ihre Geschichte im Abendland* (Göttingen: Vandenhoeck and Ruprecht, 2005); Christoph Wulf and Dietmar Kamper, eds., *Logik und Leidenschaft: Erträge Historischer Anthropologie* (Berlin: Reimer, 2002).

15. See, among others, Marianne Mischke, *Der Umgang mit dem Tod: Vom Wandel in der abendländischen Geschichte* (Berlin: Reimer, 1996).

16. Jean Baudrillard, *Symbolic Exchange and Death* (London: Sage, 1993).

17. Louis-Vincent Thomas, *Mort et pouvoir* (Paris: Payot, 1978), 10 ("Culture n'est rien d'autre qu'un ensemble organisé de croyances et de rites, afin de mieux lutter contre le pouvoir dissolvant de la mort individuelle et collective"); see also the following ground-breaking studies: Louis-Vincent

Thomas, *Anthropologie de la mort* (Paris: Payot, 1975); Vladimir Jankélévitch, *La mort* (Paris: Flammarion, 1977).

18. See Thomas Macho, *Todesmetaphern: Zur Logik der Grenzerfahrung* (Frankfurt am Main: Suhrkamp, 1987); Thomas Macho and Kristin Marek, eds., *Die neue Sichtbarkeit des Todes* (Munich: Wilhelm Fink, 2007); Reimer Gronemeyer, *Sterben in Deutschland: Wie wir dem Tod einen Platz in unserem Leben einräumen können* (Frankfurt am Main: Fischer, 2007).

19. See Hans-Dieter Bahr, *Den Tod denken* (Munich: Wilhelm Fink, 2002).

20. Martin Heidegger, *Being and Time*, trans. John Macquarrie and Edward Robinson (London: Wiley-Blackwell, 2000), 303; original German version: *Sein und Zeit* (Tübingen: Niemeyer, 1960), 258–59.

21. Bahr, *Den Tod denken*, 143.

22. Ibid., 144.

23. Blaise Pascal, *Pensées*, trans. Roger Ariew (Indianapolis, IN: Hackett, 2005), 42.

24. Bahr, *Den Tod denken*, 147–48.

25. Ibid., 150.

26. Hannah Arendt, *Der Liebesbegriff*, 63.

27. See Christoph Wulf, *Zur Genese des Sozialen: Mimesis, Performativität, Ritual* (Bielefeld, Germany: Transcript, 2005).

28. "Als ob die Welt mit ihm neu entstünde" (Hannah Arendt, *Denktagebuch*, 175).

29. Ludger Lütkehaus, *Natalität: Philosophie der Geburt* (Zug, Switzerland: Die graue Edition [part of Elsevier group], 2006), 48.

30. See Gunter Gebauer and Christoph Wulf, *Mimesis: Culture, Art, Society* (Berkeley and Los Angeles: University of California Press, 1995).

31. See Axel Michaels and Christoph Wulf, eds., *Images of the Body in India: South Asian and European Perspectives on Rituals and Performativity* (London: Routledge, 2011).

FUTURE PROSPECTS

1. See chapter 5 on historical cultural anthropology, especially notes 3–7; see also chapter 3 on anthropology in history.

2. See Christoph Wulf and Dietmar Kamper, eds., *Logik und Leidenschaft: Erträge Historischer Anthropologie* (Berlin: Reimer, 2002); Christoph Wulf, ed., *Der Mensch und seine Kultur* (Cologne: Anaconda, 2010); Erika Fischer-Lichte and Christoph Wulf, eds., "Praktiken des Performativen" (issue title), *Paragrana* 13, no. 1 (2004).

3. See Jürgen Kocka, ed., *Interdisziplinarität. Praxis—Herausforderung—Ideologie* (Frankfurt am Main: Suhrkamp, 1987).

4. See Peter Weingart, "Interdisziplinarität—der paradoxe Diskurs," *Ethik und Sozialwissenschaften* 8, no. 4 (1997): 521–29.

5. See Julie Thompson Klein, *Interdisciplinarity: History, Theory, and Practice* (Detroit, MI: Wayne State University Press, 1990), and *Crossing Boundaries:*

Knowledge, Disciplinarities, and Interdisciplinarities (Charlottesville: University Press of Virginia, 1996).

6. See, among others, Hans-Georg Gadamer, *Truth and Method* (New York: Crossroad, 1989); Paul Ricoeur, *The Rule of Metaphor: Multi-Disciplinary Studies of the Creation of Meaning in Language* (Toronto: University of Toronto Press, 1977), *Time and Narrative*, 3 vols. (Chicago: University of Chicago Press, 1984–88), and *Oneself as Another* (Chicago: University of Chicago Press, 1992).

7. See Hayden White, *Metahistory: The Historical Imagination in Nineteenth-Century Europe* (Baltimore, MD: Johns Hopkins University Press, 1973), and the resulting discussion on the role of fiction in historical science; see, among others, Peter Burke, *History and Social Theory* (Ithaca, NY: Cornell University Press, 2005); Christoph Conrad and Martina Kessel, eds., *Geschichte schreiben in der Postmoderne: Beiträge zur aktuellen Diskussion* (Stuttgart: Reclam, 1994); Jacques LeGoff, *History and Memory* (New York: Columbia University Press, 1992); Paul Veyne, *Writing History: Essay on Epistemology* (Middletown, CT: Wesleyan University Press, 1984).

8. On interpretation, see Claudia Benthien and Hans R. Velten, eds., *Germanistik als Kulturwissenschaft: Eine Einführung in neue Theoriekonzepte* (Reinbek, Germany: Rowohlt, 2002); Hugh J. Silverman, ed., *Cultural Semiosis* (New York: Routledge, 1998); Harold Aram Veeser, ed., *The New Historicism* (New York: Routledge, 1989). On deconstruction, see Michael Wimmer, "Die Kehrseite des Menschen: Probleme und Fragen der Historischen Anthropologie," in *Anthropologische Markierungen: Herausforderungen pädagogischen Denkens*, ed. Winfried Marotzki, Jan Masschelein, and Alfred Schäfer (Weinheim, Germany: Beltz, Deutscher Studienverlag, 1998), 85–112; Jacques Derrida, *L'écriture et la différence* (Paris: Éditions du Seuil, 1967), and *Of Grammatology* (Baltimore, MD: Johns Hopkins University Press, 1998); see also *The Derrida Reader: Writing Performances* (Lincoln: University of Nebraska Press, 1998).

9. See Barney G. Glaser and Anselm L. Strauss, *The Discovery of Grounded Theory* (Chicago: University of Chicago Press, 1969); Anselm L. Strauss and Juliet Corbin, "Grounded Theory: An Overview," in *Handbook of Qualitative Research*, ed. Norman K. Denzin and Yvonna S. Lincoln (Thousand Oaks, CA: Sage, 1994), 273–85; Denzin and Lincoln, *Handbook of Qualitative Research*; Eckard König and Peter Zedler, eds., *Bilanz qualitativer Forschung*, vol. 2 (Weinheim, Germany: Beltz, Deutscher Studienverlag, 1995); Uwe Flick, *An Introduction to Qualitative Research* (London: Sage, 2006); Barbara Friebertshaeuser and Annedore Prengel, eds., *Handbuch qualitative Forschungsmethoden in der Erziehungswissenschaft* (Weinheim, Germany: Juventa, 2009); Stefan Hirschauer and Klaus Amann, eds., *Die Befremdung der eigenen Kultur: Zur ethnographischen Herausforderung soziologischer Empirie* (Frankfurt am Main: Suhrkamp, 1997); Ronald Hitzler and Anne

Honer, eds., *Sozialwissenschaftliche Hermeneutik* (Opladen, Germany: Leske and Budrich, 1997); Heinz-Hermann Krüger and Winfried Marotzki, eds., *Erziehungswissenschaftliche Biographieforschung* (Opladen, Germany: Leske and Budrich, 1996); Klaus Kraimer, ed., *Die Fallrekonstruktion: Sinnverstehen in der sozialwissenschaftlichen Forschung* (Frankfurt am Main: Suhrkamp, 2000); Uwe Flick, Ernst von Kardorff, and Ines Steinke, eds., *A Companion to Qualitative Research* (London: Sage, 2004); Ralf Bohnsack, *Rekonstruktive Sozialforschung: Einführung in qualitative Methoden* (Opladen, Germany: Leske and Budrich, 2003).

10. See "Methode und Methodologie," in *Historisches Wörterbuch der Philosophie*, vol. 5, ed. Joachim Ritter and Karlfried Gründer (Basel: Schwabe, 1980), cols. 1304ff.

11. See Mike Featherstone, ed., *Global Culture: Nationalism, Globalization and Modernity* (London: Sage, 1990); David T. Goldberg, ed., *Multiculturalism* (Oxford: Oxford University Press, 1994); Jonathan Friedman, *Cultural Identity and Global Process* (London: Sage, 1994); Arjun Appadurai, *Modernity at Large: Cultural Dimensions of Globalization* (Minneapolis: University of Minnesota Press, 1996); Akhil Gupta and James Ferguson, eds., *Culture, Power, Place: Explorations in Critical Anthropology* (Durham, NC: Duke University Press, 1997); Ulrich Beck, *Power in the Global Age: A New Global Political Economy* (Cambridge: Polity Press, 2005); Richard Münch, *Globale Dynamik, lokale Lebenswelten: Der schwierige Weg in die Weltgesellschaft* (Frankfurt am Main: Suhrkamp, 1998); Anthony Giddens, *The Global Third Way Debate* (Cambridge: Polity Press, 2001); Christoph Wulf and Christine Merkel, eds., *Globalisierung als Herausforderung der Erziehung: Theorien, Grundlagen, Fallstudien* (Münster: Waxmann, 2002).

12. See Manuel Castells, *The Rise of the Network Society* (Malden, MA: Blackwell, 1996).

13. See Homi K. Bhabha, *The Location of Culture* (London: Routledge, 1994); Wolfgang Welsch, "Auf dem Weg zu transkulturellen Gesellschaften," *Paragrana* 10, no. 2 (2001): 254–84.

14. Frans de Waal, *The Ape and the Sushi Master: Cultural Reflections by a Primatologist* (New York: Basic Books/Perseus Books Group, 2001); Dominique Lestel, *Les origines animales de la culture* (Paris: Flammarion, 2001).

15. Christoph Wulf, "Globalisierung und kulturelle Vielfalt: Der Andere und die Notwendigkeit anthropologischer Reflexion," in Wulf and Merkel, *Globalisierung als Herausforderung*, 75–100.

16. Jörg Zirfas, "Globale Ethik," in Wulf and Merkel, *Globalisierung als Herausforderung*, 217–47.

17. UNESCO, *Learning, the Treasure Within: Report to UNESCO of the International Commission on Education for the 21st Century* (Paris: UNESCO, 1996).

18. See Ernst Ulrich von Weizsäcker, *Erdpolitik: Ökologische Realpolitik an der Schwelle zum Jahrhundert der Umwelt* (Darmstadt: Wissenschaftliche Buchgesellschaft, 1989); Enquête-Kommission, "Schutz des Menschen

und der Umwelt," in *Konzept Nachhaltigkeit: Vom Leitbild zur Umsetzung* (Bonn: Deutscher Bundestag, Referat Öffentlichkeitsarbeit, 1998); Agenda 21, which was ratified by more than 170 nations at the United Nations Conference for Environment and Development (UNCED) in 1992 in Rio de Janeiro; Bernd Hamm, "Für eine Kultur der Zukunftsfähigkeit," in Wulf and Merkel, *Globalisierung als Herausforderung*, 193–216; see also the Hamburg declaration of the German UNESCO Commission of 2003 (Bonn: Deutsche UNESCO Kommission), which pleaded for a decade of sustainable growth. In this context sustainability is understood as the most economic use of nonrenewable resources. Expanding this view, we now talk of future-compatible development instead of sustainable development. Future-compatible development also entails issues of human rights, cultural diversity, violence, peace, and social justice.

19. For the following observations, I am grateful for the ideas of my many colleagues in the Cluster of Excellence of Heidelberg University, Asia and Europe in a Global Context: The Dynamics of Transculturality of whose scientific advisory board I am chairman.

20. See Christine Délory, Gunter Gebauer, Marianne Krüger-Potratz, Christiane Montandon, and Christoph Wulf, eds., *Europäische Bürgerschaft in Bewegung* (Münster: Waxmann, 2011).

21. See Christoph Wulf, ed., "Kontaktzonen" (issue title), *Paragrana* 19, no. 2 (2010), with articles by John Borneman, Bruce Kapferer, and George Marcus.

22. See, respectively, Mary Louise Pratt, *Ways of Reading* (New York: Bedford/ St. Martin's, 1999), and *Imperial Eyes: Travel Writing and Transculturation*, 2nd ed. (London: Routledge, 2007); Serge Gruzinski, *Images at War: Mexico from Columbus to Blade Runner (1492–2019)* (Durham, NC: Duke University Press, 2001); and Homi Bhabha, *Location of Culture.*

Selected Bibliography

The bibliography has been divided into sections corresponding to the chapters of the book, in order to make it easier for the reader. There are also full details of works and further research in the footnotes at the end of each chapter.

Paradigms of Anthropology

CHAPTER ONE: EVOLUTION—HOMINIZATION—ANTHROPOLOGY

Changeux, Jean-Pierre. *The Physiology of Truth: Neuroscience and Human Knowledge*. Cambridge, MA: Belknap Press of Harvard University Press, 2004.

Darwin, Charles. *On the Origin of the Species by Means of Natural Selection*. Mineola, NY: Dover, 2006.

Dawkins, Richard. *The Selfish Gene*. Oxford: Oxford University Press, 2006.

de Waal, Frans. *The Ape and the Sushi Master: Cultural Reflections by a Primatologist*. New York: Basic Books, Perseus Books Group, 2001.

Eibl-Eibesfeldt, Irenäus. *Ethnic Conflict and Indoctrination: Altruism and Identity in Evolutionary Perspective*. New York: Berghahn Books, 1998.

Leakey, Richard, and Roger Lewin. *Origins Reconsidered: In Search of What Makes Us Human*. New York: Doubleday, 1992.

Leroi-Gourhan, André. *Gesture and Speech*. Trans. Anna Bostock Berger. Cambridge, MA: MIT Press, 1993.

Maasen, Sabine, Wolfgang Prinz, and Gerhard Roth, eds. *Voluntary Action: Brains, Minds, and Sociality*. New York: Oxford University Press, 2003.

Malsburg, Christoph von der, William A. Phillips, and Wolf Singer, eds. *Dynamic Coordination in the Brain: From Neurons to Mind.* Struengmann Forum Report. Cambridge, MA: MIT Press, 2010.

Markl, Hubert. *Natur als Kulturaufgabe: Über die Beziehung des Menschen zur lebendigen Natur.* Stuttgart: Deutsche Verlagsanstalt, 1986.

Maturana, Humberto, and Francisco J. Varela. *The Tree of Knowledge: The Biological Roots of Human Understanding.* Boston: Shambhala, 1992.

Mayr, Ernst. *Evolution: Die Entwicklung von den ersten Lebensspuren bis zum Menschen.* Heidelberg: Spektrum der Wissenschaft, 1982.

———. *Toward a New Philosophy of Biology: Observations of an Evolutionist.* Cambridge, MA: Belknap Press of Harvard University Press, 1988.

Morin, Edgar. *Le paradigme perdu: La nature humaine.* Paris: Éditions du Seuil, 1973.

Oeser, Erhard. *Katastrophen: Triebkraft der Evolution.* Darmstadt: Wissenschaftliche Buchgesellschaft, 2011.

Pöppel, Ernst: *Mindworks: Time and Conscious Experience.* Boston: Harcourt Brace Jovanovich, 1988.

Schrenk, Friedemann. *Die Frühzeit des Menschen: Der Weg zum Homo sapiens.* 3rd ed. Munich: Beck, 2001.

Schrenk, Friedemann, and Timothy G. Bromage, eds. *African Biogeography, Climate Change and Human Evolution.* New York: Oxford University Press, 1999.

Schrenk, Friedemann, and Stephanie Mueller. *The Neanderthals.* London: Routledge, 2009.

Wilson, Edward O. *Sociobiology: The New Synthesis.* Cambridge, MA: Harvard University Press, 1975.

Wuketits, Franz M. *The Evolution of Living Systems.* Weinheim, Germany: Wiley-VCH, 2005.

Wuketits, Franz M., and Christoph Antweiler. *Handbook of Evolution.* Weinheim, Germany: Wiley-VCH, 2005.

CHAPTER TWO: PHILOSOPHICAL ANTHROPOLOGY

Arlt, Gerhard. *Philosophische Anthropologie.* Stuttgart: Metzler, 2001.

Driesch, Hans. *The Science and Philosophy of the Organism.* New York: AMS Press, 1979.

Dux, Günter. "Für eine Anthropologie in historisch-genetischer Absicht: Kritische Überlegungen zur philosophischen Anthropologie Helmuth Plessners." In *Der Prozeß der Geistesgeschichte: Studien zur ontogenetischen und historischen Entwicklung des Geistes,* ed. Günter Dux and Ulrich Wenzel, 92–115. Frankfurt am Main: Suhrkamp, 1994.

Fischer, Joachim. *Philosophische Anthropologie: Eine Denkrichtung des 20. Jahrhunderts.* Freiburg: Karl Alber, 2008.

Gehlen, Arnold. *Gesamtausgabe.* 7 vols. Ed. Karl-Siegbert Rehberg. Frankfurt am Main: Klostermann, 1978–2004 (vols. 8–10 in preparation).

———. *Man: His Nature and Place in the World.* Trans. Clare McMillan and Karl Pillemer, with an introduction by Karl-Siegbert Rehberg. New York: Columbia University Press, 1988.

———. *Man in the Age of Technology.* New York: Columbia University Press, 1980.

Groethuysen, Bernhard. *Philosophische Anthropologie.* Munich: Oldenburg, 1969.

Honneth, Axel, and Hans Joas. *Social Action and Human Nature.* Cambridge: Cambridge University Press, 1988.

Krüger, Hans-Peter. *Zwischen Lachen und Weinen.* Vol. 1. *Das Spektrum menschlicher Phänomene.* Berlin: Akademie, 1999.

Landmann, Michael. *Fundamental Anthropology.* Washington DC: Center for Advanced Research in Phenomenology and University Press of America, 1985.

———. *Philosophical Anthropology.* Philadelphia: Westminster Press, 1974.

Plessner, Helmuth. *Gesammelte Schriften.* Ed. Günter Dux, Odo Marquard, and Elisabeth Ströker. Frankfurt am Main: Suhrkamp, 10 vols. 1980–1985.

———. *Laughing and Crying: A Study of the Limits of Human Behavior.* Evanston, IL: Northwestern University Press, 1970.

———. *Die Stufen des Organischen und der Mensch.* Vol. 4 of *Gesammelte Schriften,* ed. Günter Dux, Odo Marquard, and Elisabeth Ströker. Frankfurt am Main: Suhrkamp, 1981.

Rehberg, Karl-Siegbert. "Zurück zur Kultur? Arnold Gehlens anthropologische Grundlegung der Kulturwissenschaften." In *Kultur: Bestimmungen im 20. Jahrhundert,* ed. Helmut Brackert and Fritz Wefelmeyer, 276–316. Frankfurt am Main: Suhrkamp, 1990.

Scheler, Max. *Gesammelte Werke.* Ed. Manfred S. Frings. Bern: Francke, 1971.

———. *The Human Place in the Cosmos.* Evanston, IL: Northwestern University Press, 2009.

———. *On Feeling, Knowing, and Valuing: Selected Writings (Heritage of Sociology).* Chicago: University of Chicago Press, 1993.

———. *Selected Philosophical Essays.* Evanston, IL: Northwestern University Press, 1973.

Schüssler, Kersten. *Helmuth Plessner: Eine intellektuelle Biographie.* Berlin: Philo Verlagsgesellschaft, 2000.

Thies, Christian. *Gehlen zur Einführung.* Hamburg: Junius, 2000.

Weiner, James F. *Tree Leaf Talk: A Heideggerian Anthropology.* Oxford: Berg, 2002.

CHAPTER THREE: ANTHROPOLOGY IN THE HISTORICAL SCIENCES:
HISTORICAL ANTHROPOLOGY

Althoff, Gerd. *Die Macht der Rituale: Symbolik und Herrschaft im Mittelalter.* Darmstadt: Wissenschaftliche Buchgesellschaft, 2003.

Ariès, Philippe. *Centuries of Childhood: A Social History of Family Life.* New York: Knopf, 1962.

———. *The Hour of Our Death.* Oxford: Oxford University Press, 1991.

Ariès, Philippe, and Georges Duby. *A History of Private Life*. 5 vols. Cambridge, MA: Belknap Press of Harvard University Press, 1987–1991.

Bloch, Marc. *The Feudal Society*. Chicago: University of Chicago Press, 1964.

Bock, Gisela. "Geschichte, Frauengeschichte, Geschlechtergeschichte." *Geschichte und Gesellschaft* 14, no. 3 (1988): 364–91.

Braudel, Fernand. *The Mediterranean and the Mediterranean World in the Age of Philipp II*. New York: Harper & Row, 1992.

———. *On History*. Chicago: University of Chicago Press, 1980.

Bulst, Neithard, and Robert Jütte, eds. *Zwischen Sein und Schein: Kleidung und Identität in der ständischen Gesellschaft*. Freiburg: Karl Alber, 1993.

Burke, Peter. *The French Historical Revolution: The Annales School, 1929–89*. Stanford, CA: Stanford University Press, 1991.

Chartier, Roger. *Cultural History: Between Practices and Representations*. Ithaca, NY: Cornell University Press, 1988.

Connerton, Paul: *How Societies Remember*. Cambridge: Cambridge University Press, 1989.

de Certeau, Michel. *The Practice of Everyday Life*. Trans. Steven Rendell. Berkeley and Los Angeles: University of California Press, 1984.

Delumeau, Jean. *Sin and Fear: The Emergence of a Western Guilt Culture, 13th–18th Centuries*. New York: St. Martin's Press, 1990.

Dinzelbacher, Peter, ed. *Europäische Mentalitätsgeschichte: Hauptthemen in Einzeldarstellungen*. Stuttgart: Kröner, 1993.

Dressel, Gert. *Historische Anthropologie: Eine Einführung*. Vienna: Böhlau, 1996.

Duby, Georges. *The Three Orders: Feudal Society Imagined*. Chicago: University of Chicago Press, 1980.

Febvre, Lucien. *Martin Luther: A Destiny*. New York: E. P. Dutton, 1929.

Ginzburg, Carlo. *The Cheese and the Worms: The Cosmos of a Sixteenth-Century Miller*. New York: Penguin Books, 1982.

Gurjevitch, Aaron. *Historical Anthropology of the Middle Ages*. Cambridge: Cambridge Polity Press, 1992.

———. *Medieval Popular Culture: Problems of Belief and Perception*. Cambridge: Cambridge University Press, 1988.

Habermas, Rebekka. "Geschlechtergeschichte und 'anthropology of gender': Geschichte einer Begegnung." *Historische Anthropologie* 1, no. 3 (1993): 485–509.

Historische Anthropologie: Kultur, Gesellschaft, Alltag. Cologne: Böhlau, 1993 and subsequent years.

Knapp, Bernard A., ed. *Archaeology, Annales, and Ethnohistory*. Cambridge: Cambridge University Press, 2009.

Koselleck, Reinhart. *Futures Past: On the Semantics of Historical Time*. New York: Columbia University Press, 2004.

LeGoff, Jacques. *The Birth of Purgatory*. Aldershot: Scolar Press, 1990.

———, ed. *The Medieval World*. London: Collins & Brown, 1990.

Le Roy Ladurie, Emmanuel. *Carnival in Romans*. New York: Braziller, 1979.

———. *Montaillou: Cathars and Catholics in a French Village, 1294–1324*. London: Scolar, 1978.

Lloyd, Geoffrey Ernest Richard. *Demystifying Mentalities*. Cambridge: Cambridge University Press, 1990.

Lüdtke, Alf, ed. *The History of Everyday Life: Reconstructing Historical Experiences and Ways of Life*. Princeton, NJ: Princeton University Press, 1995.

Medick, Hans, and David Warren Sabean, eds. *Interest and Emotion: Essays on the Study of Family and Kinship*. New York: Cambridge University Press, 1984.

Mitterauer, Michael. *The European Family: Patriarchy to Partnership from the Middle Ages to the Present*. Chicago: University of Chicago Press, 1982.

Reinhard, Wolfgang. *Lebensformen Europas: Eine historische Kulturanthropologie*. Munich: Beck, 2004.

van Dülmen, Richard. *Historische Anthropologie: Entwicklung, Probleme, Aufgaben*. Cologne: Böhlau, 2000.

White, Hayden. *Metahistory*. Baltimore, MD: Johns Hopkins University Press, 1973.

CHAPTER FOUR: CULTURAL ANTHROPOLOGY

Antweiler, Christoph. *Was ist den Menschen gemeinsam? Über Kultur und Kulturen*. Darmstadt: Wissenschaftliche Buchgesellschaft, 2007.

Appadurai, Arjun. *Modernity at Large: Cultural Dimensions of Globalization*. Minneapolis: University of Minnesota Press, 1997.

Augé, Marc. *An Anthropology for Contemporaneous Worlds*. Stanford, CA: Stanford University Press, 1999.

———. *Le métier d'anthropologue: Sens et liberté*. Paris: Galilée, 2006.

Barnard, Allan. *History and Theory in Anthropology*. Cambridge: Cambridge University Press, 2000.

Barth, Fredrik, Andre Gingrich, Robert Parkin, and Sydel Silverman. *One Discipline, Four Ways: British, German, French and American Anthropology*. Chicago: Chicago University Press, 2005.

Bateson, Gregory. *Naven: A Survey of the Problems Suggested by a Composite Picture of the Culture of a New Guinea Tribe Drawn from Three Points of View*. Stanford, CA: Stanford University Press, 1958.

Benedict, Ruth. *The Chrysanthemum and the Sword: Patterns of Japanese Culture*. Boston: Houghton Mifflin, 1946.

———. *Patterns of Culture*. Boston: Houghton Mifflin, 1934.

Berg, Eberhard, and Martin Fuchs, eds. *Kultur, soziale Praxis, Text: Die Krise der ethnographischen Repräsentation*. Frankfurt am Main: Suhrkamp, 1993.

Bernard, Russel H., ed. *Handbook of Methods in Cultural Anthropology*. Walnut Creek, CA: Altamira Press, 1998.

Boas, Franz. *The Mind of Primitive Man*. New York: Macmillan, 1911.

———. *Race, Language, and Culture*. New York: Macmillan, 1940. Orig. pub. 1896.

Borneman, John, and Abdellah Hammoudi, eds. *Being There: The Fieldwork*

Encounter and the Making of Truth. Berkeley and Los Angeles: University of California Press, 2009.

Borofsky, Robert, ed. *Assessing Cultural Anthropology*. New York: McGraw-Hill, 1994.

Bourdieu, Pierre. *Outline of a Theory of Practice*. Cambridge: Polity Press, 1977; and New York: Cambridge University Press, 1977.

Bruner, Jerome S. *The Culture of Education*. Cambridge, MA: Harvard University Press, 1996.

Cerwonka, Allaine, and Lisa Malkki. *Improvising Theory: Process and Temporality in Ethnographic Fieldwork*. Chicago: University of Chicago Press, 2007.

Clifford, James, and George E. Marcus, eds. *Writing Culture: The Poetics and Politics of Ethnography*. Berkeley and Los Angeles: University of California Press, 1986.

Colleyn, Jean-Paul, and Jean-Pierre Dozon, eds. "L'Homme: L'anthropologue et le Contemporain." Special issue, *Revue francaise d'anthropologie* 185–186 (January–June 2008).

Cowan, Jane K., Marie-Bénédicte Dembour, and Richard Wilson, eds. *Culture and Rights: Anthropological Perspectives*. Cambridge: Cambridge University Press, 2001.

Das, Veena, ed. *The Oxford India Companion to Sociology and Social Anthropology*. Delhi: Oxford University Press, 2003.

Douglas, Mary. *Natural Symbols: Explorations in Cosmology*. London: Routledge, 2003.

———. *Purity and Danger: An Analysis of Concepts of Pollution and Taboo*. London: Routledge, 2005.

Dumont, Louis. *Essays on Individualism: Modern Ideology in Anthropological Perspective*. Chicago: University of Chicago Press, 1992.

———. *Homo Hierarchicus: The Caste System and Its Implications*. Trans. Mark Sainsbury. Chicago: University of Chicago Press, 1980.

Evans-Pritchard, Edward E. *Theories of Primitive Religion*. Westport, CT: Greenwood Press, 1985.

Fabian, Johannes. *Time and the Other: How Anthropology Makes Its Object*. New York: Columbia University Press, 1983.

Firth, Raymond W. *Elements of Social Organization*. Boston: Beacon, 1961.

Fischer, Manuela, Peter Bolz, and Susan Kamel, eds. *Adolf Bastian and His Universal Archives of Humanity: The Origins of German Anthropology*. Hildesheim, Germany: Olms, 2007.

Fortes, Meyer. *The Web of Kinship among the Tallensi: The Second Part of an Analysis of the Social Structure of a Trans-Volta Tribe*. London: Oxford University Press, 1949.

Frazer, James George. *The Golden Bough: A Study in Magic and Religion*. London: Macmillan, 1940.

Geertz, Clifford. *The Interpretation of Cultures: Selected Essays*. New York: Basic Books, 1973.

Gellner, Ernest. *Plough, Sword and Book: The Structure of Human History*. Chicago: University of Chicago Press, 1988.

Gluckman, Max. *Custom and Conflict in Africa*. Oxford: Basil Blackwell, 1955.

Godelier, Maurice. *Perspectives in Marxist Anthropology*. Cambridge: Cambridge University Press, 1977.

Goodenough, Ward Hunt. "Anthropology in the 20th Century and Beyond." *American Anthropologist* 104, no. 2 (2002): 423–40.

Goody, Jack. *The Expansive Moment: Anthropology in Britain and Africa, 1918–1970*. Cambridge: Cambridge University Press, 1995.

Greenblatt, Stephen. *Marvelous Possessions: The Wonder of the New World*. Chicago: University of Chicago Press, 1992.

Gruzinski, Serge: *The Conquest of Mexico: The Incorporation of Indian Societies into the Western World, 16th–18th Centuries*. Cambridge: Polity Press, 1993.

Hall, Edward T. *Beyond Culture*. New York: Anchor Books, 1978.

Harris, Marvin. *The Rise of Anthropological Theory: A History of Theories of Cultures*. Rev. ed. Walnut Creek, CA: AltaMira Press, 2001.

Herskovits, Melville J. "The Cattle Complex in East Africa." *American Anthropologist* 28, no. 3 (1926): 494–528.

Herzfeld, Michael. *Anthropology: Theoretical Practice in Culture and Society*. Malden, MA: Blackwell, 2001.

Ingold, Tim. *Key Debates in Anthropology*. New York: Routledge, 1996.

Kaschuba, Wolfgang. *Einführung in die europäische Ethnologie*. Munich: Beck, 2006.

Kilani, Mondher. *Introduction à l'anthropologie*. Lausanne: Éditions Payot, 1992.

Kitayama, Shinobu, and Dov Cohen, eds. *Handbook of Cultural Psychology*. New York: Guilford Press, 2007.

Kohl, Karl-Heinz. *Ethnologie—die Wissenschaft vom kulturell Fremden: Eine Einführung*. Munich: Beck, 1993.

Kroeber, Alfred L. *Configurations of Culture Growth*. Berkeley and Los Angeles: University of California Press, 1944.

Kroeber, Alfred L., and Clyde Kluckhohn. *Culture: A Critical Review of Concepts and Definitions*. Papers of the Peabody Museum of American Archaeology and Ethnology, 47. Cambridge, MA: Harvard University Press, 1952.

Kuper, Adam. *Anthropologists and Anthropology: The British School, 1922–1972*. London: Allen Lane, 1973.

Leach, Edmund R. *Culture and Communication: The Logic by Which Symbols Are Connected*. Cambridge: Cambridge University Press, 1976.

Leiris, Michel. *Manhood: A Journey from Childhood into the Fierce Order of Virility*. Chicago: University of Chicago Press, 1992.

Lévi-Strauss, Claude. *Structural Anthropology*. New York: Basic Books, 1999.

———. *Tristes tropiques*. New York: Penguin Books, 1992.

Lewis, Morgan: *Ancient Society*. Cambridge, MA: Belknap Press of Harvard University Press, 1964.

Lowie, Robert. *The German People: A Social Portrait to 1914*. New York: Farrar and Rinehart, 1945.

———. *The History of Ethnological Theory*. New York: Holt, Rinehart and Winston, 1937.

Malinowski, Bronislaw K. *Argonauts of the Western Pacific*. London: Routledge, 1922.

———. *A Diary in the Strict Sense of the Term*. Stanford, CA: Stanford University Press, 1989.

———. *The Ethnography of Malinowski: The Trobriand Islands, 1915–18*. London: Routledge, 1979.

———. *A Scientific Theory of Culture, and Other Essays*. Chapel Hill: University of North Carolina Press, 2002. (Orig. pub. 1944).

Marcus, George E., and Michael M. J. Fischer, eds. *Anthropology as Cultural Critique: An Experimental Moment in Human Sciences*. Chicago: University of Chicago Press, 1986.

Mauss, Marcel. *The Manual of Ethnography*. Trans. Dominique Lussier; ed. N. J. Allen. New York: Durkheim Press/Berghahn Books, 2007.

———. *Sociology and Psychology: Essays*. London: Routledge, 1979.

———. *Techniques, Technology, and Civilisation*. New York: Durkheim Press/Berghahn Books, 2006.

Mead, Margaret. *Coming of Age in Samoa: A Psychological Study of Primitive Youth for Western Civilization*. New York: Perennial Classics, 2001.

———. *Growing up in New Guinea: A Comparative Study of Primitive Education*. New York: HarperCollins, 2001.

———. *Sex and Temperament in Three Primitive Societies*. New York: Morrow Quill Paperbacks, 1980.

Michaels, Axel, and Christoph Wulf, eds. *Images of the Body in India: South Asian and European Perspectives on Rituals and Performativity*. London: Routledge, 2011.

Moore, Henrietta L. *Feminism and Anthropology*. Cambridge: Polity Press, 1988.

Moore, Jerry. *Visions of Culture: An Introduction to Anthropological Theories and Theorists*. Walnut Creek, CA: Altamira Press, 1997.

Polanyi, Karl. *Dahomey and the Slave Trade: An Analysis of an Archaic Economy*. New York: AMS Press, 1991.

Radcliffe-Brown, Alfred R. *The Andaman Islanders*. Cambridge: Cambridge University Press, 1922.

———. *Structure and Function in Primitive Society: Essays and Addresses*. London: Oxford University Press, 1965.

Rappaport, Roy A. *Ritual and Religion in the Making of Humanity*. Cambridge: Cambridge University Press, 1999.

Russell, Bernard, ed. *Handbook of Methods in Cultural Anthropology*. Walnut Creek, CA: AltaMira Press, 1998.

Sahlins, Marshall. *Culture and Practical Reason*. Chicago: University of Chicago Press, 1976.

Said, Edward. *Orientalism*. New York: Pantheon, 1978.

Sax, William S. *Dancing the Self*. Oxford: Oxford University Press, 2002.

Segal, Daniel A., and Sylvia J. Yanagisako. *Unwrapping the Sacred Bundle: Reflections on the Disciplining of Anthropology.* Durham, NC: Duke University Press, 2005.

Sluka, Jeffrey A., and Antonius Robben, eds. *Ethnographic Fieldwork: An Anthropological Reader.* Malden, MA: Blackwell, 2007.

Spindler, George. *Fifty Years of Anthropology and Education, 1950–2000: A Spindler Anthology.* Mahwah, NJ: Lawrence Erlbaum, 2000.

Stagl, Justin. *Kulturanthropologie und Gesellschaft.* 2nd ed. Berlin: Reimer, 1981.

Stocking, George W. *After Tylor: British Social Anthropology, 1888–1951.* London: Athlone Press, 1996.

———. *Observers Observed: Essays on Ethnographic Fieldwork.* History of Anthropology, 1. Madison: University of Wisconsin Press, 1983.

———, ed. *Volksgeist as Method and Ethic: Essays on Boasian Ethnography and the German Anthropological Tradition.* History of Anthropology, 8. Madison: University of Wisconsin Press, 1996.

Taussig, Michael T. *The Magic of the State.* New York: Routledge, 1997.

Todorov, Tzvetan. *The Conquest of America: The Question of the Other.* Norman: University of Oklahoma Press, 1999.

Valsiner, Jaan. *Culture and Human Development: An Introduction.* London: Sage, 2000.

Wolf, Eric R. *Europe and the People without History.* Berkeley and Los Angeles: University of California Press, 1982.

Zammito, John H. *Kant, Herder and the Birth of Anthropology.* Chicago: University of Chicago Press, 2002.

Zimmerman, Andrew. *Anthropology and Antihumanism in Imperial Germany.* Chicago: University of Chicago Press, 2001.

CHAPTER FIVE: HISTORICAL CULTURAL ANTHROPOLOGY

Anderson-Levitt, Kathryn M., ed. *Anthropologies of Education: A Global Guide to the Ethnographic Studies of Learning and Schooling.* New York: Berghahn Books, 2012.

Assmann, Aleida, and Dietrich Harth, eds. *Mnemosyne: Formen und Funktionen der kulturellen Erinnerung.* Frankfurt am Main: Fischer, 1991.

Assmann, Jan. *Religion and Cultural Memory: Ten Studies.* Stanford, CA: Stanford University Press, 2006.

Augé, Marc. *An Anthropology for Contemporaneous Worlds.* Stanford, CA: Stanford University Press, 1999.

———. *Non-Places: Introduction to an Anthropology of Supermodernity.* London: Verso, 2008.

Baudrillard, Jean, and Guillaume, Marc. *Radical Alterity.* London: distributed by MIT Press, 2008.

Bhabha, Homi K. *The Location of Culture.* London: Routledge, 1998.

Blumenberg, Hans. *Shipwreck with Spectators: Paradigm of a Metaphor for Existence.* Cambridge, MA: MIT Press, 1977.

Bodei, Remo. *Destini personali: L'età della colonizzazione delle coscienze.* Milano: Feltrinelli, 2002.

Böhme, Gernot. *Anthropologie in pragmatischer Hinsicht: Darmstädter Vorlesungen.* Frankfurt am Main: Suhrkamp, 1985.

———. *Coping with Science.* Boulder, CO: Westview Press, 1992.

Böhme, Hartmut, Franz-Theo Gottwald, Christian Holtorf, Thomas Macho, Ludger Schwarte, and Christoph Wulf, eds. *Tiere: Die andere Anthropologie.* Cologne: Böhlau, 2004.

Böhme, Hartmut, Peter Matussek, and Lothar Müller. *Orientierung Kulturwissenschaft: Was sie kann, was sie will.* Reinbek, Germany: Rowohlt, 2000.

Brackert, Helmut, and Fritz Wefelmeyer, eds. *Kultur: Bestimmungen im 20. Jahrhundert.* Frankfurt am Main: Suhrkamp, 1990.

Dilthey, Wilhelm. *Hermeneutics and the Study of History.* Ed. Rudolf A. Makkreel and Frithjof Rodi. Princeton, NJ: Princeton University Press, 1996.

Dux, Günter. *Historisch-genetische Theorie der Kultur.* Weilerswist, Germany: Velbrück, 2000.

Elias, Norbert. *The Civilizing Process.* New York: Urizen Books, 1978.

Foucault, Michel. *Discipline and Punish: The Birth of the Prison.* New York: Pantheon Books, 1977.

Gadamer, Hans-Georg. *Truth and Method.* New York: Crossroad, 1989.

Gebauer, Gunter, Dietmar Kamper, Dieter Lenzen, Gert Mattenklott, Christoph Wulf, and Konrad Wünsche. *Historische Anthropologie: Zum Problem der Humanwissenschaften heute oder Versuche einer Neubegründung.* Reinbek, Germany: Rowohlt, 1989.

Habermas, Jürgen, *The Structural Transformation of the Public Sphere: An Inquiry into a Category of Bourgeois Society.* Trans. Thomas Burger, with Frederick Lawrence. Cambridge, MA: MIT Press, 1989.

Hahn, Alois. *Konstruktionen des Selbst, der Welt und der Geschichte: Aufsätze zur Kultursoziologie.* Frankfurt am Main: Suhrkamp, 2000.

Herder, Johann Gottfried. *Philosophical Writings.* New York: Cambridge University Press, 2002.

Honneth, Axel. *The Struggle for Recognition: The Moral Grammar of Social Conflicts.* Cambridge, MA: MIT Press, 1996.

Jüttemann, Gerd, Michael Sonntag, and Christoph Wulf, eds. *Die Seele: Ihre Geschichte im Abendland.* Göttingen: Vandenhoeck and Ruprecht, 2005.

Kamper, Dietmar. *Geschichte und menschliche Natur: Die Tragweite gegenwärtiger Anthropologie-Kritik.* Munich: Hanser, 1973.

Kamper, Dietmar, and Christoph Wulf, eds. *Anthropologie nach dem Tode des Menschen: Vervollkommnung und Unverbesserlichkeit.* Frankfurt am Main: Suhrkamp, 1994.

———, eds. *Die Wiederkehr des Körpers.* 4th ed. Frankfurt am Main: Suhrkamp, 1992.

Kamper, Dietmar, Christoph Wulf, and Gunter Gebauer, eds. "Kants Anthropologie" (issue title). *Paragrana* 11, no. 2 (2002).

Kittler, Friedrich A. *Literature, Media Information Systems: Essays.* Amsterdam: Arts International, 1997.

Kontopodis, Michalis, Christoph Wulf, and Bernd Fichtner, eds. *Children, Development and Education: Cultural, Historical, Anthropological Perspectives.* Dordrecht: Springer, 2011.

Lenzen, Dieter. *Mythologie der Kindheit.* Reinbek, Germany: Rowohlt, 1985.

Liebau, Eckart, and Christoph Wulf, eds. *Generation.* Weinheim, Germany: Deutscher Studienverlag, 1996.

Michaels, Axel, and Christoph Wulf, eds. *Exploring the Senses: Emotions, Performativity, and Ritual.* London: Routledge, 2013.

Montandon, Alain, ed. *Le livre de l'hospitalité: Accueil de l'étranger dans l'histoire et les cultures.* Paris: Bayard, 2004.

Morin, Edgar. *La méthode: L'humanité de l'humanité; L'identité humaine.* Paris: Éditions du Seuil, 2001.

———. *The Nature of Nature.* New York: P. Lang, 1992.

———. *On Complexity.* Cresskill, NJ: Hampton Press, 2008.

Schings, Hans-Jürgen, ed. *Der ganze Mensch: Anthropologie und Literatur im 18. Jahrhundert.* Stuttgart: Metzler, 1994.

Sloterdijk, Peter. *Bubbles: Spheres.* Vol. 1. *Microspherology.* Trans. Wieland Hoban. Cambridge, MA: MIT Press, 2011.

Soeffner, Hans-Georg. *Gesellschaft ohne Baldachin: Über die Labilität von Ordnungskonstruktionen.* Weilerswist, Germany: Velbrück Wissenschaft, 2000.

Stagl, Justin, and Wolfgang Reinhard, eds. *Grenzen des Menschseins: Probleme einer Definition des Menschlichen.* Vienna: Böhlau, 2005.

Vernant, Jean-Pierre. *Myth and Thought among the Greeks.* London: Routledge and Kegan Paul, 1983.

von Braun, Christina. *Versuch über den Schwindel: Religion, Schrift, Bild, Geschlecht.* Zurich: Pendo, 2001.

Waldenfels, Bernhard. *The Question of the Other.* Albany: State University of New York Press; Hong Kong: Chinese University Press, 2007.

Wenzel, Horst. *Hören und Sehen, Schrift und Bild: Kultur und Gedächtnis im Mittelalter.* Munich: Beck, 1995.

Wulf, Christoph. *Anthropology of Education.* Münster: LIT Verlag, 2002.

———. *Une anthropologie historique et culturelle: Rituels, mimésis sociale et performativité.* Paris: Téraèdre, 2007.

———, ed. *Vom Menschen: Handbuch Historische Anthropologie.* Weinheim, Germany: Beltz, 1997. 2nd ed.: *Der Mensch und seine Kultur.* Cologne: Anaconda, 2010.

Wulf, Christoph, Birgit Althans, Kathrin Audehm, Gerald Blaschke, Nino Ferrin, Ingrid Kellermann, Ruprecht Mattig and Sebastian Schinkel. *Die Geste in Erziehung, Bildung und Sozialisation: Ethnographische Feldstudien.* Wiesbaden: Verlag für Sozialwissenschaften, 2011.

Wulf, Christoph, and Dietmar Kamper, eds. *Logik und Leidenschaft: Erträge Historischer Anthropologie.* Berlin: Reimer, 2002.

Wulf, Christoph, Birgit Althans, Kathrin Audehm, Constanze Bausch, Michael Göhlich, Stephan Sting, Anja Tervooren, Monika Wagner-Willi, and Jörg Zirfas. *Ritual and Identity: The Staging and Performing of Rituals in the Lives of Young People.* London: Tufnell Press, 2010.

Wulf, Christoph, Jacques Poulain, and Fathi Triki, eds. *Europäische und islamisch geprägte Länder im Dialog: Gewalt, Religion und interkulturelle Verständigung.* Berlin: Akademie, 2005 (Arabic edition, 2008; French edition, 2010).

Wulf, Christoph, Shoko Suzuki, Jörg Zirfas, Ingrid Kellermann, Yoshitaka Inoue, Fumo Ono, and Nanae Takenaka. *Das Glück der Familie: Ethnographische Studien in Deutschland und Japan.* Wiesbaden: Verlag für Sozialwissenschaften, 2011.

Wulf, Christoph, and Gabriele Weigand. *Der Mensch in der globalisierten Welt: Anthropologische Reflexionen zum Verständnis unserer Zeit; Christoph Wulf im Gespräch mit Gabriele Weigand.* Münster: Waxmann, 2011.

Core Issues of Anthropology

CHAPTER SIX: THE BODY AS A CHALLENGE

Agamben, Giorgio. *Homo Sacer: Sovereign Power and Bare Life.* Stanford, CA: Stanford University Press, 1998.

Alter, Joseph S. *The Wrestler's Body: Identity and Ideology in North India.* Berkeley and Los Angeles: University of California Press, 1992.

———. *Yoga in Modern India: The Body between Science and Philosophy.* Princeton, NJ: Princeton University Press, 2004.

Belting, Hans, Dietmar Kamper, and Martin Schulz, eds. *Quel Corps? Eine Frage der Repräsentation.* Munich: Wilhelm Fink, 2002.

Benthien, Claudia, and Christoph Wulf, eds. *Körperteile: Eine kulturelle Anatomie.* Reinbek, Germany: Rowohlt, 2001.

Böhme, Gernot. *Aisthetik: Vorlesungen über Ästhetik als allgemeine Wahrnehmungslehre.* Munich: Wilhelm Fink, 2001.

Bourdieu, Pierre. *Distinction. A Social Critique of the Judgment of Taste*, trans. Richard Nice. Cambridge, MA: Harvard University Press, 1984.

———. *Practical Reason: On the Theory of Action.* Stanford, CA: Stanford University Press, 1998.

Bull, Michael, and Les Back, eds. *The Auditory Culture Reader.* Oxford: Berg, 2003.

Classen, Constance. *The Color of Angels: Cosmology, Gender and the Aesthetic Imagination.* London: Routledge, 1998.

———, ed. *The Book of Touch.* Oxford: Berg, 2005.

Classen, Constance, David Howes, and Anthony Synnott, eds. *Aroma: The Cultural History of Smell.* London: Routledge, 1994.

Csordas, Thomas J. "The Body's Career in Anthropology." In *Anthropological Theory Today*, ed. Henrietta L. Moore, 172–205. Cambridge: Polity Press, 1999.

Diaconu, Madalina. *Tasten, Riechen, Schmecken: Eine Ästhetik der anästhesierten Sinne.* Würzburg: Könighausen und Neumann, 2005.

Drobnick, Jim, ed. *The Smell Culture Reader.* Oxford: Berg, 2006.

Elias, Norbert. *The Civilizing Process.* New York: Urizen Books, 1978.

Evans-Pritchard, Edward E. *A History of Anthropological Thought.* London: Faber and Faber, 1981.

Featherstone, Mike, Mike Hepworth, and Bryan S. Turner, eds. *The Body: Social Process and Cultural Theory.* London: Newbury Park, CA: Sage, 1991.

Feher, Michel, ed. *Fragments for a History of the Human Body.* 3 vols. New York: Zone, 1989.

Foucault, Michel. *Discipline and Punish: The Birth of the Prison.* New York: Pantheon Books, 1977.

Galimberti, Umberto. *Les raisons du corps.* Paris: Grasset, 1998.

Goody, Jack. *The Domestication of the Savage Mind.* Cambridge: Cambridge University Press, 1977.

Herzfeld, Michael. *Cultural Intimacy: Social Poetics in the Nation-State.* New York: Routledge, 2005.

Hume, Lynne. *Portals: Opening Doorways to Other Realities Through the Senses.* Oxford, New York: Berg, 2007.

Johnson, Mark. *The Meaning of the Body: Aesthetics of Human Understanding.* Chicago: University of Chicago Press, 2007.

Kamper, Dietmar, and Christoph Wulf, eds. *Die Wiederkehr des Körpers.* 4th ed. Frankfurt am Main: Suhrkamp, 1992.

———, eds. *Transfigurationen des Körpers: Spuren der Gewalt in der Geschichte.* Berlin: Reimer, 1989.

Lacan, Jacques. *Ecrits: A Selection.* Trans. Alan Sheridan. New York: W. W. Norton, 1977.

Lakoff, George, and Mark Johnson. *Philosophy in the Flesh: The Embodied Mind and Its Challenge to Western Thought.* New York: Basic Books, 1999.

Le Breton, David. *Anthropologie du corps et modernité.* Paris: Presses Universitaires de France, 2000.

———. *Le saveur du monde: Une anthropologie des sens.* Paris: Metailié, 2006.

Malsburg, Christoph, von der, William A. Phillips, and Wolf Singer, eds. *Dynamic Coordination in the Brain: From Neurons to Mind.* Struengmann Forum Report. Cambridge, MA: MIT Press, 2010.

Mauss, Marcel. *Techniques, Technology, and Civilisation.* New York: Durkheim Press/Berghahn Books, 2006.

Merleau-Ponty, Maurice. *Phenomenology of Perception: An Introduction*, trans. Colin Smith. London: Routledge, 2002.

———. *The Visible and the Invisible.* Ed. Claude Lefort; trans. Alphonso Lingis. Evanston, IL: Northwestern University Press, 1968.

Michaels, Axel, and Christoph Wulf, eds. *Images of the Body in India: South Asian and European Perspectives on Rituals and Performativity.* London: Routledge, 2011.

Rizzolatti, Giacomo, and Corrado Sinigaglia. *Mirrors in the Brain: How Our Minds Share Actions and Emotions*. Oxford: Oxford University Press, 2008.

Said, Edward. *Orientalism*. New York: Pantheon, 1978.

Scarry, Elaine. *The Body in Pain: The Making and Unmaking of the World*. New York: Oxford University Press, 1985.

Scheper-Hughes, Nancy, and Margaret Lock. "The Mindful Body: A Prolegomenon to Future Work in Medical Anthropology." *Medical Anthropological Quarterly* 1, no. 1 (1987): 6–41.

Schmitz, Herrmann. *Der Leib*. Bonn: Bouvier, 1965.

Schwarte, Ludger, and Christoph Wulf, eds. *Körper und Recht: Anthropologische Dimensionen der Rechtsphilosophie*. Munich: Wilhelm Fink, 2003.

Segal, Daniel A., and Sylvia J. Yanagisako. *Unwrapping the Sacred Bundle: Reflections on the Disciplining of Anthropology*. Durham, NC: Duke University Press, 2005.

Serres, Michel. *The Five Senses: A Philosophy of Mingled Bodies*. London: Continuum, 2009.

Shilling, Chris. *The Body and Social Theory*. London: Sage, 1993.

Singer, Wolf. *Der Beobachter im Gehirn: Essays zur Hirnforschung*. Frankfurt am Main: Suhrkamp, 2002.

Stafford, Barbara M. *Body Criticism: Imaging the Unseen in Enlightenment Art and Medicine*. Cambridge, MA: MIT Press, 1991.

Strathern, Andrew. *Body Thoughts*. Ann Arbor: University of Michigan Press, 1996.

Waldenfels, Bernhard. *Das leibliche Selbst: Vorlesungen zur Phänomenologie des Leibes*. Frankfurt am Main: Suhrkamp, 2000.

———. *The Question of the Other*. Albany: State University of New York Press; Hong Kong: Chinese University Press, 2007.

Wulf, Christoph, and Dietmar Kamper, eds. *Logik und Leidenschaft: Erträge Historischer Anthropologie*. Berlin: Reimer, 2002.

zur Lippe, Rudolf. *Am eigenen Leibe: Zur Ökonomie des Lebens*. Frankfurt am Main: Syndikat, 1978.

CHAPTER SEVEN: THE MIMETIC BASIS OF CULTURAL LEARNING

Agacinski, Sylviane, Jacques Derrida, Sarah Kofman, Philippe Lacoue-Labarthe, Jean-Luc Nancy, and Bernard Pautrat. *Mimesis des articulation*s. Paris: Aubier-Flammarion, 1975.

Auerbach, Erich. *Mimesis: The Representation of Reality in Western Literature*. Princeton, NJ: Princeton University Press, 2003.

Bandura, Albert. *Self-Efficacy: The Exercise of Control*. New York: W. H. Freeman, 1997.

Bourdieu, Pierre. *The Logic of Practice*. Stanford, CA: Stanford University Press, 1990.

Cantwell, Robert. *Ethnomimesis*. Chapel Hill: University of North Carolina Press, 1993.

Costa Lima, Luiz. *Control of the Imaginary: Reason and Imagination in Modern Times.* Minneapolis: University of Minnesota Press, 1988.

Derrida, Jacques. *Disseminations.* Chicago: University of Chicago Press, 1972.

de Tarde, Gabriel. *The Laws of Imitation.* Gloucester, MA: P. Smith, 1962.

Gebauer, Gunter, and Christoph Wulf. *Mimesis: Culture, Art, Society.* Berkeley and Los Angeles: University of California Press, 1995.

———. *Mimetische Weltzugänge: Soziales Handeln—Rituale und Spiele—ästhetische Produktionen.* Stuttgart: Kohlhammer, 2003.

———. *Spiel, Ritual, Geste: Mimetisches Handeln in der sozialen Welt.* Reinbek, Germany: Rowohlt, 1998.

Girard, René. *The Scapegoat.* Baltimore, MD: Johns Hopkins University Press, 1986.

———. *Violence and the Sacred.* Baltimore, MD: Johns Hopkins University Press, 1977.

Goodman, Nelson. *Ways of Worldmaking.* Indianapolis, IN: Hackett, 1978.

Jacoboni, Marco. *Mirroring People.* New York: Farrar, Straus, and Giroux, 2008.

Koller, Hermann. *Die Mimesis in der Antike: Nachahmung, Darstellung, Ausdruck.* Bern: Francke, 1954.

Plessner, Helmuth. *Laughing and Crying: A Study of the Limits of Human Behaviour.* Evanston, IL: Northwestern University Press, 1970.

———. "Zur Anthropologie der Nachahmung." In *Gesammelte Schriften.* Vol. 7. Ed. Günter Dux, Odo Marquard, and Elisabeth Ströker, 389–98. Frankfurt am Main: Suhrkamp, 1982.

Ricoeur, Paul. *Time and Narrative.* 3 vols. Chicago: University of Chicago Press, 1984–1988.

Rizzolatti, Giacomo, and Corrado Sinigaglia. *Mirrors in the Brain: How Our Minds Share Actions and Emotions.* Oxford: Oxford University Press, 2008.

Suzuki, Shoko, and Christoph Wulf, eds. *Mimesis, Poiesis, Performativity in Education.* Münster: Waxmann, 2007.

Taussig, Michael. *Mimesis and Alterity: A Particular History of the Senses.* New York: Routledge, 1993.

Tomasello, Michael. *The Cultural Origins of Human Cognition.* Cambridge, MA: Harvard University Press, 1999.

Walton, Kendall L. *Mimesis as Make-Believe: On the Foundations of the Representational Arts.* Cambridge, MA: Harvard University Press, 1990.

Wulf, Christoph. *Zur Genese des Sozialen: Mimesis, Performativität, Ritual.* Bielefeld, Germany: Transcript, 2005.

CHAPTER EIGHT: THEORIES AND PRACTICES OF THE PERFORMATIVE

Austin, John L. *How to Do Things With Words.* Oxford: Clarendon Press, 1962.

Bourdieu, Pierre, and Loïc J. D. Wacquant. *An Invitation to Reflexive Sociology.* Chicago: Chicago University Press, 1992.

Butler, Judith. *Excitable Speech: A Politics of the Performative.* New York: Routledge, 1997.

————. *Gender Trouble: Feminism and the Subversion of Identity*. New York: Routledge, 1990.

de Certeau, Michel. *The Practice of Everyday Life*, trans. Steven Rendell. Berkeley and Los Angeles: University of California Press, 1984.

Duttlinger, Carolin, Lucia Ruprecht, and Andrew Webber, eds. *Performance and Performativity in German Cultural Studies*. Oxford: P. Lang, 2004.

Fischer-Lichte, Erika. *Performative Aesthetics*. New York: Routledge, 2008.

Fischer-Lichte, Erika, and Christoph Wulf, eds. "Praktiken des Performativen" (issue title). *Paragrana* 13, no. 1 (2004).

————, eds. "Theorien des Performativen" (issue title). *Paragrana* 10, no. 1 (2001).

Loxley, James. *Performativity*. New York: Routledge, 2006.

Noe, Alva. *Action in Perception*. Cambridge, MA: MIT Press, 2004.

Parker, Andrew, and Eve Kosofsky, eds. *Performativity and Performance*. New York: Routledge, 1995.

Schechner, Richard. *Performance Studies*. New York: Routledge, 2006.

Schramm, Helmar, ed. *Bühnen des Wissens: Interferenzen zwischen Wissenschaft und Kunst*. Berlin: Dahlem University Press, 2003.

Tulloch, John. *Performing Culture: Stories of Expertise and the Everyday*. London: Sage, 1999.

Turner, Victor. *From Ritual to Theatre: The Human Seriousness of Play*. New York: Performing Arts Journal Publications, 1982.

Wirth, Uwe, ed. *Performanz: Zwischen Sprachphilosophie und Kulturwissenschaften*. Frankfurt am Main: Suhrkamp, 2002.

Wulf, Christoph, Michael Göhlich, and Jörg Zirfas, eds. *Grundlagen des Performativen: Eine Einführung in die Zusammenhänge von Sprache, Macht und Handeln*. Weinheim, Germany: Juventa, 2001.

Wulf, Christoph, and Jörg Zirfas, eds. *Pädagogik des Performativen*. Weinheim, Germany: Beltz, 2007.

CHAPTER NINE: THE REDISCOVERY OF RITUALS

Agamben, Giorgio. *Means without End: Notes on Politics*. Minneapolis: University of Minnesota Press, 2000.

Althoff, Gerd, Johannes Fried, and Patrick J. Geary, eds. *Medieval Concepts of the Past: Ritual, Memory, Historiography*. Cambridge: Cambridge University Press, 2002.

Bell, Catherine M. *Ritual: Perspectives and Dimensions*. New York: Oxford University Press, 1997.

————. *Ritual Theory, Ritual Practice*. New York: Oxford University Press, 1992.

Belliger, Andrea, and David J. Krieger, eds. *Ritualtheorien: Ein einführendes Handbuch*. Opladen, Germany: Westdeutscher Verlag, 1998.

Bourdieu, Pierre. "Les rites comme des actes d'institution." *Actes de la recherche en science sociales* 43 (June 1982): 58–63.

———. *Outline of a Theory of Practice*. Cambridge: Polity Press, 1977; New York: Cambridge University Press, 1977.

Collins, Randall. *Interaction Ritual Chains*. Princeton, NJ: Princeton University Press, 2004.

Douglas, Mary. *Natural Symbols: Explorations in Cosmology*. Oxford: Oxford University Press, 2002.

———. *Purity and Danger: An Analysis of Concepts of Pollution and Taboo*. Oxford: Oxford University Press, 2002.

Flusser, Vilém. *Gesten: Versuch einer Phänomenologie*. Düsseldorf: Bollmann, 1991.

Gebauer, Gunter, and Christoph Wulf. *Spiel, Ritual, Geste: Mimetisches Handeln in der sozialen Welt*. Reinbek, Germany: Rowohlt, 1998.

———, eds. *Praxis und Ästhetik: Neue Perspektiven im Denken Pierre Bourdieus*. Frankfurt am Main: Suhrkamp, 1993.

Geertz, Clifford. *The Interpretation of Cultures: Selected Essays*. New York: Basic Books, 1973.

Goffman, Erving. *Frame Analysis: An Essay on the Organization of Experience*. New York: Harper & Row, 1974.

Grimes, Ronald L. *Beginnings in Ritual Studies*. Columbia: University of South Carolina Press, 1995.

———, ed. *Research in Ritual Studies*. Methuen, MA: Scarecrow Press, 1985.

Hahn, Alois. *Konstruktionen des Selbst, der Welt und der Geschichte: Aufsätze zur Kultursoziologie*. Frankfurt am Main: Suhrkamp, 2000.

Jousse, Marcel. *Anthropologie du geste*. 3 vols. Paris: Gallimard, 1974–1978.

Kendon, Adam (1984). *Gesture: Visible Action as Utterance*. Cambridge: Cambridge University Press, 2004.

Kreinath, Jens, Jan Snoek, and Michael Stausberg, eds. *Theorizing Rituals: Issues, Topics, Approaches, Concepts*. Leiden: Brill, 2006.

McNeill, David. *Gesture and Thought*. Chicago: University of Chicago Press, 2005.

———. *Hand and Mind: What Gestures Reveal about Thought*. Chicago: University of Chicago Press, 1992.

Michaels, Axel, ed. *Ritual Dynamics and the Science of Ritual*. Vols. 1–5. Wiesbaden: Harrassowitz, 2010–2011.

Michaels, Axel, and Christoph Wulf, eds. *Emotions in Rituals and Performances*. London: Routledge, 2012.

Schmitt, Jean-Claude. *La raison des gestes dans l'Occident médiéval*. Paris: Gallimard, 1990.

Soeffner, Hans-Georg. *The Order of Rituals: The Interpretation of Everyday Life*. New Brunswick, NJ: Transaction, 1997.

Tomasello, Michael. *Origins of Human Communication*. Cambridge, MA: MIT Press, 2008.

Turner, Victor. *Drama, Fields, and Metaphors*. Ithaca, NY: Cornell University Press, 1974.

———. *From Ritual to Theatre: The Human Seriousness of Play*. New York: Performing Arts Journal Publications, 1982.

————. *The Ritual Process: Structure and Anti-Structure.* New York: Aldine de Gruyter, 1995.

van Gennep, Arnold. *The Rites of Passage.* London: Routledge & Paul, 1960.

Wulf, Christoph (with Gilles Boetsch). "Rituels" (issue title). *Hermès* 43 (2005).

Wulf, Christoph, Birgit Althans, Kathrin Audehm, Constanze Bausch, Michael Göhlich, Stephan Sting, Anja Tervooren, Monika Wagner-Willi, and Jörg Zirfas. *Das Soziale als Ritual: Zur performativen Bildung von Gemeinschaften.* Opladen, Germany: Leske and Budrich, 2001.

————. *Ritual and Identity. The Staging and Performing of Rituals in the Lives of Young People.* London: Tufnell Press, 2010.

Wulf, Christoph, Birgit Althans, Kathrin Audehm, Constanze Bausch, Benjamin Jörissen, Michael Göhlich, Ruprecht Mattig, Anja Tervooren, Monika Wagner-Willi, and Jörg Zirfas. *Bildung im Ritual: Schule, Familie, Jugend, Medien.* Wiesbaden: Verlag für Sozialwissenschaften, 2004.

Wulf, Christoph, Birgit Althans, Kathrin Audehm, Gerald Blaschke, Nino Ferrin, Ingrid Kellermann, Ruprecht Mattig, and Sebastian Schinkel. *Die Geste in Erziehung, Bildung und Sozialisation: Ethnographische Fallstudien.* Wiesbaden: Verlag für Sozialwissenschaften, 2011.

Wulf, Christoph, Birgit Althans, Gerald Blaschke, Nino Ferrin, Michael Göhlich, Benjamin Jörissen, Ruprecht Mattig, Iris Nentwig-Gesemann, Sebastian Schinkel, Anja Tervooren, Monika Wagner-Willi, and Jörg Zirfas. *Lernkulturen im Umbruch: Rituelle Praktiken in Schule, Medien, Familie und Jugend.* Wiesbaden: Verlag für Sozialwissenschaften, 2007.

Wulf, Christoph, and Erika Fischer-Lichte, eds. *Gesten: Inszenierung, Aufführung, Praxis.* Munich: Wilhelm Fink, 2010.

Wulf, Christoph, Hildegard Macha, and Eckart Liebau, eds. *Formen des Religiösen: pädagogisch-anthropologische Annäherungen.* Weinheim, Germany: Beltz, 2004.

Wulf, Christoph, Shoko Suzuki, Jörg Zirfas, Ingrid Kellermann, Yoshitaka Inoue, Fumo Ono, and Nanae Takenaka. *Das Glück der Familie: Ethnographische Studien in Deutschland und Japan.* Wiesbaden: Verlag für Sozialwissenschaften, 2011.

Wulf, Christoph, and Jörg Zirfas, eds. "Rituelle Welten" (issue title). *Paragrana* 12, nos. 1–2 (2003).

————, eds. *Die Kultur des Rituals: Inszenierungen, Praktiken, Symbole.* Munich: Wilhelm Fink, 2004.

————, eds. "Innovation und Ritual." Special issue, *Zeitschrift für Erziehungswissenschaft* 7, no. 2 (2004).

CHAPTER TEN: LANGUAGE—THE ANTINOMY BETWEEN THE UNIVERSAL
AND THE PARTICULAR

Barthes, Roland. *Image Music Text.* New York: Hill and Wang, 1977.

Briggs, Charles L. "Linguistic Magic Bullets in the Making of a Modernist Anthropology." *American Anthropologist* 104, no. 2 (2002): 481–98.

Chomsky, Noam. *Knowledge of Language: Its Nature, Origin, and Use*. New York: Praeger, 1986.

———. *Language and Mind*. New York: Harcourt Brace Jovanovich, 1972.

Eschbach, Achim, and Jürgen Trabant. *History of Semiotics*. Philadelphia, PA: J. Benjamins, 2000.

Gebauer, Gunter. *Wittgensteins anthropologisches Denken*. Munich: Beck, 2009.

Herder, Johann Gottfried. *On the Origin of Language*. Trans. John H. Moran and Alexander Gode. Chicago: University of Chicago Press, 1986.

Poulain, Jacques. *De l'homme: Élements d'anthrobiologie philosophique du langage*. Paris: L'Harmattan, 2001.

Trabant, Jürgen. *Artikulationen: Historische Anthropologie der Sprache*. Frankfurt am Main: Suhrkamp, 1998.

———. *Mithridates im Paradies: Kleine Geschichte des Sprachdenkens*. Munich: Beck, 2003.

Trabant, Jürgen, and Sean Ward, eds. *New Essays on the Origin of Language*. Hawthorne, NY: De Gruyter Mouton, 2001.

von Humboldt, Wilhelm. *On Language: On the Diversity of Human Language Construction and Its Influence on the Mental Development of the Human Species*. New York: Cambridge University Press, 1999.

———. *Schriften zur Anthropologie und Geschichte: Werke in fünf Bänden*. Ed. Andreas Flitner and Klaus Giel. Darmstadt: Wissenschaftliche Buchgesellschaft, 1960–1983.

———. *Über die Verschiedenheit des menschlichen Sprachenbaues und ihren Einfluss auf die geistige Entwicklung des Menschengeschlechts*. Paderborn, Germany: Schoeningh, 1998.

Vygotskii, Lew S. *Thought and Language*. Cambridge, MA: MIT Press, 1962.

Wittgenstein, Ludwig. *Philosophical Investigations: The English Text of the Third Edition*. New York: Macmillan, 1973.

CHAPTER ELEVEN: IMAGES AND IMAGINATION

Augé, Marc. *The War of Dreams: Exercises in Ethno-Fiction*. London: Pluto Press, 1999.

Barthes, Roland. *Camera Lucida: Reflections on Photography*. New York: Hill and Wang, 1981.

Belting, Hans. *An Anthropology of Images: Picture, Medium, Body*. Princeton, NJ: Princeton University Press, 2011.

———. *Likeness and Presence: A History of the Image Before the Era of Art*. Chicago: University of Chicago Press, 1994.

Boehm, Gottfried, ed. *Was ist ein Bild?* Munich: Wilhelm Fink, 1994.

Böhme, Gernot. *Aisthetik: Vorlesungen über Ästhetik als allgemeine Wahrnehmungslehre*. Munich: Wilhelm Fink, 2001.

Castoriadis, Cornelius. *The Imaginary Institution of Society*. Trans. Kathleen Blamey. Cambridge, MA: MIT Press, 1987.

de Kerckhove, Derrick. *The Skin of Culture: Investigating the New Electronic Reality*. Toronto: Somerville House, 1995.

Didi-Huberman, Georges. *Confronting Images: Questioning the Ends of a Certain History of Art*. University Park: Pennsylvania State University Press, 2005.

———. *Was wir sehen, blickt uns an: Zur Metapsychologie des Bildes*. Munich: Wilhelm Fink, 1999.

Flusser, Vilém. "Eine neue Einbildungskraft." In *Lob der Oberflächlichkeit: Für eine Phänomenologie der Medien*, 251–331. Bensheim, Germany: Bollmann, 1993.

———. *Into the Universe of Technical Images*. Minneapolis: University of Minnesota Press, 2011.

Gruzinski, Serge. *Images at War: Mexico from Columbus to Blade Runner (1492–2019)*. Durham, NC: Duke University Press, 2001.

Hüppauf, Bernd, and Christoph Wulf, eds. *Dynamics and Performativity of Imagination: The Image between the Visible and the Invisible*. New York: Routledge, 2009.

Imai, Yasuo, and Christoph Wulf, eds. *Concepts of Aesthetic Education*. Münster: Waxmann, 2007.

Iser, Wolfgang. *The Fictive and the Imaginary: Charting Literary Anthropology*. Baltimore, MD: Johns Hopkins University Press, 1993.

Kamper, Dietmar. *Unmögliche Gegenwart: Zur Theorie der Phantasie*. Munich: Wilhelm Fink, 1995.

———. *Zur Geschichte der Einbildungskraft*. Munich: Hanser, 1981.

———. *Zur Soziologie der Imagination*. Munich: Wilhelm Fink, 1986.

Kittler, Friedrich. *Discourse Networks, 1800/1900*. Stanford, CA: Stanford University Press, 1990.

Locke, John. *Essay Concerning Human Understanding*. Indianapolis, IN: Hackett, 1996.

Marin, Louis. *Des pouvoirs de l'image: Glosses*. Paris: Éditions du Seuil, 1993.

———. *On Representation*. Stanford, CA: Stanford University Press, 2001.

McLuhan, Marshall. *The Gutenberg Galaxy: The Making of Typographic Man*. London: Routledge & Kegan Paul, 1962.

———. *Understanding Media: The Extensions of Man*. New York: Routledge, 2001.

Mersch, Dieter. *Was sich zeigt: Materialität, Präsenz, Ereignis*. Munich: Wilhelm Fink, 2002.

Mitchell, William J. T. *Picture Theory: Essays on Verbal and Visual Representation*. Chicago: University of Chicago Press, 1994.

Mollenhauer, Klaus, and Christoph Wulf, eds. *Aisthesis/Ästhetik: Zwischen Wahrnehmung und Bewusstsein*. Weinheim, Germany: Beltz, 1996.

Mondzain, Marie-José. *Image, Icon, Economy: The Byzantine Origins of the Contemporary Imaginary*. Stanford, CA: Stanford University Press, 2005.

Panofsky, Erwin. *Meaning in the Visual Arts*. Chicago: University of Chicago Press, 1982.

———. *Studies in Iconology: Humanistic Themes in the Art of the Renaissance*. New York: Harper & Row, 1962.

Pylyshyn, Zenon. *Seeing and Visualizing: It's Not What You Think*. Cambridge, MA: MIT Press, 2003.

Sartre, Jean-Paul. *The Imaginary: A Phenomenological Psychology of the Imagination*. London: Routledge, 2004.

Schäfer, Gerd, and Christoph Wulf, eds. *Bild—Bilder—Bildung*. Weinheim, Germany: Deutscher Studienverlag, 1999.

Seel, Martin. *Aesthetics of Appearing*. Stanford, CA: Stanford University Press, 2005.

Sontag, Susan. *On Photography*. New York: Farrar, Straus and Giroux, 1977.

Weibel, Peter. *Net-Condition: Art and Global Media (Electronic Culture—History, Theory, Practice)*. Cambridge, MA: MIT Press, 2001.

Welsch, Wolfgang. *Undoing Aesthetics*. London: Sage, 1997.

Wulf, Christoph, Dietmar Kamper, and Hans Ulrich Gumbrecht, eds. *Ethik der Ästhetik*. Berlin: Akademie, 1994.

Wulf, Christoph, Jacques Poulain, and Fathi Triki, eds. *Die Künste im Dialog der Kulturen: Europa und seine muslimischen Nachbarn*. Berlin: Akademie, 2006.

CHAPTER TWELVE: DEATH AND RECOLLECTION OF BIRTH

Arendt, Hannah. *The Human Condition*. Chicago: University of Chicago Press, 1958.

Ariès, Philippe. *The Hour of Our Death*. Oxford: Oxford University Press, 1991.

Bahr, Hans-Dieter. *Den Tod denken*. Munich: Wilhelm Fink, 2002.

Baudrillard, Jean. *Symbolic Exchange and Death*. London: Sage, 1993.

Bonnet del Valle, Muriel. *La naissance, un voyage: L'accouchement à travers les peuples*. Paris: L'Harmattan, 2000.

Borneman, John, ed. *Death of the Father: An Anthropology of the End in Political Authority*. New York: Berghahn Books, 2004.

Dundes, Lauren, ed. *The Manner Born: Birth Rites in Cross-Cultural Perspective*. Walnut Creek, CA: AltaMira Press, 2003.

Enright, Dennis J., ed. *The Oxford Book of Death*. Oxford: Oxford University Press, 1983.

Jankélévitch, Vladimir. *La mort*. Paris: Flammarion, 1977.

Landsberg, Paul Ludwig. *The Experience of Death: The Moral Problem of Suicide*. London: Rockliff, 1953.

Lütkehaus, Ludger: *Natalität: Philosophie der Geburt*. Zug, Switzerland: Die graue Edition, 2006.

Macho, Thomas. *Todesmetaphern: Zur Logik der Grenzerfahrung*. Frankfurt am Main: Suhrkamp, 1987.

Morin, Edgar. *L'homme et la mort*. Paris: Éditions du Seuil, 1970.

Noys, Benjamin. *The Culture of Death*. Oxford, New York: Berg, 2005.

von Barloewen, Constantin, ed. *Der Tod in den Weltkulturen und Weltreligionen*. Frankfurt am Main: Insel, 2000.

Vovelle, Michel. *La mort et l'Occident de 1300 à nos jours*. Paris: Gallimard, 1983.

Wulf, Christoph, Birgit Althans, Julia Foltys, Martina Fuchs, Sigrid Klasen, Juliane Lamprecht, Dorothea Tegethoff. *Geburt in Familie, Klinik und Medien.* Opladen, Germany: Budrich UniPress, 2008.

Wulf, Christoph, Anja Hänsch, and Micha Brumlik, eds. *Das Imaginäre der Geburt.* Munich: Wilhelm Fink, 2008.

FUTURE PROSPECTS

Barret-Ducrocq, Françoise, ed. *Quelle Mondialisation?* Paris: Grasset, 2002.

Beck, Ulrich. *What Is Globalization?* Cambridge: Polity Press, 2000.

Beck, Ulrich, Anthony Giddens, and Scott Lash. *Reflexive Modernization: Politics, Tradition and Aesthetics in the Modern Social Order.* Cambridge: Polity Press, 1994.

Bohnsack, Ralf. *Rekonstruktive Sozialforschung: Einführung in qualitative Methoden.* 5th ed. Opladen, Germany: Leske and Budrich, 2003.

Denzin, Norman K., and Yvonna S. Lincoln, eds. *Handbook of Qualitative Research.* Thousand Oaks, CA: Sage, 1994.

Featherstone, Mike. *Undoing Culture: Globalisation, Postmodernism and Identity.* London: Sage, 1995.

Flick, Uwe. *An Introduction to Qualitative Research.* London: Sage, 2006.

Hutchinson, John, and Anthony D. Smith, eds. *Ethnicity.* Oxford: Oxford University Press, 1996.

Münch, Richard. *Globale Dynamik, lokale Lebenswelten: Der schwierige Weg in die Weltgesellschaft.* Frankfurt am Main: Suhrkamp, 1998.

Ricoeur, Paul. *Oneself as Another.* Chicago: University of Chicago Press, 1992.

Todorov, Tzvetan. *Life in Common: An Essay in General Anthropology.* Lincoln: University of Nebraska Press, 2001.

UNESCO. *Déclaration universelle de L'Unesco sur la diversité culturelle: Commentaires et propositions,* Série Diversité culturelle No. 2. Ed. Katérian Stenou. Paris: UNESCO, 2003.

Weingart, Peter. "Interdisziplinarität—der paradoxe Diskurs." *Ethik und Sozialwissenschaften* 8, no. 4 (1997): 521–29.

Wolton, Dominique. *L'autre mondialisation.* Paris: Flammarion, 2003.

Wulf, Christoph. *Anthropologie kultureller Vielfalt: Interkulturelle Bildung in Zeiten der Globalisierung.* Bielefeld, Germany: Transcript, 2006.

———, ed. "Kontaktzonen" (issue title). *Paragrana* 19, no. 2 (2010).

Wulf, Christoph, and Christine Merkel, eds. *Globalisierung als Herausforderung der Erziehung: Theorien, Grundlagen, Fallstudien.* Münster: Waxmann, 2002.

Wulf, Christoph, and Gabriele Weigand. *Der Mensch in der globalisierten Welt: Anthropologische Reflexionen zum Verständnis unserer Zeit. Christoph Wulf im Gespräch mit Gabriele Weigand.* Münster, Germany: Waxmann, 2011.

Index

abstraction, 88, 119, 121, 141, 175, 177, 257, 261

action(s), 8, 39, 42, 44–46, 49, 51–54, 63, 66–72, 96, 102, 104, 136, 139, 142–43, 145–47, 149–50, 154, 156, 181, 184–85, 188, 193–94, 197–99, 205, 221–24, 235, 249, 264–65, 285–86, 288; collective/joint, 5, 148, 220, 249; educational, 147, 152; everyday, 66, 200, 223; imaginary, 149; mimetic, 141, 143–44, 160, 179, 186, 189–90, 196–98; political, 53, 97; ritual, 145, 151–52, 155, 202, 218, 223–24, 226–27, 229–30; sacred, 180; social, 7, 90, 97, 102, 117, 141, 152, 194–98, 200–201, 233, 235; symbolic, 147, 198, 217; theory of, 46, 53, 235

adaptation, 17–21, 26–27, 39, 166, 172, 196, 198, 262, 298

Adelung, Johann Christoph, 81

adolescence, adolescent, 47, 50, 84, 140–41, 144, 148, 171, 216, 233, 265

Adorno, Theodor W., 115–16, 140, 175–76, 189, 204, 272

aesthetics, aesthetic, 8, 52, 118, 122, 128–29, 140, 143, 147, 178, 189–90, 197, 199, 208, 210, 260–61, 266, 277–78, 298; aesthetic experience, 118, 129, 135, 147, 189, 192, 210, 266

Africa, 23, 26–27, 29–32, 80, 84, 86, 90, 254, 309n29

agent, agency, 183, 214, 225

aggression, aggressive(ness), 49, 90, 148, 193, 196, 217

Alexandria, 316n13

alienation, alienating, alien, 43, 46, 71, 107–8, 238, 285

alterity, 78, 103–4, 107–9, 121, 138–39, 150–51, 173, 177–79, 189, 211, 215, 228, 266, 272, 283, 295–96. *See also* differentness; Other, the

America, 29; Latin, South America, 107; North America, 6, 55, 81, 83, 103

American Anthropological Association, 82–83, 330n104

American Museum of Natural History, 79

animals: comparison of man and, 37, 48–51, 171–72, 183–85, 217, 234, 236, 239, 246

Annales E.S.C. (French historical journal), 55–57, 61, 70–71, 315n1

anthropoids, 23–24, 26, 28–29, 166

anthropology, 1–2, 8, 114, 177–78, 205–6, 213, 242, 248, 251, 290–91, 299–303, 306n1, 330n104, 343n25; anthropological research, 6, 36, 212, 291–303, 343n25; biological, 81, 114, 305n1, 330n104; concepts of, 1, 7; cultural, 5–6, 8, 19, 23, 55, 64, 69, 75, 78, 81–84, 86, 91–92, 94, 97–101, 103–5, 107–13, 146, 153, 173–74, 199, 322n1; four-field anthropology (Boas), 77,

biotope, 30, 33, 49, 172
birds, 16–17, 22, 26
birth, 8, 10, 28, 34, 47–48, 65–66, 70, 161,
    169, 171–72, 182, 237–38, 275–77, 279,
    284–90
Bloch, Marc, 5, 57–58, 61, 70, 73, 315n7
Blondel, Charles, 57
blueprint(s), 22, 35
Boas, Franz, 2, 76–85, 91, 106, 110, 324n19;
    Boasians, 78, 82–86, 100, 110
Boccaccio, 243
body (human), 4, 6–10, 23, 31, 37–38, 43–
    45, 54, 67, 70, 117, 119–26, 138, 141,
    143, 149, 160–61, 165–82, 194, 197, 199,
    202, 206, 212–14, 219, 225, 247, 252,
    275, 290, 301; body and mind, 41, 54;
    body concepts, 165, 175; body images,
    175, 260; body language, 150, 233–34;
    body plasticity, 202, 285; body politic,
    176; disciplining the body, 119, 172,
    175, 198, 208; historical and cultural
    nature of the human body, 172–74, 178
Boethius, 242
Böhme, Gernot, 206
Bolk, Louis, 46–47, 311n2
Borneo, 32
Borscheid, Peter, 66
Bougainville, Louis Antoine de, 75
Bourdieu, Pierre, 77, 110, 174, 219, 314n40,
    342n18, 348n32
brain, 23–24, 26–31, 34–35, 51, 166–71, 180,
    184, 186, 236, 239, 314n26, 314n35,
    356n4; cerebral cortex, 169–70; develop-
    ment of, 314n26; growth of, 28, 30;
    language centers of, 9, 241; motor func-
    tion, motor system of, 28, 142; research,
    28, 48, 138, 167–68, 170–71, 181, 237;
    size of, 28, 31, 166
Braudel, Fernand, 5, 57, 60–61
Brazil, 7
Britain, Great; British, 6, 75–78, 81, 86, 88–
    89, 110, 238, 272
Broca area, 27, 241
Burke, Peter, 65, 73
Butler, Judith, 174, 213–14, 226
Buytendijk, Frederik, 50, 311n2

Cairo, 23
Cambridge (UK), 89
Canada, 76
Caneiro, Robert, 86

Capella, Galeazzo, 1–2
capitalism, 61, 87, 295
Cartesian. *See* Descartes
case studies, 6, 54, 58, 62, 68–70, 74, 144,
    152
Castoriadis, Cornelius, 181, 274
cave, cave painting, 31–32, 236, 252, 277–78
celebration(s), 70, 180, 189, 194–96, 217–
    18, 279; family celebrations, 145, 153,
    155–59
cell (biological), 14–15
Cenozoic period, 19
cerebellum, 28; cerebral, 4, 33–34, 167, 169–
    70. *See also* brain, cortex
cerebralization, 34
ceremony, ceremonies, 139, 145, 150, 158,
    180, 201, 217, 226, 228, 280; birthday,
    194–96; Christmas (Germany), 153–59;
    New Year's (Japan), 153–59; wedding
    ceremony, 8, 201, 207
Certeau, Michel de, 206
Chad, 309n28
Char, René, 266
Chicago (University of), 82, 86, 88
childhood, children, 34, 46–47, 61, 279
child-rearing, nursing, upbringing, 7, 27,
    29–30, 34, 48, 54, 117, 120, 144, 146,
    149, 152, 166, 192, 285
China, 7, 30, 32
Chomsky, Noam, 238, 243, 249
Christ, 131, 158, 266
Christianity, Christian, 60, 70, 107, 125, 130,
    137, 207, 254, 266, 279–80
Church, the; church, 71, 125, 134, 157, 207,
    226, 233, 245, 280
Cicero, 243
civilization, civilization process, 2, 40, 64,
    76, 80, 105, 117, 119–20, 124–25, 175–77
class, social, 6, 62–65, 68, 71, 145, 174, 202,
    212, 233
climate, climatic, 15, 20, 26–27, 31, 35, 297
climbers, climbing, 23–24, 166
clothing, 8, 61, 70, 129, 173
cognition, cognitive, 35, 66, 169, 207, 209,
    221, 240–44, 246–47, 259, 265, 267, 273,
    277
cohesion (social), 88–89, 103, 111, 149, 153,
    193
Coleridge, Samuel T., 272–73
colonialism, colonial, 19, 80, 87, 99–100,
    107; anti-colonial, 106–7

ity 3, 74, 114–15, 117, 133, 136, 139, 291–99, 302. *See also* methods
resources, 137, 167, 297; exhaustion, scarcity of resources, 35, 132
rhetoric(s), 118, 130–31, 243
rhythm, rhythmic, 60, 123, 133, 148, 174, 179, 206–8, 225, 227
Richardson, Jane, 84
Ricoeur, Paul, 95, 96, 204
Rimbaud, Arthur, 266
Rist, Charles, 315n1
ritual, rituals, ritualistic, rites, 70, 89, 109, 117, 134, 139, 141–42, 144–46, 149–55, 157–59, 172, 174–75, 180, 182, 193, 205, 215–35, 301; concept, range of rituals, 216–17; death, burial rituals, 216, 258, 277, 279; everyday rituals, 145, 216, 226; family rituals 144–45, 153, 155, 157–58, 226; rituals as text, 221–22
ritualization, ritualize, 123, 145–46, 149, 151, 156, 217–18
Romantics, Romantic, 81, 125
Rome, Romans, 243, 270
Ross, William David, 306n1
Rothko, Mark, 259
Rousseau, Jean-Jacques, 306n4
Rückert, Friedrich, 81
Russia, 7

sacred, the, 7, 118, 126–28, 131, 157, 177, 180, 207, 217, 227–29, 258, 285
sacrifice, 45, 122, 127, 176, 193, 232; human self-sacrifice, 279; introversion of sacrifice, 176
Sahagún, Bernardino de, 75
Sahlins, Marshall, 86–87, 219, 221
Salzgitter-Lebenstedt (Germany), 31
Samoa, 84
Sapir, Edward, 82–83; Sapir-Whorf hypothesis, 83
Sartre, Jean-Paul, 104, 273
Saussure, Ferdinand de, 91, 240
savannah, 26, 33–34
"scapegoat" (Girard), 193
Schechner, Richard, 219
Scheler, Max, 4, 37–41, 45, 48–51, 53–56, 171, 311n1
Schlegel, Friedrich von, 81
Schrenk, Friedemann, 26, 29
science, sciences, 1, 23, 35, 37, 215; biological, 3, 16, 283; cultural sciences, studies,

1, 4–5, 75, 119, 177, 205–6, 251; natural, 1, 37, 125, 132, 254; social, 1, 4, 10, 75, 103, 112, 114, 119, 136, 143, 160, 177, 206, 215, 275, 288, 294
Second World War, 57, 86, 110, 176
security, feeling of, living in, 45, 52, 123–24, 146, 156, 215, 217, 223, 233
seeing (the act of), vision, sight, 121–22, 169, 177, 180, 251, 267, 270–71; chiastic structure of vision, 206, 251, 268, 270
selection. *See* natural selection
self, the, 38, 45, 140, 143, 159, 175, 177, 197; self-consciousness, 121; self-control, 120, 176–77; self-discipline, 176; self-organization, 4, 14, 166, 168–70, 312n2; self-perception, 123, 138, 253; self-perfection, 176; self-realization, 126; self-reflection, self-interpretation, 43, 115; self-reproduction, 14, 33
semiotics, semiotic, 175, 221, 253
senses, the; sense organs in general, 7–8, 38, 40, 44, 50, 102, 117, 119–24, 138, 143, 156, 159, 169, 175, 177, 197, 206–9, 257; contact senses, 121, 124; practical sense (Bourdieu), 174
sensuality, 148, 174
sexuality, sexual, sex, 20, 48–50, 61–62, 66–67, 70, 118, 120, 122, 130–31, 138, 172, 174, 212–14, 217, 240, 257, 274; sex drive, 49, 131; sexual reproduction, 15, 20, 22, 27, 49, 138, 166
Shakespeare, William, 214
Shanidar cave (Kurdistan), 31
Shostak, Marjorie, 97
Sicily, 189
Siegfried, André, 315n1
silence, 7, 118, 134–36
Simmel, Georg, 100
simulacrum, simulacra, 257, 262
simulation, 128, 257–58, 261–63, 268, 282
Singer, Milton, 199–200
skeleton, skeletal, 15, 22–23, 26, 28, 32–33, 167
skill(s), 30, 104, 145, 179, 183–84, 186, 194, 196–97, 199, 229, 260, 278, 290, 293, 356n4; aesthetic, artistic, 30, 277; communication, 30, 33, 292; coordination, 30; cultural, 105, 167, 251; mimetic, 183–84, 186; perception, 237; poietic, 148; social, 29–30, 192, 196, 227; vocal, speech, 211, 237